Teach
Yourself
VRML 2

in 21 days

Teach Yourself
VRML 2
in 21 days

Chris Marrin
Bruce Campbell

sams
net

201 West 103rd Street
Indianapolis, Indiana 46290

Copyright © 1997 by Sams.net Publishing

FIRST EDITION

International Standard Book Number: 1-57521-193-9

Library of Congress Catalog Number: 96-70054

2000   99   98   97   4   3   2   1

Interpretation of the printing code: the rightmost double-digit number is the year of the book's printing; the rightmost single digit, the number of the book's printing. For example, a printing code of 97-1 shows that the first printing of the book occurred in 1997.

Composed in AGaramond and MCPdigital by Macmillan Computer Publishing

Printed in the United States of America

Trademarks

Publisher and President   Richard K. Swadley

Publishing Manager   Mark Taber

Director of Editorial Services   Cindy Morrow

Assistant Marketing Managers   Kristina Perry
Rachel Wolfe

Acquisitions Editor
David B. Mayhew

Development Editor
Kelly Murdock

Software Development Specialist
Bob Correll

Production Editor
Brice P. Gosnell

Copy Editors
Cheri Clark, Heather Butler

Indexer
Christine Nelsen

Technical Reviewer
John Charlesworth

Editorial Coordinator
Katie Wise

Technical Edit Coordinator
Lorraine E. Schaffer

Resource Coordinator
Deborah Frisby

Editorial Assistants
Carol Ackerman, Andi Richter, Rhonda Tinch-Mize

Cover Designer
Tim Amrhein

Book Designer
Gary Adair

Copywriter
Peter Fuller

Production
Svetlana Dominguez
Carl Pierce
Dana Rhodes
Deirdre Smith
Laura A. Smith
Rebekah Stutzman

Overview

Contents

Appendix B VRML Field and Event Types **425**

Appendix C Glossary **439**

Appendix D What's on the CD-ROM? **457**

Dedication

Chris Marrin   *To my wife, Lynn, for her patience and consistent support, even though I started this project a mere two months after our wedding!*

Bruce Campbell   *To my nuclear family in the information age.*

Acknowledgments

From Chris Marrin:

Writing a book on a technical topic like VRML is a very intensive process and it takes the support and dedication of many people to make it possible. I would like to thank my co-authors of the VRML 2 specification, Rikk Carey and Gavin Bell. Gavin had the foresight to see what VRML could be, and Rikk had the wisdom to carry it through to the end. And no text on VRML would be complete without acknowledging the contributions of the VRML community. This group has, mostly through e-mail exchanges, forged VRML into the great piece of work you see in this book. I could not mention anyone's name without slighting a dozen others, so I would just like to thank the community as a whole.

I would also like to thank my coauthor, Bruce Campbell. He has come through on countless occasions to make sure the book got out on time. Finally, I'd like to thank the great staff at Sams, without whom you would not be holding this book in your hands.

From Bruce Campbell:

I would like to acknowledge Dr. Araya Debessay at the University of Delaware who spoke and demonstrated dedication to technical excellence, to Irma Tabellione who taught me the value of collaboration and the art of management in the information age, and to the University of Wisconsin for dramatically broadening my awareness of human spirit, Mother Nature, and world culture.

Specifically related to VRML, I must give thanks to Toni Emerson and Dr. Tom Furness at the Human Interface Technology Laboratory in Seattle, WA and to all the hardworking collaborators who put together the VRML standard. And, thanks to everyone who participates on the Web with the intent of building a better tomorrow.

About the Authors

Chris Marrin is a software engineer at Silicon Graphics, Inc. and a Pioneer of VRML. He has been a key contributor to the VRML process since its inception, and is one of three primary authors of the VRML 2 specification. His main responsibility at SGI is technical liaison with the worldwide VRML community. He is also involved in projects to make VRML worlds easier to create and use.

Bruce Campbell lives in Seattle, WA and works with technologies related to 3D collaboration, such as VRML. When he is not writing, he is either teaching for Catapult training centers, performing VR related research at the Human Interface Technology Laboratory at the University of Washington, or running around somewhere in North America. He wrote Chapters 15,16, and 20, and Appendix C.

Check out his home page at `http://www.hitl.washington.edu/people/bdc`.

Introduction

3D graphics are all the rage today. We see them everywhere: in video games, advertising, even feature-length films. We have come to a point in history where we can create completely synthetic worlds that exist entirely inside a computer's memory. These worlds have been referred to in the popular media as "virtual reality," "cyberspace," or "the metaverse." These terms are great for a science fiction writer in search of a new book idea, but we are many years away from virtual worlds that are anywhere near the rich detail of the real world. However, 3D graphics give us much more than the future promise of virtual reality. They give us a powerful new tool for the presentation of information, art, and entertainment. And while I don't think virtual reality will ever overtake the real world, as so many science fiction movies would like us to believe, they will add to our repertoire of creative outlets.

The World Wide Web adds an interesting new twist to the use of 3D graphics. In the past, the presentation of art or information was limited to those who could get their work shown in an art gallery, or to someone with access to a publishing house or television studio. But, access to the Web is relatively inexpensive, so almost anyone can communicate their ideas, as long as they know how to use the tools that turn their dreams into reality.

VRML is the tool for creating 3D virtual experiences on the World Wide Web. Even though it is in its infancy, VRML will allow you to realize your visions and make them available to everyone on the Web.

The purpose of this book is to help you get started using VRML. In the next 21 chapters, I will be taking you through all the features VRML has to offer. I will start by introducing the simplest concepts, and at the end of this book you will understand and be able to use the full power of VRML. The first seven chapters will help you grasp the fundamentals of 3D graphics and will show you how to create static three-dimensional worlds. But VRML is all about dynamic, moving experiences, so in the next seven chapters I will show you how to add life to your worlds and how to give visitors the ability to interact with them. In the last seven chapters, I will describe the most advanced features of VRML and show you how to create full multimedia experiences, integrating 2D and 3D elements. Each chapter will end with a question-and-answer section, followed by exercises to help stimulate you to put together the building blocks of VRML into real, useful virtual worlds. All answers to the exercises can be found on the CD-ROM that accompanies this book at \Source\Answers.

VRML is an exciting new development. It has been a lifelong dream of mine to be involved in something with the potential to change the world in a very positive and fundamental way. VRML is the realization of that dream for me. I hope reading this book gets you as excited about VRML as I am.

Have fun!

Conventions

The computer font is used for commands, parameters, statements, and text you see on-screen.

A **boldfaced computer font** indicates text you type.

Italics indicate new terms or items of emphasis.

 New Terms are introduced in New Term boxes, with the term in italics.

 NOTE

> A Note box presents interesting pieces of information related to the surrounding discussion.

TIP

> A Tip box offers advice or teaches an easier way to do something.

> A Warning box advises you about potential problems and helps steer you clear of disaster.

WARNING

Tell Us What You Think!

As a reader, you are the most important critic and commentator of our books. We value your opinion and want to know what we're doing right, what we could do better, what areas you'd like to see us publish in, and any other words of wisdom you're willing to pass our way. You can help us make strong books that meet your needs and give you the computer guidance you require.

Do you have access to Compuserve or the World Wide Web? Then check out our Compuserve forum by typing **GO SAMS** at any prompt. If you prefer the World Wide Web, check out our site at http://www.mcp.com.

 NOTE

> If you have a technical question about this book, call the technical support line at (800) 571-5840, ext. 3668.

As the publishing manager of the group that created this book, I welcome your comments. You can fax, e-mail, or write me directly to let me know what you did or didn't like about this book—as well as what we can do to make our books stronger. Here's the information:

Fax: 317/581-4669

E-mail: newtech_mgr@sams.mcp.com

Mail: MarkTaber
          Sams.net Publishing
          201 W. 103rd Street
          Indianapolis, IN 46290

Day 1

VRML Background

The notion of 3D graphics has been very popular lately, from video games to weather simulations to movies that give us a glimpse of virtual reality, complete with virtual villains and cyberheroes. The World Wide Web has gained even more popularity. Therefore, it is natural that people would want to join the two, marrying the compelling experience of 3D to the global access of the Web.

VRML was born to solve just this problem: how to put compelling 3D onto every PC connected to the Web. In this chapter, you'll explore the phenomenon of the World Wide Web and how VRML was created to put interconnected 3D worlds onto every desktop. Here's what you'll learn:

- ☐ Why use 3D on the Web?
- ☐ A short history of VRML.
- ☐ Authoring VRML worlds.
- ☐ Tools and resources for VRML.

Why Use 3D on the Web?

The World Wide Web has grown from a curiosity on college campuses to a major force in business in fewer than five years. It seems as though there is not a TV commercial, billboard, or panel truck without the now familiar http://.... The Web is the subject of jokes, talk shows, and articles in major magazines. You can buy wine and movie tickets on the Web, see the latest shots from the space shuttle, and find out the weather in any corner of the world, as long as you know the magic incantation, http://www.weather.com/current/.

As with many of the inventions now taken for granted, no one knew what the Web would become when it was first conceived. It started out as an easier way to browse text pages on large computer databases. It was soon realized that some sort of text formatting and the capability to add images to a page were crucihal to the successful presentation of the information. Thus, the HyperText Markup Language (HTML) was born. An outgrowth of publishing standards of the late 1980s, HTML is a simple text-based file format with embedded commands (known as tags) to instruct the computer how to display the information. For instance, surrounding a word with the tags <B> and </B> causes that word to be displayed in bold. There are tags to distinguish between a heading and body text, to center text, and to create bulleted lists, to name a few. Figure 1.1 shows a simple Web page with many different tags.

Figure 1.1.

A simple HTML page with text and graphics.

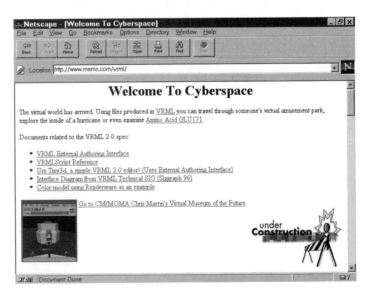

HTML also has a tag to embed images on a page, and it is here that HTML started down the path toward full multimedia integration. Brochures, magazines, and other printed material consist basically of words and images, with the occasional background color to set off a sidebar. With text formatting and embedded images, HTML can handle most of this. But this is all static information, and because it is being displayed on a computer screen, it is ideally suited to dynamic presentations with motion, sound, and interactivity.

This interactivity is easy to find at information kiosks in malls and airports where maps of the area and restaurant choices have been available for years. But these are all custom installations, created for a specific purpose. The next goal of the Web became bringing that richness of information presentation to every desktop.

Toward Media-Rich Web Content

From its earliest days, HTML had a simple form of interactivity. The user calls up Web pages by entering a Universal Resource Locator (URL), the familiar http://... form seen in every corner of the world. A displayed page can have a hyperlink: a word, phrase, or image that is associated with another URL. Instead of remembering a cryptic series of meaningless symbols, the user can click a hyperlink that says, "For more information, click here." It is from this linking capability that the Web gets its name. If you were to spread out all the pages on a giant field and connect a string from each link to each page with which it is associated, you would have a great spider web of linked information. Imagine those strings running between all the pages stored all over the world, and the term World Wide Web becomes clear.

But hyperlinks provide a very simplistic interaction. There is no animation; the user can simply jump from one page to the next. Since the beginning, this linking capability has improved. You can now go to new pages by clicking in different regions of a single image. With this capability, you can have, for example, an image of a desktop full of office equipment. Clicking on the telephone takes you to telephonic products, and clicking on the calendar takes you to time-management products. You can also have simple (and sometimes annoying) animated images. Other advances, such as forms and buttons, have made a whole new class of interaction possible. You can go to a page, look at descriptions of some wine, enter the number of bottles of that wine you want, type your credit card number, and whisk off an order to the virtual vineyard. (See Figure 1.2.)

But all of these features simply extend the paradigm of interacting with text and pictures. What if other types of information could be included on the page, in place of the images and forms? This is the technology companies have been scrambling to provide recently, and it is where 3D on the Web finds its foothold. But 3D is only one of a number of technologies being embedded on an HTML page. The two most popular browsers, Navigator from Netscape Communications and Internet Explorer from Microsoft, both have the capability to display several media types, including 3D, on a page. Displaying any of these media types is a simple matter of installing the appropriate software component, known as a plug-in module, on your computer. CosmoPlayer from Silicon Graphics is the 3D plug-in you will be using, and later I'll show you how to install it from the CD-ROM included with this book. With CosmoPlayer, you'll be able to visit and explore 3D worlds. (See Figure 1.3.)

Figure 1.2.

The Virtual Vineyards order page.

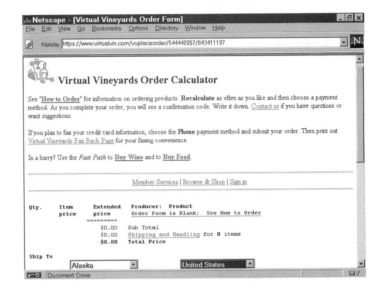

Figure 1.3.

A simple VRML world.

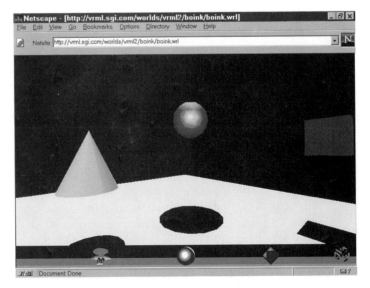

Using 3D for a Richer User Experience

Why would anyone want to put 3D on the Web? Think back to that kiosk in the airport. What if the user had a window on the screen showing the gallery she was standing in at that moment, as if there were a camera in a nearby corner. She knows that her departure gate is in building E, so she moves her view of the gallery up and through the roof to see an overview of the airport. And there, two buildings away to the right, is a building with a big, glowing E floating above it. She clicks on that building and the view drops down into it, right in front of a signpost showing the major sites. She clicks on her gate and her view moves quickly to that location. She presses Replay and the view jumps back to her current location and slowly moves toward her gate, turning to go down the breezeway, past a nice modern statue, through the next gallery and into the entrance to building E. Now it's just a right turn down the main hall, past security, and right up to her gate. She now has landmarks and an approximate walking time as she follows the path she just saw on the computer screen, with no confusion and no missed flight! Figure 1.4 shows this virtual airport lobby.

Figure 1.4.

A virtual airport lobby.

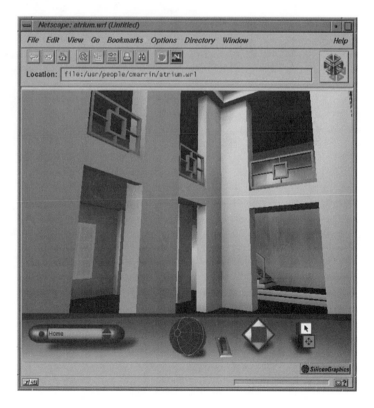

There are dozens of scenarios like this, from architectural walk-throughs of a building under construction, investigation of ancient sites that no longer exist, and virtual tours through any art gallery in the world. And, in the Louvre, you can get as close to the Mona Lisa as you want! More abstract applications of 3D are possible on the Web. A company's logo can float in front of you on the company's Web page. One click on an area called New Products and the logo slowly unfolds and becomes a room full of pedestals displaying the latest stereo or television. The products in this virtual audio-video gallery have real working buttons to demonstrate the features for you instead of forcing you to read dry brochures with still images. And, imagine how much easier it will be to put together that desk from Norway with a Web site containing animations, viewable from any angle, that show which screw goes into which predrilled hole in what order. (See Figures 1.5 and 1.6.)

Figure 1.5.

Commercial site with virtual rooms to explore products.

Figure 1.6.
Virtual help for desk construction.

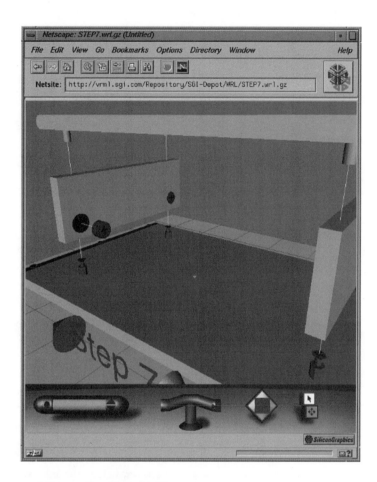

Toward a Standard 3D File Format

But how does one go about putting 3D content on the Web? Until recently, displaying 3D required enormously powerful computers. Thus, its use was limited to research and entertainment. It took a government grant or a big-budget motion picture company to afford the equipment to create and show 3D graphics. Because 3D has always been a niche, there has never been much motivation to develop a standard file format as PostScript has been for desktop publishing or HTML is for Web content.

Computer hardware has gotten much more powerful in recent years, so 3D is now becoming practical for everyone. But a common file format is needed to allow anyone browsing the Web to view 3D. VRML was designed to be that file format. VRML files are written in plain text, so they can be created using a simple text editor. This is the reason HTML experienced such explosive growth. Anyone could create an HTML document without tools designed specifically for the task. This will be an important feature of VRML until tools to create HTML documents are available to everyone.

A Short History of VRML

The origins of VRML date back to the middle of 1994, to a European Web conference in which Tim Berners-Lee talked about the need for a 3D Web standard. He coined the name VRML (Virtual Reality Markup Language) as an acronym to parallel HTML. Mark Pesce picked up on this idea and was able to persuade Brian Behlendorf at *Wired* magazine to start a mailing list called www-vrml.

The VRML mailing list was the seed from which a thriving community of artists, engineers, and visionaries grew. The name was quickly changed to Virtual Reality Modeling Language to reflect the emphasis on worlds rather than pages of text. This group produced the VRML 1 specification in record time purely through e-mail interactions. This was possible thanks in part to the fact that it was based on the Inventor file format from Silicon Graphics. Inventor is a mature file format used everywhere from universities doing research to animation houses doing special effects for movies and television. A subset of Inventor was chosen that facilitated implementation on a wide variety of platforms. Although this allowed several VRML browsers to be created, it also crippled the language to a certain extent. (See Figure 1.7.) Inventor's advanced interaction and animation capabilities were not included, so VRML 1 worlds were as still as a graveyard. So, before the ink even had a chance to dry on the specification, work was started to bring life to those virtual worlds.

A small extension to VRML, called VRML 1.1, was tried. It contained facilities to add audio clips to a scene and some very primitive animation. But because this was not nearly enough to create compelling content, VRML1.1 never saw the light of day. The VRML community set its sights on a major overhaul of the language and dubbed it VRML 2.

The Requirements

Gavin Bell was the SGI engineer primarily responsible for introducing the VRML community to Inventor. In thinking about 2, he conceived of three requirements he deemed important for 3D Web content: composability, scalability, and extensibility.

Figure 1.7.

*An early VRML 1
browser.*

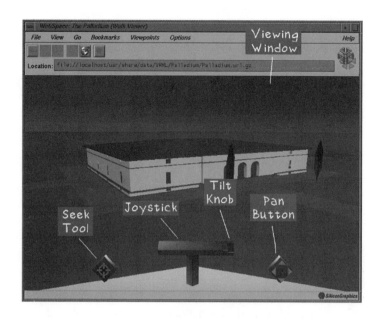

Composability allows an author to create a virtual house, scale it down, and place it on a tabletop. This table with the house model can then be placed in the office building of a virtual architecture company. This building can be placed on a city block with other buildings, which, in turn, can be placed in a city, which can be placed on a planet orbiting the sun. In this composition, each piece is independent of the rest. The full-size house can be placed on a residential street somewhere else on the planet because everything that makes it a house, from the attic light that can be switched on to the door that opens to the basement, is contained within the house model.

Scalability allows worlds of arbitrary size to be created. With VRML, it must be possible to see a galaxy, zoom in on a star system, then to a planet, then a city, a block, a park, a man sitting on a bench, and the mosquito sitting on his arm. This is difficult due to limits in the precision of computer hardware, but it is important to prevent every world from having arbitrary limits in size or detail.

Extensibility allows an author to extend the capability of the language to serve special purposes. This allows, for instance, multiuser worlds to be created or new geometric objects to be added to VRML.

The Process

In the fall of 1995, several long-standing contributors to the VRML community, led by Mark Pesce, formed the VRML Architecture Group (VAG) to steer the VRML 2 effort. The

VAG's original goal was to define the 2 spec. But it was soon clear that there was so much good design going on that the group would merely steer the existing work and approve the final specification. The group quickly developed a list of requirements, based on Bell's three tenets, for VRML 2. It was decided that there would be a period during which proposal submissions would be accepted from any company, institution, or individual who met the submission requirements. Then the proposals would be debated in the VRML community, a vote would be taken in the community, and if a single proposal won a strong majority, it would be selected as the VRML 2 spec.

Proposals were prepared by SGI, Sony, Sun, Microsoft, and many other companies and institutions. Early in the process, SGI teamed up with Sony and others to combine their efforts into a single proposal, dubbed Moving Worlds. Several of the proposals built on the VRML 1 foundation meet the requirements. As the process progressed, it was clear that Moving Worlds was the most mature of these proposals. But Microsoft took a totally new direction with its ActiveVRML proposal. It was clear that ActiveVRML and Moving Worlds were poised for a major battle.

That battle took place on the VRML mailing list. Issues both technical and political were raised and debated. When it came time to vote, two questions were posed. Respondents were asked to rate the suitability of each proposal to the needs of VRML 2, on a scale from very suitable to very unsuitable. Then, each respondent was asked to name his or her favorite proposal. In the end, Moving Worlds had a 92-percent suitability rating, and 74 percent of the respondents voted for it as their favorite. This is what Mark Pesce often refers to as "consensus," and it caused the VAG to choose Moving Worlds as the basis for VRML 2.

NOTE

ActiveVRML was later renamed ActiveAnimation and made a part of Microsoft's ActiveX toolkit. Its 3D aspects have been deemphasized in favor of a more two-dimensional animation style.

But the work was far from over. Bell, Rikk Carey, and I had the primary responsibility for bringing VRML 2 through several levels of draft standard to the final specification. But before that could happen, it had to be reviewed, changes and clarifications had to be made, and the result had to be tested to see whether our virtual worlds could solve the real-world problems I've described. A large number of contributors to the VRML mailing list made comments and suggestions, and many wrote sections for incorporation. VRML 2 was a collaborative effort of the entire community.

The uniqueness of this process of consensus building and collaboration in producing VRML 2 caught the attention of the International Standards Organization (ISO). In June of 1996, Carey went to Japan to start the process of making VRML 2 an ISO standard. The ISO committee accepted the work of the VRML community intact, moving the specification quickly through its acceptance procedures. In addition, the committee is currently looking at the VRML process as a way to speed up the slow and cumbersome ISO standards procedures.

Finishing Up

After long months of work, the release of the VRML 2 specification was announced at Siggraph '96, the preeminent 3D graphics technical conference. Carey, who had put in endless hours finishing the document, declared, "VRML 2.0 is not frozen, VRML 2.0 is done!" This was both an expression of personal relief and a plea to the community to begin focusing on content rather than further improvements to the specification.

Authoring VRML Worlds

So, there's a specification for VRML 2 and browsers to view content created for it. But how is that content created? Many tools exist for the creation and editing of 2D images because they have been around for a long time. Because HTML editors are becoming more and more commonplace, creating 2D content for the Web is now easy. But 3D is very different from HTML and 2D images, so creating content for VRML is very different as well.

Creating 3D Content

Creating 2D objects (images) is very much like a child drawing with crayons. You grab a sheet of paper, pick midnight blue, and start painting the night sky. Working with the third dimension changes the situation completely. To start, there's the issue of the work surface. Drawing a 2D picture on a 2D computer screen is easy and natural, as long as you know how to handle a mouse. But working in three dimensions on that same 2D surface requires different thinking.

Imagine cutting a hole in a shoe box and placing a block and a soda can inside. Now imagine peeking through the hole with one eye and moving the two objects so they are side by side. This is very difficult because, using only one eye, you cannot perceive depth very well. This makes it hard to know when the two dissimilar objects are at the same distance. (See Figure 1.8.)

The exercises in this book were designed to be created by hand using a simple text editor. One of the big advantages of VRML is its capability to be created in this way. Hand editing is also a great way to learn how VRML works. It is similar to the way in which HTML pages were created in the early days of the Web. Before HTML authoring tools were widely available, Web pages were handcrafted. In fact, today many authors still handcraft parts of their HTML pages for that "perfect" look.

Figure 1.8.
*Which object is
closer?*

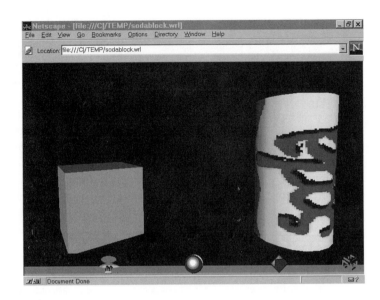

Displaying 3D Graphics

Displaying 3D graphics is very different from displaying 2D images. Objects are positioned in three dimensions but must be viewed on a two-dimensional computer display. Because the objects exist in three dimensions, it must be decided from which direction they should be viewed. To do this, I'll use the analogy of a camera. When you shoot a picture with a camera, you first aim it at the desired scene. Then you snap the picture, which places an image of the three-dimensional scene onto the flat surface of the camera film. Similarly, a 3D scene in the computer has a camera that is placed by the author to view the desired part of the scene. Then the computer draws what the camera sees onto the two-dimensional computer display. This operation is known as *rendering*.

This is a very powerful notion. To look at the scene from any angle, you simply place your virtual camera at a different viewpoint, render the image, and show it onscreen. If you move the camera little by little and render the image again at each step, you can create a walk-through of your scene. This is something you could never do with a 2D image, and it is part of the power of 3D. But this operation is as difficult as it is powerful. Rendering quickly enough to make the movement look fluid takes an enormously powerful computer. Until recently, this could be done only on big, expensive systems. But faster computer hardware has made it possible for PCs to do a good job of rendering simple scenes. Advances are happening quickly, so soon everyone will have the ability to view virtual worlds such as airports and other planets at home.

Tools and Resources for VRML

How do you get started in writing VRML 2 worlds? First, you need a way to display your work. CosmoPlayer from Silicon Graphics is included on the CD-ROM that comes with this book. After installing it, you can view some of the VRML 2 worlds included on the CD-ROM.

Installing CosmoPlayer

CosmoPlayer runs under Windows 95 and works with Netscape Navigator 2 or 3.0 or Internet Explorer 3.0. To install it, follow these steps:

1. Insert the CD-ROM into the drive.
2. Double-click My Computer.
3. Double-click on the CD-ROM icon.
4. Double-click on the icon labeled npcosmop.exe.
5. When the installation begins, follow the on-screen instructions.

Creating VRML Worlds

VRML 2 is simple enough that you will be learning how to create worlds using a simple text editor. Wordpad is an excellent choice for this task. CosmoPlayer and Wordpad will form your first authoring system for creating exciting VRML 2 worlds!

For worlds too complex to be edited by hand, you'll need to learn to use a 3D authoring tool. Some packages specifically designed for VRML are just starting to appear. Many of these new packages have features designed specifically to help the casual user create VRML worlds. Some have novel methods of helping the author solve the object placement problem mentioned before. Shadows on the walls or hash marks on the floor are used to show the position of objects relative to each other. All the author has to do is line up the shadows or guidelines, and the objects will be aligned perfectly.

Some tools that have been around for a long time have been updated for use in VRML authoring. But many of these were designed to create complex animations for TV or games, so they are often difficult to learn. When mastered, however, they are powerful tools for creating VRML content. One of the many benefits of a standard file format like VRML is that it attracts many software developers to create tools for it. This is one of the reasons VRML is gaining popularity so quickly.

Summary

In this chapter, you learned about the evolution of 3D on the Web. You saw how VRML was born and what problems exist for 3D Web authors. The shoe box example pointed out the problem a 3D author faces in positioning objects in three dimensions using a flat computer screen. You've been shown how to install a VRML browser to explore the worlds you will create.

Now explore some VRML worlds on the Web to whet your appetite for the next chapter, in which you learn to create your own world.

Q&A

Q Why would I want to use 3D on the Web? Why would I need anything more than the text and images that are already on an HTML page?

A The use of 3D on the Web has many great benefits. First, it allows a virtually infinite amount of interactivity. Viewing an image of the outside of a house is not nearly as interesting or informative as being able to walk through the front door and up to the master bedroom to check out the view. Second, 3D is much more compact than either images or text. They say that a picture is worth a thousand words. If that's true, a 3D world is worth a thousand pictures. Finally, 3D gives an author a richer medium in which to express ideas.

Q Why was VRML created from scratch, rather than from one of the existing 3D formats?

A VRML does build on the Open Inventor file format from Silicon Graphics. Inventor was intended to be a portable, cross-platform file format. Many other formats available were either proprietary or insufficient to meet the requirements of VRML. This was true because 3D had always been such a niche market that there was not enough of a need for a standard file format. The Web changed all that, so VRML was created.

Exercise

1. After loading CosmoPlayer, double-click the file labeled index.html on the CD-ROM. Here you will find links to many 3D worlds written in VRML 2. Many worlds have objects that animate when you click them. At the bottom of the window, you will notice some controls that can be used to move around in the 3D scene. Refer to the CosmoPlayer documentation, accessible from the Help menu item. To bring up the menu, click the right mouse button over the CosmoPlayer window. After you've learned how to view the content, you're ready to start writing VRML worlds of your own!

Day **2**

Basic VRML Concepts

Now that you understand how VRML relates to the Web, let me show you how to create worlds of your own. You will be creating VRML yourself, so have Microsoft WordPad or your favorite text editor ready. Give any VRML file you create a suffix of .wrl. Then, as long as you have Netscape Navigator(or Internet Explorer) and CosmoPlayer set up properly, you can just click your files and display your 3D creations.

Here's what will be covered in this chapter:

☐ 2D versus 3D graphics.

☐ What is a scene graph?

☐ Nodes and fields.

☐ Shapes and geometry.

☐ Materials and appearance.

☐ The VRML 2 file format.

2D Versus 3D Graphics

As you saw in Chapter 1, "VRML Background," there is a big difference between 2D and 3D. Although this makes it harder to work with 3D, it also gives 3D huge advantages over 2D. You can create a 3D world, populate it with interesting objects, and then walk around that world using a 3D browser such as CosmoPlayer. The only way to get similar motion using 2D is by using movies, such as MPEG, or image-based formats, such as Shockwave from Macromedia. Both of these techniques create huge files that are extremely slow to download over the Web, and are not as flexible. The only viewing angle you have is the one the author has created for you. With 3D and VRML, you can go literally anywhere in the 3D world. You can walk up to a sign to read it, look over your shoulder to see where a sound is coming from, or walk up a flight of stairs to go into a second-story office.

The compactness of 3D comes from the ability of the author to define objects as skeletons, to be filled in by the computer rendering the image. For a 2D image, you must define the color of every pixel on the screen. For 3D, you download the skeletal objects, pick a vantage point from which to view them, and then let the renderer do the rest. In VRML, the renderer can paint objects with 2D images. However, because they are repeated, they can be small and reused on many objects. For example, an image of inlaid stones could be used to represent a stone wall or a stone walkway. These images are called textures, and I will be showing you how they are used in VRML in Chapter 5, "Object Appearance."

As a VRML author, your job is to come up with an idea (often the hardest task of any job), create the skeletal models to realize your idea, and then combine these models into a VRML file. Once this is finished, you have created a virtual world. Throughout this book, I will show you how to use VRML's many features, but first, you need to learn the basics of creating the foundation of VRML, or the *scene graph*.

What Is a Scene Graph?

A scene graph is to VRML what a bitmap is to 2D graphics. It is the structure of the world being created. The VRML file format allows you to create a scene graph for your world using simple words and punctuation. Because of this you can (and will) create VRML scene graphs using a simple text editor.

A VRML scene graph comprises, among other things, a group of objects. When rendered, these objects exist in 3D space. They have depth, height, and width. VRML has many object types. The simplest are known as primitive objects because they can be described in very simple terms. The primitives available in VRML are Box, Cone, Cylinder, and Sphere.

By themselves, these primitives are not very interesting. However, in combination with one another, they can make very interesting objects. For instance, a long, thin cylinder with a cone on the end of it makes a good arrow. Replace the cone with a sphere and you have a magic wand. VRML has many other, more complex, object types, as you will see in Chapter 4, "Building Complex Objects." But for now, these primitives will allow me to illustrate the structure of a VRML scene graph.

Graphically Depicting a Scene Graph

For reasons that will become clear in Chapter 3, "Building a Scene," a VRML scene graph is very structured. It looks a lot like an upside-down tree when you draw it. Figure 2.1 shows an example of a scene graph diagram.

Figure 2.1.

A VRML scene graph.

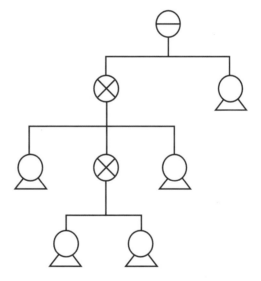

Each circle in the diagram represents a node. VRML is made up of more than 60 node types. Nodes fit together as shown in the diagram. Some have other nodes below them, connected with a line. These are known as *grouping nodes*. The node above is called the *parent* node and the nodes below it are called its *children*. Other nodes have a triangle stuck to the bottom of them. These are known as *shape* nodes. They are the actual geometry of the world, such as Sphere or Box. I will use different symbols to indicate the general node classes when drawing diagrams of a VRML scene graph, such as the preceding one. Figure 2.2 shows those symbols.

Figure 2.2.
Symbols used in scene graph diagrams.

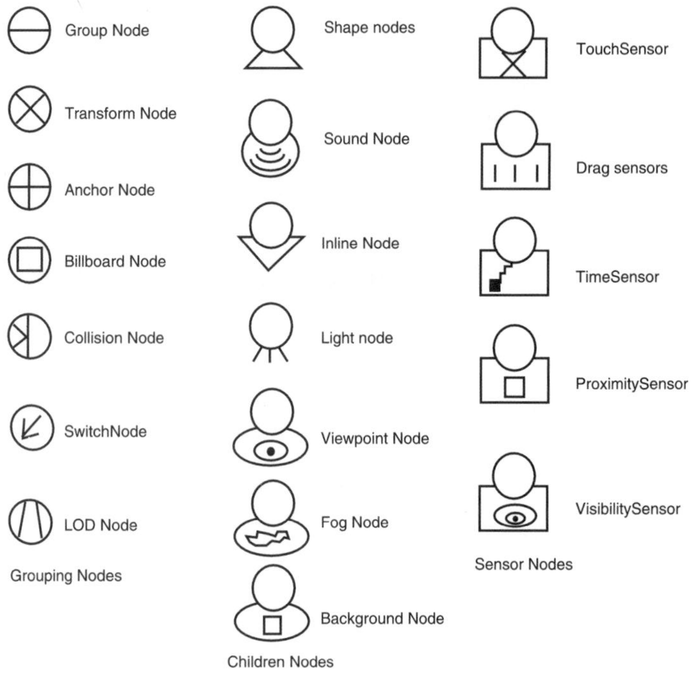

Group Node	Shape nodes	TouchSensor
Transform Node	Sound Node	Drag sensors
Anchor Node	Inline Node	TimeSensor
Billboard Node	Light node	ProximitySensor
Collision Node	Viewpoint Node	VisibilitySensor
SwitchNode	Fog Node	Sensor Nodes
LOD Node	Background Node	
Grouping Nodes	Children Nodes	

You will learn the meaning of these symbols as the week proceeds. The relationship between parent nodes and children nodes is called the *scene graph hierarchy*, and it is the most important VRML concept to learn. Chapter 3 will explain, in depth, the reason for this hierarchy. For now, I will show you simple shapes so that you can create your first VRML world!

Nodes and Fields

A node in VRML is a piece that implements some functionality. The name of the node indicates its basic function (Transform, Cone, and so on). Each node contains a list of *fields*, which hold values that define parameters for its function. For instance, the fields of the Cone node define the height of the cone and the radius at its base. These two values are all that is needed to fully define a cone. A Transform, on the other hand, is not a rendering node; it is a grouping node. Therefore, one of its fields, the children field, is a list of other nodes. I will go into more detail about grouping nodes in the next chapter. For now, look in detail at the Cone node. Here is its definition:

```
Cone {
    field        SFFloat      bottomRadius 1
    field        SFFloat      height            2
    field        SFBool        side                  TRUE
    field        SFBool        bottom          TRUE
}
```

Take a close look at the format of the preceding node description. It shows the name of the node, the names of the fields, and the numbers next to the field names in bold. These are in bold because they are the parts that can actually be typed into the VRML file format. Look at the first field entry. The word field is called as the class specifier, and the word SFFloat is called the type specifier of the bottomRadius. In this case, the value is in the field class (there are other classes of information in a node, which will be seen in Chapter 8, "Events and Routing"), and it holds an SFFloat data type. An SFFloat is a floating point number, and, in this case, it defines the radius of the bottom of the cone. The last number on this line is the default value. Every field in VRML has a default value. If you do not enter any value in the file for a certain field, it will use the default for that field. VRML tries to make the most reasonable value for each field the default, to minimize the number of fields that have to be filled in. This makes VRML easier to use and makes VRML files smaller.

 A *type specifier* in VRML is the name of the type of data stored in a field. For instance, the type specifier SFBool indicates that this field contains a single Boolean (true or false) value.

 A *class specifier* indicates one of four classes to which a field can belong. The class you will be using in the next six chapters is *field*. Field indicates that this value holds static data that is set in the VRML file and never changes. You will also be using the *exposedfield* class, which has additional capabilities. But, until Chapter 7, "Viewpoints, Sound, and Anchors," you will be using it just like the field class. The other two classes available are *eventIn* and *eventOut*. I will be describing these special classes in Chapter 8.

> **TIP**
>
> All numbers that indicate size in VRML are stated in meters. By default, a cone is two meters tall and the radius of the base is one meter. Most browsers will set the size of everything in the world according to this scale. In this case, the default cone would be a little taller than the average person. Remember this scale whenever creating a model or positioning an object in the VRML world.

The cone has four fields. As I mentioned, the `height` and `bottomRadius` fields indicate the size of the cone. The `side` and `bottom` fields allow the sides and bottom of the cone to be turned on and off. They are of the `SFBool` type, which means they can have a value of `TRUE` to turn that part of the cone on, or `FALSE` to turn that part off. For instance, you could flip the cone upside down and turn off the bottom, if you want to make an ice cream cone.

Every node in VRML has a description like the one I showed for the preceding `Cone` node. See Appendix A, "VRML Node Reference," for a complete listing of nodes using this format. Appendix A also has a short description of the function and field definitions for each node, making it a useful reference. If you look through this reference, you will see class specifiers other than field. These are for advanced animation and behavior effects, which I will explore in the second week of this book. For now, you will not be using the eventIn and eventOut classes. You will be using the exposedField class as if it were the same as field.

Shapes and Geometry

Making a VRML file with just a `Cone` node will not do anything. The `Cone` specifies only the geometry (shape) of an object, not its appearance (color). VRML also has an `Appearance` node, which I will show you in the next section, to define its color. Once you have geometry and appearance, you have enough to define a VRML object. All you need is a way to associate the color with the geometry. In VRML, you do this with the `Shape` node. Its definition looks like this:

```
Shape {
    exposedField SFNode appearance NULL
    exposedField SFNode geometry    NULL
}
```

Again, you will use exposedField just like field for now. This field is of type `SFNode`, which is a data type that holds another node. It is seen in lots of places in VRML, but here it just gives you someplace to put your geometry and appearance. The default value is `NULL` for both these fields, which is a special value meaning, "this value contains nothing." Remember I said that VRML tries to put the most reasonable default in every field? Well, a `NULL` geometry field doesn't do much, but a `NULL` appearance makes whatever geometry is in the `Shape` pure white, so it shows up. Therefore, the simplest VRML scene possible looks like this:

```
Shape {
        geometry Cone { }
}
```

Figure 2.3 shows what this world looks like.

Figure 2.3.

A simple VRML world.

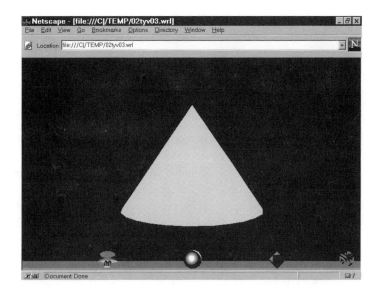

Coordinate Spaces

Where in the world does the preceding cone get placed in the world? A VRML scene graph uses a Cartesian coordinate system. Every point in the world can be described by a set of three numbers, called a coordinate. The first number is the X component, which places the object right and left in the world. The second is the Y component, which places the object up and down in the world. The third is the Z component, which places the object nearer and farther from the front of the screen.

When I talk about right and left, and so on, I am speaking in terms relative to the default initial view of the scene. If you display the cone object in Figure 2.3, the positive X direction is to the right, the positive Y direction is up, and the positive Z direction is toward you. This is known as the world coordinate system. In a 3D world, this system is fairly arbitrary. If the cone is animated and is moving right and left when you enter the world, it is moving along the X-axis. But if you walk around to its side, it is still moving on its X-axis, but now it would be moving toward and away from you.

In the next chapter, I will talk more about coordinate systems as you learn how to position objects relative to each other in the world.

Material and Appearance

The cone shown in Figure 2.3 is not very interesting because it is pure white without any highlights. The object does not even look curved. One of the biggest advantages of VRML is its capability to naturally shade objects so that they have depth and dimension. VRML gives you great control over this shading, but you have to use the Appearance node to get it.

The Appearance node holds all information pertaining to the look of an object. Here is its definition:

```
Appearance {
    exposedField SFNode material                NULL
    exposedField SFNode texture                 NULL
    exposedField SFNode textureTransform    NULL
}
```

The Appearance node is another node that has only SFNode fields. Like the Shape node, it is designed to hold other nodes containing different bits of information. The material field holds a Material node. It holds information about what color to make the object. The other two fields, texture and textureTransform, hold information about images that can be wrapped around the object for interesting effects. But I'll save talking about those until Chapter 5, "Object Appearance," when you can study appearance effects in more depth.

The Material node holds many pieces of information, all related to the color of the object. Here is how it is defined:

```
Material {
    exposedField SFFloat ambientIntensity    0.2
    exposedField SFColor diffuseColor             0.8 0.8 0.8
    exposedField SFColor emissiveColor          0 0 0
    exposedField SFFloat shininess                   0.2
    exposedField SFColor specularColor          0 0 0
    exposedField SFFloat transparency             0
}
```

As I said before, I will save a detailed discussion on how color is applied in VRML for Chapter 5. For now I will just use the simplest field, diffuseColor. This value can be thought of as the base color being reflected from the object in all directions when light hits it. Imagine a colored piece of paper. When you hold it up to the light, it looks blue, with very few shiny spots. The diffuseColor field can be thought of as the flat, or non-shiny color of the object. The diffuseColor field is of the SFColor type. This means that its value is three numbers: The first is the amount of red in the object, the second is the amount of green in the object, and the third is the amount of blue in the object. These values go from 0 (none of that color component is in the object) to 1 (the full amount of that color component is in the object). Mixing red, green, and blue allows you to create any visible color.

So, to make a red cone, I would create a Material with a red diffuseColor (a value of 1 0 0), put that in the material field of an Appearance node, and put that in the appearance field of a Shape node. The following is its definition:

```
Shape {
        appearance Appearance {
                material Material {
                        diffuseColor 1 0 0
                }
```

```
        }
        geometry Cone { }
}
```

Figure 2.4 shows what this red cone looks like in CosmoPlayer.

Figure 2.4.

A cone with a diffuse red color.

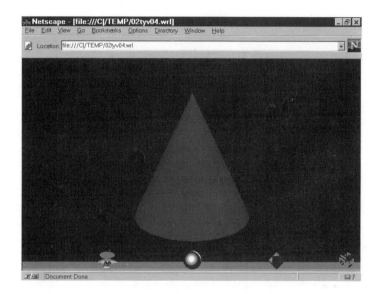

When you look at this world on your display, you will notice that the cone is not only red, but that it also has nice shading: darker at the edges and lighter in the middle, making it look three-dimensional.

The VRML 2 File Format

The CD-ROM has two files, named \figures\02tyv03.wrl and \figures\02tyv04.wrl, which you can double-click to see the cones from the preceding two examples. If you look at those files, you'll notice that they both start with the same first line:

```
#VRML V2.0 utf8
```

This is called the VRML header line, and every VRML file must start with one. It indicates that this is a VRML file, it is version 2, and that the text that follows it uses the UTF8 encoding. UTF8 is an International Standards Organization (ISO) standard that allows characters in the file to be read by a text editor. It also allows virtually any character in any language to be represented, including accented characters for Spanish, German, and French, and Japanese Kanji characters. Of course, to be able to include these characters you must have a text editor that allows them to be typed. But once they are in a VRML file, any browser can read and understand them.

The pound sign (#) must be the first character on the header line. This is actually the symbol used to enter comments into the VRML file. Whenever a VRML browser sees a pound sign, it ignores the rest of that line. Commenting your source files is a useful way to keep track of the meaning of different sections. Here are examples of comments being used:

```
# This is a tower object
Shape {
        geometry Cone { }                 # The top of the tower
        appearance Appearance {
                material Material {
                        diffuseColor 0.2 0.2 0.8 # Make the top of the
                                                 # tower a light blue
                }
        }
}
```

Indenting and Special Symbols

You have seen some examples of nodes and fields in the file format. Indenting is not necessary, but this book formats lines using indenting to show the relationship of fields to nodes and of children to parent nodes. Indenting can be done with either spaces or tabs. You can have new lines anywhere a space or a tab can appear, which is between any two words or between a word and any other symbol (such as the brace symbols ({ and })).

VRML considers the comma symbol (,) to be the same as a space, which can make for some very strange-looking files if misused. Commas are intended to separate lists of numbers. There are many places in VRML where sequences of two, three, or four number sets are used. One example of this is the Color node, which is a list of color values. Commas can be used to make this node more clear, such as in the following example:

```
Color {
        color [ 0 0 0, 0 1 0, 0.5 0.5 0.5, 1 0.5 1 ]
}
```

You could place a comma between each number if you wished, or you could omit them altogether. But using them between sets of numbers makes the file more readable and easier to fix if there are problems.

Field Data Types

Notice that in the preceding example, the number list is enclosed in bracket symbols ([ ]). Anytime you see more than one number value (where a set of three numbers, such as an SFColor, is considered one value), you must enclose them in brackets. The type of the preceding color field is MFColor. It is similar to SFColor, except that it can hold a sequence of color values. This naming convention is used throughout the VRML field types. All fields that can hold a single value start with SF (Single value Field), while all fields that can hold a sequence of values start with MF (Multiple value Field). Many SF field types (for example, SFColor) have a corresponding MF field type (for example, MFColor), which holds a sequence of the SF field type. Table 2.1 lists all the field types. A more complete description of the field types can be found in Appendix B, "VRML Field and Event Types."

Table 2.1. VRML field types.

Type	Description
SFBool	The Boolean value TRUE or FALSE.
SFFloat	A 32-bit floating point value.
SFInt32	A 32-bit signed integer.
SFTime	An absolute or relative time value.
SFVec2f	A pair of floating point values usually denoted as u, v because they are most often used to represent texture coordinates.
SFVec3f	Three floating point values usually denoted as x, y, z because they are most often used to represent a 3D position.
SFColor	Three floating point values, each between zero and one, representing the red, green, and blue components of a color.
SFRotation	Four floating point values. The first three values represent an axis (with 0,0,0 being the other point on the axis line) and the fourth value represents the angle of rotation in radians around that axis.
SFImage	A two-dimensional image with one to four color components, allowing representation of monochrome to full-color images with transparency.
SFString	A UTF8 (international character) string.
SFNode	A container for a VRML node.
MFFloat	An array of SFFloat values.
MFInt32	An array of SFInt32 values.
MFVec2f	An array of SFVec2f values.
MFVec3f	An array of SFVec3f values.
MFColor	An array of SFColor values.
MFRotation	An array of SFRotation values.
MFString	An array of SFString values.

2

Adding Nodes to the File

The main part of any VRML file is the list of nodes. After the header line, any number of nodes can be placed in sequence, as long as all the nodes can legally be placed at the top level of the file. Legal nodes are all those listed in Figure 2.2. So, a sequence of Shape nodes is a legal scene graph. This is often not desirable, though, because all shapes are centered around the coordinate 0 0 0 by default, and they would all be sitting on top of each other.

VRML has three major types of nodes. There are the nodes that must be in a specific spot; they are called the property nodes. These include Cone, which must go in the geometry field of a Shape node, and Material, which must go in the material field of an Appearance node. Then there are the grouping nodes, all of which can have children. Transform is an example of a grouping node. Then there are the children nodes, so named because they are children of a grouping node. Actually, grouping nodes can be children of other grouping nodes. This is the basis for the *scene hierarchy* concept of VRML, which I will be talking about in more detail in the next chapter. All the children and grouping nodes can be at the top level of the file.

TIP
> How can you figure out which nodes go where in a VRML file? The easiest way is to look in Appendix A. Along with the node definition and a description of its function, each entry in Appendix A shows where in the VRML file that node can go.

There are many more parts to the VRML file format that I will introduce in later chapters as needed. For now you know enough to create your own VRML worlds, starting with the exercises at the end of this chapter.

Summary

Three-dimensional graphics differ greatly from two-dimensional graphics, but both have a format in which information is stored and retrieved for display. In general terms, the 3D format is called a scene graph, which is a hierarchical representation of all the objects in a virtual world and their positions relative to each other. A scene graph is made up of nodes, which contain the shapes and descriptions of the objects. Nodes are made up of fields, which hold values describing the individual characteristics of each node. A shape is made up of geometry, which makes up its form, and appearance, which gives the geometry its color. A 3D scene graph in VRML is represented in a text file format to make it easier to edit by hand.

In Chapters 3 through 7, I will be describing the basics of scene graphs, nodes, and fields. By the end of the first week, you should be able to create your own VRML worlds populated with interesting objects. In Chapters 8 through 14, I will show you how to add animation and user interaction to your worlds. Finally, in Chapters 15 through 21, I will describe some advanced VRML capabilities, including ways to optimize your worlds, integration with HTML pages, and what might be in VRML's future.

Q&A

Q Why does it take four nodes (`Shape`, `Appearance`, `Material`, and `Cone`) to make a simple object in VRML?

A The reuse of appearances, colors, and entire shapes is common in VRML. Therefore, separating the functionality of the `Shape` node like this allows great flexibility in doing this sharing. This saves both in authoring, because you can choose from a standard set of appearances, and in download time, because you do not need to constantly redefine the same colors.

Q Why is the default material pure white, without any highlights?

A During the design of the VRML language, the choice of an appropriate default material was a big issue. It was originally going to be a nice, highlighted, gray color. This would have made simple scenes, such as the first cone example, easy and useful. But any practical VRML object is going to need a better color defined for it. Therefore, it was decided to make the color pure white; any other appearance, such as textures, would not have the interference of a material that would have to be disabled.

Exercise

1. Create a scene with three cones. One should be gold, the second should be turquoise, and the third should be pink. Make them different heights and widths so they can all be seen, even though they are sitting on top of each other.

Answer

1. Listing 2.1 shows three cones in a VRML world.

Listing 2.1. Three cones in a VRML world.

```
#VRML V2.0 utf8
Shape {
        appearance Appearance {
                material Material {
            diffuseColor 0.606383 0.432091 0
                }
        }
        geometry Cone { height 3 }
}

Shape {
        appearance Appearance {
                material Material {
            diffuseColor 0 0.49931 1
                }
        }
        geometry Cone { bottomRadius 1.8 }
}
Shape {
        appearance Appearance {
                material Material {
            diffuseColor 0.8 0.200912 0.434113
                }
        }
        geometry Cone {
                bottomRadius 0.5
                height 4
        }
}
```

Day **3**

Building a Scene

In the previous chapter, you learned the basic structure of a VRML scene graph. But how do you place objects in a scene so they are not all at 0 0 0? VRML has many powerful facilities for accomplishing this. I will show you the `Transform` node, which gives you complete flexibility in placing and orienting objects in a scene. `Transform` is also one of the nodes making up the foundation of the VRML scene hierarchy. I will also talk about this hierarchy, and explain why it is so important in creating complex and interesting worlds. Then, I will show you how to put many objects together in a single scene. Finally, I will show you how to reuse parts of a scene to simplify authoring. Here is what I'll cover today:

- ☐ Transformation and hierarchy
- ☐ Groups and transforms
- ☐ Basic geometric primitives
- ☐ Using `DEF/USE` to reuse parts of the scene

Transformation and Hierarchy

 The *World Coordinate System* is the coordinate system created by the placement of the X-, Y-, and Z-axes that all objects in a VRML scene will use for proper placement, scale, and orientation in the scene.

By default, a shape in VRML is placed with its center at 0 0 0 in the world coordinate system. To move it to another location, the Transform node is used. Here is its definition:

```
Transform {
    eventIn         MFNode          addChildren
    eventIn         MFNode          removeChildren
    exposedField    SFVec3f         center          0 0 0
    exposedField    MFNode          children        []
    exposedField    SFRotation      rotation        0 0 1   0
    exposedField    SFVec3f         scale           1 1 1
    exposedField    SFRotation      scaleOrientation 0 0 1  0
    exposedField    SFVec3f         translation     0 0 0
    field           SFVec3f         bboxCenter      0 0 0
    field           SFVec3f         bboxSize        -1 -1 -1
}
```

The Transform node has a children field that can hold a Shape node. This field is similar to the material field in the Appearance node because it has another node as its value. But it is different because it is an MFNode field, rather than an SFNode field. That means the children field can have more than one node in a list. If more than one node is placed in the children field, the nodes must be enclosed in square brackets.

Most of the other fields of Transform allow you to change the position, size, and orientation of the nodes in the children field. The fields controlling these transformations are center, rotation, scale, scaleOrientation, and translation. The translation field allows you to move the children of the Transform away from their default location of 0 0 0. The translation field contains an SFVec3f value, which gives the new position around which to center the shape. Here is an example, Listing 3.1, in which I will move a red cone to the position 4 5 0.

TYPE   Listing 3.1. A transformed cone.

```
Transform {
      translation 4 5 0
      children Shape {
            appearance Appearance {
                  material Material {
                        diffuseColor 1 0 0

                  }                      }
            geometry Cone { }

      }
}
```

Figure 3.1 shows the scene graph diagram for this simple world. This diagram is trivial, but you'll find that using diagrams like this is invaluable when you start building more complex scenes.

Figure 3.1.

The scene graph for a transformed red cone.

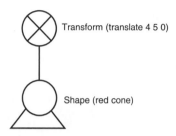

Transform (translate 4 5 0)

Shape (red cone)

Notice that I did not use brackets to enclose the contents of the children field because there is only one child in the list. When viewed from the front, this example will move the center of the cone four units to the right and five units up. If the Transform had multiple children, each would be moved the same amount; therefore, their position relative to each other would not change. But, they would move relative to any shapes not under that Transform.

This notion of relative movement is very important. The preceding scene didn't change much because I moved the only object in the scene. It might shift a little to the right and up when you first view it, but there is nothing else in the world with which to compare it, so the Transform is not very useful. Let me add another object to the scene in Listing 3.2.

Type **Listing 3.2. VRML scene with red and green cones.**

```
Transform {
    translation 4 5 0
    children Shape {
        appearance Appearance {
            material Material {
                diffuseColor 1 0 0
            }
        }
        geometry Cone { }
    }
}
Shape {
    appearance Appearance {
        material Material {
            diffuseColor 0 1 0
        }
    }
    geometry Cone { }
}
```

As I mentioned in Chapter 2, "Basic VRML Concepts," a VRML file can contain any number of nodes, as long as they are either children or grouping nodes. So, in the preceding scene, the first shape, the red cone, is moved by its parent Transform, but the second shape, the green cone, is not a child of the Transform, so it will stay at 0 0 0. Figure 3.2 shows what the scene looks like, and Figure 3.3 shows its scene graph diagram.

Figure 3.2.

Scene with a red cone and a green cone. The red cone is translated 4 5 0, relative to the green cone.

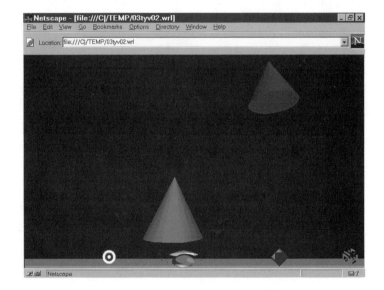

Figure 3.3.

Scene graph diagram of the scene.

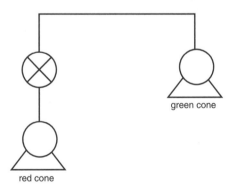

As I mentioned in the last chapter, a Transform can be a child of another Transform. So, the Transform and the Shape at the top level of the file could be made children of another Transform and moved together. The following code with related Figures 3.4 and 3.5 is an example where I do this, plus add a third cone, to show the relationships between all the objects in the scene. In Listing 3.3, I will put a Transform around the red and green cones, move it back (by translating them in the Z-axis), and add a blue cone.

TYPE | **Listing 3.3. VRML scene with a red, green, and blue cone.**

```
Transform {
      translation -2 0 -6
      children [
            Transform {
                  translation 4 5 0
                  children Shape {
                        appearance Appearance {
                              material Material {
                                    diffuseColor 1 0 0
                              }
                        }
                        geometry Cone { }
                  }
            }
            Shape {
                  appearance Appearance {
                        material Material {
                              diffuseColor 0 1 0
                        }
                  }
                  geometry Cone { }
            }
      ]
}
Shape {
      appearance Appearance {
            material Material {
                  diffuseColor 0 0 1
            }
      }
      geometry Cone { }
}
```

Figure 3.4.

The scene from Figure 3.2 with the two cones moved back and a blue cone added.

Figure 3.5.

Scene graph diagram of the scene.

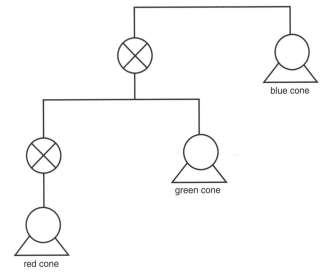

Scale and Rotation

The Transform node performs three operations related to manipulating its children. In addition to changing the children's position, as we have seen, the Transform node can also alter the size of its children, and their orientation. The size is changed with the `scale` field, which is an `SFVec3f`, just like the `translation` field. But in this case, the three values independently change the size of the children relative to the three axes. The default of 1 1 1 makes the children their normal size. Making any dimension 2 will stretch the children to twice their original size in that dimension. Making it 0.5 would squeeze the children to one-half their normal size. Making all three numbers the same scales the children uniformly, but making them different values will stretch the objects into different shapes. For instance, the scene in Figure 3.6 is a cone with a scale of 3 1 1, so it is stretched along the X-axis, making its base an oval, rather than a circle.

Figure 3.6.

A cone with a scale factor of 3 1 1.

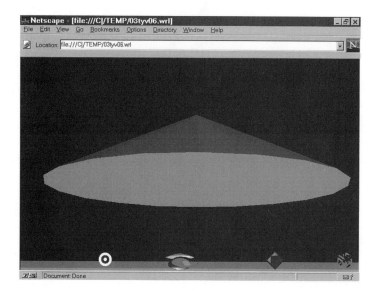

The orientation of children of a `Transform` is changed with the `rotation` field, which is an `SFRotation` field type. The `SFRotation` is more complicated than `SFVec3f`, but can be easily understood with an analogy. Take a soda can and stick a pencil through the middle of the can horizontally. Now, spin the pencil and the soda can will spin around the center of the pencil. Take the pencil out and try to push it through again, but this time at a 45° angle. Now when you spin the pencil, the can does something interesting. If you keep the pencil at the same 45° angle you started with, the can starts upright, spins onto its side, goes back to being upright again, and so on. Figure 3.7 illustrates this.

Figure 3.7.

Spinning a soda can about a pencil.

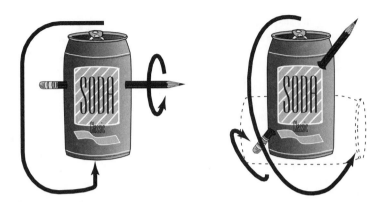

The pencil forms the *axis of rotation* for the soda can. Whatever direction the pencil goes through the can, that is the axis about which the can will rotate. In fact, the pencil doesn't even have to go through the can. If it doesn't, the can will orbit around the pencil, as if attached to it with a string. This is how the SFRotation value is specified, with four numbers. The first three define the axis of rotation, and the fourth defines the angle the object should rotate, relative to its initial position. Here is an example of a rotation:

```
rotation 0 1 0 1.57
```

To find the actual axis, you draw a line from 0 0 0 to the axis value in the SFRotation. In this case, the line goes from 0 0 0 to 0 1 0, which goes along the Y-axis. The angle is in radians, which is not as common as degrees, but easy once you get used to it. Just remember that 2Π or about 6.28 radians are in a circle. So, 3.14 is 180°, 1.57 is 90°, and 0.78 is 45°. The preceding example will rotate the object counterclockwise, when looking from the top, and 90° about a vertical axis.

Why counterclockwise? Rotations in VRML follow something called the right-hand rule. The axis in this example goes from 0 0 0 to 0 1 0. That is the positive Y direction. This is very important. Every axis has a direction. Now, if you grasp this axis line with your right hand and your thumb is pointing in the direction of the axis, and if you look at the axis with your thumb pointing toward you, your fingers curve around the axis in the counterclockwise direction. (See Figure 3.8.) This is the direction an SFRotation will rotate an object.

Figure 3.8.

The right-hand rule.

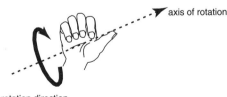

axis of rotation

rotation direction

TIP

The relationship between radians and degrees is a linear one. To calculate radians based on degrees, multiply the number of degrees by .017444. Before you multiply, make sure the degrees number is between -360 and 360. Subtract or add 360 to the number of degrees until you get it in this range because adding or subtracting 360 degrees to any angle maintains that same angle in a VRML world. The following are some sample conversions:

Degrees	x .017444 =	Radians
45	x .017444 =	.78
90	x .017444 =	1.57
180	x .017444 =	3.14
-90	x .017444 =	-1.57
17	x .017444 =	.30

center **and** scaleOrientation

There are two more fields in the `Transform` node that deal with altering the children, the `center` and `scaleOrientation` fields. The `center` field sets the point about which the rotation occurs. As already mentioned, the axis of rotation is the line that goes through the origin, `0 0 0`, and the axis part of the `SFRotation`. Changing the `center` field from its default of `0 0 0` will cause the rotation axis to still have the direction of the original axis, but it will go through the `center` point instead of the origin. This is often useful if you want to rotate an object along it edge, such as the base of a cone.

The `scaleOrientation` field changes the axes along which the object scales. By default, the `scaleOrientation` is `0 0 1 0`, which means a rotation of 0 radians about the Z-axis. The axis is arbitrary because you are not rotating. This will cause the X-scale value (the first number of the `scale` `SFVec3f`) to scale along the X-axis, and so on. But changing `scaleOrientation` essentially rotates the axes. A value of `1 0 0 1.57` will rotate the axes 90° about the X-axis, which will interpret a `scale` value of `2 3 4` differently than the usual X Y Z orientation. This scale value of `2 3 4` will scale the object by 2 along the X-axis, by 4 about the Y-axis, and by 3 about the Z-axis.

TIP

Although the `center` field is extremely useful in offsetting the rotation of an object, the `scaleOrientation` field is rarely used. Don't worry about mastering it right now.

Listing 3.4 is a Transform that manipulates an object in every way possible.

| TYPE | **Listing 3.4. VRML scene demonstrating transformations.** |

```
Transform {
      translation 0 -2 0
      scale 3 1 1
      scaleOrientation 0 1 0 -0.78
      rotation 0 0 1 0.78
      center 0 1 0
      children Shape {
            appearance Appearance {
                  material Material {
                        diffuseColor 1 0 0
                  }
            }
            geometry Cone { }
      }
}
Shape {
      appearance Appearance {
            material Material {
                  diffuseColor 0 1 0
            }
      }
      geometry Cone { }
}
```

Figure 3.9 shows the result of these manipulations. The red cone is translated -2 along the Y-axis. That places its tip just touching the base of the green cone. Then it is rotated 45° about the Z-axis, and the center of rotation is at the tip of the cone. Finally, it is scaled, and the scaleOrientation is -45° tilted about the Y-axis, which causes the base of the cone to be elliptical, but canted at a 45° angle.

Composite Hierarchical Transformations

I've shown you hierarchies: placing multiple children in a Transform node, some of which might themselves be Transform nodes, but with still more children. Now I want to show you one of the most important concepts of transformation hierarchies: *composition*. The human body provides an excellent example of composition. When you move your forearm, it hinges at the elbow, and everything from your forearm to your fingertips moves together. When you move your wrist, your hand and fingers move, and so on, all the way down to the last knuckle on your fingers. You can think of your fingers as children of your hand, which is a child of your arm, which is a child of your torso. Your body is a big scene graph!

Figure 3.9.

Cone with all transformations applied to it.

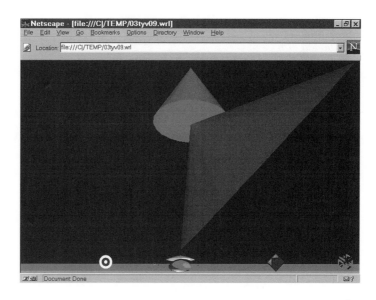

 Composition is the act of putting smaller pieces together to make a larger whole. For example, the English composition you created in grade school was a composition of multiple, simple sentences you put together to make one large essay.

Figure 3.10 is a scene graph diagram of a human arm. The Transform nodes make up the joints, and the shapes make up the various bones in your arm.

When you rotate the shoulder Transform, the entire arm, right down to the fingertips, rotates with it. Because of the hierarchy, they are all considered children of the shoulder, so they all move just like a real arm. When the elbow Transform rotates, the forearm, hand, and fingers move, but not the upper arm or the shoulder Transform. They are above the elbow in the hierarchy. All of the transforms in this scene graph affect only the parts of the arm below them. This makes the arm scene graph behave just like a real arm.

There are many examples of this hierarchical relationship in the real world. All the parts of a car, the body, the wheels, the interior, and the engine, can be placed under a car Transform. When you move the car by changing the translation field of its transform, all the parts move. Each wheel has its own Transform, with the tire and hubcap as children. When you rotate the wheel transform, all parts of the wheel rotate, but the rest of the car does not. Doors, fireplugs, and even trees are all represented with hierarchy in VRML.

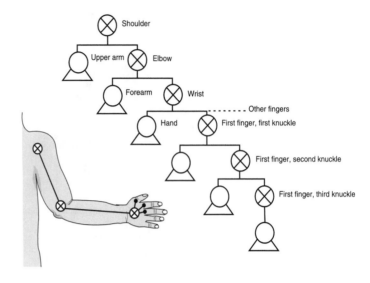

Figure 3.10.
*The human arm
as a VRML scene
graph diagram.*

Groups and Transforms

So far, I've mentioned only Transforms in talking about hierarchy. There are many other grouping nodes that can have children. I will discuss all of them in later chapters. For example, I'll discuss the Anchor node in Chapter 7, "Viewpoints, Sound, and Anchors," the Billboard node in Chapter 12, "Movies, Switches, and Billboards," and the Collision node in Chapter 18, "Collision." All these nodes can have children. The simplest grouping node is Group. Here is its definition:

```
Group {
    eventIn       MFNode    addChildren
    eventIn       MFNode    removeChildren
    exposedField  MFNode    children        []
    field         SFVec3f   bboxCenter      0 0 0
    field         SFVec3f   bboxSize        -1 -1 -1
}
```

This node has a children field just like Transform. It is used to collect nodes and to create hierarchies that do not need transformations applied to them. However, this might not seem very useful for the nodes you have seen. Geometric primitives really need to be transformed or they will sit on top of each other. But I will show you nodes such as the Sensor and Interpolator nodes in Chapter 9, "Adding Behavior to Objects," that do not benefit from transformation, so the Group node can be used to collect together these nodes.

The Group node has two other fields, ignoring the eventIn values for the moment, bboxSize, and bboxCenter. These fields appear in the Transform node as well. They allow you to give a "hint" to the VRML browser about the total size and location of the children of this node. The bboxSize field is set to the size of a box surrounding the children in all three dimensions, and the bboxCenter specifies the center of this box. If this box is not specified (or set to its default size of -1 -1 -1), the VRML browser must compute the value itself. For complex objects comprising many primitives, this could be a very time-consuming operation.

Basic Geometric Primitives

So far, I have told you about only one geometric primitive, Cone. In the next chapter, I will talk about more complex geometric nodes that give you great flexibility in creating interesting shapes. But, for now, let me show you three other primitives that are often useful: Box, Sphere, and Cylinder.

```
Box {
    field       SFVec3f size   2 2 2
}
Sphere {
    field SFFloat radius    1
}
Cylinder {
    field       SFBool      bottom      TRUE
    field       SFFloat     height      2
    field       SFFloat     radius      1
    field       SFBool      side        TRUE
    field       SFBool      top         TRUE
}
```

Like the Cone, these three all have simple parameters specifying their shape and size (size for Box, radius for Sphere, and height and radius for Cylinder). Cylinder also has SFBool fields, like Cone, to turn its different parts on and off. This allows a single cylinder with different colors on the sides and ends to be created, such as the following in Listing 3.5.

TYPE **Listing 3.5. VRML scene of a multicolored cylinder.**

```
Shape {
    appearance Appearance {
        material Material {
            diffuseColor 1 0 0
        }
    }
    geometry Cylinder {
        top FALSE
        bottom FALSE
    }
}
```

continues

Listing 3.5. continued

```
Shape {
    appearance Appearance {
        material Material {
            diffuseColor 0 0 1
        }
    }
    geometry Cylinder {
        side FALSE
    }
}
```

Here, I am using the fact that two objects have the same default position to my advantage. I have created two objects: a red cylinder with the end caps turned off, and a blue one with only the end caps turned on. The appearance is that of a single Cylinder with red sides and blue ends, as shown in Figure 3.11.

Figure 3.11.

A cylinder with different colors on the sides and ends.

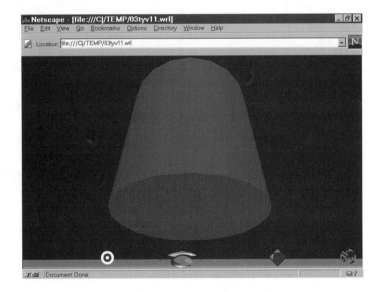

Using transformation hierarchies and the sphere, cylinder, and box geometric primitives, a wide variety of shapes can be created. Figure 3.12 shows two interesting complex objects made up entirely of these four primitives.

Figure 3.12.
A big bird and a harp, both created with a combination of cones, boxes, spheres, and cylinders.

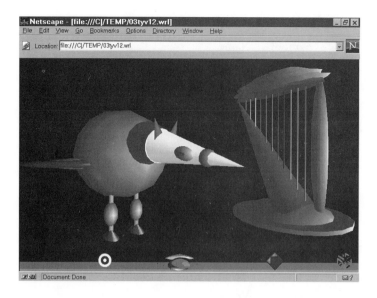

Using DEF/USE to Reuse Parts of the Scene

If you want a world made up of 16 blue spheres, arranged in a square pattern, you would need 16 sphere shapes and 16 Transform nodes to position them. But VRML gives you tools to avoid this duplication of work, DEF and USE. These two modifiers can be placed wherever a node name is allowed. The DEF keyword is followed by a name, and then a node description. This node now has a name defined for it. Legal names can be as short as one character long, but must start with a letter. Letters include symbols in other languages, such as Japanese Kanji characters, and accented characters. Following the first letter may be any letter, number, or any of the characters in Table 3.1.

Table 3.1. Special characters allowed in a VRML DEF name.

Symbol	Name
!	Exclamation point
$	Dollar
%	Percent
&	Ampersand
(	Left parenthesis
)	Right parenthesis
*	Asterisk

continues

Table 3.1. continued

Symbol	Name
/	Forward slash
:	Colon
;	Semicolon
<	Less than
=	Equal
>	Greater than
?	Question mark
@	Commercial at
^	Hat
_	Underscore
`	Accent grave
|	Vertical bar
~	Tilde

Once a node is named using DEF, you can place the keyword USE, followed by that same name, in place of a node name. This node is now instantiated where the USE is placed. It is as if the node had been retyped, but with two important distinctions. First, you save space in the file because the node does not appear twice. Second, if you change the size, color, or any other aspect of the node you instanced, both renditions of that node will get changed. Listing 3.6 is a simple example of using the same appearance to create a red box and a red cylinder.

TYPE **Listing 3.6. VRML scene demonstrating appearances.**

```
Shape {
        appearance DEF Red Appearance {
                material Material { diffuseColor 1 0 0 }
        }
        geometry Box { }
}
Shape {
        appearance USE Red
        geometry Cylinder { }
}
```

Notice that when I instanced the Appearance node, everything inside it, including the Material node, was instanced. This is very powerful. You can create a Transform node containing a very complex hierarchy, name it with DEF, and then instantiate it with USE many times. This not only saves a lot of typing, but it also allows a VRML browser to be more efficient in drawing these objects, because it is just repeating the same operations over and over.

Listing 3.7 is the blue sphere example previously mentioned.

TYPE **Listing 3.7. VRML scene demonstrating reuse.**

```
*** begin code listing ***DEF RowOfSpheres Group {
     children [
          Transform {
               translation -6 -6 0
               children Shape {
                    appearance Appearance {
                         material Material {
                              diffuseColor 0 0 1
                         }
                    }
                    geometry Sphere { }
               }
          }
          Transform {
               translation -2 -6 0
               children Shape {
                    appearance Appearance {
                         material Material {
                              diffuseColor 0 0 1
                         }
                    }
                    geometry Sphere { }
               }
          }
          Transform {
               translation 2 -6 0
               children Shape {
                    appearance Appearance {
                         material Material {
                              diffuseColor 0 0 1
                         }
                    }
                    geometry Sphere { }
               }
          }
          Transform {
               translation 6 -6 0
               children Shape {
                    appearance Appearance {
                         material Material {
                              diffuseColor 0 0 1
                         }
                    }
```

3

continues

Listing 3.7. continued

```
                    geometry Sphere { }
          }
        }
      ]
  }
Transform {
      translation 0 4 0
      children USE RowOfSpheres
}
Transform {
      translation 0 8 0
      children USE RowOfSpheres
}
Transform {
      translation 0 12 0
      children USE RowOfSpheres
}
```

In this example, I'm creating a row of blue spheres along the X-axis. This row has a Y value of -6, because that is where I want the first row to be. I then group these spheres together so that I can name them. Creating a Group in order to associate a name with a reusable composition is a good use of the Group node. Now I can instance my row of spheres three more times to make four rows. I place the instances under Transform nodes so that I can translate them up in the Y direction to get the regular grid I want. The resulting spheres can be seen in Figure 3.13.

Figure 3.13.

Four rows of four spheres using DEF and USE.

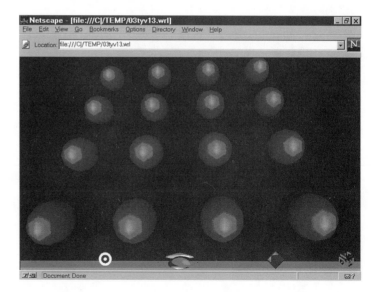

Summary

In order to place objects relative to each other, VRML provides you with the ability to transform the position and orientation of your objects. The Transform node contains a list of children, which can be the set of shapes to be transformed. By transforming one object and not another, you can position them relative to each other. Then, that group of one transformed object and one untransformed object can be placed under another Transform node to move it relative to another object. This nesting of transformations and shapes is called the transformation hierarchy and is a cornerstone of VRML. A Transform node basically determines where in the virtual world the origin of a set of objects (its children) will be. This Transform effectively creates a local coordinate space for its children. Every node in VRML operates in this local coordinate space.

VRML has several simple geometric shapes that you can use to build much more complex objects—thanks to this object hierarchy. These shapes include the Box, Cone, Cylinder, and Sphere. You can also save space and effort in constructing your worlds with the DEF/USE constructs. These allow you to name nodes (either shapes or entire transformation hierarchies) then reuse them just by using that name.

The hierarchical concepts of VRML allow you to construct objects with joints. In Chapter 9, you'll see how to move these joints to make animated characters. But first, in the next two chapters, I will show you many more ways to create interesting geometric shapes.

Q&A

Q Why are there not more primitive shapes available as nodes in VRML 2?

A First of all, the primitives that are available are all easily defined in a few fields. That makes the VRML nodes clear and precise. Second, the box, sphere, cone, and cylinder shapes all have well known rendering algorithms that make them attractive to use from a performance standpoint. You will learn in Chapter 19, "Prototyping," that you can create additional primitives yourself using the prototyping capabilities of VRML 2. Prototyping is very powerful and there are many issues and capabilities you need to understand before I can show you how to use them properly. Still, if you do create a prototype of a basic shape, there will be no guarantee it will work well with the VRML browser. These primitives do guarantee high performance.

Q Couldn't I have created all these objects using VRML 1?

A Yes. The goal of VRML 1 was to define a standard for representing three-dimensional worlds. When the VRML 2 standard set out to add action to 3D worlds, the geometry features stayed pretty much the same, yet the node descriptions changed to open the door for using the best methods of adding animation and user interaction to a VRML scene.

Q Are there any disadvantages of using DEF and USE for reuse?

A DEF and USE work so well because of the architecture of computers. When the parser reads the nodes from the VRML file text, it puts each node in a memory location and associates it with that memory location whenever it uses that node during rendering. So, whenever the USE is encountered, the computer does not put another copy in memory, but instead keeps a pointer to the original. Therefore, once you've created a pointer in memory, whatever happens within the original also happens to the copy. If this is not the intended effect, you should not use the USE statement. But when you do, you save typing time, network download time, browser loading time, computer memory usage, and rendering time.

Exercises

1. It is time to start building a homestead. To start, create two trees for the front yard. Make a cypress tree from a Sphere and Cylinder, and make a pine tree from a Cone and a Cylinder.

2. Create a large flat Box, which will define your property. Make it grassy green. Place a row of three cypress trees at one side of the property, and place two pine trees in the front yard.

Answers

☐ Because of code length, you can find the complete VRML files for the preceding exercises on the CD-ROM at \Source\Answers.

Day 4

Building Complex Objects

So far, I've shown you how to create a VRML scene with simple shapes transformed to change their position, size, and orientation. I've also shown you how to create objects with complex hierarchies so you could imagine how to allow a puppet's arms to be moved and a car's wheels to be turned. Now I will show you several geometric objects that take you far past the simple cone, box, sphere, and cylinder you've seen so far. These allow you to easily create complex shapes to make your worlds interesting and compelling. Here is what I'll cover:

- [ ] Using the `IndexedFaceSet`
- [ ] Using lines and points
- [ ] Using elevation grids
- [ ] Creating extrusions for use in a VRML scene
- [ ] Using text in a VRML scene
- [ ] Combining geometries to make complex objects

The `IndexedFaceSet`

In addition to the simple geometric primitives you've learned about so far, VRML also lets you define arbitrarily shaped patches of flat surfaces. Each patch is like cutting out different shapes from a piece of paper. The shapes are defined by giving a list of `SFVec3f` points, and then describing the order in which these points should be connected. It's like a connect-the-dots game. You draw a straight line between consecutive points, you connect the last point to the first, and the area contained within these lines is painted with the color in the `Appearance` node, just like the primitive shapes. The node that creates shapes like this is the `IndexedFaceSet`. It is a complex node, so I will present its VRML node definition after I tell you a little bit about it. First of all, it can contain several shapes like the one I just described. Each shape is called a face, and the `IndexedFaceSet` gets its name from the fact that it can have many of these faces in one node.

Two rules govern the definition of these faces. First, all the points of the shape must be *coplanar*. This means that if you drew all the points in three-dimensional space, you must be able to place a flat sheet, or plane, into that space and have all the points lie on it. This plane doesn't have to be parallel to the X-, Y-, or Z-axes; however, it must be positioned so that all the points lie in it. For instance, the three points 0 0 0, 0 1 0, and 1 0 0 all lie in the XY plane. If you place a flat sheet into the world, aligned with the X-axis and the Y-axis, all three of these points would lie on it. Likewise, 0 0 0, 0 0 1, and 1 0 1 all lie in the XZ plane. But what about 1 0 0, 0 1 0 and 0 0 1? These lie in a plane, too. This plane, though, is at a 45° angle to all three axes. In fact, any three points lie in a plane because a plane is defined by three points in space.

The simplest shape you can make with an `IndexedFaceSet` is a triangle. Connecting the three sets of points I showed you in the preceding paragraph will all create triangles. The next simplest shape has four points. A triangle will always be coplanar. But a shape created with four points will not always be coplanar. If all four points do lie in a plane, the shape is known as a *quadrilateral*.

> Creating a face that is not coplanar yields undefined results. Some browsers will render it wrong and others will not render it at all. Make sure you always define planar faces. One way to ensure this is to always make your faces triangular.

The second rule governing faces is that, by default, every face must be *convex*. A convex face means that a line drawn between any two points in the face will be entirely inside the face. Figure 4.1 shows an example of a convex versus non-convex face.

Figure 4.1.

Convex versus non-convex faces.

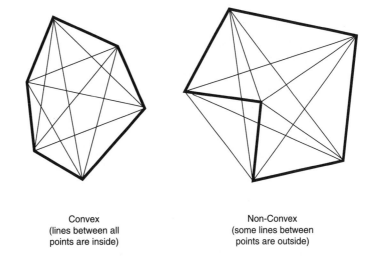

Convex
(lines between all
points are inside)

Non-Convex
(some lines between
points are outside)

There is a field in the IndexedFaceSet that can override this requirement, but rendering non-convex faces can be expensive, so it is usually best to make all your faces convex. Figure 4.2 shows how you would convert a non-convex face into two or more convex ones.

Figure 4.2.

Splitting a face to make it convex.

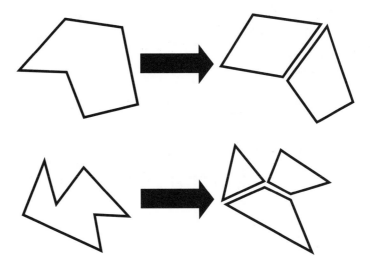

With those two rules defined, you are ready to be introduced to the IndexedFaceSet node:

```
IndexedFaceSet {
    eventIn       MFInt32 set_colorIndex
    eventIn       MFInt32 set_coordIndex
    eventIn       MFInt32 set_normalIndex
    eventIn       MFInt32 set_texCoordIndex
    exposedField  SFNode  color            NULL
    exposedField  SFNode  coord            NULL
    exposedField  SFNode  normal           NULL
    exposedField  SFNode  texCoord         NULL
    field         SFBool  ccw              TRUE
    field         MFInt32 colorIndex       []
    field         SFBool  colorPerVertex   TRUE
    field         SFBool  convex           TRUE
    field         MFInt32 coordIndex       []
    field         SFFloat creaseAngle      0
    field         MFInt32 normalIndex      []
    field         SFBool  normalPerVertex  TRUE
    field         SFBool  solid            TRUE
    field         MFInt32 texCoordIndex    []
}
```

As you can see, the IndexedFaceSet is very complex. It is easily the most complex node in VRML. That is because it is very flexible in allowing you to create different shapes. Because it is so complex, I will show you another version, this time with only the fields I will be covering in this chapter. I will be covering the other fields in later chapters, but for now, here is the simplified IndexedFaceSet:

```
IndexedFaceSet {
    exposedField  SFNode  coord       NULL
    field         SFBool  ccw         TRUE
    field         SFBool  convex      TRUE
    field         MFInt32 coordIndex  []
    field         SFBool  solid       TRUE
}
```

That helps you focus on the most often used fields first, doesn't it? Before I show you how to use these fields, I need to introduce one more node, Coordinate. The Coordinate node is placed in the coord field of the IndexedFaceSet, just like the Material node goes in the material field of the Appearance node. It looks like this:

```
Coordinate {
    exposedField MFVec3f point  []
}
```

This node holds the list of points, to be used in the IndexedFaceSet, in the point field. The point field is an MFVec3f, which means it holds a list of SFVec3f values. Listing 4.1 is an example of a simple IndexedFaceSet with one face, a square.

Listing 4.1. VRML scene showing a square.

```
Shape {
    geometry IndexedFaceSet {
        coord Coordinate {
            point [ 0 0 0, 1 0 0, 1 1 0, 0 1 0 ]
        }
        coordIndex [ 0, 1, 2, 3, -1 ]
    }
}
```

The Coordinate node holds four points, which define a square in the XY plane, assuming you connect the points in order. This ordering is given in the coordIndex field, containing the sequence in which the points should be connected. Each value of coordIndex is an index into the list of coordinate points. The last value is -1, which indicates the end of the index list. The -1 is not necessary in this case because the list automatically ends when the last index is reached, but I usually include it for completeness. The -1 will be necessary for the first face coordinate index list in the next example, where I will place more than one face in a single IndexedFaceSet. Figure 4.3 shows what this face looks like, and you can examine it by going to the file 04tyv03.wrl on the CD-ROM.

Figure 4.3.

A simple IndexedFaceSet *of a square.*

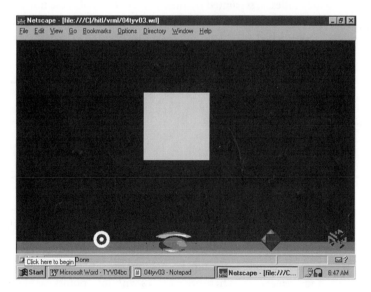

When you browse this world, notice that the face is completely flat. If you look at it edge on, it disappears. Unlike the simple geometric primitives, this face has no thickness. But because the IndexedFaceSet can have many faces in a single node, you can create objects with thickness by creating several faces that enclose a volume. The box is the simplest example of this. Listing 4.2 is a box, created with a single `IndexedFaceSet` node.

TYPE | **Listing 4.2. VRML scene showing a box.**

```
Shape {
    geometry IndexedFaceSet {
        coord Coordinate {
            point [ -1 -1  1, 1 -1  1, 1 1  1, -1 1  1,
                    -1 -1 -1, 1 -1 -1, 1 1 -1, -1 1 -1 ]
        }
        coordIndex [ 0, 1, 2, 3, -1,
                     5, 4, 7, 6, -1,
                     1, 5, 6, 2, -1,
                     4, 0, 3, 7, -1,
                     4, 5, 1, 0, -1,
                     3, 2, 6, 7, -1 ]
    }
}
```

This box is made up of six faces, with four sides each. So, the `coordIndex` list has six sets of four indexes, separated by the -1 value. Each of these index values refers to one of the eight points in the point list. Figure 4.4 shows a wireframe version of the cube, with the points and faces marked.

Figure 4.4.

A cube made up of six faces of an `IndexedFaceSet`.

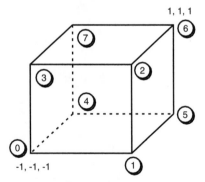

The preceding example points out a very important and powerful concept of the `IndexedFaceSet`. There are six faces with four points each, which means I need a total of 24 points. But the `point` field of the `Coordinate` node only has eight points. Where did the other 16 points come from? Notice that the `coordIndex` field specifies each of the eight points three times, because three faces have that point in common. This reusability of points can save a lot of space in the file and is the reason why the point ordering (using the `coordIndex` field) is separated from the point list itself. It is also the reason why the point list is kept in a separate node, rather than a field of the `IndexedFaceSet`. You can instantiate the `Coordinate` node and reuse the entire point list in more than one `IndexedFaceSet`.

There are three flags of interest in the simplified `IndexedFaceSet` node shown above, `ccw`, `convex`, and `solid`. I talked about the `convex` field when I was discussing the convex requirement of creating faces. By default, this is `TRUE`, which means that you must create only convex faces for this node. But, if you set this flag to `FALSE`, you can create any type of face, convex or non-convex, and the VRML browser will do the right thing.

The `ccw` and `solid` fields have to do with another optimization of VRML. By default, only one side of a face gets rendered. Go back to the example world shown in Figure 4.3, `04tyv03.wrl`, and walk around to the back of the square. You will see that it is not there! In 3D graphics, it is easy for the computer to know which side of a face is being rendered so it can choose to render only one side. This is useful when rendering "solid" objects, which are objects whose faces enclose a volume. Most objects in the real world are solid, such as a block of wood. Even the walls of a glass have thickness. If you create a football in VRML out of several faces in an `IndexedFaceSet`, it can be considered solid because you probably never intend to go "inside" the football. If the renderer never renders the inside faces, because it knows they will never be seen, it can avoid rendering half the polygons. To use this feature, you need to know how to indicate to the renderer which side of a face is on the inside and which is on the outside of the object.

Distinguishing the inside from the outside faces is done by looking at the direction the points are connected when they are being viewed. If the points are connected in a counterclockwise direction, the front of the face is visible by default. If you view the other side of the object, the ordering will appear reversed and the renderer will be able to tell this is the inside of the face, and skip it. If all faces of an `IndexedFaceSet` are ordered so their outsides are counterclockwise, the object can be considered solid and rendered faster. The `ccw` field allows this rule to be changed. When set to `FALSE`, faces that are ordered clockwise are considered to be the outside faces. The `solid` field allows this behavior to be turned off altogether. When `solid` is set to `FALSE`, faces are rendered regardless of their ordering, and the `ccw` field is ignored. This allows a house to be built with infinitely thin walls. Whether on the inside or outside of the house, you will see the walls when `solid` is `FALSE`.

I have just scratched the surface of the `IndexedFaceSet` node. It gives you the most freedom to create any shape you can imagine. In upcoming chapters, I will show many more of its capabilities.

Lines and Points

I've shown you how the IndexedFaceSet node can allow you to make complex, solid objects. But VRML can also draw objects without dimension, lines, and points. Lines are drawn with the IndexedLineSet node. It is conceptually very similar to the IndexedFaceSet, but because it renders one-dimensional lines rather than solid objects, it is quite a bit simpler. The following is its definition:

```
IndexedLineSet {
    eventIn        MFInt32    set_colorIndex
    eventIn        MFInt32    set_coordIndex
    exposedField   SFNode     color           NULL
    exposedField   SFNode     coord           NULL
    field          MFInt32    colorIndex      []
    field          SFBool     colorPerVertex  TRUE
    field          MFInt32    coordIndex      []
}
```

As with the IndexedFaceSet, I will only explain the fields that render the geometry. So, only the coord and coordIndex fields are of interest right now. They perform the same function as their counterparts in the IndexedFaceSet. But, rather than rendering solid faces, the IndexedLineSet simply draws lines connecting the points, according to the order specified in the coordIndex. Although all the features of the Appearance node affect the color applied to the faces of an IndexedFaceSet, only the emissiveColor (described in the next chapter) affects the IndexedLineSet. Therefore, no shading of the lines is done. Lines appear in the color specified in the emissiveColor.

To complete the set, there is the PointSet. It is similar to IndexedLineSet except that it draws points rather than lines. Here is its definition:

```
PointSet {
    exposedField   SFNode    color    NULL
    exposedField   SFNode    coord    NULL
}
```

The PointSet node is the simplest of the three. Ignoring the color field, as you have with the other two nodes, you have only a holder for the Coordinate node, the coord field. The PointSet node does not have a coordIndex field like the other two because this field defines *connectivity*, or the order of connection, between points. Because the PointSet does not connect points, but simply draws them as individual dots, it does not need the coordIndex. The PointSet is useful for drawing star fields and swarms of bees.

The following is an example of a Coordinate node, containing a list of points that I will render as a face, a set of connected lines, and a set of points. I will offset them from each other so you can see them side by side. Listing 4.3 and Figure 4.5 show the resultant world.

4

TYPE   **Listing 4.3. VRML scene showing use of** `Coordinate` **field.**

```
Transform {
    translation -15 0 0
    children Shape {
        appearance Appearance {
            material Material {
                diffuseColor 0.6 0 0.2
            }
        }
        geometry IndexedFaceSet {
            coord DEF C Coordinate {
                point [
                    6 8 0,     5 9.2 0,   4 9.5 0, 3 9.6 0,
                    1.8 9 0,   1.1 8 0,   0.7 7 0, 0.3 5 0,
                    0.6 3 0,   2 1.2 0,   3 0.9 0, 5 1.3 0,
                    8.3 3 0,  10 3.3 0,  12 2 0,  11.9 4 0,
                    11.2 5 0, 9.3 6 0,   7.5 5 0, 3.8 2 0,
                    2 2 0,     1 4 0,    1.4 6 0, 2.2 7 0,
                    3.5 8 0,   5 8.4 0 ]
            }
            coordIndex [
                 0,  1,  2,  3,  4,  5,  6,  7,  8,  9,
                10, 11, 12, 13, 14, 15, 16, 17, 18, 19,
                20, 21, 22, 23, 24, 25 ]
        }
    }
}

  Shape {
    appearance Appearance {
        material Material {
            diffuseColor 0 1 1
        }
    }
    geometry IndexedLineSet {
        coord USE C
        coordIndex [
             0,  1,  2,  3,  4,  5,  6,  7,  8,  9,
            10, 11, 12, 13, 14, 15, 16, 17, 18, 19,
            20, 21, 22, 23, 24, 25, 0 ]
    }
}
Transform {
    translation 15 0 0
    children Shape {
        appearance Appearance {
            material Material {
                diffuseColor 1 1 1
            }
        }
        geometry PointSet {
            coord USE C
        }
    }
}
```

4

Figure 4.5.

Example usage of the Coordinate *field in geometry-based nodes.*

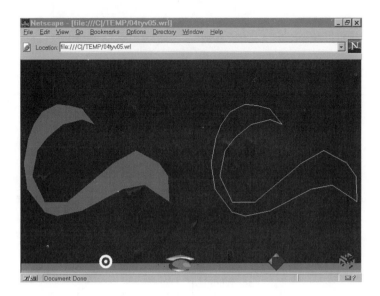

Notice how I defined the point list only once, in the IndexedFaceSet, and instantiated it for the other two nodes.

 TIP

Look at the last coordIndex value in the IndexedLineSet. There is an additional index value of 0 there. This is because, when connecting points in the IndexedFaceSet, there is an implicit connection made between the last index and the first. This allows the shape to become solid so it can be filled with color. But the IndexedLineSet does not get filled in; it does not make this implicit connection and must be done manually.

 WARNING

As of the writing of this book, CosmoPlayer does not yet support the Extrusion, ElevationGrid, or Text nodes. CosmoPlayer for SGI machines can view all these objects.

4

Elevation Grid

VRML allows you to create worlds, and worlds usually need some land mass upon which the visitors to your world may walk. The ElevationGrid node was created for just this purpose. It defines a grid of regularly spaced points, on the XZ (horizontal) plane. You then specify a Y value for each point in the grid. The Y values are placed in a list, one for each point on the grid. Collectively, this list is known as a *height map*. Like the IndexedFaceSet, ElevationGrid has many of the same fields. I will discuss this later once you have mastered the basics. So, here is a simplified definition:

```
ElevationGrid {
    field      MFFloat   height         []
    field      SFBool    ccw            TRUE
    field      SFBool    solid          TRUE
    field      SFInt32   xDimension     0
    field      SFFloat   xSpacing       0.0
    field      SFInt32   zDimension     0
    field      SFFloat   zSpacing       0.0
}
```

The ccw and solid fields perform the same function as the fields with the same names in the IndexedFaceSet. They control which side of the ElevationGrid is visible. Four fields control the grid of points onto which the height map is applied. The xDimension and zDimension fields define the number of points in each dimension. The xSpacing and zSpacing fields determine how far apart points are from one another in each dimension. Finally, the height field is the list of Y values placed at each grid point, starting in the lower-left corner of the grid and proceeding along the X dimension, followed by the Z dimension. The number of values in the height field is the number of grid points in the X dimension times the number of grid points in the Z dimension. Listing 4.4 is an example of a simple 3×3 ElevationGrid. Figure 4.6 shows the resulting shape.

TYPE **Listing 4.4. VRML scene of an ElevationGrid.**

```
Shape {
    appearance Appearance {
        material Material { diffuseColor 1 1 0 }
    }
    geometry ElevationGrid {
        height     [ 4, 3, 2, 3, 5, 4, 1, 3, 6 ]
        xDimension 3
        zDimension 3
        xSpacing   3
        zSpacing   2
    }
}
```

Figure 4.6.

Image produced from the ElevationGrid *example from Listing 4.4.*

 TIP

Combining the X and Z values at each grid point, with the Y value in the height field, you could construct an SFVec3f value to describe the location of that point in space. In fact, you could create an identically shaped object with the IndexedFaceSet node. But the ElevationGrid allows you to represent the shape with one-third the amount of data, because you are only supplying the Y values at each point rather than all three.

The ElevationGrid is important to cartographers, who have sets of height maps for virtually every corner of the earth. These can be translated to VRML ElevationGrid nodes for use in VRML worlds. Figure 4.7 shows the island of Maui, Hawaii, as an ElevationGrid.

Figure 4.7.

*A VRML world showing
the island of Maui,
Hawaii as an*
`ElevationGrid`.

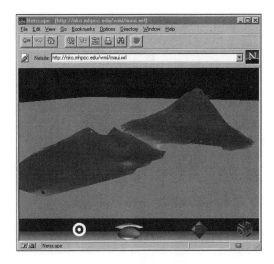

Extrusion

The `ElevationGrid` node provides a very efficient way of representing a certain type of shape. VRML has another node that is very good at representing a different type of shape in a very compact way. It is called the `Extrusion` node. You've probably seen the children's toy where you place a cutout of a shape (for example, a star) into a press, squeeze clay through the cutout, and out comes long strands of clay in the shape of the cutout. This is the idea behind the `Extrusion` node. It lets you define the cutout, or *cross section*, and a line passing, lengthwise, through the center of the shape, called the *spine*. It then extrudes the cross section along the spine. (See Figure 4.8.)

Figure 4.8.

*Extruding a cross
section along a spine.*

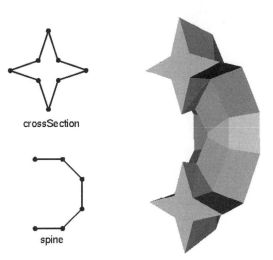

crossSection

spine

Here is the definition of the Extrusion node:

```
Extrusion {
    field    SFBool        beginCap        TRUE
    field    SFBool        ccw             TRUE
    field    SFBool        convex          TRUE
    field    MFVec2f       crossSection
                                           [ 1 1, 1 -1, -1 -1, -1 1, 1 1 ]
    field    SFBool        endCap          TRUE
    field    MFRotation    orientation     0 0 1 0
    field    MFVec2f       scale           1 1
    field    SFBool        solid           TRUE
    field    MFVec3f       spine           [ 0 0 0, 0 1 0 ]
}
```

Like the IndexedFaceSet and ElevationGrid, I've left out a few fields that I will discuss later. But, even with that, the Extrusion node has many fields. This gives it great flexibility beyond simple extruded shapes, made with the crossSection and spine fields. For instance, the scale field allows the cross section size to be changed at each point in the spine. This allows you to change the profile of your extruded shape. It has a real-world analogy to a lathe. A lathe spins a piece of wood, and the woodworker cuts indentations into it, which become circular undulations in the surface. This is how baseball bats and table legs are made. The scale field is a pair of SFVec2f values, each one corresponding to a point on the spine. The two components of the SFVec3f scale the horizontal and vertical dimension of the crossSection separately, allowing shapes with oval cross sections, rather than just circular cross sections. The scale value is multiplied by each point in the crossSection. A value of 1 makes it normal size, 0.5 squeezes it to half its original size, and a value of 2 stretches it to twice the size. Figure 4.9 shows the effects of scale on an extruded shape.

Figure 4.9.

The effects of scale
on an extruded shape.

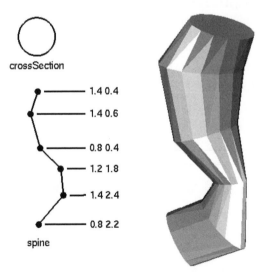

Notice, in the shape of Figure 4.9, how the crossSection is an approximation of a circle, made with many individual points, but the ends of the shape are oval. That is because the scale at the ends scales the two dimensions of the cross section differently. Listing 4.5 is the VRML code used to create the image in Figure 4.9.

TYPE   **Listing 4.5. VRML scene showing an Extrusion.**

```
Extrusion {
    crossSection [
          1 0, 0.92388 0.382683,
        0.707107 0.707106, 0.382684 0.923879,
        1.26759e-06 1, -0.382682 0.92388,
        -0.707105 0.707108, -0.923879 0.382685,
        -1 2.53518e-06, -0.923881 -0.382681,
        -0.707109 -0.707105, -0.382687 -0.923878,
        -3.80277e-06 -1, 0.38268 -0.923881,
        0.707104 -0.70711, 0.923878 -0.382688, 1 0 ]
    scale [
        1.4 0.4, 1.4 0.6,
        0.8 0.4, 1.2 1.8,
        1.4 2.4, 0.8 2.2 ]
    spine [
        0 -5 0, 2 -2.8 0,
        1.8 -0.8 0, 0.2 0.8 0,
        -0.6 3.4 0, 0 5 0 ]
}
```

The Extrusion node also has an orientation field. Like the scale field, it contains a list of values, one to be applied at each spine point. But, rather than SFVec2f values used to scale the cross section, these are SFRotation values, used to set the orientation of the crossSection at each spine point. Normally, the cross section is oriented to be at an angle halfway between the two spine edges on either side. Just like the corner of a picture frame joins two edges at a 45° angle, a right angle turn in the spine will angle the crossSection at 45° to that turn, making a nice, mitered edge. (See Figure 4.10.)

Figure 4.10.

The default
crossSection
angle.

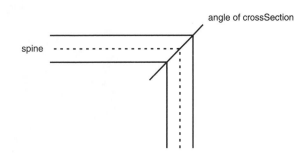

The orientation field allows the crossSection to be rotated from this default orientation. It is most often used to impart twist in the cross section. The cross section is considered to be in the XZ (horizontal) plane, for the purpose of applying orientation. Twist can be applied by giving a rotation axis of 0 1 0, which is the Y (vertical) axis. The rotation angle then specifies the twist in the cross section at that spine point. Figure 4.11 shows twist applied to a cross section with a four-pointed star pattern. Listing 4.6 is the VRML code that produces Figure 4.11.

TYPE **Listing 4.6. Another VRML scene using an Extrusion.**

```
Extrusion {
    crossSection [
        0 2, 0.5 0.5,
        2 0, 0.5 -0.5,
        0 -2, -0.5 -0.5,
        -2 0, -0.5 0.5,
        0 2 ]
    orientation [
        0 1 0  0,
        0 1 0  0.349065,
        0 1 0  0.698132,
        0 1 0  1.0472,
        0 1 0  1.39626,
        0 1 0  1.74533 ]
    spine [
        0 -5 0, 0 -3 0,
        0 -1 0, 0 1 0,
        0 3 0, 0 5 0 ]
}
```

Figure 4.11.

An extruded shape with a twist.

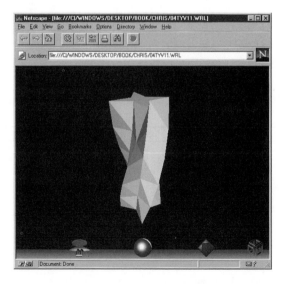

The Extrusion node also has several fields used to control its appearance. The beginCap and endCap fields allow the ends of the object to be closed off with a flat cap, just like the Cylinder node. The convex field informs the browser that the crossSection is or is not convex, allowing the same optimization in drawing the caps as you saw in the IndexedFaceSet. Finally, the ccw and solid fields allow you to render only the inside, only the outside, or both sides of the object. The ccw value refers to the crossSection. With a default value of ccw, if the crossSection runs counterclockwise, as viewed from above, the outside of the object will be visible. Otherwise, only the inside will be visible. If the ccw field is set to FALSE, this notion is reversed. Setting the solid flag to TRUE makes both sides of the object visible. The value of ccw would not matter in this case.

WARNING

Setting solid and convex to FALSE allows the most flexibility in the creation of an extruded object. You never need to worry about the shape you are creating. But, they will also make many browsers run slower when drawing this object. Most browsers are especially sensitive to the solid flag because it can make them render twice as many polygons. Most extruded objects are solid shapes. They are intended to be viewed from the outside only. Therefore, leaving the solid field TRUE is especially important to get maximum performance from your browser.

Text

The last geometric object to discuss is the Text node. This allows you to place lines of text in your world. The text produced is flat, meaning that viewing it is invisible when viewed from the side. Here is its definition:

```
Text {
  exposedField   MFString  string     []
  exposedField   SFNode    fontStyle  NULL
  exposedField   MFFloat   length     []
  exposedField   SFFloat   maxExtent  0.0
}
```

The fontStyle field holds a FontStyle node, which controls how the text looks and how it is laid out. I will explain that feature in detail in the next chapter. The string field holds the text strings to be rendered. The string field is an MFString field, which means it can take several strings. Each string is rendered on its own line. The spacing between each line, by default, is the height of the characters. This can be changed using the FontStyle node.

The maxExtent field allows you to define the maximum width you want the text to occupy. If a text string is shorter than this, it is rendered normally. But if it is longer, the string is squeezed to fit the given width. Each browser renders characters with slightly different widths, because the fonts on many machines have slight variations in the definition of each character. The maxExtent field allows you to ensure text will fit in a specified width (for instance, on a sign), regardless of the browser used. The default of 0.0 allows lines of text to be as long as they need to be.

The length field, like the maxExtent field, allows you to manipulate the width of the text. But rather than a single value restricting the maximum width, length allows you to specify the exact width of each line of text individually. If the text is shorter than this width, it is stretched. If it is longer, it is squeezed. This gives you the capability to typeset each line of text. You can use this to make each line the same width, to achieve text justification like a word processor provides. Or, you can set the width of each individual line, ensuring that the text will look exactly the same, regardless of the browser used to view the world. If you give fewer values in the length field than there are lines of text in the string field, the last length entry will be used to set the width of the remaining lines of text. You can set all lines of text to the same width (accomplishing text justification) by simply placing a single value in the length field.

Figure 4.12 is a world showing all the capabilities of the Text node. Many of the features shown here require the use of the FontStyle node, which I will talk about in the next chapter.

Figure 4.12.

A world showing all the capabilities of the Text *node.*

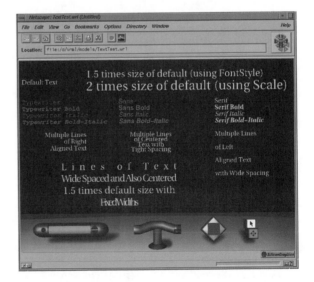

Combining Geometry into Complex Objects

You have now seen all the geometric object types available in VRML. The most interesting objects are those comprising several different object types. For instance, a storefront may use an IndexedFaceSet for the walls, a flattened Box for the door, a Text node with the name of the store written across the top of the front wall, and an Extrusion for the streetlight out front. Using the hierarchical concepts you learned in the previous chapter, you can place all these objects relative to each other, and put them all together under a single Group node. Then, using the instantiation feature, you can have many copies of your storefront, making an entire city of stores!

Summary

VRML has many geometry nodes with which you can create many interesting shapes. The IndexedFaceSet is the most versatile of these. With it you can create literally any other shape in VRML. Lines and points can also be created with the IndexedFaceSet and PointSet. These are very similar to IndexedFaceSet, but they simply draw lines and points, rather than fill in polygons.

Due to the flexibility of the IndexedFaceSet, it takes a lot of space in the file format to create a shape this way. For more efficiency, VRML has several nodes designed to create specific kinds of shapes very efficiently. The ElevationGrid node is used to create a rectangular surface with height specified in the node. This makes the ElevationGrid three times smaller than the same shape created with an IndexedFaceSet. It is used to make topographic map shapes and to build terrain. The Extrusion node allows you to create tubes and curved sheets very efficiently. Finally, the Text node allows you to create flat text by simply specifying the text strings to render.

The most interesting shapes are obtained when you combine separate geometric pieces, using the transformation hierarchy to position objects relative to each other. In the next chapter, I'll show you how to add color to these shapes to make them more realistic and interesting.

Q&A

Q Isn't there any feature of VRML 2. I can use to avoid the disappearing text situation?

A There are a few things you can do to keep text visible longer for a visitor to a VRML world. First, you can include the Text node inside of the Billboard node that I will show you in Chapter 16, "Making Efficient Scenes." Billboards automatically move relative to the user to face its contents toward the camera. Second, you can add other geometry in your scene that prohibits the user from moving to a place where the text is viewed from the side. If you visit an art gallery-based world, you will see many examples of effective uses of walls and other objects to keep the user viewing the exhibits from head on.

Q **The `IndexedFaceSet` node seems to be the most flexible node for creating geometric objects in VRML. Is there anything it can't represent?**

A No. The `IndexedFaceSet` is a catch-all node. You've probably noticed how cumbersome it would be to have to create a coordinate for every significant point in an object. Well, that technique also creates very large VRML files that are not so great when considering network bottlenecks and hard drive utilization. You'll continue to see improvements in VRML for defining geometry without specifying each coordinate in the object. Yet, the `IndexedFaceSet` will always be an alternative way to denote any geometry.

Q **What is the easiest way to create a terrain using the `ElevationGrid` node?**

A They say that truth is stranger than fiction. I create mine using a topographical map of an existing land mass. Take some see-through graph paper and lay it over a topographical map. Then note the elevation at each point of intersection of the graph paper. Choose a unit of measure for each square on the paper and then put the `ElevationGrid` node together using the elevations you wrote down. Someday, if VRML catches on as I expect it to, you'll be able to download the terrain for any existing terrain in the world—or, perhaps the Moon, Mars, Venus, and so on!

Exercises

1. Create a house to put on the property you made in the last chapter. Make four walls using the `IndexedFaceSet` node, including cutouts for a doorway and windows. Make a roof using an extruded shape. Add a chimney using another extrusion. Make sure the chimney penetrates the wall so it can be seen from both the inside and outside.

2. Replace the simple Box you used for the ground with an `ElevationGrid`, to give yourself a piece of virtual property with nice, rolling hills.

3. Put a welcome mat at the front door of your house, made from a `Box` node and a `Text` node.

Answers

☐ Because of code length, you can find the complete VRML files for the preceding exercises on the CD-ROM at `\Source\Answers`.

Day 5

Object Appearance

The Appearance node of VRML is used to apply color to a geometric model. In the previous chapters, you've used the Material node and, more specifically, the diffuseColor field to apply this color. But VRML has the capability to apply much more rich appearances to geometry. This includes 2D images applied to the object, ways to adjust the shininess and brightness of an object, and even ways to apply a different color at each vertex of the object. In this chapter, I will show you all the techniques available to do these things. I will also show you how to change the appearance of objects created with the Text node. Here is what I will cover today:

☐ Using textures
☐ Transforming textures
☐ Customizing the texture
☐ Changing text font style
☐ Advanced material usage
☐ Using per-vertex color

Textures

So far, I have shown you how to apply color to an object using the `diffuseColor` field of the `Material` node. But you can also add color by wrapping a 2D image, called a *texture*, around the surface of an object. It's just like stretching fabric over a chair, or applying wallpaper to a wall. The image follows the contours of the object as needed. In VRML, any JPEG image can be used as a texture. Some browsers, including CosmoPlayer, also allow you to use GIF images as textures because they are so popular in HTML pages. Textures are added using the `ImageTexture` node. Here is its definition:

```
ImageTexture {
  exposedField MFString  url       []
  field        SFBool     repeatS   TRUE
  field        SFBool     repeatT   TRUE
}
```

The `ImageTexture` node is placed in the `texture` field of the `Appearance` node. The `url` field has a string, which is the filename of the image you want to wrap onto the object.

About URLs

You might be familiar with the term *URL* if you already have experience on the World Wide Web. It stands for *Universal Resource Locator*, and it usually looks something like the following:

`http://www.marrin.com/vrml/museum.wrl`

This string is a request to a computer (known as a *server* because it serves information to you) for a piece of information. This could be an image file, an HTML file, or, in the preceding example, a VRML file for display in your VRML browser. The `http://` part identifies this as using the *Hypertext Transfer Protocol*. This tells the server the language in which you are expecting to receive the information. The `www.marrin.com` part is the name of the server containing the information. The `/vrml/museum.wrl` part is the directory and filename of the information.

When you request a VRML file from the Web (usually by clicking on a hyperlink in an HTML document), a request similar to the preceding one is sent to a server, and then the text file containing the VRML world is received by your VRML browser. The browser then interprets the meaning of this file and renders the world it contains. If the VRML world contains other URL strings (like the one put into the `ImageTexture` node), they can be either *relative* or *absolute*. An absolute URL is one with a complete request string, like the preceding example. But a relative URL adds the address used to retrieve the original VRML file to this URL request. A relative URL takes the original address, minus the filename (the `museum.wrl` part in

---

5

the preceding example), as the prefix for the new URL. For instance, if the VRML world in the preceding example contained the following `ImageTexture` node:

```
ImageTexture {
 url "myImage.jpg"
}
```

a request would be made to fetch the image at the following:

```
http://www.marrin.com/vrml/myImage.jpg
```

This makes it much easier to specify the locations of the images and other files used in your VRML worlds. You just place them in the directory with the original world and use relative addressing.

Notice that the `url` field of the `ImageTexture` node is an `MFString`. This means it can contain several strings. This allows you to list several URLs, and the browser will retrieve the first one in the list that exists and that it understands. This allows you, for example, to list both JPEG and GIF images in the `ImageTexture` node. Because JPEG images are typically smaller, your browser will try to load those first. But, if your browser does not recognize the JPEG format, it can try the next URL. If it does recognize the GIF format, it can retrieve this image and use it as its texture.

VRML has several nodes with `url` fields. All these `url` fields can reference an absolute or relative URL in the manner discussed here.

Listing 5.1 is an example that maps an `ImageTexture` to a `Box` and a `Sphere`.

TYPE **Listing 5.1. VRML scene showing textured box and sphere.**

5

```
Transform {
  translation -2 0 0
  children
      Shape {
          appearance DEF A Appearance {
              material Material { }
              texture ImageTexture {
                  url "WildLife.gif"
              }
          }
          geometry Box { }
      }
}
Transform {
  translation 2 0 0
  children
      Shape {
          appearance USE A
          geometry Sphere { }
      }
}
```

The Appearance now has an ImageTexture in addition to the Material. Notice that I did not set the diffuseColor of the material. This is because the texture is used instead of the diffuseColor. The object is still shaded, darker on the sides, lighter in the center, but the color is being provided by the texture image. (See Figure 5.1.)

Figure 5.1.

An image textured onto a box and sphere.

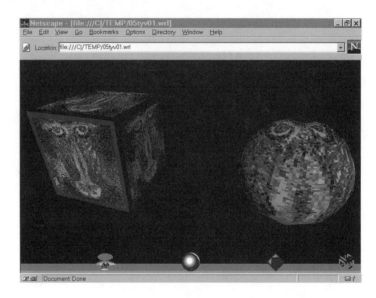

WARNING

At the time this book was published, the plug-in technology for Internet Explorer 3.0 had not yet completely stabilized. In fact, during testing, the Internet Explorer browser was unable to load some of the more basic examples in this text. Most of the VRML community continues to use Netscape Navigator with VRML plug-ins, yet Microsoft has committed to delivering plug-in technology for Internet Explorer. If you are using Internet Explorer to view the .wrl files in this book, be wary of this situation and check with Microsoft's Web site for information about fixes and new releases for Internet Explorer.

Notice the difference in the way the image is wrapped around the objects. On the box, the image appears once on each face. On the sphere, the image is stretched around the horizontal diameter, and squeezed to a point at the top and bottom poles. This is the *default texture mapping* for these two shapes. Every shape has a default mapping. In the next chapter, I will show you how to change those defaults. But for now, Table 5.1 shows the defaults for all the shapes.

5

Table 5.1. Default texture mapping for all geometric shapes.

Shape	Mapping
Box	One copy of the texture on each face.
Cone	Wrap once around the base, with the seam at the back. Squeeze all points at the top. Image is cut out at the lower-left corner and placed on the bottom cap, appearing right side up when bottom is tilted toward you.
Cylinder	Wrap once around horizontal diameter, with the seam at the back. Image is cut out at the lower-left corner and placed on the top and bottom caps, appearing right side up when the bottom or top is tilted toward you.
ElevationGrid	One copy of the texture is laid on the grid.
Extrusion	Wrap once around cross-section diameter, horizontally. Place once along spine, vertically.
IndexedFaceSet	Mapping is determined by measuring the dimensions along the major axes. The longest dimension is used to determine the horizontal mapping. The second longest dimension determines the vertical mapping. Image is projected onto the shape using these dimensions. (See Figure 5.2.)
IndexedLineSet	No textures are applied to this shape.
PointSet	No textures are applied to this shape.
Sphere	Wrap once around the horizontal diameter, with the seam at the back. Squeeze image at the top and bottom of the sphere, to a single point at the top and bottom.
Text	Image is cut out to fit a single copy of the texture over the entire block of text.

The mapping of the IndexedFaceSet is complicated. Figure 5.2 illustrates it.

When you apply a texture map, you are mapping a point on the texture to a point on the surface of the object. To make this explanation simpler, I will refer to points on the texture in terms of s and t values, where s is the horizontal coordinate of the image and t is the vertical coordinate. For instance, in Figure 5.2, the lower-left corner of the image has an s,t value of 0,0. And the upper-right corner has an s,t value of 1,1. Later in this chapter, I'll show you how to use these texture coordinates in a powerful way, but for now, just notice how they are used to describe the default mapping of the IndexedFaceSet.

Figure 5.2.

Mapping of textures to the IndexedFaceSet.

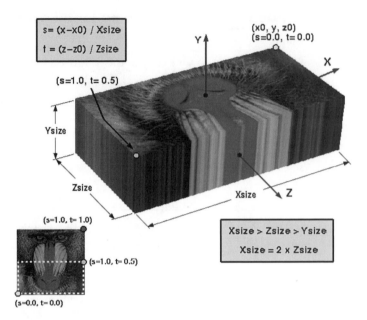

To create a default mapping for an IndexedFaceSet, you first figure out which are the two largest dimensions of your object. In Figure 5.2, this is X and Z. Then you apply the texture to the plane formed by these dimensions. The horizontal direction of the texture is mapped to the larger dimension (X in the example), and the vertical direction (Z in the example) is mapped to the smaller dimension. The texture is mapped square. This means that the s direction of the texture is always mapped from 0 to 1 because it will always be the larger dimension. The t direction will map from 0 to something less than 1. The maximum t value is computed with the following ratio:

$$t_{maximum} = \frac{dimension_{smaller}}{dimension_{larger}}$$

The texture is mapped in the positive direction. In Figure 5.2, this means that the texture is mapped from an s value of 0 to an s value of 1 in the positive X direction. In the positive Z direction, the texture maps from a t value of 0 to a t value of the Z dimension divided by the X dimension, or 0.5.

The ImageTexture node has two more fields, repeatS and repeatT. These allow you to control what happens when the object has more surface area than the texture can cover. Normally, if the texture cannot cover the entire object, it simply repeats. When the renderer comes to the end of the texture in one direction, it starts back at the beginning of the texture in that direction. By default, this does not happen. But in the next section, I'll show you how to control the texture to squeeze it into a smaller space, so it will repeat. If you want only a single copy of the texture in a particular direction, you can set repeatS or repeatT to FALSE. In the next section, when I show you how to change the way a texture is mapped to an object, I'll show you how these flags affect the mapping of the texture to the object.

VRML handles textures with four different component values. So far, I have shown you the most common texture type, which is a three-component, or RGB, texture. The term RGB refers to the fact that these images contain separate values for the three primary colors of light: red, green, and blue. With these three colors, you can make literally any color in the rainbow. All JPEG images are three-component textures, because they are full color. A three-component texture simply paints onto the object, in place of the diffuseColor.

A one-component texture is sometimes called an *intensity map*. That's because, rather than replacing the diffuseColor, it is multiplied by it to produce the final color. An intensity map can be converted into a three-component texture by simply multiplying its value by each component of the diffuseColor value. This is often useful for creating floor tile patterns of different colors. The texture is used to establish the pattern and the diffuseColor is used to set the overall tile color. CosmoPlayer will recognize a GIF image with only gray values as a one-component texture.

Both one- and three-component textures can have an additional transparency component, known as an *alpha channel*. With an alpha channel, each pixel in the texture can be given an opacity value of 0 (fully transparent) to 1 (fully opaque). This turns a one-component texture into a two-component, and a three-component texture into a four-component. This is extremely useful in creating trees and other non-rectangular shapes. Rather than creating a complex shape from an IndexedFaceSet, and then applying a texture to it, you can create a rectangular IndexedFaceSet and apply a texture with transparency to make the complex shape. CosmoPlayer recognizes the transparency feature of GIF images to add an alpha channel to one- or three-component textures. For an example of a GIF file that supports transparency, open the shaft.gif file in your Web browser and notice that the pixels around the elevator shaft pick up whatever background color you have set in your browser. The pixels are transparent and will let you see through them in a VRML world, also. I'll discuss transparency more in Chapter 16, "Making Efficient Scenes," when I discuss background objects.

Transforming Textures

The example shown in Figure 5.1 shows two objects with their default texture mappings. But, you are not limited to these defaults in VRML. There are two ways to change the default way textures are applied to objects. The first uses the TextureTransform node. The following is the Transform node definition:

```
TextureTransform {
  exposedField  SFVec2f   center       0 0
  exposedField  SFFloat   rotation     0
  exposedField  SFVec2f   scale        1 1
  exposedField  SFVec2f   translation  0 0
}
```

The `TextureTransform` node is placed in the `textureTransform` field of the `Appearance` node. It does just what its name implies. It scales, rotates, and translates the texture on the object. Setting the scale field to 2 2, will scale the texture *s* and *t* coordinates of the texture by 2. This can be confusing. Rather than making the texture larger on the object, it makes it smaller. This is because, rather than scaling the texture image up and then applying the larger texture to the object, it scales the *s* and *t* coordinates used to map the texture to the object, so the texture has to shrink down to fit on an object of the same size. The same thing happens with `translation` and `rotation`. A `translation` field of 0.5 0.5 will place a point in the center of the texture at the lower-left corner of the object. The appearance is that the texture has shifted by a value of -0.5 -0.5.

 TIP

The easiest way to remember how texture translations work is to imagine a frame over the texture (the dotted lines in Figure 5.2 show this). Remember that when you scale or translate, you are actually changing the box around the texture rather than the texture itself. Whatever is inside this box (repeating the image as needed if you scale up), is placed in the same spot the original texture is placed. (See Figure 5.3.)

Figure 5.3.
Scale, translation, and rotation of a texture.

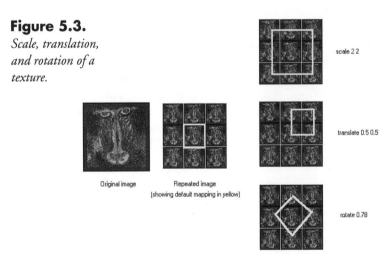

Original image

Repeated image
(showing default mapping in yellow)

scale 2 2

translate 0.5 0.5

rotate 0.78

Figure 5.4 shows four square `IndexedFaceSet` shapes. The first has a default texture applied. The second has a texture scaled by a value of 2 2. It appears half as big. The third is translated by a value of 0.5 0.5. The texture is moved down half the image distance and to the left. The last shape has a texture rotated by a value of 0.78. The image is rotated at a 45° angle in the clockwise direction (because the box around the image rotated counterclockwise). Listing 5.2 is the VRML code to produce these shapes.

TYPE **Listing 5.2. VRML scene showing texture transformations.**

```
Transform {
 translation -6 0 0
  children Shape {
     appearance Appearance {
        material DEF M Material { }
        texture DEF T ImageTexture { url "fish.jpg" }
     }
     geometry DEF IFS IndexedFaceSet {
        coord Coordinate {
           point [ -1 -1 0, 1 -1 0, 1 1 0, -1 1 0 ]
        }
        coordIndex [ 0, 1, 2, 3 ]
     }
  }
}
Transform {
  translation -2 0 0
  children Shape {
     appearance Appearance {
        material USE M
        texture USE T
        textureTransform TextureTransform { scale 2 2 }
     }
     geometry USE IFS
  }
}
Transform {
  translation 2 0 0
  children Shape {
     appearance Appearance {
        material USE M
        texture USE T
        textureTransform TextureTransform { translation 0.5 0.5 }
     }
     geometry USE IFS
  }
}
Transform {
  translation 6 0 0
  children Shape {
     appearance Appearance {
        material USE M
        texture USE T
        textureTransform TextureTransform { rotation 0.78 }
     }
     geometry USE IFS
  }
}
```

5

Figure 5.4.

Four shapes with transformed textures. From left to right they are default, scaled, translated, and rotated.

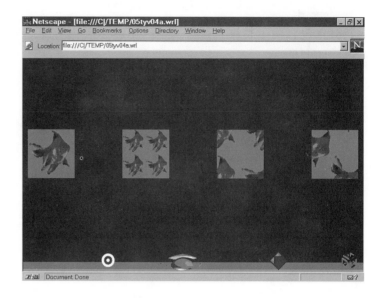

The center field allows the point about which the texture is rotated to be changed. In the preceding example, the texture is rotated around the lower-left corner of the texture (*s,t* coordinate 0 0), which is the default. The center field allows the rotation point to be moved to another point on the texture. A value of 0.5 0.5 would move the rotation point to the center of the texture. Negative values of center are legal, as are values greater than 1. These would move the center to a point outside the base texture.

TIP

It is not very obvious how you would combine fields of the TextureTransform to come up with a transformed coordinate. You get a different result depending on the order you apply the fields. Here's how the VRML browser does it. Start with the *s,t* coordinates, and then apply the following:

1. The translation field
2. The center field
3. The rotation field
4. The scale field

Lastly, apply the negated center field. Adding in the center field and then subtracting it back out allows you to offset the rotation without having the center field affect the final translated position.

5

Customizing the Texture Application

The other way a texture's application can be modified is with the use of the `TextureCoordinate` node. In the previous section, I explained about the s and t coordinates controlling the mapping of the texture to the shape. The `TextureTransform` modifies these coordinate values by applying a transformation to them. But `TextureCoordinate` allows you to control the value of the s,t coordinates at each vertex of a shape. Here is its definition:

```
TextureCoordinate {
  exposedField  MFVec2f  point  []
}
```

Only `IndexedFaceSet` and `ElevationGrid` allow the use of `TextureCoordinate`. Each of these shapes has a `texCoord` field into which you can place a `TextureCoordinate` node. The `point` field takes a list of `SFVec2f` values that are the s,t values to use at each coordinate. For the `IndexedFaceSet`, there are two ways to use the texture coordinates in the `point` list. If the `IndexedFaceSet` has an empty `texCoordIndex` field, there is a one-to-one mapping of texture coordinates to points in the `Coordinate` node. If the `texCoordIndex` field is not empty, it is used to select texture coordinates in the same way as the `coordIndex` field is used for selecting points from the `Coordinate` node. Listing 5.3 is a VRML code example that will show the same image you see in Figure 5.4, but it uses a `TextureCoordinate` node rather than a `TextureTransform` node.

TYPE **Listing 5.3. VRML scene using `TextureTransform` node.**

```
Transform {
  translation -6 0 0
  children Shape {
      appearance DEF A Appearance {
          material DEF M Material { }
          texture ImageTexture { url "fish.jpg" }
      }
      geometry DEF IFS IndexedFaceSet {
          coord DEF C Coordinate {
              point [ -1 -1 0, 1 -1 0, 1 1 0, -1 1 0 ]
          }
          coordIndex [ 0, 1, 2, 3 ]
          texCoord TextureCoordinate {
              point [ 0 0, 1 0, 1 1, 0 1 ] # default mapping
          }
      }
  }
}
Transform {
  translation -2 0 0
  children Shape {
      appearance USE A
```

5

continues

Listing 5.3. continued

```
                geometry DEF IFS IndexedFaceSet {
                    coord USE C
                    coordIndex [ 0, 1, 2, 3 ]
                    texCoord TextureCoordinate {
                        point [ 0 0, 2 0, 2 2, 0 2 ] # scale by 2 2
                    }
                }
            }
        }
    Transform {
      translation 2 0 0
      children Shape {
            appearance USE A
            geometry DEF IFS IndexedFaceSet {
                coord USE C
                coordIndex [ 0, 1, 2, 3 ]
                texCoord TextureCoordinate {
                    point [ 0.5 0.5, 1.5 0.5,
                            1.5 1.5, 0.5 1.5 ] # translate by 0.5 0.5
                }
            }
        }
    }
    Transform {
      translation 6 0 0
      children Shape {
            appearance USE A
            geometry DEF IFS IndexedFaceSet {
                coord USE C
                coordIndex [ 0, 1, 2, 3 ]
                texCoord TextureCoordinate {
                    point [ 0 0, 0.707 0.707,
                            0 1.414, -0.707 0.707 ] # rotate by 0.78 radians
                }
            }
        }
    }
}
```

Notice that to get the various transformed texture coordinate points, I simply applied the transform value in the comment. For scale, you multiply the value; for translation, you add the value; and for rotation, you rotate the points counterclockwise, relative to 0 0.

Very often you will use TextureCoordinate to do fine adjustment of a texture. For instance, you could take a photograph of a building and use that as a texture for a structure in your virtual world. The face of the building may be an IndexedFaceSet with holes cut for the windows and doorways. You will often need to use a TextureCoordinate node in this case to line up the spots for the windows and doors in the texture, with the holes cut for them in the IndexedFaceSet.

5

Changing Text Font Style

The Text node displays a common looking font with a height of 1 by default. But the FontStyle node can be used to change this, and much more. Here is its definition:

```
FontStyle {
    field   SFString    family          "SERIF"
    field   SFBool      horizontal      TRUE
    field   MFString    justify         "BEGIN"
    field   SFString    language        " "
    field   SFBool      leftToRight     TRUE
    field   SFFloat     size            1.0
    field   SFFloat     spacing         1.0
    field   SFString    style           "PLAIN"
    field   SFBool      topToBottom     TRUE
}
```

The FontStyle node is placed in the fontStyle field of the Text node. The family and style fields allow you to change the look of the font. They both take SFString values in which you can place one of several strings that select some general appearance characteristics of the font. The family field can have the string SERIF for a serif font, SANS for a sans-serif font, or TYPEWRITER for a fixed pitch font. Typically, a serif font is one that looks a lot like the one you're reading right now. A sans-serif font is simpler, and many systems use a font called Helvetica for it. A fixed pitch font is one where all characters are the same width. The code examples in this book are in a fixed pitch font. The style field modifies the font family's appearance. The allowed values here are PLAIN for a font with no style modifications, BOLD for a heavier font, ITALIC for a slanted font, and BOLDITALIC for a font that is both heavy and slanted. These apply to the family attribute to create 12 possible font styles.

NOTE

> As of the printing of this book, there is discussion underway to allow the name of any font available on the system to be used in the family field. If allowed, this would greatly increase the usefulness of the FontStyle node.

The size field allows you to change the height of the font. By default, the size is 1, which means the font should be tall enough so that lines of text can be spaced vertically at 1 unit spacing. This does not set an absolute height for every character, but every font has a notion of how tall it must be to look acceptable when lines are spaced at this distance. This line spacing can be adjusted from this default with the spacing field. This value is multiplied by the size field to determine how much distance there will be from the top of one line of text to the next. Here is a simple example of these four fields in action. I will show you four Text nodes, each with a different FontStyle. The first uses the default FontStyle, the second will change the family and style fields, the third will change the size, and the fourth will change the spacing, with that same size. (See Figure 5.5.) Take a look at Listing 5.4.

5

TYPE **Listing 5.4. VRML scene demonstrating the Text node.**

```
Transform {
  translation -16 0 0
  children Shape {
      geometry Text {
          string [ "VRML",
                   "is the wave",
                   "of the future" ]
          fontStyle FontStyle {           }
      }
  }
}
Transform {
  translation -9 0 0
  children Shape {
      geometry Text {
          string [ "VRML",
                   "is the wave",
                   "of the future" ]
          fontStyle FontStyle {
              family "SANS"
              style "BOLDITALIC"
          }
      }
  }
}
Transform {
  translation -2 0 0
  children Shape {
      geometry Text {
          string [ "VRML",
                   "is the wave",
                   "of the future" ]
          fontStyle FontStyle {
              size 2
          }
      }
  }
}
Transform {
  translation 10 0 0
  children Shape {
      geometry Text {
          string [ "VRML",
                   "is the wave",
                   "of the future" ]
          fontStyle FontStyle {
              size 2
              spacing 1.5
          }
      }
  }
}
```

Figure 5.5.

An example of text strings formatted differently through the use of the fontStyle *field.*

The justify field allows you to align a certain point on each text string with the origin. The default of LEFT causes the string in each row to align its left edge with the Y-axis. The value of MIDDLE aligns the center of each row with the Y-axis. And RIGHT makes the left edge of each string with the Y-axis. The justify field can take a second string as well; this controls the horizontal justification. If the second string has its default value of FIRST, the baseline of the first line of text is placed along the X-axis. If it is BEGIN, the top of the first line is placed along the X-axis. If it is MIDDLE, the center of the entire block of text is placed at the X-axis. Finally, if it is END, the bottom of the last line of text is placed along the X-axis.

The horizontal, leftToRight, and topToBottom fields are used together to change the direction the text flows from its default of left-to-right, top-to-bottom. Setting the horizontal field to FALSE changes the direction the text is rendered from left-to-right for characters in a line to top-to-bottom. The characters still appear upright, but they now travel vertically down, rather than horizontally from the left. In this case, lines of text will run left-to-right, and now the size and spacing fields will control the horizontal spacing of lines.

But even the flow of characters to the left or down can be altered. Setting leftToRight to FALSE will cause text to flow from the right to the left. If horizontal is TRUE, this means that characters in a single text string run from right to the left. If horizontal is FALSE, it means that each line of text goes horizontally from the right to the left. Likewise, if topToBottom is set to FALSE, text lines will flow up rather than down, with horizontal TRUE, or characters in a line will flow up rather than down, if horizontal is FALSE.

VRML uses the UTF8 standard to allow you to place virtually any character from any language into a string. This means that the Text node can display a character in any language. But there are some languages (most notably, Korean), in which the appearance of some characters is slightly different, even though it is represented by the same character code in UTF8. Because of this, the language field can be given a string that is a country identifier. These identity strings are standardized, and are short abbreviations such as en_us for US English, or zh_CN for Chinese.

Advanced Material Usage

I have described the diffuseColor field of the Material node. It is used to define a color for an object. But there are several other fields in the Material node to control object color, including the transparency of the object. The color fields base their characteristics on the qualities of light used to give realistic shading to VRML worlds. I will talk more about the relationship between light and the Material node in the next chapter. For now, I will give a brief explanation of each field in the Material node.

I have already mentioned emissiveColor, when I was describing the IndexedLineSet and PointSet nodes. This field controls the color given off by the object that is not dependent on the external light source striking it. Because lighting does not affect an IndexedLineSet or PointSet, they get their color from emissiveColor. This is useful when you want to make objects that emit light in the real world, such as neon tubes or light bulbs.

The ambientIntensity field is essentially a brightness control for the object. It is an SFFloat value that is multiplied by the other colors on the object to make it brighter. It is intended to simulate ambient light, or light that does not come from any particular light source. In the real world, the dark areas of an object are not totally dark because small amounts of light bounce around from everywhere. That's what keeps objects in a shadow from being totally black, and it is what ambientIntensity simulates.

The specularColor and shininess fields are used together to simulate shiny objects. These values depend the most on a particular light source. So, I'll save a detailed explanation for the next chapter. For now, just remember that a high shininess value makes an object look more like metal and a low value makes an object look like fabric.

Finally, the Material node has a transparency field. If this field is 1, the object is totally transparent, and if 0, it is totally opaque. Values in-between allow you to see the object, but you can see through it. This is an excellent way to simulate a drinking glass or windshield.

Using Per-vertex Color

Sometimes you need more control over an object color than just specifying its overall color. Just as you can specify the texture coordinates at each vertex of an IndexedFaceSet or ElevationGrid, you can also specify the color to use. These are known as per-vertex colors, and they are specified by adding the Color node to the color field of an IndexedFaceSet or ElevationGrid. Here is the Color node definition:

```
Color {
  exposedField MFColor color []
}
```

It is very similar to the Coordinate and TextureCoordinate nodes. And like those nodes, it is controlled with a colorIndex field. If this field is empty, there is a one-to-one mapping between coordinates and color values. But if it contains values, they are used to select colors for use at each vertex. In this case, it must follow the same format as the coordIndex field, including the -1 entries at the end of each face definition. If you give each vertex of a single face a different color, the colors for that face will blend from one to the other, over the entire surface of the face. Listing 5.5 is a simple example of a triangle with a red, green, and blue vertex. (See Figure 5.6.)

Listing 5.5. VRML scene showing a per-vertex colored triangle.

TYPE

```
Shape {
  geometry IndexedFaceSet {
      coord Coordinate {
          point [ 0 0 0, 1 0 0, 0.5 1 0 ]
      }
      coordIndex [ 0 1 2 ]
      color Color {
          color [ 1 0 0, 0 1 0, 0 0 1 ]
      }
  }
}
```

5

NOTE

The image in Figure 5.6 was captured while using CosmoPlayer for the SGI platform. The subtle gradation you see in the grayscale was actually in color. At the time of this book writing, the Color node was not implemented in the Windows 95 version of CosmoPlayer.

The colorPerVertex flag can be used to apply the colors in the Color node per-face rather than per-vertex. Setting this flag to FALSE will cause one color to be applied to an entire face. If the colorIndex field is empty, one color is selected from the Color node, in order, for each face. If the colorIndex field is not empty, it must contain one index entry for each face, without any -1 entries.

Figure 5.6.

A simple object with a color per-vertex.

The values in the Color node replace only the diffuseColor field of the Material node. If the material contains specularColor, emissiveColor, or ambientIntensity, these colors are still applied, just as they would be if the diffuseColor were being used. If both texture and Color nodes are present, the color is applied to the texture if it is a one component texture (intensity map), and it is ignored if it is a color texture.

Summary

Textures are 2D images applied to the surface of objects, using the ImageTexture node. These textures are wrapped around objects using texture coordinates, points on the texture image expressed as *s* and *t* values. There are default mappings of these texture coordinates onto the object, which can be modified indirectly with the TextureTransform node, or directly by specifying texture coordinates using the TextureCoordinate node. The attributes of the Text node can also be modified with the FontStyle node. This allows the font appearance and size, the spacing of lines, and the direction of text layout to be modified. The Material node has many color components that can be used to vary the appearance of an object, from shiny to subdued. Objects can be made to look partially transparent and they can appear to emit their own light. Color can also be applied directly to each vertex of an object, which is smoothly shaded over the surface, for efficiency and special effects.

Q&A

Q **In this chapter, you mention that red, green, and blue are the primary colors. I remember learning in second grade that red, blue, and yellow were primary. Who is right?**

A We both are. The primary colors of pigmentation are magenta, cyan, and yellow. Because children do a lot of painting and drawing in grade school, they are taught about pigmentation in order to mix colors properly on a canvas. Also, because magenta is close to red and cyan is close to blue, those more common color names are taught to children. The primary colors of light are red, green, and blue. A television represents all color by mixing these three colors. VRML represents colors as they are used for producing colored light. It is easier to represent black and white using this model. By the way, the secondary colors of light, obtained by mixing two of the primary colors, are magenta (red and blue), cyan (green and blue), and yellow (red and green).

Q **So, then, how do I represent yellow in VRML?**

A I usually use 1 1 .85 (full red, full green, and 85 percent blue) for a bright yellow color. Go ahead and start from there and vary each number slightly until you get the yellow you want.

Q **Should I use per-vertex coloring to represent shadows on an object?**

A It is true that VRML objects don't cast shadows. Per-vertex coloring can appear to show a shadow. But, unfortunately, per-vertex shading does not realistically emulate the nature of light. If you really need to produce realistic shadows on your objects, consider creating texture maps that show the appropriate shadowing based on the physical properties of light. These are tricky to calculate by hand, but there is software available that can help you do this based on setting some basic parameters. Worlds that have been texture shadowed look really beautiful to visit. Unfortunately, they require tremendous computing power, which is not available on a typical home computer yet. I'll talk about the nature of light in Chapter 6, "Using Lights."

Exercises

1. Add a wood texture to the outside of your house. Place a gravel roof on top, make the fireplace brick, and put wallpaper on the inside walls.

2. Add per-vertex color to the terrain around your house to make a nice dirt path leading to the front door and put some white snow on the hilltops.

Answers

☐ Because of code length, you can find the complete VRML files for the preceding exercises on the CD-ROM at \Source\Answers.

Day 6

Using Lights

In the last chapter you learned how to change the appearance of a VRML object in various ways. But most of the appearance characteristics you applied depend on a light source somewhere in the VRML world to give the object the color you see. Up until now, that light source has been automatically generated for you, pointing in the direction you are currently looking. Now I will show you how to add lights of various colors and types to the scene. These can be used to highlight pictures on the wall, or to make one room bright while another is dimly lit. These lights interact with the Appearance node to give the object its final color. Here is what you will learn about today:

- ☐ Lighting 3D models
- ☐ Simple VRML lighting
- ☐ Advanced VRML lighting
- ☐ Material, texture, and lighting
- ☐ Geometric normals

Lighting 3D Models

A 3D virtual world attempts to mimic the real world as closely as possible. Objects are often shaped to reflect a real-world counterpart; they are positioned relative to each other as they would be in the real world, and photographic textures are used to improve realism. But, most important, when rendering 3D worlds, an attempt is made to duplicate the process the human eye goes through when looking at a scene, whether it be a room full of furniture or a sweeping mountain landscape.

The human visual system operates by receiving light reflected by objects in the world. It then separates the light spatially and spectrally to make out the shape, location, and color of objects. Light from the sun shines through a window, reflects off a light colored wall, bounces off a vase in a room, and is picked up by the eye. The sun is yellow, the wall is light blue, and the vase is red. All these colors combine, and the eye sees a red vase with a purple cast.

In a virtual world, calculating every bit of light from every possible source is not practical for real-time rendering, so shortcuts are needed. First, the light striking an object is only computed at the vertex points. An object whose shape is defined by an `IndexedFaceSet` with 20 points in a `Coordinate` node will only have to compute the light striking those 20 points. This computation results in a color value for each vertex. The actual surface of a face is colored by smoothly transitioning, or *interpolating*, between the colors at the vertex points. This approximation is often very convincing. Look at the examples in the previous chapters. The sides of the spheres you've seen are darker than the front. This is what makes the sphere look curved, and is done with the simple shading process I just described.

Before the color of a vertex can be computed, the renderer must know the source of all the light in the scene. Some light is spontaneously generated by the object itself. This is from the `emissiveColor` and `ambientIntensity` fields of the `Material` node, which I briefly described in the previous chapter. But most of the color of an object comes from external light sources. In all the worlds you've seen so far, CosmoPlayer has been creating such a light for you. It's called a *headlight* and is positioned to always look in the same direction you are. But now I will show you how to add your own lights to the scene. These can be used in place of the headlight to add more realism to a scene. For instance, you can place a light in a lamp object so that it appears all objects in a room are lit by that lamp.

Each light added to a scene requires that the renderer do more work. Adding many lights (more than eight, for example) could significantly decrease the performance of your world. So, throughout this chapter, I'll be talking about the expense of lighting and how to keep the number of lights in the scene low.

6

Simple VRML Lighting

The simplest type of light in a VRML scene is the `DirectionalLight` node. The following is its definition:

```
DirectionalLight {
  exposedField  SFFloat  ambientIntensity  0
  exposedField  SFColor  color             1 1 1
  exposedField  SFVec3f  direction         0 0 -1
  exposedField  SFFloat  intensity         1
  exposedField  SFBool   on                TRUE
}
```

This light doesn't really have a position in the scene, so it is not appropriate for placing a light in a lamp model. It is intended to add primary light sources, such as the sun, to the world. In fact, the headlight automatically created by CosmoPlayer is made with a `DirectionalLight`. The defaults shown here would create a perfectly good headlight if you could make the light follow you around as you walk through the world. I will show you how to do that when I discuss the many methods for interacting with a user next week, but for now, let me show you how the `DirectionalLight` works.

The `direction` field sets the direction the light shines. The light coming from this node takes the form of parallel rays. Most light comes from a single source, such as a lightbulb. But, because the sun is a point of light very far away, you can think of its light rays as being parallel. This makes the `DirectionalLight` very efficient for use in computing the light reflecting from an object. This is due to the fact that the rays of light hit all parts of an object at the same angle. Figure 6.1 compares parallel light rays to point light rays. As shown in the figure, with point light rays you would have to compute the direction of the light for every vertex, which is very expensive. A `DirectionalLight` avoids this computation, and is, therefore, the most efficient light to use in a scene.

Figure 6.1.

Comparing parallel light rays to point light rays.

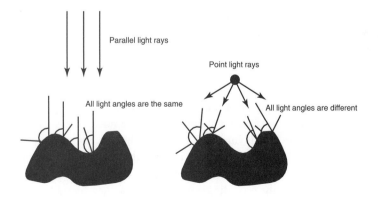

Figure 6.2 shows an example of two directional lights in a simple scene. Each light is pointing in the opposite direction along the X-axis; therefore, both sides of the sphere and cone are lit. When lights are added to a scene, CosmoPlayer turns off the automatic headlight, so the fronts of the objects in this example are dark. Listing 6.1 is the VRML code used to produce this scene.

TYPE   **Listing 6.1. VRML scene with two directional lights.**

```
Group {
  children [
  DirectionalLight {
      direction 1 0 0
  }
  DirectionalLight {
      direction -1 0 0
  }
  Transform {
      translation -2 0 0
      children Shape {
          appearance Appearance {
              material Material {
                  diffuseColor 0.3 0.3 0
              }
          }
          geometry Cone { }
      }
  }
  Transform {
      translation 2 0 0
      children Shape {
          appearance Appearance {
              material Material {
                  diffuseColor 0 0 0.4
              }
          }
          geometry Sphere { }
      }
  }
  ]
}
```

Note that the objects don't block the light reaching each side. VRML does not support shadows, so directional lights reach one side of all objects, regardless of their position in a scene. In fact, if you use a directional light as the sun in your world, it will light all objects, even when they are inside a room with no windows! To avoid this often undesirable effect, the DirectionalLight node is *scoped*. This means that it lights only objects contained in its group. In the preceding example there is a Group node at the top of the scene, containing all nodes as children. That means both lights will affect both objects. If I were to move the lights so that one was a child of each Transform node, each light would affect only the object in that Transform. (See Figure 6.3.)

Figure 6.2.

Objects lit by two directional lights pointing in opposite directions along the X-axis.

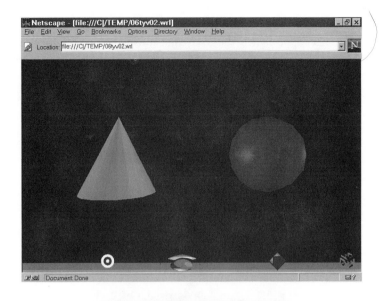

Figure 6.3.

Directional lights scoped so that only one shines on each object.

Scoping directional lights in this way not only allows you to control which objects are lit by which light, but it is also more efficient to render. If different parts of a scene are affected only by certain lights, fewer lights need to be considered when rendering each object.

Other fields in the DirectionalLight node are used to control different aspects of the light. The on field allows the light to be turned on and off. This might not seem very interesting for a light—why not just leave it out of the scene if you don't want it on? However, I will show you how to turn the light on and off from within the scene in Chapter 8, "Events and Routing."

The color and intensity fields are used in the computation of the vertex color for the objects. They apply light of the given color and intensity to the object, which is mixed with the object's own color to produce a final shade for that vertex. For example, a blue light shining on a red object will make it look purple. Many interesting effects can be obtained from this, including light shining through colored glass and light coming from colored neon.

Finally, the ambientIntensity field is added to the ambientIntensity field of the object's Material node. The total ambient intensity is then multiplied by the diffuseColor and added to the overall color of the object to make it brighter. This simulates the effect in the real world where rooms with many bright lights tend to make all objects brighter, even those in dark corners. This is because light scatters from the numerous reflections, and even from interactions with particles in the air.

Advanced VRML Lighting

The DirectionalLight node is an efficient way to add simple lighting to a scene. But VRML has two other lighting nodes that can be used for interesting effects. The first is the PointLight. You can place a light inside a lamp object to give the appearance that a room is lit by that lamp. This effect is done with a PointLight. Here is its definition:

```
I would rather eliminate the prior reference. Not necessary -bdcPointLight {
    exposedField    SFFloat    ambientIntensity  0
    exposedField    SFVec3f    attenuation       1 0 0
    exposedField    SFColor    color             1 1 1
    exposedField    SFFloat    intensity         1
    exposedField    SFVec3f    location          0 0 0
    exposedField    SFBool     on                TRUE
    exposedField    SFFloat    radius            100
}
```

The PointLight node has the same ambientIntensity, color, intensity, and on fields as the DirectionalLight node. But, rather than having a direction field, it has a location field, which positions the light in its local coordinate system. As shown in Figure 6.1, the PointLight node radiates light in all directions, from a single point source. You cannot see this source because, in VRML, light radiates from an invisible origin. It is only when the light reflects off other objects that you can detect its presence. Figure 6.4 shows an example of a scene with a point light source. The light is emitted from a sphere and lights three cones placed around it.

6

Figure 6.4.

A sphere with a spotlight at its center, showing the effect of the light on three cones surrounding it.

I made the background to this world a dark blue so you could see that the sphere that contains the light is completely black. Why is that? The light is at the center of the sphere. Therefore, it is lighting it from the inside. Because there is no headlight in this world, there is nothing lighting the outside of the sphere. Actually, if you look closely enough, you will see that the sphere is very dark gray. By default, the Material node has a small amount of ambientIntensity, so the sphere does have a bit of shading. The cones are all lit on the side facing the point light. This is the strength of the PointLight node: It lights the objects all around it on the side facing it, so it realistically duplicates the look of a real-world light source.

The scope of a PointLight is very different from that of the DirectionalLight. The local coordinate system of the light does affect its position, but not which objects are affected by its luminance. Instead, its effects are limited by its radius field. The value in the radius field gives the limit beyond which objects are no longer lit by the light. The intensity of its effect on objects is diminished by their distance from it, as well. Objects further away are affected less than objects that are nearer, just as in the real world. The rate at which the intensity drops off with distance is controlled by the attenuation field. This is an SFVec3f field that contains three floating point values. To arrive at the intensity of the illumination from a light at any distance from it, you would perform the calculation shown in Figure 6.5.

Figure 6.5.

Calculation to arrive at the intensity of illumination from a light at any distance from it.

$$length = \sqrt{normal[0]^2 + normal[1]^2 + normal[2]^2}$$

Here, the final *illumination* at a given *distance* is computed from the three components of `attenuation` and the `intensity` field of the `PointLight`, as shown. These three attenuation values give you lots of flexibility in adjusting the drop-off rates of particular lights. For instance, light in the real world follows a distance squared rule. This means that the intensity of the light at 20 meters is four times less than the intensity at 10 meters. To duplicate this effect, you might give a value of `0 0 0.01`, with the default `intensity` of `1.0`. That way, at 10 meters, the illumination will be `1.0`, but at a distance of 20 meters the illumination will be only `0.25`, and therefore, follow the distance squared rule.

The most advanced, and compute-intensive, light available in VRML is the `SpotLight`. The `SpotLight` node is very similar to the `PointLight` node. But, just like a real spotlight, it shines its light in a cone pattern, so it falls on a flat surface in a circular pattern. Here is its definition:

```
SpotLight {
  exposedField  SFFloat  ambientIntensity  0
  exposedField  SFVec3f  attenuation       1 0 0
  exposedField  SFFloat  beamWidth         1.570796
  exposedField  SFColor  color             1 1 1
  exposedField  SFFloat  cutOffAngle       0.785398
  exposedField  SFVec3f  direction         0 0 -1
  exposedField  SFFloat  intensity         1
  exposedField  SFVec3f  location          0 0 0
  exposedField  SFBool   on                TRUE
  exposedField  SFFloat  radius            100
}
```

This has all the fields of the `PointLight`, plus three new fields: `beamWidth`, `cutOffAngle`, and `direction`. The `direction` defines the center of the cone of light being emitted. The `beamWidth` is an angle from this centerline to the edge of the light cone; it defines where the light just starts to drop off. If you look at a real spotlight, you'll notice that when it shines on a flat surface, there is a circle of bright light, with edges that taper off into darkness. These "soft" edges are accomplished in the `SpotLight` node with the `cutOffAngle` field. This value is an angle, also measured from the centerline, that defines the edge of the cone where the spotlight no longer illuminates. In the area of the cone between the `beamWidth` and `cutOffAngle`, the beam intensity linearly falls from the value of `intensity` to `0`. (See Figure 6.6.)

6

Figure 6.6.

The relationship between the direction, beamWidth, *and* cutOffAngle *fields.*

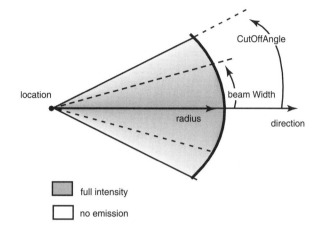

Figure 6.7 shows an example of a scene with a SpotLight shining on an IndexedFaceSet to show the illumination circle. This image shows a problem with the SpotLight node. Although the IndexedFaceSet in Figure 6.7 looks like a flat plane, it is actually composed of about 100 small triangles. This was done because the illumination from the spotlight is computed only at the vertices of the faces. In order to get nice, circular illumination from the spotlight, you need to compute the color at many vertices. Even with the number of triangles in this object, the edge of the lit circle is slightly ragged. The number of triangles chosen to represent the surface is a compromise between complexity and well-formed edges. Using this technique to get a nice spotlight effect must be used sparingly or the performance of your worlds will suffer.

Figure 6.7.

A spotlight shining on a surface.

Material, Texture, and Lighting

The lights introduced in this chapter interact with the color and intensity values of the Material node and also with the texture colors. Theoretically, color is computed at each pixel, across the surface of the objects. But, as I have shown in the previous chapter, color is actually computed only at each vertex. The factors that go into this color computation are the lights illuminating this object, its Material node, and the texture applied to the object. Because the texture is a 2D array of color values, it is incorporated into the equation after the vertex color is computed. The renderer attempts to make the texture take the place of the diffuseColor in the calculation of the color at each pixel. But, this is often approximated for performance reasons.

The Material node has three color values: diffuseColor, emissiveColor, and specularColor. It also has a shininess field and ambientIntensity field. These are factored into the calculation used to determine the color at each vertex, along with the light sources hitting each vertex. The emissiveColor brightens the color at each vertex, regardless of the other factors involved. The diffuseColor is affected linearly by the intensity and the angle of approach of the light hitting the vertex. The ambientIntensity adds color according to the intensity of the lights, but does not depend on the angle of approach of the light.

The specularColor and shininess fields are used together to simulate shiny objects. These values depend on the light sources the most. In the real world, if a light source is reflected directly back into your view by a shiny object, the spot reflecting the light will be especially bright. Everywhere around that spot that is not at precisely the correct angle to the light source will not reflect the light into your view and will be much darker. The shininess field controls how bright this spot is when at the right angle, as well as how close to the right angle the object has to be to reflect. A low value of shininess means the spot will not be very bright, but it will reflect over a larger angle. A high value will reflect only within a small angle, but it will be a very bright reflection. The specularColor controls the color of the shiny spot. Making this color white gives objects with a high shininess value a metallic look, because the shiny spots turn bright white, just like in real life. But making the specularColor something different from the color of the object gives a pearlescent effect. The shiny spot turns a totally different color from the rest of the object, making it look like a pearl or an opal.

Introducing Geometric Normals

I have been talking about the angle of approach of the light rays affecting the specular reflection and also the diffuse color component. But how is this angle computed? Look back at Figure 6.1. It shows the angle at which the light is striking the object. It also shows lines sticking straight out from the object at the point where the light ray is striking it. This is called the *normal* of the object at that point. The angle between this normal and the light ray is the angle of approach. If these two lines are parallel, it means the object is perfectly perpendicular to the light at that point, and there will be a high specular component (a shiny spot) at that point.

Because colors are computed only at each vertex, only the normals at the vertices, or the *vertex normals*, are important for this computation. By default, vertex normals are automatically generated for each object. For the simple primitives, these normals are computed as you would imagine. Normals for boxes are perpendicular to each face. For cones and cylinders, they are perpendicular to the top and bottom faces and follow a line from the center of the object through the vertices for the sides. For spheres, each normal follows a line from the center of the sphere through the vertices at the surface. Notice that in the case of the box, each vertex has more than one normal, because there is a normal pointing in the direction of each face. As I pointed out in Chapter 3, "Building a Scene," each vertex of a box is shared by three faces, but the sphere has only one normal per vertex. (See Figure 6.8.)

Figure 6.8.

Single versus multiple normals per vertex.

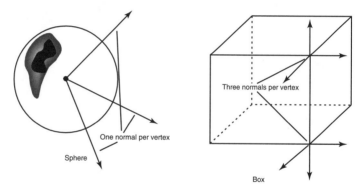

Having one normal per vertex on a sphere allows there to be smooth shading between facets. Having three normals per vertex causes each face of a box to be in sharp contrast to the adjoining face. This is the desired look for these objects. But for some shapes, it is not clear whether the seam between facets should be sharp or smooth. To help VRML decide this, the IndexedFaceSet, ElevationGrid, and Extrusion nodes have a creaseAngle field. The creaseAngle field gives the angle between facets in radians, above which multiple normals will be generated for each vertex. It is from this that you will start to see a crease between the faces. Figure 6.9 shows two Extrusion nodes with different values of creaseAngle. The shape on the left has a default value of 0, and the shape on the right has a value of 0.5 radians. Note how smooth the sides of the right shape are while the sharp edge still has a crease.

6

Figure 6.9.

An extruded shape with different values of `creaseAngle`.

Normals can also be controlled directly using the `Normal` node. This node is placed in the `normal` field of the `IndexedFaceSet` and `ElevationGrid` nodes. Here is its definition:

```
Normal {
  exposedField  MFVec3f  vector []
}
```

The vector array contains normals as `SFVec3f` values. A line drawn from the origin `0 0 0` to the point defines the normal.

Creating Normals

To give the renderer consistent normal values for its angle of approach calculation, normal values must be *normalized*. This term is a bit confusing because it sounds like normal. It means that the length of the vector from the origin to the normal point must be equal to one. A normal of `0 1 0` has the length of one. For more complicated values, the length is easily computed with the formula shown in Figure 6.10.

Figure 6.10.

Formula to compute more complicated values.

$$illumination = \frac{intensity}{attenuation[0]+attenuation[1] \times distance+attenuation \times r^2}$$

6

A normal of any length can be normalized by simply computing its *length* with the preceding formula, and then dividing the X, Y, and Z components by this value. For example, the vector value 1 2 3 has a length of about 3.74. Dividing each component by this value gives a normalized value of 0.267 0.535 0.802.

If you wanted to compute a normal pointing from the vertex of a face to a point light source, you would subtract the vertex position from the light position, and then normalize the result. For example, for a vertex at 4 5 6 and a light at 10 15 20, the difference is 6 10 14, the length is 18.2, and the normal is 0.329 0.549 0.768.

In the case of the IndexedFaceSet, the assignment of normals to coordinate points is controlled by the normalIndex field, with the same rules as those used to assign texture coordinates. If this field is empty, normals have a one-to-one mapping with the coordinates in the point field of the Coordinate node. If normalIndex has values, they follow the same structure as the coordIndex field, with the same number of index values per face, and a -1 to separate face indexes. The ElevationGrid node assigns normals to each point in the grid, in the same order as the values in the height field.

To control the assignment of single or multiple normals for each vertex, a normalPerVertex flag is available in both nodes. This field follows the same rules as the colorPerVertex field. For the ElevationGrid node, if normalPerVertex is FALSE, one normal per rectangular grid box is assigned. For the IndexedFaceSet node, if normalPerVertex is FALSE and the normalIndex field is empty, there is a one-to-one mapping between normals and faces. If normalPerVertex is FALSE and the normalIndex field is not empty, the geometry contains one index per face, without any -1 values.

Summary

VRML worlds can be enhanced through the use of lighting. The lighting model in VRML mimics real-world lighting as closely as possible while maintaining real-time rendering. I've shown you several different types of lights that can be used for different purposes in a scene. These lights interact with the texture and material applied to an object to produce the final object colors. Light is reflected from objects to the viewer. Objects with a high specular content reflect shiny spots and appear metallic. This specularity is controlled by the angle of approach of the light, relative to the viewer. By default, light reflects along a line parallel to the surface of the object. This line is called the normal of the surface, and can be changed to make objects look smoother or to achieve special effects.

6

Q&A

Q **Can you explain why a directional light passes through objects without casting a shadow?**

A Sure. Adding light to a scene is a time-consuming process. In VRML, each object is lit solely by the effect of the light on that object, irrespective of any other object in the scene, including objects between it and the light source. Calculating shadows would take too long for the browser to keep up with a user's interaction with the scene. Each time the camera moved or an object moved, the shadows would have to be recalculated. There is a subfield of computer science that does study all the effects of light in a scene. That field is called *ray tracing*, and many of the techniques used by ray tracers are used in virtual reality rendering. Ray tracing artists sometimes wait up to a week for a scene to render. Once it is done, they frame it and consider it art. Creating animations out of ray-traced scenes can take months. Still, if you are interested, you should find a book on ray tracing and read the first few chapters. Most texts do a really great job of explaining the process, and you will quickly realize which features are used by a VRML browser and which ones are not. In a nutshell, ray tracing traces a ray of light from each pixel on the screen and works its way back to the objects in the scene. So, the more pixels, the more calculations. And, the more objects, the more calculations. VRML browsers work off the same basic process. So, scenes with lights in them render dramatically faster as you make the browser window smaller. Why? The number of pixels in the window drops off rapidly as you decrease the window size. Make your windows smaller when you are testing out your lights and you will save time.

Q **In Figure 6.7, wouldn't I be better off using a texture that produces the lighting effect than creating all those triangles?**

A Yes. I agree with you—especially if you can eliminate the light altogether, because it is only shining on one or a few objects. Textures work especially well if the light source is very close to the textured object. In that case, the light looks realistic from all angles in the scene. There is specialized software that will create a bitmap based on a light source you identify. In fact, the browsers of tomorrow might be able to do that on-the-fly when they determine it will be easier to manipulate the texture than recalculate the light for all those vertices. As I say this, I realize that this has some bearing on the discussion of the LOD node in Chapter 16, "Making Efficient Scenes." If you can, keep this in mind as you read about the LOD node in the Q&A section of Chapter 16.

6

Q Aren't lights important for the realism of my scene?

A Lighting will definitely be an opportunity for VRML browsers of the future to make a difference in the quality of the worlds they can reproduce. But for now, the headlight seems to be enough for most users to enjoy a VRML scene. If you study art history, you will study the periods of mankind's art. The first art done on cave walls was all 2D. The first 3D paintings ignored the effects of directional light as if using an `AmbientLight` node. Now, most painters are trained in the science of lighting. We are just turning the corner into 3D environments. Those capabilities will be exciting for quite a while without the added benefit of perfect lighting.

Exercises

1. Add a table and chairs to the inside of your house. Make a lamp hanging from the ceiling with a `PointLight` shining on the table.

2. Add a pedestal and vase next to the table. Add a marble texture to the base, making it slightly shiny to simulate real marble. Put a shiny gold vase on top of the pedestal. Put a spotlight on the wall, shining on the pedestal and vase.

Answers

☐ Because of code length, you can find the complete VRML files for the preceding exercises on the CD-ROM at `\Source\Answers`.

6

Day 7

Viewpoints, Sound, and Anchors

By now you have learned most of the geometric capabilities of VRML 2. It's now time to make your worlds more interesting. In this chapter, I'll show you how to set an initial viewpoint in your world so visitors start out at a spot you choose for them. I'll also show you how to add many viewpoints to lead your visitors to different interesting vistas in your world. Then I'll show you how to add ambient sound to add depth and interest. Finally, I'll show you how to give visitors the ability to click on objects to go to different worlds or other Web content, just like hyperlinks in HTML! Here's what I'll cover today:

- ☐ Introduction to navigation
- ☐ Adding viewpoints
- ☐ Ambient sound
- ☐ Adding sound with locations in the scene
- ☐ Anchors

Introduction to Navigation

Visitors to your virtual worlds are navigating in an environment you create for them. In all the examples you've seen so far, the controls available allow users to walk in your world. Other methods of navigation are available, including examination, where you simulate picking up an object and looking at it from all sides, and flying, where you can move through the world with your feet off the ground. Many browsers allow you to change these modes through a button on the screen or a pop-up menu. CosmoPlayer has a right mouse pop-up that lets you switch between the walk and examination interface. But, VRML also has a NavigationInfo node to allow you to change this when you design the world. That way, you can start your visitors off with the appropriate interface. The following is the definition of the NavigationInfo node:

```
NavigationInfo {
  eventIn        SFBool      set_bind
  exposedField   MFFloat     avatarSize        [ 0.25, 1.6, 0.75 ]
  exposedField   SFBool      headlight         TRUE
  exposedField   SFFloat     speed             1.0
  exposedField   MFString    type              "WALK"
  exposedField   SFFloat     visibilityLimit   0.0
  eventOut       SFBool      isBound
}
```

As always, I'll save discussion of the eventIn and eventOut for later. The type field allows you to set the type of interface for the user. The default, "WALK", gives the user the walking interface you have seen up until now. This value can also be the strings "EXAMINE" or "FLY" to give the user these interfaces. Notice that this field is an MFString. That means you can place more than one string in this field, and the browser will choose the first string it recognizes. For example, you can place the strings "FLY" and "WALK" in the type field. If a user opens this world in a browser that does not understand the flying interface, it will choose the walking interface instead.

In fact, the type field can have any string that might be recognized by some browser. Your browser might understand the string SGI_GAMEVIEWER, which might be recognized by another browser that enables an interface used for playing games. Any browser not understanding the string SGI_GAMEVIEWER would attempt to recognize another string in the list, or revert to the default walking interface. By agreement, strings specific to a certain browser are prefixed by the company name and an underscore. This prevents two companies from accidentally picking the same name. Figure 7.1 shows CosmoPlayer with the EXAMINE interface set.

Figure 7.1.

Example of an object viewed with the EXAMINE *navigation type.*

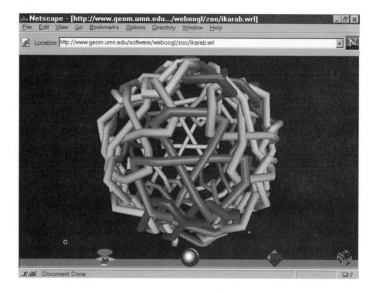

Avatars

When you move around a 3D world with the walk interface, there is actually an embodiment of yourself in the 3D world, known as an *avatar*. This avatar gives you a height and dimensions, so you can walk up hills and not pass through walls. Your avatar is actually a cylinder with the eyes (your current view of the world) near the top. The size of this avatar, by default, has a 0.25 meter radius and is 1.6 meters tall. It can also step over objects as tall as 0.75 meters. Any taller than this, and the avatar will run into the object instead. You can create a staircase for your avatar to climb, as long as each step is less than 0.75 meters. These values are set in the avatarSize field. You can change the size of avatars visiting your world using this field. You can make everyone in the world giants or ants.

This need to define the avatar has to do with *collision detection* and *terrain following*. I will be talking about these in Chapter 18, "Collision." For now, just remember that collision detection is what prevents you from walking through walls, and is used in the walking and flying interfaces. And, terrain following is what allows you to keep your feet on the ground as you walk up stairs and hills; it is used only in the walking interface.

The speed field allows you to control the rate at which visitors walk through your world. This is a floating point value and merely gives an average rate of travel when a user is walking. Many browsers (including CosmoPlayer) allow you to vary your walking speed with some interface. The default speed value of 1.0 makes you walk forward or backward at one meter per second

7

on average. You can often walk faster or slower than this by varying the mouse position. The speed field allows you to have users travel quickly through large worlds, or travel slowly and carefully through small worlds.

The NavigationInfo node has two more fields. The headlight field allows you to turn the automatic headlight I mentioned in the last chapter on and off. The visibilityLimit field is a floating point value that allows you to control how far a user can see in your world. Typically, objects beyond this number of meters from your current view will not be rendered. This allows you to optimize the performance of your worlds by not rendering distant objects. VRML has many ways to obscure the fact that these objects are disappearing, which I will discuss in Chapter 16, "Making Efficient Scenes."

Adding Viewpoints

The nature of a 3D virtual world is to allow a user to wander around at will. But it is often useful for the author of a world to set up special viewing spots, or *viewpoints*, that are of interest. It is especially important to set up an initial, or entry, viewpoint so that the user is brought into the world at the best point. Viewpoints are added to a VRML world with a Viewpoint node. The following is the Viewpoint node definition:

```
Viewpoint {
    eventIn        SFBool       set_bind
    exposedField   SFFloat      fieldOfView    0.785398
    exposedField   SFBool       jump           TRUE
    exposedField   SFRotation   orientation    0 0 1 0
    exposedField   SFVec3f      position       0 0 10
    field          SFString     description    ""
    eventOut       SFTime       bindTime
    eventOut       SFBool       isBound
}
```

The Viewpoint node is one of the most powerful nodes in VRML, and I will be showing you all its capabilities in Chapter 14, "Animated Viewpoints and Binding." But, for now, I want to concentrate on the fieldOfView, orientation, position, and description fields. These four fields are used to set up the opening camera viewpoint for the scene.

The position and orientation fields set the location in the world of the viewpoint and set the direction the viewpoint is looking, respectively. If this is the first viewpoint encountered in the VRML file text when reading from top down, it will be the user's initial view upon entry into the world. The orientation field cannot only turn the viewpoint horizontally, but it can also be used to tilt the view up or down, so you can have the user look up at the top of a hill, or down into the heart of a valley. (See Figures 7.2 and 7.3.)

Figure 7.2.

Looking down at a scene from above.

Figure 7.3.

Looking up at the building from Figure 7.2.

The `fieldOfView` field simulates the lens in a camera. When you look at objects in a scene, an object looks smaller when it is far away than when it is close. This is called *perspective*, and is one factor that makes 3D virtual worlds look realistic. Every human eye perceives perspective about the same. Objects at 1 meter and at 1,000 meters from the eyes have the same relative sizes for everyone because people's eye lenses are similar. But a camera lens can change this apparent difference dramatically.

About Cameras and Field of View

A wide-angle lens makes close objects look smaller to allow large objects to be photographed at a small distance. But, because of the way optics works, getting just a little farther away from the object makes it look much smaller. So, the size difference between a close object and one farther away is exaggerated. This is very useful when you want to draw the viewer's eye to a nearby subject, or when you want to photograph a wide, sweeping vista and there are no close-up objects in the way.

A telephoto lens, on the other hand, does just the opposite. It makes far away objects look about the same size as nearby objects, allowing you to photograph something far away with great detail. But, because there is little size difference between nearby and distant objects, the illusion of depth is impaired and the scene does not look very three-dimensional. This is useful when you want a close-up of a bird in a distant tree, for example.

A wide-angle lens is said to have a wide field of view, because you can see very wide, distant objects. A telephoto lens is said to have a narrow field of view, because you can't take in distant objects that are much wider than nearby ones.

The `fieldOfView` field in the `Viewpoint` node sets the field of view for this viewpoint as an angle in radians. It defines the angle from the center of the user's view (set by the `orientation` field) to the tallest object visible at a given distance. (See Figure 7.4.) A very narrow angle (around `0.1` radians) will limit your vision to distant objects that are not much taller than close ones, so this gives you a telephoto effect. A very large angle (around `1.5` radians) will allow you to take in huge distant objects, so this gives you a wide angle effect. The default value of `0.785398` gives a field of view that approximates the human eye.

Figure 7.4.

Comparison between a telephoto and wide-angle effect using `fieldOfView`.

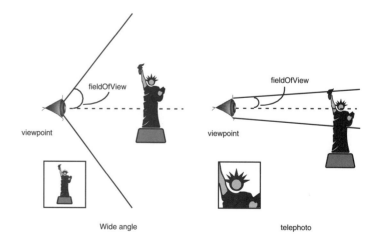

The Viewpoint node also has a description field. This field contains a string to use as descriptive text for a browser-defined user interface to viewpoints. In CosmoPlayer, the right mouse button gives the user a list of viewpoints to which the user may be automatically taken. The text for each viewpoint in this menu is taken from the description field. If the description field is left empty, this Viewpoint node does not appear in the viewpoint list. This allows you to create some viewpoints the user can access from the menu, and others that are not directly accessible by the user. These "invisible" viewpoints will be discussed in Chapter 14 when I discuss advanced viewpoint usage.

Ambient Sound

So far, you've created worlds that are silent. But, adding sound to a world can make even a simple world much richer and more interesting. A world set in a moonlit, starry night is just not complete without a cricket chirping and an owl hooting in the distance. VRML gives you a sound capability with the Sound node. The following is its definition:

```
Sound {
  exposedField   SFVec3f   direction      0 0 1
  exposedField   SFFloat   intensity      1
  exposedField   SFVec3f   location       0 0 0
  exposedField   SFFloat   maxBack        10
  exposedField   SFFloat   maxFront       10
  exposedField   SFFloat   minBack        1
  exposedField   SFFloat   minFront       1
  exposedField   SFFloat   priority       0
  exposedField   SFNode    source         NULL
  field          SFBool    spatialize     TRUE
}
```

The Sound node has many powerful capabilities, but, for now, I just want to show you the simplest way to use it to produce *ambient sound*. Playing ambient sound means your world has sound that seems to come from everywhere, and plays continuously. But to play any sound at all, you need a file containing an audio clip. You've probably come across audio files when visiting some Web pages. These are files that are downloaded to your computer and played over your speakers. Sounds can include someone delivering a speech, or the sound of glass breaking. Audio files are given to the Sound node by placing an AudioClip node in the source field. Here is the definition of the AudioClip node:

```
AudioClip {
  exposedField   SFString   description      ""
  exposedField   SFBool     loop            FALSE
  exposedField   SFFloat    pitch           1.0
  exposedField   SFTime     startTime       0
  exposedField   SFTime     stopTime        0
  exposedField   MFString   url             []
  eventOut       SFTime     duration_changed
  eventOut       SFBool     isActive
}
```

Taken together, the Sound and AudioClip nodes have lots of fields. I'll get into all of them eventually, but first let me show you a very simple ambient sound example. This example has a flat cube on which you can walk. There is also an ambient sound playing in the world. Take a look at Listing 7.1.

TYPE **Listing 7.1. VRML scene demonstrating ambient sound.**

```
Shape {
  geometry Box { size 20 0.2 20 }
}
Sound {
  source AudioClip {
      url "cricket.wav"
      stopTime -1
      loop TRUE
  }
  minBack 1000
  minFront 1000
  maxBack 1000
  minFront 1000
  spatialize FALSE
}
```

You can explore this world and hear the sound by going to the file ambientSound.wrl on the CD-ROM. Look at the fields used in the AudioClip node first. The url field specifies the sound file. This is a WAVE format file, which is a common Web audio format. The loop field is set to TRUE, which causes this clip to play over and over. The stopTime field indicates when the sound should stop playing. The -1 value is special, and indicates that the sound should never stop.

TIP

The startTime and stopTime fields hold SFTime values. These are floating point numbers that indicate the amount of time, in seconds, that has passed since midnight GMT, January 1, 1970. Don't worry, you'll never have to compute that number. In the file format, about the only value you'll ever set is -1. This value actually means "before the beginning of time" to VRML. Whenever a stopTime value is earlier in time than a startTime value, it is interpreted as meaning that the audio clip should not be stopped by stopTime. Setting loop to TRUE in this case will cause the sound to play forever.

Now look at the fields of the Sound node. The source field holds the AudioClip to use. The next four fields, minBack, minFront, maxBack, and maxFront, are all used to set the range over which the sound is heard. Sounds in VRML actually emanate from a point in the world. By default, this is 0 0 0 in the coordinate space (Transform node) containing the Sound node. The maxFront and maxBack fields define a distance from this origin beyond which sound will not be heard at all. For now, I have set these values to a very large distance so the sound is heard virtually everywhere. The minFront and minBack fields define the distance from the sound source at which sound volume starts decreasing. I want the sound to be the same volume everywhere, so I have made these very large, as well. I'll explain the spatialize field, as well as show you many interesting uses for the range fields, in the next section.

Adding Sound with Locations in the Scene

I mentioned that sound is emanated from a point in the VRML world. But there is more to it than that. Sound is actually spatialized in VRML. This means that the sound volume you hear depends on the emanation point. In many browsers, the stereo effect heard also depends on the direction of the sound. Some browsers, such as CosmoPlayer, even change complex characteristics of the sound to enhance the spatial effect.

In the previous section, I turned off this spatial effect by setting the spatialize field to FALSE. This can be done when the sound should be perceived as coming from all directions. The cricket sound in the last example is a good use for non-spatialized sounds.

However, you have some control over the sound source. You can control the size of the area in which the sound is heard. This is done with the minBack, minFront, maxBack, and maxFront fields. The Sound node is directional, set by the direction field. This is a normalized direction vector, just like the normals you saw in the last chapter. The minFront and maxFront fields determine the sound range in the direction of the direction field. The other two fields determine the range in the opposite direction. This is done because many sounds are louder when you are standing in front of the sound source. This is true of loudspeakers and people talking. The sound in front of the source is at its maximum volume, set with the intensity field, when you are closer than the minFront distance. Beyond this, the volume drops off evenly, until you read the maxFront distance, at which point the sound is no longer heard. The same process happens behind the sound with the minBack and maxBack fields. These four fields actually form an *ellipsoidal volume* of sound. The sound intensity you hear from the side of the source is determined by the size of the ellipsoid along the side, as determined by the four range fields. (See Figure 7.5.)

7

Figure 7.5.

Determining the sound ellipsoid from the minBack, maxBack, minFront, *and* maxFront *fields.*

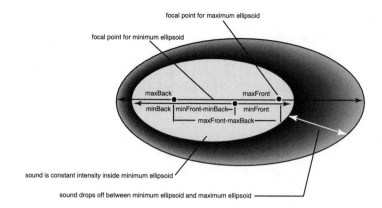

An ellipsoid can be determined from two focal points and a distance from the focal points to the edge of the ellipsoid. For the Sound node, one focal point for the minimum and maximum ellipsoids is the sound source. The other focal point for the minimum ellipsoid is found by taking the difference between the minFront and minBack values, and the distance is the minBack distance. The maximum ellipsoid is found by performing the corresponding operations with the maxFront and maxBack values.

Listing 7.2 is an example of spatialized sound with two sources centered around two boxes in the world. You can walk around the spatializedSound.wrl file on the CD-ROM to see how the sound spatialization works.

TYPE **Listing 7.2. VRML scene demonstrating spatialized sound.**

```
Transform {
  translation 5 0 0
  children [
      Shape {
          geometry Box { }
      }
      Sound {
          source AudioClip {
              url "owl.wav"
              stopTime -1
              loop TRUE
          }
          minBack 1
          minFront 3
          maxBack 3
          maxFront 10
          direction -1 0 0
      }
  ]
}
```

```
Transform {
  translation -5 0 0
  children [
      Shape {
          geometry Box { }
      }
      Sound {
          source AudioClip {
              url "bird.wav"
              stopTime -1
              loop TRUE
          }
          minBack 1
          minFront 3
          maxBack 3
          maxFront 10
          direction 1 0 0
      }
  ]
}
```

In the preceding world, I have directed the sound sources toward each other. If you stand halfway between the two sources, you should hear the owl coming out of the right speaker and the bird chirping coming out of the left speaker. When you stand near the right box, the owl should be loud and the bird should be very soft. The reverse is also true. Many interesting effects can be achieved with spatialized sound.

I've been using WAVE files as my audio sources. But MIDI sounds can also be used. MIDI files use the Musical Instrument Digital Interface standard to encode music in an electronic format. MIDI files are music files stored as a series of notes, rather than actual audio information. Therefore, for soundtrack audio, they are a much more efficient storage method.

The Sound and AudioClip nodes have other fields to give you even more flexibility. The AudioClip node has a pitch field, to allow you to slow down or speed up sounds. Setting pitch to 0.5 will cause sounds to play at half speed. This will cause voices to be lower in pitch and the sound will take twice as long to play. A pitch of 2.0 will cause sounds to play twice as fast, causing voices to sound like chipmunks. There is also a description field in AudioClip that allows you to put a textual description with the audio that the browser may choose to display. This is useful when the audio is muted or when the user is deaf.

The Sound node has a priority field. Many computers have difficulty playing more than a few sounds at a time. If too many sounds are within range, the priority field can be used to select which sounds get played and which get skipped. For example, if you are in a world with a doorbell telling you to answer the door, you will probably still want to hear it, even if many other background sounds are playing. You would set the doorbell sound as a high priority (a priority of 1.0 is the highest priority), while leaving the background sounds at a lower priority. When the doorbell needs to be played, some other sounds may stop, and then continue when the doorbell sound is finished.

7

Anchors

In HTML Web pages, you can click on a highlighted piece of text, or an image, and be taken to a new page hyperlinked to that highlight. A hyperlink is a URL of another piece of media, such as an HTML page, an image, or a VRML world. You can also place hyperlinks in your VRML world with the Anchor node. Here is the Anchor node's definition:

```
Anchor {
  eventIn       MFNode    addChildren
  eventIn       MFNode    removeChildren
  exposedField  MFNode    children       []
  exposedField  SFString  description    ""
  exposedField  MFString  parameter      []
  exposedField  MFString  url            []
  field         SFVec3f   bboxCenter     0 0 0
  field         SFVec3f   bboxSize       -1 -1 -1
}
```

The children, bboxCenter, and bboxSize fields are the same as those in the Group node. The Anchor node has the same characteristics as other grouping nodes, in that it contains a list of children nodes. But the children of an Anchor can be clicked on to take the user to a new URL, specified in the url field. Like the URL in the ImageTexture and AudioClip nodes, the URL can be relative or absolute. But, unlike these other nodes, this URL is not limited to an image or audio file. It can be a file of any type that is understood by your browser. In the case of CosmoPlayer, this is any file format understood by Netscape or Internet Explorer.

The description field contains a string that has some descriptive information about the link. The browser can choose to display this string when the children of the Anchor are highlighted. In most browsers, highlighting occurs when the user's mouse is over the Anchor children. CosmoPlayer changes the look of the mouse cursor and displays the description field during highlighting. Listing 7.3 is an example of using the Anchor node. It shows a Cone and a Cylinder, both of which are children of the Anchor.

TYPE **Listing 7.3. VRML scene using the Anchor node.**

```
Anchor {
  url "http://vrml.sgi.com/"
  description "Silicon Graphics VRML Web Site"
  children [
      Transform {
          translation 0 2 0
          children Shape {
              appearance Appearance {
                  material Material {
                      diffuseColor 0 0.6 0.8
                  }
              }
              geometry Cone { bottomRadius 1.5 }
```

```
            }
        }
        Shape {
            appearance Appearance {
                material Material {
                    diffuseColor 0.8 0.9 0
                }
            }
            geometry Cylinder { }
        }
    ]
}
```

The Anchor node also has a parameter field that allows communication with an HTML browser for advanced integrated media applications. I'll discuss these in detail in Chapter 20, "Creating a Composite Multimedia Document."

Summary

The many navigation functions of the VRML browser can be controlled with the NavigationInfo node. This includes selection of the user interface and the size of the avatar, the user's embodiment in the VRML world. Viewpoints can be set to give users an interesting view on entry and also to give them a selection of interesting vistas of the virtual world. The Sound node is another means of enhancing the user experience by adding ambient or spatial sound in the world. Adding sound at the same location as an object makes even simple objects seem more lifelike. Finally, the Anchor node gives visitors to your world very simple interaction capabilities. An Anchor creates a hyperlink so that when users click on the linked object, they are taken to the linked content. All these facilities give the author simple ways to enhance the user involvement in the virtual world.

Q&A

Q You say that I am an avatar when I walk around a scene. If I can't see myself, why should I consider myself an avatar?

A VRML is being used both for designing detailed avatars and creating worlds for multiple people to visit at the same time. Already, you can visit worlds on the Web where you can walk around and see other avatars in the world. Each of those other avatars represent another person who has recently loaded the same world in a browser and is exploring the world at the same time you are. Many of these worlds allow you to chat with other avatars using a chat server provided by the world host. There are many VRML authors who are focusing on creating avatars for people to use while walking around shared virtual worlds. It seems that creative people will

7

want to create exotic avatars using the geometry capabilities of VRML, as well as the animation and texturing features. Someday soon, you may even be able to walk into a virtual store and try on virtual clothing. As people get more used to using avatars, I won't be surprised if you get the ability to see the virtual hands and legs of your avatar under control of the VRML browser. This will help eliminate the need for using a mouse to interact with VRML scenes and make interaction more natural.

Q Anchors are great for hyperlinking around the Web, but isn't it disruptive to be jumping in and out of a world?

A Yes, I think so. If you are worried about this side effect of anchors, you will be really impressed with the techniques I will show you in Chapter 20, "Creating a Composite Multimedia Document," as they will help you get around that problem. In Chapter 20, I will introduce the concept of frames. With frames, your visitors will be able to click an anchored object and open that link in a different subwindow in the browser. That window within the browser window is called a frame and lets you do a bang-up job of providing 3D visuals while providing additional reference text. In fact, you'll be able to use VRML worlds within an encyclopedia-like interface.

Q If I use an Anchor node to give access to a document that I don't maintain, isn't there a chance the link won't work one day? If so, is there anything I can do to deactivate the link?

A Yes. This is an unfortunate fact about hyperlinks. Everyone on the Web is trying to deal with dead links. You can always copy the linked material to your own server and even write an agent to go get a new copy every week or so. I will talk about a different naming convention in Chapter 15, "Enriching Your Scene and Reusing Objects," that should help with some of the invalid URLs. But even in the URNs I discuss, there won't be help with material that has been completely taken off the Web. On the other hand, if a link is no longer active, the VRML browser should not blow up or anything. You shouldn't have to worry about deactivating your links. And, don't hold your breath waiting for the Web to settle down.

Exercises

1. Add a speaker in the corner of your scene. Put a sound source playing a MIDI-track in the speaker. Add an ambient wind noise to the outside of the house.

2. Add three viewpoints to your house. The entry viewpoint should be standing in the path looking at the outside of the house. The second should be standing in the doorway. The third should be inside, at the table, looking in the direction of your new speaker.

Answers

☐ Because of code length, you can find the complete VRML files for the preceding exercises on the CD-ROM at \Source\Answers.

7

Day **8**

Events and Routing

Up until now, you have created VRML worlds that have been, for the most part, static. Today, I introduce the topics of behavior and interaction, which make up the heart of VRML. These are the major features, added by the designers of VRML 2, that distinguish it from VRML 1. You will start with the basics today: events and routing. Understanding these two is crucial in using all the other advanced features of VRML 2. Today, you will learn the following:

- [ ] Bringing 3D worlds to life
- [ ] Creating a route
- [ ] Fields and events
- [ ] Sensing objects with the TouchSensor

Bringing 3D Worlds to Life

As you learned yesterday, VRML allows you to create interesting worlds of objects: Anchors can link you to other worlds and pages, you can animate to a given viewpoint, and you can add sounds to make the world more life-like. But the virtual world is motionless, and the user can do little but walk around and see the sites.

 TIP

> VRML gives you three ways to bring your worlds to life without adding behaviors to objects:
>
> ☐ `Anchor` nodes can link to other VRML worlds or HTML pages.
>
> ☐ The browser user interface allows users to animate to predefined viewpoints using the `Viewpoint` node.
>
> ☐ The `Sound` node can be used to add the extra dimension of ambient sounds to your worlds.

You will now see how to change all that. VRML allows the user to add behavior and interaction to the virtual world. Behavior allows objects in the scene to move, it allows object appearance to change, and it can start and stop audio clips and animated textures (which you will learn about in Chapter 11, "Allowing Users and Objects to Interact"). Interaction allows the user to control these behaviors while exploring the world you have created. The user can touch an object to start it moving, slide a knob to control light intensity, or simply run into a wall and produce a sound. The user's proximity to an area of your world can also trigger behaviors.

Communicating Between Nodes

The position, size, and orientation of an object is controlled by its parent transformation. These parameters are entered into the fields of the `Transform` node when the file is created, but you can also change these fields while your world is being explored. For example, the following is a little scene featuring the red cone I introduced way back in Chapter 2, "Basic VRML Concepts." Figure 8.1 shows the figure created by this segment.

```
Transform {
    translation 0 5 0

    children [
        Shape {
            geometry Cone { }
            appearance Appearance {
```

```
            material Material {
                diffuseColor 1 0 0
            }
        }
      }
    ]
}
```

Figure 8.1.

A cone translated 5 units in the Y direction.

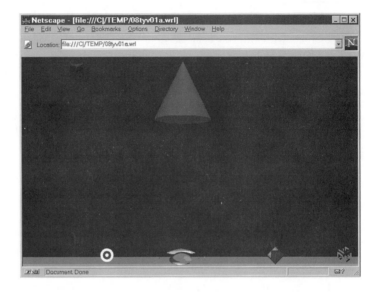

This is your good friend, the red cone, translated 5 units. Now, if you were to change the translation to 4 5 0 while the user is watching, the cone would jump four units to the right.

Changing Fields

The fields of many nodes can be changed on-the-fly. These changes are made by sending *events* to the node. An event is a message sent to the node informing it that one of its fields should be changed. In the preceding example, the following message is sent to the Transform node:

```
"Please change the value of your translation field to 4 5 0"
```

When this event is received, the node makes the change, the scene is redrawn, and the user sees the cone jump.

You can think of the node as having a set of mail slots into which requests can be placed. There is one slot for each field that can be changed in the node. These slots are called eventIns, and every node has its own set. Every eventIn has a name so that when an event is sent, the sender can place it in the appropriate slot. The content of the message is a piece of data with one of the VRML field types. (See Appendix A, "VRML Node Reference.") In the preceding example, the data type is SFVec3f. Only events of the correct type can be received by an eventIn. All other types generate an error.

The eventIn is the destination of an event. But the event must also have a source, known as an eventOut. Many nodes have one or more eventOuts that generate an event based on stimuli. This can be anything from user interaction with the scene (as you will see later in this chapter with the TouchSensor node), the movement of the user through the scene (the ProximitySensor, introduced in Chapter 11), or even the passage of time (the TimeSensor node, described later in this chapter). Just like eventIns, eventOuts have a fixed data type. An eventOut is connected to an eventIn using a *route*.

Creating a Route

In VRML, routes are the wiring that make animation and user interaction possible. The ROUTE command looks like this:

```
ROUTE Node1.isActive TO Node2.set_on
```

The names Node1 and Node2 are user-defined names of nodes. In order to create a route, the node with the eventOut and the eventIn must be named using the DEF construct. Here's a simple example of routing:

```
DEF MySensor TouchSensor { }

DEF MyLight DirectionalLight { }

ROUTE MySensor.isActive TO MyLight.set_on
```

I'll discuss the TouchSensor node a bit later. For now, just assume it has an isActive eventOut. This is routed to the set_on eventIn of the DirectionalLight, which corresponds to its on field. When this event is sent, the light is turned on or off, depending on the value (TRUE or FALSE) of the event. Notice that the type of both the isActive eventOut and the set_on eventIn is SFBool. Only like types can be routed, or an error will be generated.

NOTE

Make sure you match the types of an eventIn and eventOut. If not, CosmoPlayer will put up an error dialog box, but will continue running, and the route will be disabled.

Many eventOuts can be routed to the same eventIn, a capability known as *fan-in*. If two events are sent to the same eventIn, the time of their arrival is used to determine which is handled first. If two events were to arrive at precisely the same time, the order would be undefined, although this is rarely the case. An eventOut can *fan-out*, or be connected to many eventIns. Together, these allow very flexible routing between nodes.

Fields and Events

A node can contain four classes of data: field, exposedField, eventIn, and eventOut. I've talked about field, eventIn, and eventOut, and now, you'll look at exposedField. But first, take a look at how to find out what fields and events a node contains. The following is a node definition from the node reference in Appendix A:

```
Group {
  eventIn       MFNode  addChildren
  eventIn       MFNode  removeChildren
  exposedField  MFNode  children      []
  field         SFVec3f bboxCenter    0 0 0
  field         SFVec3f bboxSize      -1 -1 -1
}
```

Notice the items in bold. These are values you are able to enter into the file format when defining this node. The rest are simply used to identify the class and type of the fields and events. eventIn, eventOut, and exposedField names can be used in routes, but not when defining a node. The general syntax of this node description format is the node name, followed by an open bracket, followed by a list of fields and events, followed by a close bracket. The general syntax for each field or event entry is

```
class type name default
```

Each of the preceding items is replaced by their corresponding legal values. Legal class names are shown in Table 8.1.

Table 8.1. VRML data class types.

Class	Description
eventIn	An event received by the node
eventOut	An event sent by the node
field	A private node member
exposedField	A public node member

A Legal type is one of the VRML data types described in Table 8.2. (A more detailed description can be found in Appendix B, "VRML Field and Event Types.")

Table 8.2. VRML data types.

Type	Description
SFBool	The Boolean value TRUE or FALSE.
SFFloat	A 32-bit floating point value.
SFInt32	A 32-bit signed integer.
SFTime	An absolute or relative time value.
SFVec2f	A pair of floating point values usually denoted as (u, v) because they are most often used to represent texture coordinates.
SFVec3f	Three floating point values usually denoted as x, y, z because they are most often used to represent a 3D position.
SFColor	Three floating point values, each between 0 and 1, representing the red, green, and blue components of a color.
SFRotation	Four floating point values. The first three values represent an axis (with 0,0,0 being the other point on the axis line), and the fourth value represents the angle of rotation in radians around that axis.
SFImage	A two-dimensional image with one- to four-color components, allowing representation of monochrome to full-color images with transparency.
SFString	A UTF8 (international character) string.
SFNode	A container for a VRML node.
MFFloat	An array of SFFloat values.
MFInt32	An array of SFInt32 values.
MFVec2f	An array of SFVec2f values.
MFVec3f	An array of SFVec3f values.
MFColor	An array of SFColor values.
MFRotation	An array of SFRotation values.
MFString	An array of SFString values.
MFNode	An array of SFNode values.

The <name> is the identifier of the field or event that is used in the file format for the node, or in a route. Finally, the default value only appears in the field and exposedField entries. It is the value that field will have if it is not specified by the user in the file format.

In Appendix A you will find a reference for every node in VRML, using the preceding format. This should help you remember not only names of fields and events for a given node, but also what the default values are for all fields.

eventIn

Most, but not all, eventIns correspond to a field in the node. For instance, the `translation` field of the `Transform` node has a corresponding eventIn named `set_translation`. In fact, fields of a node are not accessible at all. The only way they can be changed is by having a corresponding eventIn. While most fields have this, a few do not. This allows some nodes to be lightweight, therefore being easier and faster to implement.

Some nodes have eventIns that do not correspond to any field of that node, but provide additional functionality for it. For example, the `Transform` node has an `addChildren` eventIn. When this event is sent, the passed children nodes are added to the list of children of this transform.

eventOut

Most nodes that have an eventIn corresponding to a field also have an eventOut corresponding to that same field. For example, the `translation` field of the `Transform` node, in addition to a `set_translation` eventIn, also has a `translation_changed` eventOut. This event is sent whenever the `set_translation` eventIn is received. In effect, the `translation` value is passed through from the eventIn to the eventOut. This allows the chaining of events through many nodes. Here is an example of how this chaining works:

```
DEF T1 Transform { }
DEF T2 Transform { }
DEF T3 Transform { }
ROUTE T1.translation_changed TO T2.set_translation
ROUTE T2.translation_changed TO T3.set_translation
```

Now, whenever T1 receives a `set translation` event, the change propagates to the other two transforms.

Field

You've been using fields since Chapter 2. A field can be set to a particular value in the file format, or it can be changed when its node receives a corresponding eventIn. But, it is important to understand that the field itself cannot be changed on-the-fly by the author. The field is known as private to the node. The fact that it can be changed is because the corresponding eventIn exposes it. This is important because some fields are not exposed. I will discuss this when I talk about scripting in Chapter 10, "Scripting."

exposedField

I've been talking about how the `translation` field of the `Transform` node has a corresponding `set_translation` eventIn and `translation_changed` eventOut. But, if you refer to the `Transform` node entry in Appendix A, you will not see either of these names. That is because translation is an exposedField. exposedField is a powerful VRML data class that serves many purposes. First, it is a shorthand way of saying that a field has a corresponding eventIn and eventOut. The name of the eventIn is always the field name with a `set_` prefix, and the name of the eventOut is always the field name with a `_changed` suffix.

The exposedField class also defines how the corresponding eventIn and eventOut behave. For all exposedFields, when an event comes in, the field value is changed (with a corresponding change to the scene appearance), and an eventOut is sent with the new field value. The exposedField class designation is important when I begin the discussion on scripting in Chapter 10. An exposedField is accessible to a script whereas a field is not.

TIP

When using an exposedField name (like `translation`) in a route, you can use just the original name, without adding `set_` or `_changed`. VRML understands which name to use from the context of the ROUTE statement (eventOut on the left, eventIn on the right). For instance, if A and B are both transforms,

ROUTE A.translation **TO** B.translation

is the same as

ROUTE A.translation_changed **TO** B.set_translation

Sensing Objects with the TouchSensor

You can route the `translation_changed` of one `Transform` to the `set_translation` of another. The `set_translation` of that node can, in turn, be routed to the `translation_changed` of another in an endless event chain; however, nothing much would happen. The first transform's value would never change, so an event would never be seen. Therefore, the second transform would never change, and so on. There needs to be a node that can generate an event to start what is known as an event cascade. If such a node is wired to the first transform, when the event is generated, it would cascade through the chain, changing all the field values along the way.

In general, VRML nodes that can generate events are known as sensors.

NEW TERM In VRML, a *sensor* is a node that sends events out based on user interaction with the scene. Some sensors react when the user touches or drags an object in the world. Others send events when the user's avatar moves through certain regions. And still others send purely time-based events. I will show you all these in the coming chapters.

The TouchSensor is one of the simplest, but most useful, sensors. When placed in a list of children under a grouping node, it will sense interactions with the shapes in that list. It acts as a sensor for its sibling nodes. Its siblings don't have to be simple Shape nodes. If there is a grouping node in the list that has Shape nodes as children, those shapes are considered siblings of the TouchSensor as well.

```
Group {
    children [
        Group {
            children [
                TouchSensor { }

                Shape {
                    geometry Cone { }
                }

                Group {
                    children [
                        Shape {
                            geometry Box { }
                        }
                        Shape {
                            geometry Sphere { }
                        }
                    ]
                }
            ]
        }

        Shape {
            geometry Cylinder { }
        }
    ]
}
```

The TouchSensor will sense interaction with the cone, box, and sphere, but not with the cylinder.

But what sort of interaction can you do? First take a look at the definition of the TouchSensor from Appendix A:

```
TouchSensor {
    exposedField SFBool   enabled TRUE
    eventOut     SFVec3f  hitNormal_changed
    eventOut     SFVec3f  hitPoint_changed
    eventOut     SFVec2f  hitTexCoord_changed
    eventOut     SFBool   isActive
    eventOut     SFBool   isOver
    eventOut     SFTime   touchTime
}
```

The `isOver` and `isActive` Events

Notice that `enabled` is the only field that can be entered in the file format. Everything else in the `TouchSensor` is an event generator. The simplest eventOuts are `isOver` and `isActive`. These are a direct reflection of the user's interaction with the objects being sensed. Assuming you are using a mouse, the `isOver` event is generated with a value of `TRUE` whenever the mouse is on top of any of the sibling geometry. When the mouse is no longer over the shapes, an `isOver` value of `FALSE` is sent.

An `isActive` event of `TRUE` is generated when you select the sibling shapes. This is usually done by clicking the mouse button when you are over one of the shapes. These two events are independent of each other. When you move the mouse over a shape, an `isOver` `TRUE` is generated. Then, if you click down over the shape, `isActive` `TRUE` is generated. If you are holding down the mouse button and you move the mouse off the shape, an `isOver` `FALSE` is generated; however, `isActive` remains `TRUE`.

When you press the mouse and the `TouchSensor` generates an `isActive` `TRUE`, no other `TouchSensor` in the scene will generate events of any kind. This is known as a *grab*, because it behaves as if the `TouchSensor` were grabbing all the movements of the mouse and not letting any other sensor have them. This way, if you were to create a virtual push-button, you would not get any confusing events from any other nearby `TouchSensor`s between the time the mouse button is pressed and released.

Other Styles of Input

The VRML specification is very careful to use general wording in describing the type of interaction possible with the `TouchSensor`. Even though almost all VRML worlds are explored on a PC-style computer with a mouse, it is not required. For example, many 3D input devices are becoming available, such as a data glove (which senses the movement of your fingers), and even something called a "spaceball!"

With a device other than a mouse, the `isOver` and `isActive` events can mean very different things. For example, a data glove is a device that you place over your hand like a glove. When you move your hand or your fingers, a hand moves in the virtual world to mimic your motions. This virtual hand takes the place of the mouse cursor, but can move around in the scene, not just on the surface of the computer screen. Because of this, the `isOver` event may be generated when you are

---

close to the sibling shapes, rather than when it appears that the mouse cursor is on top of the shape. Likewise, isActive may be generated when you make a grabbing gesture, rather than clicking a mouse button.

Some experimental devices even exist that provide resistance to your real hand when your virtual hand collides with an object in the scene. Don't be surprised to someday see VRML worlds that you can really reach out and touch!

The isOver event is typically used for locate highlighting, a common user-interface aid. When an isOver TRUE event is sent, the object can be made brighter, made to jump up above other objects, or even changed to a different shape. This helps the user know that this object can be clicked to perform some action.

The isActive event can be used to perform an action when the user clicks on the object. This could be as simple as turning a light on and off (as you will see in the next example), or as complicated as starting an animation of multiple objects complete with sound.

The following is an example of how to use isOver and isActive:

```
Group {
    children [
        DEF TS TouchSensor { }
        Shape {
            appearance Appearance {
                material Material {
                    diffuseColor 0 0.5 0
                }
            }
            geometry Sphere { }
        }
        DEF Highlight DirectionalLight {
            color 1 0 0
            on FALSE
        }
        DEF ActiveLight DirectionalLight {
            color 0 0 1
            on FALSE
        }
    ]

    ROUTE TS.isOver TO Highlight.set_on
    ROUTE TS.isActive TO ActiveLight.set_on
}
```

In the preceding example, you are using the isOver and isActive events to turn separate DirectionalLights on and off. The lights are different colors so you can see their different effects. You can try this example by loading the CD-ROM and double-clicking 08tyv01.wrl. Figure 8.2 shows the example with the cursor to the side. Figure 8.3 shows the same example with the cursor over the sphere.

Figure 8.2.

Example with DirectionalLights turned off.

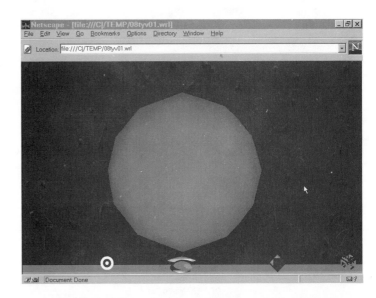

Figure 8.3.

Example with the isOver event detected.

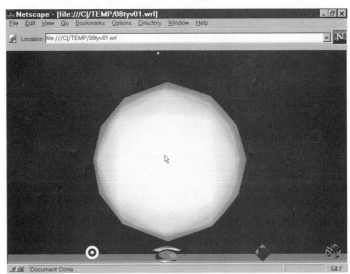

The `touchTime` event

The `isActive` and `isOver` events are direct reflections of the mouse. But these only can be wired to `SFBool` eventIns. Using them for any other purpose would require writing a script. A common use for the `TouchSensor` is starting and stopping time-based actions. For example, a doorbell has a button that, when pressed, sounds a chime. Doing this would require routing the start time for the sound from the time the doorbell was clicked. To perform this common operation, the `TouchSensor` has a `touchTime` eventOut. This sends an `SFTime` when the user presses and releases the mouse button while over the object. This can be routed directly to the AudioClip's `startTime` eventIn. Listing 8.1 shows how to use `touchTime`.

TYPE | **Listing 8.1. Using the `TouchSensor` to activate an audio clip.**

```
Group {
    children [
        DEF TS TouchSensor { }
        Shape {
            appearance Appearance {
                material Material {
                    diffuseColor 0 0.5 0
                }
            }
            geometry Sphere { }
        }
        Sound {
            maxBack 1000
            maxFront 1000
            source DEF Audio AudioClip {
                url "horse.wav"
            }
        }
    ]

    ROUTE TS.touchTime TO Audio.startTime
}
```

Now, when you click on the sphere, a `touchTime` event is sent to the `startTime` of the AudioClip. The value is the time the mouse button was released while over the sphere. This causes the AudioClip to play the sound immediately. Try it out for yourself: Load the CD-ROM and double-click `08tyv02.wrl`.

The Vector Events

The `TouchSensor` can generate three more events: `hitPoint_changed`, `hitNormal_changed`, and `hitTexCoord_changed`. These events are generated whenever the mouse moves, as long as the cursor is over the object. They give information about the surface of the object under the current position of the cursor. Table 8.3 describes the values sent.

Table 8.3. The `TouchSensor` vector eventOuts.

eventOut Name	Information
hitPoint_changed	The 3D point
hitNormal_changed	The normal to the surface at the point
hitTexCoord_changed	The 2D texture coordinate at the point

These three events are typically reserved for advanced applications, such as interactive object placement and simulating the HTML feature of performing operations based on the region of an image where the user clicked.

The `hitPoint_changed` event sends an `SFVec3f` value. This value is the position on the surface of the object that is currently under the mouse pointer. Using this value, the user can move another object to its position, thereby attaching the second object to the surface of the first.

The `hitNormal_changed` event sends an `SFVec3f` value. This value is the object's surface normal at the point currently under the mouse pointer. It can be used to rotate the object being placed so that it rests flush against the stationary object.

The `hitTexCoord_changed` event sends an `SFVec2f` value. This value maps a point on the surface of the object to the pixel value in the texture being applied. For instance, take a flat rectangle with a texture mapped normally to it. Placing the mouse pointer over the center of the rectangle will send a `hitTexCoord_changed` event with the values `0.5 0.5`.

 TIP

> If you multiply the texture coordinates by the width and height of the texture being applied to the object, you will get the exact pixel on the surface of the object directly under the mouse.

8

Summary

In the VRML file format, fields contained in nodes are given initial values to define the characteristics of those nodes. You can change these values after the world is loaded by sending events to the nodes. These changes can affect the color of an object or its position in the world. Events are propagated by routing an eventOut of one node to an eventIn of another. All events are typed, just like all fields. Routing can be done only between an eventOut and an eventIn of the same type. Some fields have an implicit eventIn and eventOut, and these are known as exposedFields. When an event is received by an exposedField, the value in its field is changed and the new value is also sent out. Other nodes contain eventOuts and eventIns not associated with any field. For instance, sensors send events as the result of some stimulation from the user.

Q&A

Q **Why is there an exposedField if it's just a combination field of eventIn and eventOut?**

A The exposedField has additional meaning. Whenever its eventIn is received, it sets its field and sends its eventOut with the new value. If they were separate entries, this would not necessarily be true. Also, you can use the field name in a ROUTE statement, and set_ or _changed will be inferred.

Q **If I use fan-in to route many eventOuts to a single eventIn, how do I control what order events get sent?**

A All events in VRML have a *timestamp*: the time the event was received. The order is defined by this timestamp. Rarely, two events with the same timestamp can be received by an eventIn. In this case, the order is undefined. This can be easily avoided by not routing two events from the same node to a single eventIn.

Q **Why would I ever want to use the enabled exposedField of the TouchSensor?**

A The enabled exposedField allows you to turn off the TouchSensor. You might have a game where a door is opened when a button is pressed, but you might have to solve a puzzle before the door can be opened. Therefore, you can have the TouchSensor disabled at first. Then, a puzzleSolved eventOut can be routed to the enabled exposedField to allow the door to be opened when the puzzle is solved.

Exercises

1. Add a light to your house model. This light must turn on when the light switch is pressed and turn off when released. In Chapter 10, you'll learn how to create a custom node, called a Script, to make the light stay on until another action turns it off. For now, simply add the geometry for the light switch button and the routes to turn it on and off. Use the PointLight in the ceiling lamp from Chapter 6, "Using Lights." When you click your light switch, the room should brighten until you release it.

2. Add a click sound (available on the CD-ROM as click.wav) to the house. Make it play when the user presses the light switch.

Answers

1. Listing 8.2 shows the code added to the VRML world. Figure 8.4 shows the room with the light turned off, and Figure 8.5 shows the room with the light turned on.

Listing 8.2. A TouchSensor, light switch, and routes added to the lamp over the table in the house.

TYPE

```
Transform {
    children Shape {
        appearance Appearance {
            material Material {
                ambientIntensity 0.253968
                diffuseColor    1 0.900511 0.314236
                specularColor   0.872449 0.247119 0.254214
                emissiveColor   0 0 0
                shininess       1
                transparency    0
            }
        }
        geometry Box { }
    }

    translation    -8.78759 -18.1029 7.45529
    rotation       -0.000227473 -0.707107 0.707107  3.14114
    scale          0.0669011 0.00500155 0.119573
    scaleOrientation 0 0 1  0
}
Transform {
    children     [
        Shape {
            appearance Appearance {
                material Material {
                    ambientIntensity 0.293166
```

8

```
                    diffuseColor    0.26801 0 0
                    specularColor   0.607143 0.132784 0.175795
                    emissiveColor   0 0 0
                    shininess       0.157143
                    transparency    0
                }
            }
            geometry Cylinder { }
        }
        DEF LightTS TouchSensor { }
    ]
    ROUTE LightTS.isActive TO Light1.set_on

    translation    -8.78702 -18.0978 7.43382
    rotation       -7.90819e-12 -0.707107 0.707107  3.14159
    scale          0.035691 0.0164668 0.0356887
    scaleOrientation 0 0 1  0
}
```

Figure 8.4.

Room with light turned off (switch is not pressed).

Figure 8.5.
Room with light turned on (switch is pressed).

2. The same TouchSensor used to turn the light on and off can be used to activate the sound. The touchTime eventOut is routed to an AudioClip node, just like in Listing 8.1. Listing 8.3 shows the Sound node and the ROUTE.

Listing 8.3. The same TouchSensor as the one used in Exercise 1 activates the click sound.

TYPE

```
Sound {
    location -8.78702 -18.0978 7.43382
    source DEF LightClick AudioClip {
        url "click.wav"
    }

    minFront 30
    maxFront 30
    minBack  15
    maxBack  15
}

ROUTE LightTS.touchTime TO LightClick.startTime
```

Day 9

Adding Behavior to Objects

In the preceding chapter, you learned about simple interaction. But switching a light on and off with a TouchSensor is not very compelling by itself. In this chapter, I'll talk about the simplest ways of getting objects to move, change their color, and perform other interesting behaviors. These tasks will all be accomplished with a set of nodes built into VRML called interpolators. I'll also introduce the driving force behind interpolators, the TimeSensor. Here's what you'll learn about today:

- [ ] Object interpolation
- [ ] Moving objects
- [ ] Changing objects over time
- [ ] Rotating objects
- [ ] Morphing
- [ ] Other interpolators

Object Interpolation

In the preceding chapter, I talked about moving a cone by sending an event to the set_translation eventIn of the Transform node. But what is the source of that event? In Chapters 10, "Scripting," and 11, "Allowing Users and Objects to Interact," you'll learn that you can generate this event in many ways. But first, I'll talk about the simplest method: the interpolator nodes.

An interpolator node has a list of numeric values, known as *keys*, and a list of values to interpolate, called *key values*. The type of the key value is determined by the particular interpolator node you're using. I will first introduce the ScalarInterpolator, which outputs (and whose key values are) SFFloat values. Here is its definition:

```
ScalarInterpolator {
    eventIn      SFFloat set_fraction
    exposedField MFFloat key         [ ]
    exposedField MFFloat keyValue    [ ]
    eventOut     SFFloat value_changed
}
```

Every interpolator has a set_fraction eventIn. When this event is received, its value is matched to one of the keys. If a match is found, the key value corresponding to that key is sent out. If the value is between two consecutive keys, an event is generated that is an interpolation between the key values corresponding to the two keys. For instance, here is an example of using the ScalarInterpolator:

```
ScalarInterpolator {
    key      [ 0, 1 ]
    keyValue [ 3, 6.4 ]

}
```

If a set_fraction value of 0 is received, the value 3 is sent out. If 1 is received, 6.4 is sent out. If 0.5 is received, a value of 4.7 is sent out. Here's the general interpolator formula that gave that value:

```
value = f / (k2 - k1) * (v2 - v1) + v1
```

In the preceding formula, f is the set_fraction eventIn value, k1 is the first key, k2 is the second key, v1 is the first key value, and v2 is the second key value. This is called a *linear interpolation*, because an input value halfway between two keys produces an output value halfway between the two key values. This rule applies to all the interpolators, although for some it's a bit harder to compute. That is the great thing about interpolator nodes: They do all the work. All you have to do is provide the keys and key values.

9

Moving Objects

Now I'll take you back to the example in the preceding chapter in which I wanted to move the cone. To do this, VRML has a `PositionInterpolator` node that generates an SFVec3f value. This value can be routed to the `set_translation` field of a `Transform` node to move the children of that transform. Here is what it looks like:

```
PositionInterpolator {
    eventIn      SFFloat  set_fraction
    exposedField MFFloat  key          [ ]
    exposedField MFVec3f  keyValue     [ ]
    eventOut     SFVec3f  value_changed
}
```

Here's the cone example from the preceding chapter, with a `PositionInterpolator` added to move it:

```
DEF T Transform {
    translation 0 5 0
    children [
        Shape {
            geometry Cone { }
            appearance Appearance {
                material Material {
                    diffuseColor 1 0 0
                }
            }
        }
    ]
}
DEF P PositionInterpolator {
    key      [ 0,    1 ]
    keyValue [ 0 5 0, 4 5 0 ]
}
ROUTE P.value_changed TO T.set_translation
```

The preceding code moves the cone from 0 5 0 to 4 5 0 when the set_fraction eventIn goes from 0 to 1. But this scene will not do anything because nothing is routed to the set_fraction eventIn. How is the set_fraction event generated?

Changing Objects Over Time

The most common source for an interpolator's set_fraction eventIn is a TimeSensor node. This node generates time-related eventOuts, either continuously or at a specified start time for a specified duration. The following is its definition:

```
TimeSensor {
    exposedField SFTime   cycleInterval 1
    exposedField SFBool   enabled       TRUE
```

```
exposedField  SFBool   loop              FALSE
exposedField  SFTime   startTime         0
exposedField  SFTime   stopTime          0
eventOut      SFTime   cycleTime
eventOut      SFFloat  fraction_changed
eventOut      SFBool   isActive
eventOut      SFTime   time
}
```

I'll go into much more detail about the TimeSensor in Chapter 13, "Timing Events and Cycles," but for now, I'll just show how to use it to drive an interpolator. The TimeSensor is controlled by the startTime and stopTime exposedFields. These are both SFTime values, and they define when the TimeSensor will start and stop sending eventOut values. They are expressed in absolute calendar and are pretty much never set to anything other than 0 or -1 in the file format. A value of 0 means "a really long time ago," and -1 means "a little bit longer ago than that." By default, both values are 0, which means that the TimeSensor started and stopped long ago, so it is not currently running. Setting stopTime to a value that is chronologically before startTime makes the TimeSensor run forever. So, if you set the stopTime to -1 in the VRML file, the TimeSensor starts running when you enter the world and never stops.

The TimeSensor can generate several types of eventOut values, but for now, I'll discuss only fraction_changed. This eventOut generates increasing SFFloat values from 0 to 1 as time proceeds. The cycleInterval field specifies the number of seconds it takes for fraction_changed to go from 0 to 1. After generating the last value (1), what happens next is up to the loop field. If loop is false (which is the default), no more values are generated when fraction_changed reaches 1. If it is true, fraction_changed immediately goes back to 0 and begins generating increasing values again. This pattern of output of the fraction_changed eventOut is known as a sawtooth curve and is shown in Figure 9.1.

Figure 9.1.

The output of TimeSensor *with* loop TRUE *and* FALSE.

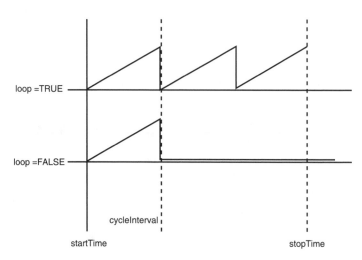

The values are generated continuously, meaning that as soon as one value is processed by the eventIn to which it is routed, another value is generated. The `fraction_changed` eventOut is just what is needed to run the `PositionInterpolator`. Here it is added to the earlier example:

```
DEF T Transform {
    translation 0 5 0

    children [
        Shape {
            geometry Cone { }
            appearance Appearance {
                material Material {
                    diffuseColor 1 0 0
                }
            }
        }
    ]
}

DEF P PositionInterpolator {
    key      [ 0,     1 ]
    keyValue [ 0 5 0, 4 5 0 ]
}

DEF TS TimeSensor {
    stopTime -1
    loop     TRUE
}

ROUTE TS.fraction_changed TO P.set_fraction
ROUTE P.value_changed TO T.set_translation
```

TIP

Notice how I used spacing to line up the keys and key values in the preceding `PositionInterpolator`. Lining them up in this way can improve readability and make it easier to add keys later.

I set up the `TimeSensor` to run forever (by setting `stopTime` to -1) and to loop continuously (by setting `loop` to `TRUE`). Now the cone will move to the right, snap back to the left, and move to the right again, over and over. It will take 1 second to carry out this motion because that is the default value of `cycleInterval`.

This snapping back to the left business, however, can be distracting. I want the cone to move from left to right, and then from right to left, back and forth like a pendulum. I can do that with a small change to the `PositionInterpolator` values. Here is how that change would look:

```
DEF P PositionInterpolator {
    key      [ 0,     0.5,    1 ]
    keyValue [ 0 5 0, 4 5 0,  0 5 0 ]
}
```

Notice that all I did was add a third key and keyValue pair and make the middle key 0.5. This will make the cone move to the right twice as fast because it is arriving at 4 5 0 when the TimeSensor is just halfway through its cycle (at the fraction value of 0.5). But, when there, it will reverse itself as the fraction value goes from 0.5 to 1, and it will move back to 0 5 0. The cone will still "snap back" as the fraction changes from 1 to 0 at the end of the cycle, but because the key value at 0 is the same as the key value at 1, you will not see any movement. The cone will just bounce back and forth forever. Try 09tyv01.wrl on the CD-ROM to see the moving cone in action.

Rotating Objects

Up until now, I have been talking about changing an object's position. But another useful interpolator, the OrientationInterpolator, is used to change an object's orientation in the scene. Here is its definition:

```
OrientationInterpolator {
    eventIn      SFFloat      set_fraction
    exposedField MFFloat      key          [ ]
    exposedField MFRotation   keyValue     [ ]
    eventOut     SFVec3f      value_changed
}
```

It is normally routed to the rotation exposedField of a Transform node. The keyValue is an SFRotation, which sets the desired orientation of the object.

NOTE   Notice I am using both the term *rotation* and the term *orientation* to describe the operation of the OrientationInterpolator. There is an important reason for this. Rotation describes an operation performed on an object, specifying that you need to rotate this object so many degrees about this axis. Orientation describes the current angular position of the object, in its local coordinate space. This will become important in the following section as you see how the OrientationInterpolator rotates an object from one orientation to another.

As you learned before, an SFRotation value describes an axis about which to rotate an object and the angle by which to rotate it. But now, you'll want to go from one orientation to another, using the OrientationInterpolator. In the simplest example of this procedure, you have two SFRotation key values, one at a key of 0 and the other at a key of 1. I'll also restrict this simple example to have the same axis of rotation for both values. As the set_fraction value changes, the object smoothly rotates about the axis, from the angle in the first value to the angle in the second. Here is an example of a simple rotation:

```
DEF T Transform {
    children [
        Shape {
            geometry Cone { }
            appearance Appearance {
                material Material {
                    diffuseColor 1 0 0
                }
            }
        }
    ]
}
DEF P OrientationInterpolator {
    key     [ 0,     1 ]
    keyValue [ 0 0 1 0, 0 0 1 3.14 ]
}

DEF TS TimeSensor {
    stopTime -1
    loop     TRUE
}

ROUTE TS.fraction_changed TO P.set_fraction
ROUTE P.value_changed TO T.set_rotation
```

The first SFRotation value, 0 0 1 0, will start the object at its default orientation. The second, 0 0 1 3.14, will finish at an orientation about halfway around. Because it is rotating about its Z-axis, you will see the cone spin counterclockwise.

TIP

How can you know that this cone would spin counterclockwise? You can find the answer using the *right-hand rule*. This is the same rule you used in Chapter 3, "Building a Scene," to figure out which way the rotation field of the Transform node would orient an object. If you were to grab the rotation axis with your right hand, with your thumb pointing in the direction of the axis, your fingers would wrap around the axis in the direction of rotation. In this case, your thumb would point out of the screen and your fingers would be wrapped in a counterclockwise direction.

Complex Rotation

Let's say you have an object that looks like the letter *T*. You want it to start in an upright orientation, rotate to the right, and then fall on its face. This operation is shown in Figure 9.2.

Figure 9.2.

*Dual rotation
of an object.*

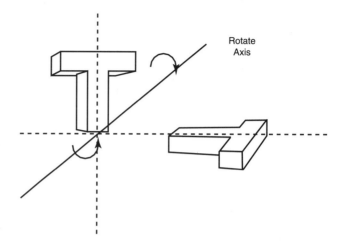

In this example, you are rotating the object twice—once about the Y-axis and once about the Z-axis. The first part is easy. You simply rotate 90° about the Y-axis. But, next you have to rotate the object so that it is lying face down. To reach this position, you must give it a final orientation *relative to the original orientation.* So, instead of simply rotating the object about the Z-axis to lay it over on its side, you must rotate it about the Y- and Z-axes together. To do this, think of a rotation axis that is diagonal to all three major axes. The object would hinge around that diagonal to the right, which would both lay it down and twist it clockwise. The result would be an object lying face down.

If you had just two key values in the OrientationInterpolator, one not rotated and one with the object lying face down, the object would twist and fall in one smooth motion. But, I have an orientation between those two that rotates the object clockwise about the Y-axis. The interpolator looks like this:

```
OrientationInterpolator {
    key      [ 0, 0.5, 1 ]
    keyValue [ 0 1 0 0,
               0 1 0 1.57
               0.577 0.577 -0.577 2.07 ]
}
```

After the initial 90-degree rotation about the Y-axis, to get to the final position of lying on its face, it just needs to fall straight down to the right. No additional twisting will occur. That's not very obvious, and it happens because the transition between the middle key value and the final one changes the direction of the axis. When going from one key value to the next, the OrientationInterpolator figures out the simplest rotation between the two and then performs that rotation. In this case, it simply makes the object fall without any additional twist.

How did I arrive at the axis of 0.577 0.577 -0.577? Imagine a box aligned with the major (X, Y, Z) axes. This axis runs from the lower-left edge closest to you to the upper-right edge farthest away. Now, apply the right-hand rule and you'll see that this axis will make an object turn to the right and twist it so that it's facing down. Because the axis is perfectly diagonal, all three values must be the same. And, because the length of the axis must be equal to one (as you learned in Chapter 3), the number comes out to 0.577. The Z component is negative to get the axis to point into the screen and cause the proper rotation. Rotating by the angle of 2.07 causes the object to lie perfectly flat on its face. Figure 9.3 shows the process of rotating a box using the right-hand rule.

Figure 9.3.

Rotating a box using the right-hand rule.

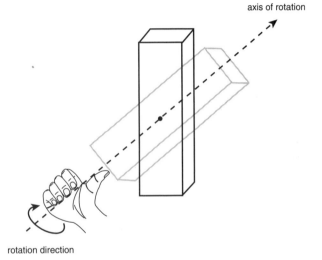

axis of rotation

rotation direction

TIP

Why is the angle 2.07? Well, 1.57 would be 90 degrees, but the object needs to rotate a bit more because it is actually rotating in two directions. To be honest, I picked that number through trial and error. There is a formula to compute it, but you'll often find that you can avoid an awful lot of math with VRML by just playing with some values until your world behaves the way you want it to.

The code for the entire falling-T animation is given in Listing 9.1. Its outcome is shown in Figure 9.4.

TYPE   **Listing 9.1. The falling-T animation.**

```
#VRML V2.0 utf8
DEF T Transform {
    center 0 -2 0
    children [
        Shape {
            geometry Box { size 1 4 1 }
            appearance Appearance {
                material Material {
                    diffuseColor 1 0 0
                }
            }
        }

        Transform {
            translation 0 2 0
            children [
                Shape {
                    geometry Box { size 3 1 1 }
                    appearance Appearance {
                        material Material {
                            diffuseColor 1 0 0
                        }
                    }
                }
            ]
        }
    ]
}

DEF P OrientationInterpolator {
    key      [ 0,                          0.5
               0.8,                        1 ]
    keyValue [ 0 1 0 0,                    0 1 0 1.57,
               0.577 0.577 -0.577 2.07, 0.577 0.577 -0.577 2.07 ]
}

DEF TS TimeSensor {
    stopTime -1
    loop     TRUE
    cycleInterval 5
}

ROUTE TS.fraction_changed TO P.set_fraction
ROUTE P.value_changed TO T.set_rotation
```

Notice that the T is made up of two boxes that are children of the same animating Transform node. This makes them move together as one object, which is what you want. Also, notice the extra key/keyValue pair at a key of 0.8. This pair does two things. First, it causes the falling animation to go faster than the twisting animation (1.5 seconds for the fall versus 2.5 seconds for the twist), which makes the animation look a little more natural. Also, it delays for a second after the fall and allows you to see the object in its final position. Notice how I altered the center of rotation in the animating Transform. This technique causes the object to rotate from its base rather than its midpoint. Combining the capabilities of the OrientationInterpolator with the Transform node can give you a wide variety of animation effects.

Figure 9.4.

The T in the middle of falling.

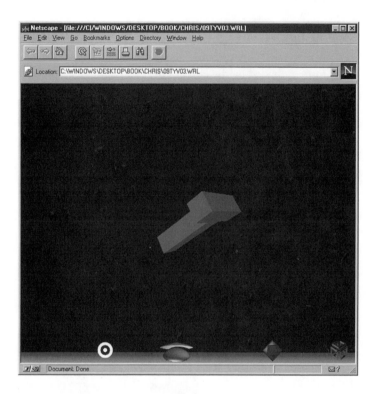

Morphing

Up until now, I've been talking about routing interpolators to a Transform node. This is the most common use of interpolation but by no means the only one. One of the most interesting effects available with interpolators is called morphing. With this effect, you can change the shape of an entire object. You've probably seen this effect in TV commercials and music videos, in which cars turn into tigers and a child becomes an old man.

The VRML CoordinateInterpolator does all the work of changing one object into another. You simply give a list of points for the object with its starting shape and a second list with its final shape. Associate these with two keys and connect a TimeSensor, and you've created a morph. Here is what the CoordinateInterpolator looks like:

```
CoordinateInterpolator {
    eventIn       SFFloat set_fraction
    exposedField MFFloat key              [ ]
    exposedField MFVec3f keyValue         [ ]
    eventOut      MFVec3f value_changed
}
```

Notice that the key values are of type MFVec3f, just as in the PositionInterpolator. What is the difference? The difference can be seen in the type of the value_changed eventOut, which is an MFVec3f. The number of key values is always a multiple of the number of keys, and the former divided by the latter defines the number of points in the object at each step of the interpolation. For instance, if you had 6 keyValues and 2 keys, the object would be a triangle (6 / 2 = 3). Let me show you an example. I will make a box whose top twists around, back and forth. First of all, I will have to make an IndexedFaceSet that looks like a box, because a box can't be morphed. My box is defined like the following code, and Figure 9.5 shows its outcome:

```
IndexedFaceSet {
    coord Coordinate {
        point [ -1 -1  1, 1 -1  1, 1 1  1, -1 1  1,
                -1 -1 -1, 1 -1 -1, 1 1 -1, -1 1 -1 ]
    }
    coordIndex [ 0, 1, 2, 3, -1,
                 5, 4, 7, 6, -1,
                 1, 5, 6, 2, -1,
                 4, 0, 3, 7, -1,
                 4, 5, 1, 0, -1,
                 3, 2, 6, 7 ]
}
```

Figure 9.5.

A box made from an
IndexedFaceSet.

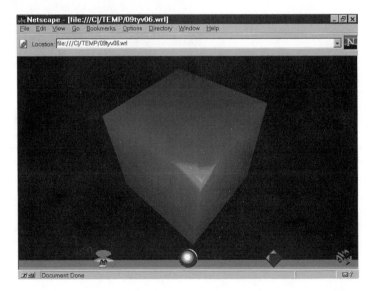

Now, I'll change the point list to show the top of the box in a twisted orientation (see Figure 9.6):

```
IndexedFaceSet {
    coord Coordinate {
        point [ -1 -1  1, 1 -1  1, 1 1  0,  0 1  1,
                -1 -1 -1, 1 -1 -1, 0 1 -1, -1 1  0 ]
    }
    coordIndex [ 0, 1, 2, 3, -1,
                 5, 4, 7, 6, -1,
                 1, 5, 6, 2, -1,
                 4, 0, 3, 7, -1,
                 4, 5, 1, 0, -1,
                 3, 2, 6, 7 ]
}
```

Figure 9.6.

A box with a twisted top.

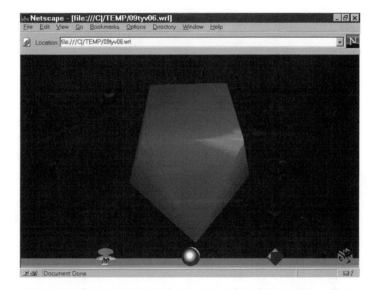

Notice that I did not change the coordIndex values, but only the point values. So, now I can combine the points from the two IndexedFaceSets and place them in a CoordinateInterpolator. Listing 9.2 shows the final animated box.

TYPE   **Listing 9.2. The animated box.**

```
#VRML V2.0 utf8

Transform {
    children [
        Shape {
            appearance Appearance {
                material Material {
                    diffuseColor 1 0 0
                }
            }
            geometry IndexedFaceSet {
                coord DEF C Coordinate {
                    point [ -1 -1  1, 1 -1  1, 1 1  1, -1 1  1,
                            -1 -1 -1, 1 -1 -1, 1 1 -1, -1 1 -1 ]
                }
                coordIndex [ 0, 1, 2, 3, -1,
                             5, 4, 7, 6, -1,
                             1, 5, 6, 2, -1,
                             4, 0, 3, 7, -1,
                             4, 5, 1, 0, -1,
                             3, 2, 6, 7 ]
            }
        }
    ]
}

DEF I CoordinateInterpolator {
    key      [ 0, 0.5, 1 ]
    keyValue [ -1 -1  1, 1 -1  1, 1 1  1, -1 1  1,
               -1 -1 -1, 1 -1 -1, 1 1 -1, -1 1 -1,
               -1 -1  1, 1 -1  1, 1 1  0,  0 1  1,
               -1 -1 -1, 1 -1 -1, 0 1 -1, -1 1  0,
               -1 -1  1, 1 -1  1, 1 1  1, -1 1  1,
               -1 -1 -1, 1 -1 -1, 1 1 -1, -1 1 -1 ]
}

DEF TS TimeSensor {
    stopTime -1
    loop      TRUE
    cycleInterval 5
}

ROUTE TS.fraction_changed TO I.set_fraction
ROUTE I.value_changed TO C.set_point
```

The CoordinateInterpolator can do much more than a simple two-step morph like the one
I've shown here. It can do complex, multipart animations to simulate rippling water or
wiggling Jell-O. It can also animate the spine in an Extrusion node to create octopus tentacles
or a scorpion's tail. It is one of the most versatile of all the interpolators.

9

Other Interpolators

Several more interpolators are included in VRML. All are used in exactly the same way. Only the type of data being interpolated is changed. The ColorInterpolator can modify the colors of a Material node. NormalInterpolator can change the values of a normal node to make shadows and reflections dance and glint from an object. The ScalarInterpolator is a basic building block from which many other interpolations can be built. The definitions of all these can be found in Appendix A, "VRML Node Reference."

The most interesting animated effects can be seen when interpolators are combined. You can cause the little box that does the twist to dance around the room by combining an OrientationInterpolator for spinning, a PositionInterpolator for moving, and a CoordinateInterpolator for twisting. When you build up layer on layer of interpolation, there is no limit to the effects you can create.

Take a look at spider.wrl on the CD-ROM. Click the spider to see it animate. This natural-looking animation was created with multiple interpolators, using a technique called *motion capture*. With this technique, a real-life actor's body is wired with sensors, and his movements are recorded onto a computer. These movements are converted into VRML interpolators (and a few legs are added), and the result is a realistic-looking spider, trying (unsuccessfully) to scare an all-too-jaded audience. (See Figure 9.7.)

Figure 9.7.

A scary spider.

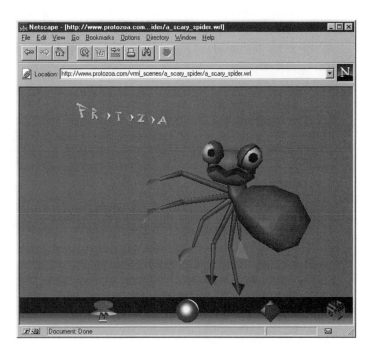

Summary

Interpolation is an easy and powerful technique for adding animation to your worlds. You simply give a set of keys, which are points in time when the interpolator should be sending out a particular value. Then you give the key values to be sent out for each key. In the time between each key value, values between the keys are computed and sent. You can do a complex animation with only a few keys and key values.

VRML has a wide array of interpolators to directly manipulate objects in various ways. Additionally, it has several that can be used in conjunction with other capabilities that I will describe in the next chapter. The PositionInterpolator moves objects around in the scene. The OrientationInterpolator rotates objects around a given axis. Combining several interpolators allows you to perform complex animations and can bring characters in your worlds to life!

Q&A

Q Why can't a box be morphed?

A There are actually two reasons: first, because a box's fields are not exposed, and second, because it is not created from points, but rather from size parameters. So, a CoordinateInterpolator cannot be routed to it, and its top cannot be moved relative to its bottom.

Q Why do I need to use more than two keys when I am rotating an object in a full circle?

A If you give two key values to rotate in a full circle, they would both be the same because you want to start and stop in the same place. So, the OrientationInterpolator would not know you wanted to rotate at all. Even if you gave three values, one at 0°, one at 180°, and one back at 0°, the interpolator would not know which direction it should rotate. Therefore, you must give at least four interpolated values to rotate in a full circle in the direction you want to go.

Q I want to make a bouncing ball that bounces up, slows down, and then speeds up as it falls back down. I tried doing this with three key values, one on the ground, one in the air, and one back on the ground. But, it doesn't look right. Why not?

A Interpolators in VRML perform linear interpolation. That means that it takes an equal amount of time at each point between any two key values. So, your animation is smoothly going from the ground to the top of the arc, instantly reversing its direction, and then going smoothly from the top of the arc to the ground. To make the ball slow down on the way up and speed up on the way down, you need to add more key values so it takes more time (and moves more slowly) as it arrives at the top of the arc. About five key values in each direction are usually enough to get a realistic appearance.

Q What would I ever use the `ScalarInterpolator` for?

A There are a few nodes that can receive an SFFloat eventIn. For instance, it can be used to vary the pitch on an AudioClip to make a police siren sound. Or, you can vary the intensity on a light. You can also route the output of the ScalarInterpolator to a Script node to perform more complex interpolations. I will explain this in the next chapter.

9

Exercises

1. Add an opening door to your house model. Create a front door that, when you click it, opens inward.

2. Using the twisting box from the CoordinateInterpolator example, make the box hop to the right during the first twist. Then make it hop back, then left, then forward on each subsequent twist. Hint: Although it is possible to create the hopping motion with a single PositionInterpolator, it is much easier to do with two.

Answers

1. Here is the animated door added to the house model, and Figure 9.8 shows its outcome.

```
Transform {
    children DEF DoorTransform_15 Transform {
        children [
            # TouchSensor which activates the door
            DEF DoorTS TouchSensor { }'

            # TimeSensor controlling the opening door interpolation
            DEF DoorTimer TimeSensor {
                cycleInterval 2
                startTime 0
            }

            # interpolator to open the door
            DEF DoorInterp OrientationInterpolator {
                key [ 0, 1 ]
                keyValue [ 0 0 1  0,
                           0 1 0  2 ]
            }

            # door
            Transform {
```

```
                    children Shape {
                        appearance Appearance {
                            material Material {
                                ambientIntensity 0.251748
                                diffuseColor 0.502714 0.295535 0.191551
                                specularColor 0.265851 0.126509 0.126509
                                emissiveColor 0 0 0
                                shininess 0.928571
                                transparency 0
                            }

                            texture ImageTexture {
                                url "wood.2.gif"
                            }

                            textureTransform TextureTransform {
                                translation 0.02 0
                                rotation 0
                                scale 2.75845 2.68335
                                center 0.48 0.5
                            }
                        }

                        geometry Extrusion {
                            crossSection [ 0.6 1,
                                          0.6 -0.8,
                                          0.4 -1,
                                          -0.4 -1,
                                          -0.6 -0.8,
                                          -0.6 1,
                                          0.6 1 ]
                            orientation [ 0 0 1  0,
                                          0 0 1  0 ]
                            scale [ 1 1,
                                    1 1 ]
                            solid FALSE
                            spine [ 0.00177229 -0.102792 0,
                                    0 0 0 ]
                        }
                    }

                rotation 1 0 0  1.57081
                }

                # door knob
                Transform {
                    children Shape {
                        appearance Appearance {
                            material DEF _19 Material {
                                ambientIntensity 0.25
                                diffuseColor 0.384722 0.266993 0
                                specularColor 0.757576 0.738847 0.590386
                                emissiveColor 0 0 0
                                shininess 0.0666667
                                transparency 0
                            }
```

```
            }
            geometry Sphere {
                radius 0.0794814
            }
        }

        translation 0.432649 -0.0298636 0.0785782
        rotation 0 0 1  0
        scale 1 1 0.5
        scaleOrientation 0 0 1  0
    }

    # plate behind the door knob
    Transform {
        children Shape {
            appearance Appearance {
            material USE _19
        }

        geometry Box {
            size 0.15 0.3 0.05
        }
    }

    translation 0.431907 -0.068912 0.023141
    rotation 0 0 1  0
    scale 1 1 0.627858
    scaleOrientation 0 0 1  0
    }
]
rotation 0 0 1  0
center -0.6 0 0
}

ROUTE DoorTS.touchTime TO DoorTimer.set_startTime
ROUTE DoorTimer.fraction_changed TO DoorInterp.set_fraction
ROUTE DoorInterp.value_changed TO DoorTransform_15.set_rotation
```

Figure 9.8.

The door to the house, already opened.

2. The following is the hopping cube, and Figure 9.9 shows its outcome.

```
#VRML V2.0 utf8

Transform {
    translation 0 -1 0

    children Shape {
        appearance Appearance {
            material Material { }
        }
        geometry Box { size 10 0.2 10 }
    }
}

DEF T2 Transform {
children DEF T1 Transform {
    translation -1 0 1
    children [
        Shape {
            appearance Appearance {
                material Material {
                    diffuseColor 1 0 0
                }
            }
            geometry IndexedFaceSet {
                coord DEF C Coordinate {
                    point [ -1 -1  1, 1 -1  1, 1 1  1, -1 1  1,
                            -1 -1 -1, 1 -1 -1, 1 1 -1, -1 1 -1 ]
```

```
                    }
                    coordIndex [ 0, 1, 2, 3, -1,
                                 5, 4, 7, 6, -1,
                                 1, 5, 6, 2, -1,
                                 4, 0, 3, 7, -1,
                                 4, 5, 1, 0, -1,
                                 3, 2, 6, 7 ]
                }
            }
        ]
    }
}

DEF I CoordinateInterpolator {
    key     [ 0 0.125 0.25 0.375 0.5 0.625 0.75 0.875 1 ]
    keyValue [ -1 -1  1, 1 -1  1, 1 1  1, -1 1  1,
               -1 -1 -1, 1 -1 -1, 1 1 -1, -1 1 -1,
               -1 -1  1, 1 -1  1, 1 1  0,  0 1  1,
               -1 -1 -1, 1 -1 -1, 0 1 -1, -1 1  0,
               -1 -1  1, 1 -1  1, 1 1  1, -1 1  1,
               -1 -1 -1, 1 -1 -1, 1 1 -1, -1 1 -1
               -1 -1  1, 1 -1  1, 1 1  0,  0 1  1,
               -1 -1 -1, 1 -1 -1, 0 1 -1, -1 1  0,
               -1 -1  1, 1 -1  1, 1 1  1, -1 1  1,
               -1 -1 -1, 1 -1 -1, 1 1 -1, -1 1 -1,
               -1 -1  1, 1 -1  1, 1 1  0,  0 1  1,
               -1 -1 -1, 1 -1 -1, 0 1 -1, -1 1  0,
               -1 -1  1, 1 -1  1, 1 1  1, -1 1  1,
               -1 -1 -1, 1 -1 -1, 1 1 -1, -1 1 -1
               -1 -1  1, 1 -1  1, 1 1  0,  0 1  1,
               -1 -1 -1, 1 -1 -1, 0 1 -1, -1 1  0,
               -1 -1  1, 1 -1  1, 1 1  1, -1 1  1,
               -1 -1 -1, 1 -1 -1, 1 1 -1, -1 1 -1 ]
}

DEF PInterp1 PositionInterpolator {
    key [ 0     0.1 0.125 0.15  0.25  0.35 0.375 0.4
          0.5  0.6 0.625 0.65  0.75  0.85 0.875 0.9   1 ]
    keyValue [ 0 0 0, 0 1.6 0, 0 2 0, 0 1.6 0,
               0 0 0, 0 1.6 0, 0 2 0, 0 1.6 0,
               0 0 0, 0 1.6 0, 0 2 0, 0 1.6 0,
               0 0 0, 0 1.6 0, 0 2 0, 0 1.6 0, 0 0 0 ]
}

DEF PInterp2 PositionInterpolator {
    key [ 0 0.25 0.5 0.75 1 ]
    keyValue [ -1 0 1, 1 0 1, 1 0 -1, -1 0 -1, -1 0 1 ]
}

DEF TS TimeSensor {
    stopTime -1
    loop       TRUE
    cycleInterval 5
}

ROUTE TS.fraction_changed TO I.set_fraction
ROUTE I.value_changed TO C.set_point
```

```
ROUTE TS.fraction_changed TO PInterp1.set_fraction
ROUTE TS.fraction_changed TO PInterp2.set_fraction
ROUTE PInterp1.value_changed TO T1.set_translation
ROUTE PInterp2.value_changed TO T2.set_translation
```

☐ You can also find the VRML files to the preceding exercise questions on the CD-ROM at \Source\Answers.

Figure 9.9.

The hopping cube in the middle of a hop.

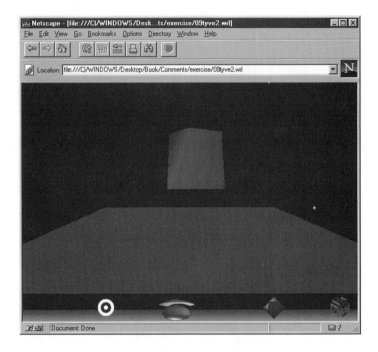

Day 10

Scripting

You've learned about ways to make your virtual world move by using interpolators, and a simple way to interact with it by using the TouchSensor. But what if you want to interact with the scene in a way that is not supported by these nodes? What if you want to click a door and have it open only if the correct combination has been entered into a nearby keypad? The Script node was created for just this purpose. You'll learn about it in this chapter. Here's what I'll cover today:

- ☐ Why use scripting?
- ☐ Creating a Script node.
- ☐ Executing a script with an eventIn.
- ☐ Writing a script using VRMLScript.
- ☐ Script eventOuts and fields.
- ☐ Accessing other nodes.
- ☐ The Browser interface.
- ☐ Other scripting languages.

Why Use Scripting?

In Chapter 8, "Events and Routing," you learned how the TouchSensor can be routed directly to a light to turn it off and on. Press and the light goes on; release and it goes off. But what if you wanted the light to go on and stay on when you click, and then go off when you click again? You can use the Script node to do this and lots more.

The Script node allows you to create your own fields and events, and then define the way they work by writing a *script*, or sequence of user-defined instructions. VRML supports several programming languages for writing scripts, including the popular Java language. Java is a very powerful language but can be difficult to learn. So, I'll be showing you how to write scripts in a simple language called VRMLScript, which is supported in CosmoPlayer.

If you've never written a computer program, don't worry. VRMLScript makes this task easy.

Creating a Script Node

In the preceding chapter, you learned about interpolators. These are a good model for what a Script node does. An interpolator receives an event and then, using the event value and data from its fields, computes a new value and sends it out. Scripts don't always do this. Sometimes they just take in an event and store its value. Sometimes they just modify the event value without using any stored data and then send it back out. But these four steps of event receipt, data manipulation, data storage, and event generation describe the complete operation of a Script node.

TIP

Every script can have four components:

☐ Some number of eventIns, which cause the script to execute when an event is received

☐ Functions that execute when an eventIn is received

☐ Fields used by the functions to store intermediate data between script executions

☐ EventOuts sent by the functions during script execution

Here is the definition of a Script node:

```
Script {
  exposedField MFString url            []
  field        SFBool   directOutput   FALSE
  field        SFBool   mustEvaluate   FALSE
```

10

```
# And any number of:
eventIn         eventTypeName eventName
field           fieldTypeName fieldName initialValue
eventOut        eventTypeName eventName
}
```

Notice that the first three elements are normal fields as in any other node. But, the definition then says you can have "any number of" fields, eventIns, and eventOuts. A Script node allows you to define your own interface. It's a lot like creating your own type of node. You could even add all the fields and events of, for instance, a ScalarInterpolator and reimplement its functionality in a script that you wrote. Although you wouldn't want to do that because the ScalarInterpolator already exists, you might want to do something similar.

Fields and Events in a Script Node

Let's say you want to have a flashing warning light above a doorway. Here's an example in which the light is a sphere that changes from dark red (off) to bright red (on). You carry out this task by using a ColorInterpolator, like this:

```
Shape {
    appearance Appearance {
        material DEF Mat Material {
            diffuseColor 0 0.5 0
        }
    }
    geometry Sphere { }
}

DEF Timer TimeSensor {
    loop      TRUE
    stopTime -1
}
DEF Interp ColorInterpolator {
    key      [ 0 0.5 0.51 1 ]
    keyValue [ 0.2 0 0, 0.2 0 0, 1.0 0 0, 1.0 0 0 ]
}

ROUTE Timer.fraction_changed TO Interp.set_fraction
ROUTE Interp.value_changed TO Mat.set_diffuseColor
```

Now, what if you want the light to flash red when there is danger, but green when there is not? You would need to change the state of the flashing from danger to safety, and then use that state to determine which color to flash. This is known as a simple state machine, but VRML does not have an existing node that can perform this task. The Script node is ideally suited to allow you to create such a machine. First, I will set up the fields and events of the Script node. I'll need an SFBool eventIn to set the state, a field to keep the current state around, a flashing eventIn from the TimeSensor, and a color eventOut. Here is the definition for my state machine Script node:

```
Script {
    eventIn  SFBool     danger    # TRUE if we are in danger state
    eventIn  SFFloat     flash     # fraction from TimeSensor
    field SFBool state FALSE       # holds current danger state
    eventOut SFColor     color     # color output to light

    url "..."                      # script to implement flasher
}
```

Notice that the format of the fields and events I've added is the same as the one used by Appendix A, "VRML Node Reference." I introduced you to this format in Chapter 8, "Events and Routing." I used it to add the two eventIns, the field, and the eventOut to the Script node.

NOTE

> The Script node does not allow user-defined exposedFields because they have predefined functionality. When an exposedField receives an event on its eventIn part, the field part is set to that value, and that value is sent through the eventOut part. That functionality is not automatically provided in the Script node, so exposedField is not allowed. But you can add this functionality yourself. You would simply define a separate eventIn, field, and eventOut. Then, when the eventIn is received, you would execute a script that would set the field and send the eventOut.

Adding the Script

The script to implement your state machine is placed in the url field. You can place a URL here, which gives the location of a file containing the script. This URL is specified like all the other nodes with a url field; it is a relative or absolute path to a file containing the script. But VRMLScript can be added in another way. By placing vrmlscript: at the beginning of the URL rather than http:, you can put the script right in the VRML file. This convenience is one of the major advantages over a language like Java, which must be compiled separately. So, here's the script for my state machine:

```
"vrmlscript:
    function danger(value) {
        // simply set the current state of the machine
        state = value;
    }

    function flash(value) {
        if (state) {
            // we are in the danger state
            if (value < 0.5)
```

10

```
            // show the dark red color
            color = new SFColor(0.2, 0, 0);
        else
            // show the bright red color
            color = new SFColor(1, 0, 0);
    }
    else {
        // we are in the safe state
        if (value < 0.5)
            // show the dark green color
            color = new SFColor(0, 0.2, 0);
        else
            // show the bright green color
            color = new SFColor(0, 1, 0);
    }
}"
```

WARNING

As of the writing of this book, CosmoPlayer has not yet been released. It does not support the new SFColor function. The file named 10tyv02.wrl on the CD-ROM shows another method that works in the current version of CosmoPlayer.

I'll go into detail about how to write a script later in this chapter. For now, notice the following three things:

☐ The functions written have the same names as the eventIns.

☐ The state field is used like a variable in the script.

☐ The statement color = sends the color eventOut.

That's all there is to using the fields and events from the Script node in the script. If you didn't understand the preceding statements, don't worry. They will become clear soon.

Executing a Script with an EventIn

The first thing to understand about a script is that it has *functions* containing instructions that are executed to do the task for which the script was written. In the preceding example, the danger function performed the simple task of saving its value in the state field. It contains a single instruction to accomplish this task, known as an assignment statement. But how does this function get executed? In VRMLScript, the function with the same name as an eventIn of the Script node is executed when an event is received by that eventIn. This is called an eventIn function.

An eventIn function is passed two pieces of information: the value received by the eventIn and the time it was received (called the *timestamp* of the event). These are listed as parameters of the function, in parentheses, after the function name. In the case of the danger function, the value is named value, but there is no timestamp. Why is that?

TIP

> VRMLScript is very flexible and forgiving in what can be in the list of parameters of a function. If you have no parameters, the function is still executed, but you don't have access to the value or the timestamp of that event. This is often useful if you know that the event can have only one possible value, in which case you just need to know that the event happened, not what its value is. You can have one parameter, as in my example, in which case you can use the value but not the timestamp. Because I did not need the timestamp in my example, I omitted it. If you list two parameters, the timestamp is available in addition to the value. This is often useful when you need to send a time value to a TimeSensor or AudioClip. You can list more than two parameters in an eventIn function, but the parameters after the initial two are ignored.

Writing a Script Using VRMLScript

If you are familiar with programming at all, you will recognize the VRMLScript code listed previously. VRMLScript is similar to many other script programming languages, from BASIC to Perl. In fact, it is a subset of JavaScript, the easy-to-use scripting language for HTML pages. I will avoid a full-blown VRMLScript tutorial here. I will introduce you to the most important concepts, which will allow you to write most of the scripts you will ever need.

The most important concepts of VRMLScript are assignment, expressions, and the if statement. I will show you how to use those now.

Assignment

An assignment statement looks like this:

```
state = value;
```

The equal sign (=) is called the assignment operator. You'll see more operators when I talk about expressions. This will be the most used operator in your programming bag of tricks. It replaces the variable on the left side of the operator with the value contained in the variable on the right. A variable in VRMLScript is a name that holds a value whose type is one of the

10

19 VRML data types. If a variable is new (never before used in this function), it does not have a value yet. Whatever is assigned to it determines its type. Here are two statements:

```
a = 5;
a = "Hello";
```

If a is new, assigning a 5 to it makes it a numeric variable and places the value 5 in it. You can think of it as being an SFInt32, because that type could hold the number 5. The next statement places the string Hello into the variable. Its type is changed from an SFInt32 to an SFString.

You can store values temporarily while the function is executing this way. But when the function is complete, the values are lost because they are temporary variables. To preserve a value after the function is complete, you must define a field in the Script node and store the value there.

Expressions

The left side of an assignment statement is a variable into which a value is stored. But the value on the right side can be much more than a simple number or string (known as a constant) or another variable. It can also be an *expression*. An expression is a combination of variables and operators that computes a value. Sometimes this value is assigned to another variable, as you have seen. Sometimes it is used in other types of statements (as I will show you next).

Here is an expression:

```
a * 5
```

This takes the current value of a and multiplies it by the number 5. You can build up complicated expressions in this way:

```
a + 5 * b / c
```

This expression multiplies 5 by b, divides the result by c, and then adds a to the result. But why is a added last? Shouldn't the operations go from right to left, or something?

Order of Evaluation

The order of evaluation of an expression follows the rules of operator precedence. These rules govern the order in which operations get performed. In VRMLScript, multiplication and division have higher precedence than addition; so, they are performed first. These two have the same precedence as each other; so, they are performed from left to right. Table 10.1 is the table of operator precedence for VRMLScript.

Table 10.1. Operators in VRMLScript.

Operator Type	Operator	Comments
Comma	,	
Assignment	= += -= *= /= %=	Right to left
	<<= >>= >>>= &=	
	^= ¦=	
Conditional	?:	Tertiary operator
Logical OR	¦¦	
Logical AND	&&	
Bitwise OR	¦	
Bitwise XOR	^	
Bitwise AND	&	
Equality	== !=	
Relational	< <= > >=	
Bitwise shift	<< >> >>>	
Add/subtract	+ -	
Multiply/divide	* / %	
Negate/increment	! ~ - ++ --	Unary operators
Call, member	() []	

Notice that not all operators are performed from left to right. Assignment (which is considered an operator from the standpoint of precedence) is performed from right to left. Thus, you can use an expression like this:

```
a = b = c + 7
```

This expression performs the addition first because it is higher precedence; it then assigns the result to b, and then to a. Operator precedence exists to make writing expressions easier. In arithmetic, you most often want to perform multiplication before addition, so it is given higher precedence. But what if you want to perform an operation in a different order? Then you can use parentheses to tell VRMLScript the order you want:

```
a = (b + c) * d;
```

This expression performs the addition first.

The Assignment Operator

Do you notice how I've started using the assignment operator in expressions? Assignment is very different from any other operator because it actually stores information and sometimes sends events. But, it can also be used wherever any other operator is used. The following expression is legal:

```
a = (b = c + 7) * d;
```

This adds 7 to c and assigns the result to b; it then takes that same result, multiplies it by d, and assigns that result to a. This is a very powerful notion, and it allows you great flexibility in forming complex expressions.

NOTE

> Here is an illegal expression:
>
> ```
> (a + b) = c * d;
> ```
>
> This is illegal because the value produced when you add c and d is not a variable into which you can store the result of the multiplication. The right part of an assignment operator must be an expression that produces a variable into which a value can be stored. A simple variable is the only type of these you have looked at. But as you will soon see, other storable expression types can also be assigned a value.

10

Expressions with Strings

You can have expressions with strings as well. The expression

```
a = 'Hello ' + 'there';
```

places the string Hello there into a. This is called *concatenation* and it allows strings to be built up from pieces. For instance, you could have an eventIn called info of type SFString. When it comes in, you can do this:

```
function info(value) {
    a = 'http://' + value;
}
```

Now a contains a string that looks like a URL that you might be able to use to get an ImageTexture or an AudioClip.

Consider the following expression:

```
a = "Hello number " + 1;
```

This is concatenating a string to a number. How is that possible? VRMLScript has the capability to convert numbers to an equivalent string in this case. So, a would contain `Hello number 1`.

Type Conversions

VRMLScript performs many conversions like the preceding code involving a string and a number. Table 10.2 describes what conversions happen for each VRML data type.

Table 10.2. Rules for combining VRML fields and events.

Type	Rules
SFString	Combining an `SFString` with any scalar type produces an `SFString`. Use `parseInt()` or `parseFloat()` to convert an `SFString` to a scalar.
Scalar types SFBool SFInt32 SFFloat SFTime	Combining scalar types in an expression promotes to the larger type, as follows (wide to narrow): `SFTime`, `SFFloat`, `SFInt32`, `SFBool`. Assigning a scalar expression to a fixed variable (field or eventOut) of a scalar type, converts to the type of the fixed variable.
Vector types SFVec2f SFVec3f SFRotation SFColor	Combine only with like types. Dereferencing (`foo[1]`) produces a value of type `SFFloat`.
SFImage	Assignment (=) and selection (.) are the only allowed operations. Can assign only `SFImage` type.
SFNode	Assignment (=) and selection (.) are the only allowed operations. Can assign only an `SFNode` type.

Type	Rules
MF types MFString MFInt32 MFFloat MFVec2f MFVec3f MFRotation MFColor MFNode	Combine only with like types. Dereferencing (`myArray[3]`) produces the corresponding SF type. Dereferenced SF types follow the same rules as normal SF types.

Notice that I've grouped the data types into categories. This grouping makes it easy to remember how data conversion takes place.

TIP

When trying to understand these conversion rules, remember that only the scalar types use all the operators listed; so, they are the ones most often involved in conversion. Also, remember the rule about combining SFStrings and scalar values (scalars convert to SFString), and that dereferencing MF values produces the corresponding SF value. The rest is easy.

Dereferencing

I want to discuss one more type of operator. In the operator precedence table, this operator is listed as [ ]. This is the *dereferencing operator*, and it is used to pick out a single element from any of the MF data types. It is also used to pick out a single scalar value from any of the vector types. Here's an example (assume that `myMFVec3f` is a variable containing an `MFVec3f`):

```
myMFVec3f[2] = SFVec3f(0, 0, 0);
```

This assigns the `SFVec3f` value on the right of the assignment operator to the third element of the `MFVec3f`. It's the third element because arrays in VRML start at 0 (element 0 is the first element, element 1 is the second, and so on). What happens when you dereference an MF type is simple. The result is the corresponding SF type.

The dereferencing operator is just like any other, except that it returns a variable into which a value can be stored. Therefore, just as with a simple variable name, it can be used on the left side of an assignment operator. The value placed inside the brackets can be any scalar expression, which is truncated to an integer to do the dereferencing. Therefore, you can use this:

```
a = new SFFloat(5.9);
b = new SFInt32(4);
myMFVec3f[a + b] = myMFVec3f[2];
```

The addition produces an index value of 9 (with truncation, the digits past the decimal point are discarded, so 9.9 becomes 9). So, the SFVec3f value at index 2 is assigned to the SFVec3f element at index 9 of the same array.

TIP

Often, when dealing with floating-point numbers that need to be converted to an integer, you want to round the value rather than truncate. That means you want values lower than 0.5 to become 0 and values of 0.5 or higher to become 1. To do this in the preceding example, you add 0.5 to the result, like this:

```
myMFVec3f[a + b + 0.5] = myMfVec3f[2];
```

Now the value is 10.4, which truncates to 10. If a were 5.4, the value would be 9.9, which would truncate to 9.

The if Statement

Several statements in VRMLScript do interesting "algorithmic" kinds of things. But, by far, the most used is the if statement. It looks like this:

```
if (a > b) c = d;
```

This says that if the value of a is greater than the value of b, assign d to c. Otherwise, just skip it. You can also use this:

```
if (a > b)
    c = d;
else
    e = f;
```

This example adds to the condition: If a is not greater than b, assign f to e instead. One way or another, something will get assigned! The expression contained in the parentheses is the *conditional expression*. If it is true, the following statement is performed. Otherwise, the statement in the else clause, if any, is performed. But what does true mean? In VRMLScript, it means that the value of the conditional expression is not 0.

Comparison Operators

One of the most important operations performed in the conditional expression is the comparison of two values. VRMLScript has a complete set of comparison operators, as shown in Table 10.3.

Table 10.3. Comparison operators.

Operator	Test Performed
<	Less than
<=	Less than or equal to
==	Equal to
!=	Not equal to
>=	Greater than or equal to
>	Greater than

The operators compare the values on either side. If the comparison is true (for instance, 5 > 4 is true, but 4 == 6 is false), the result is 1; otherwise, it is 0.

You can compare either numbers (with the type conversion rules stated in Table 10.1) or strings. When comparing strings less than and greater than, refer to the dictionary order of the string. Comparing a string to a number first converts the number to a string, just like in the concatenation operator.

Boolean Operators

In addition to comparison operators, a conditional expression can use Boolean operators. These normally take the results of two comparison operations and produce another TRUE or FALSE result. For instance, the AND operator ('&&') will produce a TRUE result only if both comparisons are true. Table 10.4 lists the complete set of Boolean operators.

Table 10.4. Boolean operators.

Operator	Name	Test Performed
!	NOT	If value is 0, the result is 1; otherwise, it's 0
&&	AND	If both values are 1, the result is 1; otherwise, it's 0
||	OR	If either value is 1, the result is 1; otherwise, it's 0

The Boolean operators are very useful in combination with the comparison operators. Here's an example:

```
if (a < b && c > d) ...
```

This statement says that if both a is less than b and c is greater than d, carry out the following statement.

What if you want more than one statement to be executed if a condition is true? VRMLScript has a compound statement to allow for this situation. If you surround a series of statements with braces—{ and }—they are taken as a single statement. So, you can use the following:

```
if (a < b) {
    c = d;
    e = f + 5;
}
else {
    c = 0;
}
```

Notice that I placed braces around the else clause, even though it is a single statement. This is legal in VRMLScript, although unnecessary.

Script EventOuts and Fields

As I mentioned before, VRMLScript creates variables automatically when you first assign to them. But some variables are already defined when a function begins execution. All fields and eventOuts defined in the Script node appear as predefined variables, and these variables behave differently from automatically created variables.

A field variable can have values assigned to it, and its value can be used in an expression, just as with an automatically created variable. But its type cannot be changed. Here is a Script node:

```
Script {
    eventIn SFFloat e
    field   SFInt32 f

    url: "vrmlscript:
        function e(value) {
            f = value;              // legal
            a = value;              // legal, a is an SFFloat
            a = f;                  // legal, a is an SFInt32
            f = new SFVec3f(0, 0, 0); // illegal
        }"
}
```

In the first assignment, the SFFloat value is converted (truncated) to an SFInt32 value and assigned to the field variable. This is different from the behavior of the next two assignments. The variable a is automatically created; so, it gets the type of the value assigned to it. When a different type is assigned, the type of a is changed. The last assignment is illegal because it is attempting to put an SFVec3f value into a field variable that is an SFInt32. If f were an automatically created variable, this would be legal. But because it is a field variable, its type cannot be changed.

An eventOut variable follows the same rules as a field variable. But, in addition, when you assign to an eventOut variable, it sends the corresponding value as an eventOut.

Accessing Other Nodes

One of the data types handled by VRMLScript is the SFNode type. A variable of type SFNode can be used in a way different from any other data type. The SFNode variable corresponds to a node somewhere in the VRML scene. That node could have been entered into a field of the Script node (either directly or with the USE construct), or it could be the value of an event sent to the Script node. The SFNode variable can be used to access the eventIns and eventOuts of this node. Here's an example:

```
Script {
    field SFNode nodeIn

    url "vrmlscript:
        function nodeIn(value) {
            // assume node being passed in is a Transform
            a = value.translation_changed;
            a[0] += 1;
            value.set_translation = new SFVec3f(1, 0, 0);
        }"
}
```

This script gets the current value of the translation field, adds 1 to the x component, and then sends the result back. Note three interesting things here. First, by reading the value of the eventOut (actually the eventOut component of the translation exposedField), you're getting the last value sent from it. If no value has ever been sent, you get the value the exposedField was set to in the original file. Second, you are dereferencing the SFVec3f variable and adding one to it in its place, using the add and assign operator. Third, you are sending the resultant value as an event to the eventIn component of the translation exposedField. VRMLScript makes it easy to access any eventIn, eventOut, or exposedField of a node to which it has an SFNode variable.

Working with SFNodes

What happens if you try to access an eventIn or eventOut that does not exist in an SFNode variable? VRMLScript generates an error and does not perform the operation. And how do you know that the preceding SFNode is a Transform node so that you can avoid this error? Sometimes you just assume that you know. As the author, you can be sure to send a node of only a single type. Most of the time, that technique works just fine. But if you want to be clever and send nodes of various types to the same eventIn, you can do this, too. The SFNode has a method to get the type name (for example, Transform) so that you can test for this. Let's say you can receive either a Transform node or a Material node and do something different with each. You would do the following:

10

```
function nodeIn(value) {
    if (value.getName() == 'Transform')
        value.set_translation = new SFVec3f(0, 0, 0);
    else if (value.getName() == 'Material')
        value.set_diffuseColor(0, 1, 0);
}
```
The preceding script resets the translation if the node is a Transform, and it sets the diffuseColor to green if it is a Material. If the node is neither, the script does nothing.

The Browser Interface

A script can be used to access fields and events in the Script node and in nodes for which the script has an SFNode variable. But, the script also has access to other facilities as well. Two objects are available to every script: the Browser object and the Math object. These are called static objects because you do not create them. They simply exist for your use. The Browser object has a set of methods to access features of the browser that aren't related to specific data types or fields of the Script node. For example, you can create new VRML nodes on-the-fly, like this:

```
a = Browser.createVRMLFromString('Box { }');
```

After this statement is executed, a will contain a Box node. Technically speaking, it contains an MFNode with one element, which is a Box SFNode. This is important because the string can be any legal VRML file (without the header line), which means it can contain more than one node. So, an MFNode variable is returned to hold any nodes created. After you have this Box node, you can insert it into a scene like this:

```
node.set_geometry = a;
```

Assuming that node is a Shape node, this makes the Box the geometry for that shape.

Here is a list of all the methods available in the Browser object:

```
SFString getName()

SFString getVersion()

SFFloat getCurrentSpeed()

SFFloat getCurrentFrameRate()

SFString getWorldURL()

void replaceWorld(MFNode nodes)

SFNode createVrmlFromString(SFString vrmlSyntax)
```

10

```
SFNode createVrmlFromURL(MFString url, Node node, SFString event)

void addRoute(SFNode fromNode, SFString fromEventOut,
SFNode toNode, SFString toEventIn)

void deleteRoute(SFNode fromNode, SFString fromEventOut,
SFNode toNode, SFString toEventIn)

void loadURL(MFString url, MFString parameter)

void setDescription(SFString description)
```

The other static object available performs basic math functions. Here is an example of using the Math object:

```
c = Math.sqrt(a * a + b * b);
```

This statement takes the square root of a squared plus b squared. The Math package has a full range of math operations, plus a set of properties that make useful values, such as pi, available. Here is a list of methods and properties on the Math object:

Properties:

```
E, LN10, LN2, PI, SQRT1_2, SQRT2
```

Methods:

```
abs(number)

acos(number)

asin(number)

atan(number)

ceil(number)

cos(number)

exp(number)

floor(number)

log(number)

max(number1, number2)

min(number1, number2)

pow(base, exponent)

random()

round(number)

sin(number)

sqrt(number)

tan(number)
```

VRMLScript has two other functions that are useful in working with strings and numbers. They are parseInt and parseFloat. Here is an example of using them:

```
a = parseInt('12');        // Returns a SFInt32 of 12.
b = parseInt('1C', 16);    // Parses a hexadecimal value.
                           //      Returns a SFInt32 of 28.
c = parseFloat('2.75');    // Returns a SFFloat of 2.75.
d = parseInt('2.75');      // Returns a SFInt32 of 2.
```

These are useful in combining an SFString with a scalar value and having the result be a scalar value.

Other Scripting Languages

As I mentioned before, VRMLScript is just one choice for scripting in VRML. Java is enjoying popular support in VRML browsers. It might well end up being the most universally accepted language for VRML. JavaScript is another popular choice, but it has gained less of this early acceptance because it is not as well developed as Java. VRMLScript is by far the simplest language available in any VRML browser, which makes it ideally suited as a first scripting language.

NOTE

> Because VRMLScript is a subset of JavaScript, many browsers supporting VRMLScript today (including CosmoPlayer) will probably migrate to full JavaScript support eventually. When that happens, you will still have all the capabilities I talked about here, plus many more.

This chapter is not intended as an exhaustive tutorial on VRMLScript. Many more features are available than are covered here. Java is another excellent choice for scripting if you have a more complex script to write. You can pick up any of the excellent books on learning Java, including the one in this series, *Teach Yourself Java in 21 Days*, also published by Sams.net.

Summary

Scripting in VRML provides you with a tremendously flexible and powerful way to extend the capabilities of VRML. The Script node can be configured with an unlimited number and type of eventIns and eventOuts. When an eventIn is received by a Script node, a corresponding function is executed. This function can set fields internal to the Script node, perform complex algorithms, and send events out to other nodes in the world.

Although VRML allows for the support of any of a number of languages, VRMLScript is easy to learn and allows scripts to be included directly in the VRML file. VRMLScript is a subset of JavaScript; therefore, it shares many of the same features. VRMLScript has a full set of statements and expressions to allow you to create scripts that perform many arithmetic, string manipulation, and algorithmic tasks. VRMLScript also gives you simple access to the fields and eventOuts defined in the Script node. In the coming chapters, I'll show you many ways to combine the Script node with other nodes to make interesting and lively worlds.

Q&A

Q Why doesn't VRML have enough built-in nodes to avoid the need for a Script node?

A An infinite variety of node types would be needed for VRML to cover all possible authoring needs. The Script node, combined with a small set of built-in nodes, gives the best combination of flexibility and simplicity.

Q How do I pass a node into VRMLScript so I can access all its eventIns and eventOuts?

A I mentioned before that you can send an SFNode event to VRMLScript, and then access all its eventIns and eventOuts. But, you can also include an SFNode field in the Script node and include a node that the script can access at any time. Here is how you would do that:

```
Script {
    field SFNode myNode USE T1
}
```

Assuming T1 is a node that has been previously defined, it can now be used any time from within the script simply by using myNode.

Q Can I have more than one Script node in a VRML world?

A Absolutely. Typically you will use a Script node to serve a single purpose. You can have as many Script nodes in your world as you have animations or user interactions to control.

Exercise

1. You have a house. It has a door that opens. Now you need to make sure that it's secure. Create a combination lock for the front door. Require the correct combination to be entered before you can click the door to open it.

Here's a hint: You need to make buttons to press for entering the combination. I recommend three disks made of Cylinders, with numbers on their surfaces or different colors to distinguish them. You can make two scripts, one to figure out when the correct sequence is entered and one to prevent the door from opening unless the other script tells it that the door is unlocked. Alternatively, you can make one script and put both functions in it. Good luck!

Answer

1. Here is the combination lock code. Figure 10.1 shows the combination lock on the outside of the door. Notice the little red light I added below the doorknob to indicate when the door is unlocked.

```
# The light on the door knob indicating when the door is unlocked.
# this is actually under the Transform with the rest of the door.
Transform {
    children Shape {
        appearance Appearance {
            material DEF LockLight Material {
                ambientIntensity 0.266839
                diffuseColor 0.285207 0 0
                specularColor 0.150101 0 0.457407
                emissiveColor 0 0 0
                shininess 0.740541
                transparency 0
            }
        }

        geometry Box {
            size 0.04 0.04 0.04
        }
    }

    translation 0.43 -0.16 0.06
}

DEF LockScript Script {
    eventOut    SFBool      unlocked
    eventOut    SFColor     lightColor
    eventIn     SFTime      b1
    eventIn     SFTime      b2
    eventIn     SFTime      b3
    field       MFInt32     combo [ 3, 1, 2 ]
    field       SFInt32     numPressed 0
    field       SFColor     color 0.8 0 0
    url "vrmlscript:
        function b1() {
            if (combo[numPressed] == 1) ++numPressed;
            else numPressed = 0;
        }
```

```
                function b2() {
                    if (combo[numPressed] == 2) ++numPressed;
                    else numPressed = 0;
                }

                function b3() {
                    if (combo[numPressed] == 3) ++numPressed;
                    else numPressed = 0;
                }

                function eventsProcessed() {
                    if (numPressed == 3) {
                        unlocked = true;
                        lightColor = color;
                    }
                }
            }"
    }
    Transform {
        children Shape {
            appearance Appearance {
                material Material {
                    ambientIntensity 0.256
                    diffuseColor 0.372322 0.371574 0.373173
                    specularColor 0.890909 0.887832 0.890909
                    emissiveColor 0 0 0
                    shininess 0.127551
                    transparency 0
                }
            }

            geometry Box {
                size 0.14 0.35 0.05
            }
        }

        translation -9.09794 -18.3371 7.59
        rotation 0 -0.0161792 0.999869  3.14159
    }

    Transform {
        children [
            DEF LockB1TS TouchSensor { }
            Shape {
                appearance Appearance {
                    material Material {
                        ambientIntensity 0.25
                        diffuseColor 0.540541 0 0
                        specularColor 0.577569 0 0.126303
                        emissiveColor 0 0 0
                        shininess 0.772973
                        transparency 0
                    }
                }
```

```
                    geometry Cylinder {
                        height 0.0833062
                    }
                }
            ]

        translation -9.09714 -18.231 7.61743
        rotation 1 0 0  1.60316
        scale 0.0416517 0.375487 0.0416533
        scaleOrientation 0 0 1  0
    }

    Transform {
        children [
            DEF LockB2TS TouchSensor { }
            Shape {
                appearance Appearance {
                    material Material {
                        ambientIntensity 0.253969
                        diffuseColor 0 0.122449 0
                        specularColor 0.071925 0.356628 0
                        emissiveColor 0 0 0
                        shininess 0.0810811
                        transparency 0
                    }
                }

                geometry Cylinder {
                    height 0.0833062
                }
            }
        ]
        translation -9.09619 -18.3328 7.61571
        rotation 1 0 0  1.5708
        scale 0.0416517 0.375487 0.0416532
        scaleOrientation 0 0 1  0
    }

    Transform {
        children [
            DEF LockB3TS TouchSensor { }
            Shape {
                appearance Appearance {
                    material Material {
                        ambientIntensity 0.25
                        diffuseColor 0.015119 0.331798 0.399133
                        specularColor 0.00438452 0.0962214 0.115749
                        emissiveColor 0 0 0
                        shininess 0.0972973
                        transparency 0
                    }
                }

                geometry Cylinder {
                    height 0.0833062
                }
```

```
        }
    ]
    translation -9.09735 -18.4381 7.61219
    rotation 1 0 0  1.60316
    scale 0.0416517 0.375487 0.0416532
    scaleOrientation 0 0 1  0
}

ROUTE LockB1TS.touchTime TO LockScript.b1
ROUTE LockB2TS.touchTime TO LockScript.b2
ROUTE LockB3TS.touchTime TO LockScript.b3
ROUTE LockScript.unlocked TO DoorTimer.set_enabled
ROUTE LockScript.lightColor TO LockLight.set_diffuseColor
```

Figure 10.1.

*The combination lock.
Notice that the red light
under the doorknob is lit,
indicating that the door
has been unlocked.*

Day 11

Allowing Users and Objects to Interact

In Chapter 8, "Events and Routing," you learned how to use the TouchSensor to interact with objects simply by clicking them or moving your mouse over them. But the TouchSensor has many more interaction capabilities. VRML also provides several other nodes that allow you to create many kinds of interactions. Instead of sensing that the user is taking some single action, such as clicking the mouse button, these nodes sense movement. This motion can be the movement of the mouse across the surface of the object, or the movement of the viewer within the scene. I will first show you how to use the advanced, motion-based events of the TouchSensor. Then I will show you more sensor nodes, called the *drag sensors*, that allow you to slide objects along a table or spin a record on a turntable. Next, you'll learn about the ProximitySensor, which senses the viewer's movement through the world, as well as other viewing-oriented sensors. Finally, I'll show you how to put sensors together with timers, interpolators, and scripts to create interesting and useful user-interface components for your VRML worlds.

Here's what I'll cover:

- ☐ Sensing with the `TouchSensor`
- ☐ Dragging objects
- ☐ Advanced manipulation
- ☐ Sensing the user's location
- ☐ Other types of sensors

Sensing with the `TouchSensor`

In Chapter 8, I showed you how to use the `TouchSensor` to trigger events on other nodes. I also provided a short description of the vector events of the `TouchSensor`. These eventOuts are sent whenever the mouse moves and is over the object being sensed. First, here is a review of the `TouchSensor`:

```
TouchSensor{
    exposedField      SFBool      enabled                 TRUE
    eventOut          SFVec3f     hitNormal_changed
    eventOut          SFVec3f     hitPoint_changed
    eventOut          SFVec2f     hitTexCoord_changed
    eventOut          SFBool      isActive
    eventOut          SFBool      isOver
    eventOut          SFTime      touchTime
}
```

The vector events are `hitNormal_changed`, `hitPoint_changed`, and `hitTexCoord_changed`. Each one sends events at each movement of the pointing device while the cursor is on top of the object, whether or not the mouse button is pressed.

NOTE

> Remember the sidebar in Chapter 8 titled "Other Styles of Input"? In general, when I talk about the `TouchSensor` or any of the other sensors I will soon be showing you, I'm assuming that a mouse is being used as the pointing device. This is, by far, the most common pointing device, but others are possible. For instance, when I say that events are generated when the mouse "is on top of" the object, I mean that the mouse cursor appears to be sitting on the object from your current viewpoint. But a 3D input device might interpret this as meaning "when the pointer is within a certain distance from the object." For now, I'll continue to talk in terms of a mouse cursor. But, remember this in case you ever come across a browser using a different type of user input.

The `hitPoint_changed` **Event**

The `hitPoint_changed` event is the easiest to understand of the three vector events, so I'll talk about it first. It just sends out the `SFVec3f` value of the point on the surface of the object over which the mouse is currently sitting. I will show you a simple example: moving a cube along the surface of a plane. Figure 11.1 shows what the scene will look like, and Listing 11.1 shows you how it is implemented:

TYPE **Listing 11.1. Moving a cube along the surface of a plane.**

```
Transform {
    children [
        DEF TS TouchSensor { }            Shape {
                appearance Appearance {
                    material Material {
                        diffuseColor 0 0.8 0
                    }
                }
                geometry Box { size 10 0.5 5 }
            }
    ]
}
DEF T Transform {
    children [
        Transform {
            translation 0 1.25 0
            children[
                Shape {
                    appearance Appearance {
                        material Material {
                            diffuseColor 0.9 0.9 0.9
                        }
                    }
                    geometry Box { }
                }
            ]
        }
    ]
}
ROUTE TS.hitPoint_changed TO T.set_translation
```

Figure 11.1.

The "moving box on a plane" example.

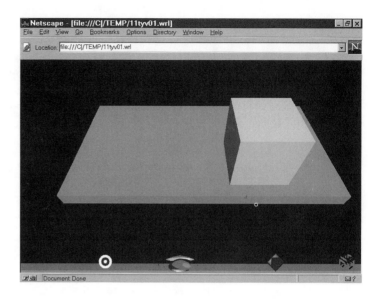

Notice that when you run this world, the box moves around on the plane whenever the mouse moves on the plane. That is because the `hitPoint_changed` event is generated whenever the mouse moves over the plane, regardless of whether the mouse button is pressed. This example presents a problem. Whenever the event is generated, the box moves to that spot, and when it does, it obscures the plane below. When that happens, the `TouchSensor` stops generating events and the box stops moving until the mouse moves off of it and back onto the plane. This problem can be solved with another sensor, the `PlaneSensor`, which I discuss later in the "Dragging Objects" section of this chapter.

The `hitNormal_changed` Event

I talked about normals in Chapter 6, "Using Lights." Normals are used to describe to the browser a line that is perpendicular to the object at every point on its surface. All objects in VRML have flat, or faceted, surfaces. But normals allow you to simulate a curved surface by allowing you to have a normal that is not actually perpendicular to the flat object surface. It is, instead, perpendicular to the surface of an idealized curved object, for which the simpler faceted object is a stand-in. Normals allow you to smooth the edges of objects, as you saw in Chapter 8.

The fact that normals are perpendicular (or *normal*) to the surface can be used in another way. If you want to place a skyscraper on a globe, you want it to stick straight up in the air. You want it to be normal to the surface of the globe at the position where it is placed. (See Figure 11.2.)

Figure 11.2.

Two skyscrapers on a globe.

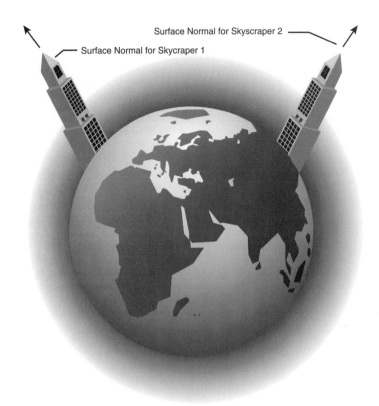

Surface Normal for Skyscraper 2

Surface Normal for Skycraper 1

11

If you want to place a skyscraper on a globe, you can use the normal of the globe surface at the point of placement to set the rotation of the skyscraper. You can create an interactive placement tool using a TouchSensor to sense the globe. When you pick a point on the surface, the hitPoint_changed eventOut gives you the point picked, and the hitNormal_changed eventOut gives you the normal at that point. Then the skyscraper can be placed, using the normal to set the rotation of a Transform, and the point to set the translation. The skyscraper is made a child of the Transform, and you have placed it on the globe.

But hitNormal_changed gives you an SFVec3f, and the rotation field of a Transform takes a SFRotation. How do you use the normal? It's possible, but a lot of math is involved. Fortunately, VRMLScript handles this task for you. You simply construct an SFRotation object like this:

```
rot = new SFRotation(new SFVec3f(0, 1, 0), normal);
```

In the preceding code sample, normal is the value generated by hitNormal_changed. When you create an SFRotation in this way, it creates the rotation value that would rotate *from* the first vector *to* the second. My *from* vector is a vertical line, and my *to* vector is the hit normal.

The result will be to create a rotation value that will rotate an object, so that a vertical line through it will be parallel to hit normal. This is just what I want to make my skyscraper stand up straight on the surface of the globe. Listing 11.2 shows the complete example.

Type **Listing 11.2. Placing a skyscraper on a globe.**

```
#VRML V2.0 utf8
Group {
    children [
        DEF TS TouchSensor { }                Shape {
                appearance Appearance {
                    material Material {
                        diffuseColor 0 0 0.6
                    }
                }
                geometry Sphere { radius 3 }
            }
    ]
}
DEF T Transform {
    scale 0.1 0.1 0.1
    translation 0 3.5 0
    children[
        Shape {
            appearance Appearance {
                material Material {
                    diffuseColor 0.9 0.8 0.8
                }
            }
            geometry IndexedFaceSet {
                coord    Coordinate {
                    point [ -1.2 -5 1.2, 1.2 -5 1.2,
                            -1.2 0 1.2, 1.2 0 1.2,
                            1.2 -5 -1.2, 1.2 0 -1.2,
                            -1.2 -5 -1.2, -1.2 0 -1.2,
                            -1 0.4 1, 1 0.4 1,
                            1 0.4 -1, -1 0.4 -1,
                            -1 3.2 1, 1 3.2 1,
                            1 3.2 -1, -1 3.2 -1,
                            -0.4 3.8 0.4, 0.4 3.8 0.4,
                            0.4 3.8 -0.4, -0.4 3.8 -0.4,
                            -0.4 4.6 0.4, 0.4 4.6 0.4,
                            0.4 4.6 -0.4, -0.4 4.6 -0.4,
                            0 5 0 ]
                }                coordIndex
                [ 0, 1, 2, -1, 2, 1, 3, -1,
                    1, 4, 3, -1, 3, 4, 5, -1,
                    4, 6, 5, -1, 5, 6, 7, -1,
                    6, 0, 7, -1, 7, 0, 2, -1,
                    2, 3, 8, -1, 8, 3, 9, -1,
                    3, 5, 9, -1, 9, 5, 10, -1,
                    5, 7, 10, -1, 10, 7, 11, -1,
                    7, 2, 11, -1, 11, 2, 8, -1,
                    8, 9, 12, -1, 12, 9, 13, -1,
```

11

```
                        9, 10, 13, -1, 13, 10, 14, -1,
                        10, 11, 14, -1, 14, 11, 15, -1,
                        11, 8, 15, -1, 15, 8, 12, -1,
                        12, 13, 16, -1, 16, 13, 17, -1,
                        13, 14, 17, -1, 17, 14, 18, -1,
                        14, 15, 18, -1, 18, 15, 19, -1,
                        15, 12, 19, -1, 19, 12, 16, -1,
                        16, 17, 20, -1, 20, 17, 21, -1,
                        17, 18, 21, -1, 21, 18, 22, -1,
                        18, 19, 22, -1, 22, 19, 23, -1,
                        19, 16, 23, -1, 23, 16, 20, -1,
                        20, 21, 24, -1, 21, 22, 24, -1,
                        22, 23, 24, -1, 23, 20, 24, -1,
                        6, 1, 0, -1, 6, 4, 1, -1 ]
            }
        }
    ]
}
DEF S Script {
        field         SFNode          touch           USE TS
        eventIn       SFBool          isActive
        eventOut      SFRotation      rot
        eventOut      SFVec3f         pos
        url "vrmlscript:
            function isActive(value) {
                if (value) {
                    pos = touch.hitPoint_changed;
                    rot = new SFRotation(new SFVec3f(0, 1, 0),
                    touch.hitPoint_changed);
                }
            }"
}
ROUTE TS.isActive TO S.isActive
ROUTE S.rot TO T.set_rotation
ROUTE S.pos TO T.set_translation
```

WARNING

As of the writing of this book, many of the VRML 2 features covered in this chapter are not implemented in CosmoPlayer for the PC. To use these features, try one of the other VRML browsers available. CosmoPlayer for SGI is compatible with CosmoPlayer for the PC and has all the sensors implemented.

Notice how I made an SFNode of the TouchSensor available to the script. That way, I can read the hitNormal_changed and hitPoint_changed values when the mouse button is pressed. I don't need continuous events of these values. When the mouse button is pressed, I perform the rotation calculation and send out the new position and orientation values. Notice, also, how I offset the position of the skyscraper in the positive y direction. This places the base of the skyscraper at 0 0 0 in its local coordinate space so that it will rotate about the base, rather than about its center, when it is placed on the globe.

The `hitTexCoord_changed` Event

The last vector event to cover is the `hitTexCoord_changed` eventOut. Unlike the other two vector events, this is an `SFVec2f` event, because it is indicating the texture coordinate of the point under the mouse cursor. I talked about texture coordinates in Chapter 5, "Object Appearance." They allow you to "pin" a certain point on the texture to a point on the object surface. Some objects have a default placement of the texture. For instance, the `Box` node places one copy of the texture on each face, and the `Cylinder` wraps one copy of the texture around its body. You can adjust these placements by using the `TextureTransform` node to stretch, rotate, or push the texture around on the object. Both the automatic texture placement and the texture transformation implicitly create a texture coordinate at each vertex of the object. The `IndexedFaceSet` and `ElevationGrid` can use the `TextureCoordinate` node to override this implicit texture coordinate generation. But either way, a texture coordinate is always associated with every point on the surface of the object.

NOTE

> The `hitTexCoord_changed` eventOut generates the texture coordinate corresponding to the point under the mouse cursor. The texture coordinate can come from the implicit texture application of the primitive nodes, or from an explicit `TextureCoordinate`. The object does not even need to have a texture applied to it. All objects have texture coordinates.

A texture coordinate has an extremely useful function. It allows your 3D objects to act like an *imagemap* in HTML. An imagemap allows a user to click an image on an HTML page and have the clicked spot perform a specific function. This could be a hyperlink, a script run on the server, or a locally executed JavaScript function. An HTML author can define several independent areas, of various shapes and sizes, on each imagemap to allow a single image to carry out many different functions. It is often used to design attractive buttons to take a user to various locations on a Web page.

Here is an example of a similar function in VRML, using the `hitTexCoord_changed` event. I will create a sphere with a red spot in the middle. This spot is created with a texture map. Whenever I click in the middle of the spot, a sound is played; if I miss the spot, the sound does not play. Figure 11.3 shows the sphere with the spot. Listing 11.3 is the VRML that implements it.

TYPE **Listing 11.3. The sphere with a spot.**

```
Group {
    children [
    DEF TS TouchSensor { } }
        Shape {
            appearance Appearance {
                material Material { }
                texture ImageTexture {
                    url "redspot.jpg"
                }
            }
            geometry Sphere { }
        }
        Sound {
            maxBack 1000
            maxFront 1000
            source DEF Audio AudioClip {
                url "horse.wav"
            }
        }
    ]
}
DEF S Script {
        field       SFNode touch USE TS
        eventIn     SFBool isActive
        eventOut    SFTime trigger
        url "vrmlscript:
                function isActive(value, timestamp) {
                    if (value) {
                        tex = touch.hitTexCoord_changed;
                        if (tex[0] > 0.25 && tex[0] < 0.75 &&
                            tex[1] > 0.25 && tex[1] < 0.75) {
                            trigger = timestamp;
                        }
                    }
                }"
}
ROUTE TS.isActive TO S.isActive
ROUTE S.trigger TO Audio.startTime
```

This is an easy task to carry out with texture coordinates because they map to a flat, 2D image. Trying to use the hitPoint_changed or hitNormal_changed values in this case would make it almost impossible to know when you actually clicked the spot. This technique makes possible many kinds of interesting user interfaces, including animated objects, in which buttons are not always visible, so the user must click them as they go by.

Figure 11.3.

A sphere with an active spot.

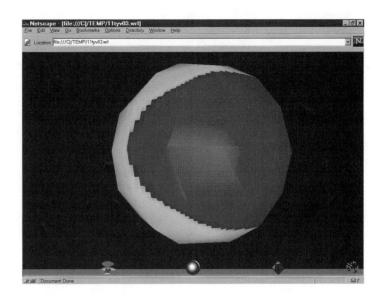

Dragging Objects

The earlier example, in which `hitPoint_changed` was used to drag a box around, is not a very good implementation of that function. When dragged to the side, the box jumped into the plane; sometimes the box obscured the plane, preventing any movement. VRML has a sensor, the `PlaneSensor`, designed specifically for this dragging task. Here is its definition:

```
PlaneSensor {
    exposedField    SFBool    autoOffset             TRUE
    exposedField    SFBool    enabled                TRUE
    exposedField    SFVec2f   maxPosition            -1 -1
    exposedField    SFVec2f   minPosition            0 0
    exposedField    SFVec3f   offset                 0 0 0
    eventOut        SFBool    isActive
    eventOut        SFVec3f   trackPoint_changed
    eventOut        SFVec3f   translation_changed
}
```

The first things to notice are the eventOuts. The `PlaneSensor` has an `isActive` eventOut just like the `TouchSensor`. But the other two eventOuts have no analogs. The `translation_changed` eventOut is generated whenever the mouse moves while the mouse button is pressed. It generates `SFVec3f` values that lie on an imaginary horizontal plane. This plane runs through the point on the object where the user clicked. Because the imaginary plane is horizontal, after the click point is established, the y value of `translation_changed` stays the same. The x and z values change as the user moves the mouse. Going back to the cube dragging example, I will show you how to accomplish the same thing using the `PlaneSensor`. Listing 11.4 shows its code.

11

TYPE | **Listing 11.4. Using the `PlaneSensor` to drag a cube.**

```
Group {
    children [
        DEF PS PlaneSensor { }
        DEF T Transform {
            translation 0 1.25 0
            children [                    Shape {
                    appearance Appearance {
                        material Material {
                            diffuseColor 0.9 0.9 0.9
                        }
                    }
                    geometry Box { }
                }
            ]
        }
    ]
}
Shape {
    appearance Appearance {
        material Material {
            diffuseColor 0 0.8 0
        }
    }
    geometry Box { size 10 0.5 5    }
}
ROUTE PS.translation_changed TO T.set_translation
```

Two differences in behavior exist between this example and the one using the TouchSensor hitPoint_changed eventOut. First, in this example, the box can be moved only when you click it. Second, after you click the box, the translation_changed eventOut sends values that are on an imaginary plane. Because of this, the box never sticks or jumps, as in the other example.

TIP

Notice how the PlaneSensor is grouped with the box, but is not under the Transform moving the box. This fact is very important. Placing the PlaneSensor under the Transform to which it is routed causes the translation_changed eventOut values to be affected by the changing transformation. This causes unpredictable movement that is hard to control and is very undesirable. Grouping the PlaneSensor and Transform, and then placing the object to be moved under the Transform, is almost always the scene structure you will use to accomplish a task like this.

The PlaneSensor also has the capability to restrict movement using the minPosition and maxPosition fields. Their default values indicate that no restriction should be performed. Making the minPosition values less than or equal to the maxPosition values restricts the translation_changed eventOut to values between those two limits. You can make a slide control, like the ones that appear on some stereo equalizers and light dimmers, by making either both x or both y values the same. For instance, the following PlaneSensor slides an object vertically between 0 and 10:

```
PlaneSensor {
        minPosition 0 0
        maxPosition 0 10
}
```

Relative Dragging

In the earlier example of dragging the box, you can click and drag the box to a new position. If you release and drag it again, it moves from where it was to where you drag it. This seems like the obvious behavior; however, it is not always the desired one, and it can be changed. The offset and autoOffset fields allow a great deal of flexibility in how the PlaneSensor behaves. By default, they are set up to perform the most common behavior, dragging an object around on a plane.

Actually, here's how the PlaneSensor works. When you click an object, an imaginary, horizontal plane is formed at the click point. At this point, translation_changed generates an event with a value of 0 0 0 plus the value of offset. With the default settings, the first time you click you get a translation_changed value of 0 0 0. Because the box is at 0 0 0, you get a smooth dragging effect from the current location of the box. As you drag, translation_changed continues to output values relative to where you first clicked with the offset added in. When you release the box, translation_changed stops generating events, and the box stays where it was last placed. If you were to click again and if the offset were still 0 0 0, the box would snap to 0 0 0. You might then be at one edge of the screen with the box moving around near the center. This outcome is not desirable, but it is exactly what would happen if autoOffset were FALSE. With autoOffset TRUE, whenever you release the mouse button, the last value output from translation_changed is placed in offset. Now, the next time you click the box, the offset added will be its last position, and it will start moving from its current position.

In some cases, you might not want the automatic offsetting behavior. For instance, if you are making a color setting tool, you might want to click an object textured with a splash of many colors. Wherever you click, you want the color in that spot to be the current color. Therefore, it is important to get an absolute position in this case, with no changing offset.

Other PlaneSensor **Capabilities**

The PlaneSensor also has an enabled exposedField, just like the TouchSensor. It can be used if you want to allow your object to be moved only under certain circumstances (such as after a puzzle is solved). It also has a trackPoint_changed eventOut, which is similar to translation_changed, except that it is not offset and does not get restricted by minPosition and maxPosition. It is raw output from the PlaneSensor for advanced applications.

Advanced Manipulation

VRML has two other drag sensors, the SphereSensor and the CylinderSensor. These share many features in common with the PlaneSensor. They both have the enabled exposedField and the automatic offsetting functionality. They also have both a massaged eventOut, like translation_changed, and a raw eventOut, like trackPoint_changed. I will show examples of how to use each of these sensors.

The CylinderSensor

Just as the PlaneSensor allows you to drag an object along a plane, the CylinderSensor allows you to drag an object in a circle. Here is its definition:

```
CylinderSensor {
    exposedField    SFBool      autoOffset          TRUE
    exposedField    SFFloat     diskAngle           0.262
    exposedField    SFBool      enabled             TRUE
    exposedField    SFFloat     maxAngle            -1
    exposedField    SFFloat     minAngle            0
    exposedField    SFFloat     offset              0
    eventOut        SFBool      isActive
    eventOut        SFRotation  rotation_changed
    eventOut        SFVec3f     trackPoint_changed
}
```

The CylinderSensor has a rotation_changed eventOut, which is an SFRotation, so it can be routed directly to the rotation field of a Transform. Two analogies describe the behavior of this eventOut, and both are used in the CylinderSensor. First is the cylinder behavior. If you place your hand on a roll of paper towels and move it up and down, you are mimicking the cylinder behavior of the CylinderSensor. Second is the disk behavior. If you place your finger on a record player turntable and spin it, you are duplicating the disk behavior. (See Figure 11.4.)

Figure 11.4.
*The cylinder and disk
behavior of the*
`CylinderSensor.`

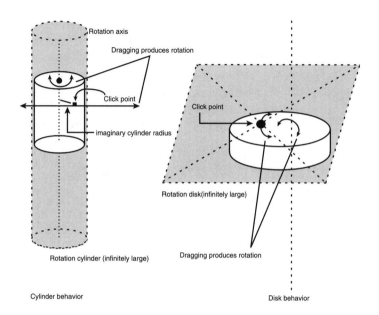

The `CylinderSensor` changes between these two styles of interaction automatically, based on the current viewing angle. The `CylinderSensor` always rotates about the Y-axis. Imagine that it is sensing a `Cylinder` in its default position. Looking at the cylinder head on, you can grab its side. When you do this, an imaginary cylinder forms that is infinitely tall. The radius of the cylinder is the distance from the rotation axis (the Y-axis) to the point clicked. By default, this gives you the cylinder behavior. Moving the mouse from side to side sends out `rotation_changed` events, relative to the initial point clicked, just as with the `PlaneSensor`.

If you rotate the scene so that you can see the top of the cylinder, you can grab that instead. Now when you click, the `CylinderSensor` creates an imaginary, infinitely large disk along the X-Z plane, centered on the Y-axis. Moving the mouse around in a circle sends out `rotation_changed` events, and you get the record player behavior.

Switching between these two behaviors does not occur because you clicked the side or top of the cylinder. Very often, you'll want to spin an object whose sides and top aren't well-defined. The switching depends on the angle at which you are currently viewing the object being sensed. The switching angle is set using the `diskAngle` exposedField. If the angle between the rotation axis of the `CylinderSensor` and the direction you're looking is less than `diskAngle`, (that is, you are looking at the object from the top or bottom), the disk behavior is used. If not, the cylinder behavior is used. (See Figure 11.5.)

Figure 11.5.

Using diskAngle *to determine when to switch behaviors.*

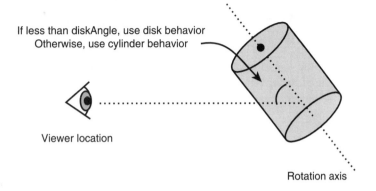

If less than diskAngle, use disk behavior
Otherwise, use cylinder behavior

Viewer location

Rotation axis

Notice that the default diskAngle is small, about 15 degrees. That means that you get the disk behavior only when you are looking at the very top or very bottom of the object. This usually feels right, because you are using the disk behavior only when your spinning motion would be circular. If you were to use the disk behavior at a larger angle, your motion would be elliptical, which is much less intuitive. At these larger angles, dragging in a straight line to spin the object, as if you were pushing a rolling pin on a table, is more natural.

Like the PlaneSensor, the CylinderSensor has the capability to restrict the rotation of the object, using the maxAngle and minAngle exposedFields. It also has the same offset and autoOffset exposedFields, to allow relative movement. Finally, it has a trackPoint_changed eventOut that, like the PlaneSensor, gives the raw position on the imaginary cylinder or disk.

The SphereSensor

The last member of the drag sensor group is the SphereSensor. The PlaneSensor drags objects on a flat plane, and the CylinderSensor spins objects about a fixed axis. But the SphereSensor allows objects to spin around a point in space, at its local origin. It is useful in allowing objects to be manipulated by the user. Connected like the object in the previous PlaneSensor example, the user can grab and spin the object in all directions. This makes object examination tasks easy to implement. Here is its definition:

```
SphereSensor {
    exposedField      SFBool        autoOffset            TRUE
    exposedField      SFBool        enabled               TRUE
    exposedField      SFRotation    offset                0 1 0 0
    eventOut          SFBool        isActive
    eventOut          SFRotation    rotation_changed
    eventOut          SFVec3f       trackPoint_changed
}
```

Unlike the PlaneSensor and CylinderSensor, the SphereSensor has no capability to restrict movement of the object. But it does have the same relative offset and raw event output features as the other two.

Sensing the User's Location

I have been talking about sensors that send events when the user manipulates the scene in some way with the mouse. But there is another class of sensors that detect movement of the user through the scene. The most commonly used of these is the `ProximitySensor`. This node sends out events when the user enters or exits a defined region of the scene. While inside that region, it reports the user's location during movement. Here is its definition:

```
ProximitySensor {
        exposedField    SFVec3f     center              0 0 0
        exposedField    SFVec3f     size                0 0 0
        exposedField    SFBool      enabled             TRUE
        eventOut        SFBool      isActive
        eventOut        SFVec3f     position_changed
        eventOut        SFRotation  orientation_changed
        eventOut        SFTime      enterTime
        eventOut        SFTime      exitTime
}
```

The region being sensed is set with the `size` and `center` exposedFields. These define a rectangular region, with its sides parallel to the major axes, in the local coordinate space of the `ProximitySensor`. Like all other sensors, it has an `isActive` eventOut. This event goes `TRUE` when the user enters the region, and it goes `FALSE` when the user exits. Additionally, on entry, the `enterTime` event is generated, and on exit, the `exitTime` is generated. These generate `SFTime` events, which can be routed directly to a `TimeSensor` to start or stop an animation, or to an `AudioClip` to start or stop a sound playing.

Listing 11.5 is a simple example that uses the `ProximitySensor`. In it, a `ProximitySensor` starts a sound playing when you enter and stops it when you exit. The world has a floor to designate the area being sensed.

TYPE   **Listing 11.5. The `ProximitySensor` example.**

```
DEF PS ProximitySensor {
        center 0 5 0
        size 10 10 10
}
Shape {
        appearance Appearance {
                material Material {
                        diffuseColor 0 0.6 0.2
                }
        }
        geometry Box { size 10 0.2 10 }
}
```

```
Sound {
        source DEF Audio AudioClip {
                url "furelise.mid"
                loop TRUE
        }
}
ROUTE PS.enterTime TO Audio.startTime
ROUTE PS.exitTime TO Audio.stopTime
```

You can go to 11tyv05.wrl on the CD-ROM to try out this world. When you enter, the world is silent. But if you walk forward over the floor, the song begins to play. If you walk off the floor, it stops. To do this, I routed the enterTime to the startTime of the AudioClip to start the sound. Then I routed the exitTime to the stopTime of the AudioClip to stop it.

The ProximitySensor also generates position_changed and orientation_changed events when the user is inside the region. These can be used for many interesting effects. For instance, if routed to a Transform, they make an object follow the user around the scene.

Other Types of Sensors

One more sensor is available in VRML, the VisibilitySensor. It generates events when a rectangular region enclosing a part of the scene comes into or leaves the user's view. Here is its definition:

```
VisibilitySensor {
    exposedField    SFVec3f    center      0 0 0
    exposedField    SFBool     enabled     TRUE
    exposedField    SFVec3f    size        0 0 0
    eventOut        SFTime     enterTime
    eventOut        SFTime     exitTime
    eventOut        SFBool     isActive
}
```

The VisibilitySensor is very similar to the ProximitySensor because it has a region, defined by size and center, as well as the isActive, enterTime, and exitTime events. The region defined is an invisible area that should enclose the objects being sensed. If this region and, therefore, any objects contained within it go out of the user's view, isActive goes FALSE and an exitTime event is generated. Likewise, when the region comes back into view, isActive goes TRUE and an enterTime event is generated. The VisibilitySensor is useful for stopping complex animations when they are not visible, or for playing a sound that asks a user to turn around to see something interesting.

WARNING

The definition of *visibility* is implementation-dependent in VRML. For some browsers, it means that the object in question is in front of the user's view. This is true even if the object is not visible because a nearby wall is obscuring it. For other browsers, the object might actually have to be rendered before it is considered visible. Remember this when using the VisibilitySensor to create an effect. Also remember that the VisibilitySensor is only sensing the invisible rectangular region defined within it. If this region is too big, the sensor might indicate that objects are visible when they actually are not. If it is too small, objects might be visible when the VisibilitySensor says they are not.

Summary

In order to interact with your virtual worlds, you need some sort of input mechanism. VRML has several of these. The TouchSensor is the simplest. It sends an event when the user clicks on an object in the world. This event can then be used to ring a doorbell, change the color of an object, or start an animation. Dragging objects is also important. It allows you to turn a volume control or slide a can on a table. VRML provides three drag sensors: the PlaneSensor, the CylinderSensor, and the SphereSensor. These allow you to slide and spin objects and assert control over them. You can also sense the user's location in the world. The ProximitySensor sends an event when the user's view moves into or out of a given region. This can be used to start an animation when the user gets close to it or to make a creature sense your presence and hop away. VRML also has a VisibilitySensor, which sends events when any part of a defined region is visible. This can allow you to perform optimizations on your world by letting you turn off animations when they are not visible, or even loading entire pieces of the world when they come into view. The VRML sensors afford a new level of user involvement with the virtual world.

Q&A

Q Why doesn't the SphereSensor have the capability to restrict movement like the PlaneSensor and CylinderSensor?

A Because the SphereSensor allows objects to be oriented at any angle, there would be no way to give meaningful values for this restriction.

11

Q I like the ability to drag objects in a VRML scene, but how do I control where they are dropped?

A I will discuss a real-life example. I created a Chinese Checker world that lets the user drag a marble across the playing board in order to move a marble to a new spot. But, in Chinese Checkers, not all locations on the board are legal places for a marble to rest. In fact, a real Chinese Checkers board has small holes in the board to indicate where a marble can legally move. I created a script that compared the hit_point on the board to the nearest legal move. The script evaluated the current hit_point and returned the valid translation for the marble. I used the valid translation to move the marble to that place. To be cute, I added an animation that rolled the marble to the right spot and shook the marble a bit as it came to a stop.

Q So, I can use a script to create any drag and drop behavior I want?

A Yes. In theory, you can have an object move along any other object and then pass the hit_point to a script that can modify the transformation in any way mathematically possible. But the VRML browser will probably react slower than if you used one of the available sensors designed for the task of visually dragging and dropping objects. The extra processing requirement of the script will eventually limit your ability to enrich your world further. These scripts can get tricky and are outside the scope of this book. Still, it is important to know that the scripting you read about in Chapter 10, "Scripting," adds powerful capabilities to VRML.

Exercises

1. In your house, add a ProximitySensor that turns the light on and off automatically. Have the light come on immediately when you enter the room but wait 10 seconds after you leave to turn off.

2. Create a vase using an Extrusion node, and place it on a pedestal in the center of the house. Now, using a SphereSensor, allow a user to grab and examine the object from all sides. When the user releases the object, return it to its initial orientation.

Answers

☐ Because of code length, you can find the VRML files for the preceding exercises on the CD-ROM at \Source\Answers.

Day 12

Movies, Switches, and Billboards

In Chapter 9, "Adding Behavior to Objects," you learned how to do simple animation using interpolators. In Chapter 10, "Scripting," you learned how scripting can allow great flexibility in adding life to your worlds. Now you will learn about a different kind of animation. You'll learn how to apply moving textures to objects, to simulate fire and television sets. You'll also learn how to switch between different objects to simulate motion. Then you'll learn how to keep a flat object facing you, to give it a three-dimensional effect. Finally, you'll learn how to combine these techniques with scripting, for some simple yet interesting effects.

Here's what you'll cover today:

☐ The `MovieTexture` node

☐ Movies and sound

☐ Starting and stopping movies

☐ Switching scene components

☐ Using billboards

☐ Animated sprites

The `MovieTexture` Node

You learned about the `ImageTexture` node in Chapter 5, "Object Appearance." It allows you to wrap a 2D image around an object to give it a much more complex appearance than it would have with just a solid color. The `MovieTexture` node gives you this same capability to apply an image to an object, but that image can move on the surface. It can do this because the MovieTexture node uses a movie format, such as MPEG, rather than an image in a static format, such as JPEG. You might have visited Web sites with links you can click to view a movie, complete with audio. But these are two-dimensional, just like a still image. The `MovieTexture` node allows these same movies to be applied as a moving texture on an object. Here is its definition:

```
MovieTexture {
    exposedField SFBool    loop              FALSE
    exposedField SFFloat   speed             1
    exposedField SFTime    startTime         0
    exposedField SFTime    stopTime          0
    exposedField MFString  url               []
    field        SFBool    repeatS           TRUE
    field        SFBool    repeatT           TRUE
    eventOut     SFFloat   duration_changed
    eventOut     SFBool    isActive
}
```

Notice that the `MovieTexture` has many of the same fields as an `ImageTexture`. The `url`, `repeatS`, and `repeatT` fields all do the same thing in both nodes. But the `url` field contains a movie file in `MovieTexture`, rather than a static image file. Also notice that all the rest of the fields of the `MovieTexture` node are the same as those in the `AudioClip` node, which I introduced in Chapter 7, "Viewpoints, Sound, and Anchors." This includes `startTime`, `stopTime`, `duration_changed`, `isActive`, and `loop`. Again, these fields serve the same purpose in both. But instead of controlling the playback of an audio clip, the fields in the `MovieTexture` control the playback of a movie.

Let me show you a simple example of a use for `MovieTexture`. This example will place a short movie on a simple box:

```
Shape {
    appearance Appearance {
        material Material { }
        texture DEF M MovieTexture {
            url "somersault.mpg"
            stopTime -1
            loop TRUE
```

12

```
        }
    }
    geometry Box { }
}
```

The MovieTexture node is placed in the same field as the ImageTexture node. This movie will start playing when the scene is loaded and will continue looping forever. You can try out this example by running 12tyv01.wrl on the CD-ROM. Notice that the movie is mapped on each face of the box, just like a static texture would be. Figure 12.1 shows this box with the movie textured on all its surfaces.

Figure 12.1.

A box with a movie wrapped on it.

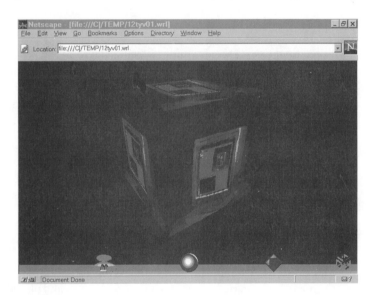

Movies and Sound

In the preceding example, you saw the movie playing on the surface of the box. That movie has audio with it, but the example is silent. What happened to the sound? Well, the sound has to have someplace in the scene from which to emanate, just like the AudioClip. In fact, the MovieTexture can be placed in the source field of the Sound node, just like the AudioClip. The following is an example of that. I'll place the audio for the movie at the center of the box.

```
Shape {
    appearance Appearance {
        material Material { }
        texture DEF M MovieTexture {
            url "somersault.mpg"
            stopTime -1
            loop TRUE
```

```
        }
    }
    geometry Box { }
}

Sound {
    source USE M
    maxBack  1000
    maxFront 1000
}
```

The Sound node will now play the audio portion of the movie while it is being displayed on the cube. Using the same node for both audio and video allows the browser to keep the two in perfect synchronization.

Because the MovieTexture audio is being played by the Sound node, all the capabilities of playing an AudioClip are available. You can set the distance at which the sound can be heard, and the sound will spatialize (the sound will seem to come from your right or your left, depending on your position in the world relative to the sound source). This way, by putting the sound source inside the box, it appears that the texture on the box is truly the source of the sound.

You can also place the sound in an object somewhere in front of, or to the side of, the textured object, to make the sound appear to come from a nearby speaker. Combining spatialized audio with moving textures allows for a very convincing television or movie theater effect.

Starting and Stopping Movies

Up until now, I've only shown you movies that run continuously. But just like the AudioClip, a movie can be started, stopped, continued, looped, and played at other than normal speeds.

WARNING

VRML allows a lot of flexibility in the implementation of MovieTexture. A browser may not support all combinations of speed and direction. It is not uncommon for a browser to turn off audio if the movie is playing backwards or at a speed other than normal. You need to be careful not to rely on a feature like this when adding a MovieTexture to your worlds.

VRML tries to be consistent in its definition and use of similar concepts. Therefore, nearly all the rules of playing and stopping a movie are the same as for a sound. One major difference is in the name of the speed control field. In the AudioClip node, this field is called pitch, because speeding up a sound tends to raise its pitch. But in the MovieTexture node, it is called speed, because that is its major function, to change the speed at which the movie plays. But when a movie speeds up, the sound increases in pitch (unless it is turned off), just like in the AudioClip node. So, from the perspective of sound, the speed and pitch fields perform the same function.

The duration_changed event also has the same function in both the MovieTexture and AudioClip nodes. It can be used to read the current length of the movie and to generate an event when the loading of the movie is complete. This event can be used to display information about the movie or to disable some function (like keeping a door locked) until the movie is loaded and ready to play.

Switching Scene Components

Movies are a simple way to add motion to your worlds. But VRML has another node that gives greater flexibility in animation and special effects. It is the Switch node, and it allows you to switch between different groups of objects. The switching is under complete control of the author, which means it must be programmed to do a particular task using a Script node. The following is the definition of the Switch node:

```
Switch {
   exposedField    MFNode  choice      []
   exposedField    SFInt32 whichChoice -1
}
```

Notice that the default value of whichChoice is -1. This value indicates that no child should be chosen. A simple way of hiding and revealing an object in a scene is to have a Switch with a single choice, then changing whichChoice to -1 to hide the object and 0 to reveal it. With multiple children in the choice field, they are selected in increasing order, from first to last, starting with a whichChoice value of 0.

The simplest use of a Switch is to change an object's appearance between two sets of geometry. Let's say I have a display case and I want to show a beautiful flower in it. But if I go away for a long time, I want the display case to show a dead flower, because I was away too long and did not water it enough. I can use a Switch node with two children: one is a live flower and the other is a dead one. I can build a script that, after a specified time-out is reached (generated by a TimeSensor), switches from the live flower geometry to the dead flower geometry. (See Figure 12.2.)

I'll show you another, simpler, example. In the following example, I will show a box. When I click the box, I will change it to a cone. When I click the cone, it will change back to a box, and so on. Listing 12.1 is the example.

12

Figure 12.2.

A live flower and a dead flower.

TYPE

Listing 12.1. Switching between a box and a cone with a Switch node.

```
DEF TS TouchSensor { }
DEF MySwitch Switch {
    whichChoice 0
    choice [
        Shape {
            appearance Appearance {
                material Material {
                    diffuseColor 0 1 0
                }
            }
            geometry Box { }
        }

        Shape {
            appearance Appearance {
                material Material {
                    diffuseColor 0 0.2 1
                }
            }
            geometry Cone { }
        }
    ]
}

DEF MyScript Script {
    eventIn SFTime switchTime
    eventOut SFInt32 whichChoice

    url "vrmlscript:
        function switchTime() {
```

12

```
        if (whichChoice == 0)
            whichChoice = 1;
        else whichChoice = 0;
    }"
}

ROUTE TS.touchTime TO MyScript.switchTime
ROUTE MyScript.whichChoice TO MySwitch.whichChoice
```

The script is very simple. It looks at the last value output and changes it to the opposite whenever the object is touched.

 TIP

> How can you test the last value sent from the whichChoice eventOut, before you've ever sent out the first event? VRML defines a default initial value for every eventOut, even those created by the author in a Script node. For SFInt32 eventOuts, the starting value is always 0. You can use this known initial state, like I did in the previous example, to do tests that will affect subsequent event generation. The starting value for all field types is 0, (0 0 0 for SFVec3f, and so on), except for SFTime. Its initial value is -1, which indicates a value just before the beginning of time.

I'll talk more about Switch nodes when I combine them with the next topic, Billboards.

Using Billboards

VRML allows the placement of 3D objects in a 3D world. However, VRML also has a way to effectively use 2D objects in the world, as well. The game community calls these objects *sprites*. Used effectively, they can increase the richness of your worlds while achieving maximum rendering performance.

NEW TERM   A *sprite* is a 2D bitmap that looks three-dimensional. It is named after a mythological fairy that could move very quickly. When rendered in a 3D world, it looks like a normal object but can be rendered much more quickly, because it consists of a single image rather than many separate polygons. A sprite has the disadvantage that you can only see it from one angle, but for some applications (such as monsters chasing you in a game), it works well.

The problem with 2D objects is that they are flat. If you look at them from the side, they disappear. To be effective, sprites need to always face the viewer. VRML has a special node to make this possible, called the `Billboard` node. The following is the `Billboard` node definition:

```
Billboard {
  eventIn       MFNode    addChildren
  eventIn       MFNode    removeChildren
  exposedField  SFVec3f   axisOfRotation   0 1 0
  exposedField  MFNode    children         []
  field         SFVec3f   bboxCenter       0 0 0
  field         SFVec3f   bboxSize         -1 -1 -1
}
```

Notice that the `Billboard` node has all of the same fields as the `Group` node, which I introduced in Chapter 3, "Building a Scene." In fact, `Billboard` does everything that `Group` does, with one additional function: It always keeps its children aligned with the viewer. It's sort of like a `Transform` node, which automatically adjusts its `rotation` field to keep its children aligned with the viewer. It does this with the exposedField `axisOfRotation`. This field defines a hinge about which children rotate to keep them aligned with the viewer. By default, it is a vertical line, which causes the objects to rotate about the Y-axis so that they always face the viewer.

If you make a textured, flat `IndexedFaceSet` the child of the `Billboard`, you have created a sprite. Sprites are often used for distant trees. At a distance, a tree looks about the same from any angle. So, by using tree images textured onto flat objects, and `Billboard` nodes, you can make a convincing grove of trees without thousands of polygons. Sprites are also useful in games, to make richly detailed creatures, and in architectural walkthroughs, for artifacts such as lamps and vases.

 TIP

> Sprites are perfect for objects that are symmetrical, meaning they look the same from all sides. Vases are a great example of this. If you walk around a vase that is a sprite under a `Billboard` node, you really can't tell the difference from a vase made from lots of polygons. Trees look fairly symmetrical from a distance, which is why they work well as sprites. Bowling balls, table lamps, and flower pots all work well as sprites.

I will create a scene with two sprites, a tree and a vase. The following code is a simple example of sprites, and Figure 12.3 shows the results of the code:

```
Transform {
    translation -3 0 0
    children Billboard {
        children Shape {
            appearance Appearance {
                texture ImageTexture {
                    url "vase.gif"
                }
            }
```

```
            geometry DEF IFS IndexedFaceSet {
                coord Coordinate {
                    point [ -1 -1 0, 1 -1 0, 1 1 0, -1 1 0 ]
                }
                coordIndex [ 0, 1, 2, 3 ]
            }
        }
    }
}

Transform {
    translation 3 0 0
    children Billboard {
        children Shape {
            appearance Appearance {
                texture ImageTexture {
                    url "tree.gif"
                }
            }
            geometry DEF IFS IndexedFaceSet {
                coord Coordinate {
                    point [ -1 -1 0, 1 -1 0, 1 1 0, -1 1 0 ]
                }
                coordIndex [ 0, 1, 2, 3 ]
            }
        }
    }
}
```

Figure 12.3.

Vase and tree sprites.

Notice that the Billboard node has a general list of children. So far, I have only shown you a flat textured object in this list. Sprites are by far the most common use for Billboards, but not the only one. Any shape or group of shapes can be a child of a `Billboard`. The shape will keep the same side of all the objects facing the viewer at all times. This is often useful in signposts the user should be sure to read, or an ominous statue whose eyes always follow you. Many tricks are possible with the `Billboard`.

Another feature of the `Billboard` I have not yet shown you is the use of different values for `axisOfRotation`. For example, having an axis angled slightly off-vertical is useful if your trees are on a hillside. But non-vertical axes are rarely used. The most interesting variant for `axisOfRotation` happens when you set its value to `0 0 0`. This is a special value that causes the objects to face the viewer, regardless of the viewer's orientation.

With the axis set to the default, the objects will only rotate along the Y-axis to maintain their orientation relative to the viewer. If you raise up your view and fly over a sprite, you will see the flat edge; it will not rotate up to match your view. But, with the special value of `0 0 0`, the object will rotate about a point in the center of the object, to present the same face to the viewer no matter what the viewer's orientation. This can be very disconcerting. The objects seem to float in space, almost stuck to the front of the screen. However, it can be useful in special cases, such as representing spheres as sprites, and it allows extremely fast sprite rendering because it can be displayed flat, no matter what the viewing angle.

Animated Sprites

You've just learned about sprites: flat images that always face the viewer. You've also learned how to use a `Switch` to change between several objects. Combining these two gives you a powerful tool for simple, yet compelling, animated objects. You've probably seen flipbooks, those booklets with simple cartoon drawings on the edge of the pages. Flip the pages and the cartoon seems to animate. Flipbook animations are now seen on many Web pages, with logos that seem to spin or messages that scroll up the screen.

Flipbook animations can be used in VRML as well. You simply create a series of images to form the animation sequence, make sprites out of them, and then make the sprites children of a `Switch`. Now, when you switch quickly between the children, you see a flipbook animation in your VRML world. As an example of this, I'll use a character from the popular video game, DOOM. In this example, the monster is a sprite. He will always face you. But when you click him, he will go through an animated death sequence, and you will be rid of him. Figure 12.4 shows the series of sprites used in the animation. Listing 12.2 shows the VRML for how this is done. Figures 12.5 and 12.6 show the monster before and after you click it.

Figure 12.4.

Sprite images used in DOOM animation.

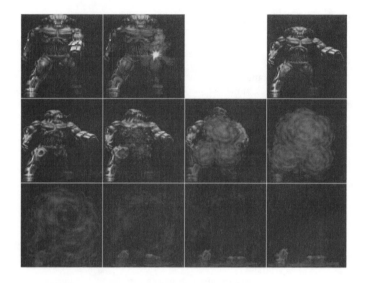

TYPE   **Listing 12.2. Animated sprite.**

```
DEF TS TouchSensor { }

DEF MySwitch Switch {
    whichChoice 0
    choice [
        Shape {
            appearance Appearance {
                texture ImageTexture {
                    url "cyberdemon/cdie00a.gif"
                }
            }
            geometry DEF IFS IndexedFaceSet {
                coord Coordinate {
                    point [ -1 -1 0, 1 -1 0, 1 1 0, -1 1 0 ]
                }
                coordIndex [ 0, 1, 2, 3 ]
            }
        }
        Shape {
            appearance Appearance {
                texture ImageTexture {
                    url "cyberdemon/cdie0a.gif"
                }
            }
            geometry USE IFS
        }
        Shape {
            appearance Appearance {
                texture ImageTexture {
                    url "cyberdemon/cdie1a.gif"
                }
```

continues

Listing 12.2. continued

```
            }
          geometry USE IFS
        }
        Shape {
            appearance Appearance {
                texture ImageTexture {
                    url "cyberdemon/cdie2a.gif"
                }
            }
          geometry USE IFS
        }
        Shape {
            appearance Appearance {
                texture ImageTexture {
                    url "cyberdemon/cdie3a.gif"
                }
            }
          geometry USE IFS
        }
        Shape {
            appearance Appearance {
                texture ImageTexture {
                    url "cyberdemon/cdie5.gif"
                }
            }
          geometry USE IFS
        }
        Shape {
            appearance Appearance {
                texture ImageTexture {
                    url "cyberdemon/cdie6.gif"
                }
            }
          geometry USE IFS
        }
        Shape {
            appearance Appearance {
                texture ImageTexture {
                    url "cyberdemon/cdie7.gif"
                }
            }
          geometry USE IFS
        }
        Shape {
            appearance Appearance {
                texture ImageTexture {
                    url "cyberdemon/cdie8a.gif"
                }
            }
          geometry USE IFS
        }
    ]
}
```

12

```
DEF Time TimeSensor {
    cycleInterval 0.7
}

DEF MyScript Script {
    eventIn SFFloat fraction
    eventOut SFInt32 whichChoice

    url "vrmlscript:
        function fraction(value) {
            whichChoice = value * 8;
        }"
}

ROUTE TS.touchTime TO Time.startTime
ROUTE Time.fraction_changed TO MyScript.fraction
ROUTE MyScript.whichChoice TO MySwitch.whichChoice
```

Figure 12.5.

The monster before clicking.

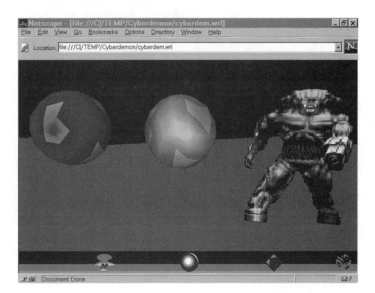

Another technique where the Switch node is used with sprites is called the *dynaboard*. With this technique you can use a series of 2D images to simulate a complete 3D object. The images are snapshots of a real-life object, taken at different angles. The dynaboard is created in a way similar to the preceding animated sprite. But, instead of cycling through the sprites to see an animation, you show the most appropriate image for the current viewing angle. This is done using a ProximitySensor to sense which direction the viewer is currently looking.

Figure 12.6.

The monster after clicking.

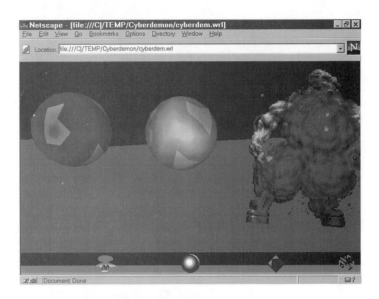

Summary

Using the MovieTexture node, VRML allows you to use movies as textures, just like still images. These movies are controlled with time events, such as the AudioClip node. The sound portion of a movie can be placed in the source field of a Sound node to allow the audio to be positioned in the world. VRML also has a Switch node that can be used to switch between sets of geometry to show objects in different states, like a flower when it is alive, and again, when it has died. Sprites can be created in a VRML world by placing a 2D image as a texture on a flat object, using the Billboard node to keep it always facing the viewer. By combining a Switch node, a Billboard node, and a sequence of sprite images, you can create animated sprites that can either run continuously, or can be controlled by user interaction or Script nodes to react to some other action. All these features give you more tools to use in the creation of interesting animated worlds.

Q&A

Q How can I play a movie backwards?

A The speed field of the MovieTexture is set to -1 to play the movie backwards at normal speed.

Q What happens if I set a whichChoice value in a Switch that is out of range of the children it has?

12

A Setting a value of -1 in the whichChoice field chooses none of the children. Any other value out of the range of children present yields undefined results.

Q Can a MovieTexture be used for a sprite rather than an ImageTexture?

A Yes. Any number of objects, with any texture or material, can be a child of a Billboard node. In fact, a movie can provide a much richer sprite animation than flipping through images with a Switch node.

Exercises

1. Place a grove of trees on the top of the hill on your property. Use tree.gif on the CD-ROM as the image.

2. Add a television set to your house. Give it an on/off switch and have it play somersault.mpg (available on the CD-ROM) when switched on. Have the screen go black when it is off.

Answers

1. The following is the code for the trees added to the house world, and Figure 12.7 shows its outcome:

```
# trees for hilltop
    DEF HillTree Transform {
        translation 30 -14 -30
        scale 3 3 3
        children Billboard {
            children Shape {
                appearance Appearance {
                    texture ImageTexture {
                        url "tree.gif"
                    }
                }
                geometry DEF IFS IndexedFaceSet {
                    coord Coordinate {
                        point [ -1 -1 0, 1 -1 0, 1 1 0, -1 1 0 ]
                    }
                    coordIndex [ 0, 1, 2, 3 ]
                }
            }
        }
    }
    Transform {
        translation 5 3 0
        children USE HillTree
    }
    Transform {
        translation -5 1 -3
        children USE HillTree
    }
```

12

Figure 12.7.
House world with billboard trees in the distance.

2. The following is the VRML code for the television added to the house, and Figure 12.8 shows its outcome:

```
# Box containing the TV
Transform {
    children Shape {
        appearance Appearance {
            material Material {
                ambientIntensity 0.297422
                diffuseColor 0.501339 0.321021 0.135513
                specularColor 0.0794227 0.0300707 0.0207978
                emissiveColor 0 0 0
                shininess 0.0212766
                transparency 0
            }
        }

        geometry Box { }
    }

    translation -8.23169 -17.9952 6.20224
    rotation 0 0 1  0
    scale 1 1 0.689943
    scaleOrientation 3.70875e-06 5.25319e-06 1  0.0621774
}
```

12

```
#TV leg
Transform {
    children DEF TVLeg Shape {
        appearance Appearance {
            material Material {
                ambientIntensity 0.263158
                diffuseColor 0.345455 0.163262 0.122622
                specularColor 0.212121 0.107475 0
                emissiveColor 0 0 0
                shininess 0.0486486
                transparency 0
            }
        }

        geometry Cylinder {
            height 0.370026
        }
    }

    translation -9.00118 -19.1802 6.66578
    rotation 1 2.23508e-09 -5.1173e-09  3.14159
    scale 0.136496 1.08138 0.136497
    scaleOrientation 1.27681e-06 1 -1.51529e-07  0.0168298
}

# TV leg
Transform {
    children USE TVLeg

    translation -7.45754 -19.1802 5.72157
    rotation 0 0 1  0
    scale 0.136496 1.08138 0.136497
    scaleOrientation 1.28542e-06 -1 1.5263e-07  0.0167161
}

# TV leg
Transform {
    children USE TVLeg

    translation -7.45737 -19.1802 6.66786
    rotation 0 0 1  0
    scale 0.136496 1.08138 0.136497
    scaleOrientation 1.28542e-06 -1 1.5263e-07  0.0167161
}

# TV leg
Transform {
    children USE TVLeg

    translation -9.0049 -19.1802 5.7245
    rotation 0 0 1  0
    scale 0.136496 1.08138 0.136497
    scaleOrientation 1.28542e-06 -1 1.5263e-07  0.0167161
}

# TV On/off knob
Transform {
```

12

```
        children [
            DEF TVTouchSensor TouchSensor { }
            Shape {
                appearance Appearance {
                    material Material {
                        ambientIntensity 0.246754
                        diffuseColor 0.416216 0.0707851 0.14109
                        specularColor 0.372973 0.00253723 0.00126432
                        emissiveColor 0 0 0
                        shininess 0.0108108
                        transparency 0
                    }
                }

                geometry Cylinder {
                    height 0.226299
                }
            }
        ]
        translation -9.03393 -18.7664 6.90634
        rotation 1 -3.94403e-08 3.68034e-08  1.5708
        scale 0.11315 0.562639 0.113149
        scaleOrientation -2.96629e-05 -1 4.49747e-05   0.00119604
    }

    # TV screen
    Transform {
        children DEF TVSwitch Switch {
            whichChoice 0
            choice [
                Shape {
                    appearance Appearance {
                        texture ImageTexture {
                            url "night.sky.gif"
                            repeatS FALSE
                            repeatT FALSE
                        }

                        textureTransform TextureTransform {
                            translation 0 0
                            rotation 4.71239
                            scale 1.25581 1.15598
                            center 0.5 0.5
                        }
                    }

                    geometry DEF TVScreen Extrusion {
                        crossSection [ -0.2 -0.8,
                                        0 -0.6,
                                        0 0.6,
                                       -0.2 0.8 ]
                        solid FALSE
                        spine [ 0 -0.8 0,
                                0.2 -0.6 0,
                                0.2 0.6 0,
                                0 0.8 0 ]
```

```
            }
        }

        Shape {
            appearance Appearance {
                texture DEF TVMovie MovieTexture {
                    url "somersault.mpg"
                    repeatS FALSE
                    repeatT FALSE
                    loop TRUE
                    stopTime    1
                }

                textureTransform TextureTransform {
                    translation 0 0
                    rotation 4.71239
                    scale 1.25581 1.15598
                    center 0.5 0.5
                }
            }

            geometry USE TVScreen

        }

        DEF TVScript Script {
            eventIn SFTime start
            eventOut SFInt32 doSwitch
            eventOut SFTime startMovie
            eventOut SFTime stopMovie
            field SFBool running FALSE
            url "vrmlscript:
                function start(value) {
                    running = !running;
                    if (running) {
                        doSwitch = 1;
                        startMovie = value;
                    }
                    else {
                        doSwitch = 0;
                        stopMovie = value;
                    }
                }"
        }
    ]
}

    translation -8.23275 -17.8858 6.87947
    rotation 0.57735 -0.57735 0.57735  2.0944
}

ROUTE TVTouchSensor.touchTime TO TVScript.start
ROUTE TVScript.doSwitch TO TVSwitch.set_whichChoice
ROUTE TVScript.startMovie TO TVMovie.set_startTime
ROUTE TVScript.stopMovie TO TVMovie.set_stopTime
```

12

Figure 12.8.

The television in the house, with the movie running.

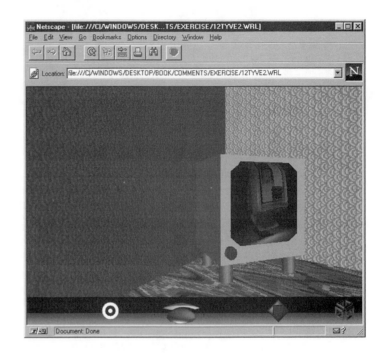

Day 13

Timing Events and Cycles

In Chapters 9 through 12, you learned how to create animated geometry and sprites and how to make moving textures. Now I will go into detail about the engine behind all these animations, the `TimeSensor` node. This node is the unsung hero of many VRML worlds. It can be used to emit a constant pulse, fire off an event some time in the future, and provide a sliding ramp of values to run interpolated animations. The `TimeSensor` node sometimes seems very complex, but I will use this chapter to uncover its secrets and make it one of the most useful nodes in your repertoire. Here is what I will cover today:

- ☐ The basics of timing
- ☐ Setting events in the future
- ☐ Using `isActive` to indicate when a timer is running
- ☐ Using the `cycleTime` and `time` outputs

The Basics of Timing

I introduced you to the TimeSensor in Chapter 9, "Adding Behavior to Objects," when I showed you how to use it to control interpolation. I showed you how to make it run continuously and how to start it with a TouchSensor. But the TimeSensor can do much more than that. Its many fields and events give it a wide variety of functions. I'll show you many of these functions, and as time goes on, you'll find many more uses on your own. But first, I'll review the TimeSensor's definition:

```
TimeSensor {
  exposedField   SFTime    cycleInterval     1
  exposedField   SFBool    enabled           TRUE
  exposedField   SFBool    loop              FALSE
  exposedField   SFTime    startTime         0
  exposedField   SFTime    stopTime          0
  eventOut       SFTime    cycleTime
  eventOut       SFFloat   fraction_changed
  eventOut       SFBool    isActive
  eventOut       SFTime    time
}
```

As you saw in Chapter 9, the fraction_changed eventOut can be routed to any of the interpolators. It can also be routed to a script for more complex control tasks. The TimeSensor operates over a time interval. The cycleInterval exposedField sets this interval, in seconds, and allows it to be changed on-the-fly. Normally, the timer begins its interval at the time in startTime and stops when the cycle is complete or when stopTime is reached. But if loop is set to TRUE, the cycle repeats until stopTime is reached. If stopTime is set to a value earlier than startTime, the timer runs forever.

The fraction_changed event generates events continuously. This means that when a node's eventIn is routed to it, that node is presented with a new fraction_changed eventIn as soon as it finishes processing the last fraction. Browsers must ensure that these events are not constantly being processed and preventing anything else from happening in the world. Many browsers handle the continuous events from the TimeSensor specifically to accomplish this task. The fraction_changed field generates a *ramp output*, which means that the first value it generates (at startTime) is 0, and it then generates ever-increasing events until it reaches 1. It takes the number of seconds in cycleInterval to complete this sequence. The ramp generated by fraction_changed is shown in Figure 13.1. This figure shows all the values that go into making up this ramp. It also shows the isActive eventOut, which generates a TRUE value at startTime and a FALSE value at the end of cycleInterval.

Figure 13.1.

The anatomy of a timing ramp.

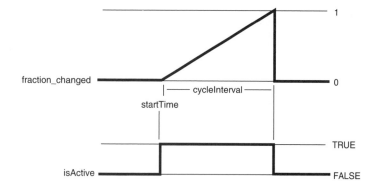

The stopTime exposedField allows you to stop the ramp before it completes. For instance, say that you start a TimeSensor with a cycleInterval of 10 seconds. But you also set the stopTime to the startTime value plus five seconds. The ramp starts at startTime, and then stops halfway through the cycle, when it reaches 0.5. The fraction_changed sends out the 0.5 value and then stops generating values. If you then set startTime to the current time, fraction_changed starts generating values, from 0 again.

TIP

It is important to remember that the value of fraction_changed is completely dependent on the values of startTime and cycleInterval. It doesn't matter if the ramp was interrupted by stopTime. As long as startTime is greater than stopTime, the ramp will run, starting from 0 at startTime and running to 1 at startTime + cycleInterval. If you want a ramp to continue where it left off, you set startTime to

startTime = currentTime - (stopTime - startTime)

This would make the value of fraction_changed at the current time the same as it was when it was interrupted by stopTime. You would also have to set stopTime to 0, to ensure that it was less than startTime, so that the timer starts running again.

Setting the loop field to TRUE allows you to create a timer that generates ramps continuously. When the value of fraction_changed reaches 1, it immediately returns to 0 and begins generating increasing values again. It carries out this action as long as stopTime is less than startTime or is in the future. Figure 13.2 shows what this timing cycle looks like.

13

Figure 13.2.
The timer output when
loop *is* TRUE.

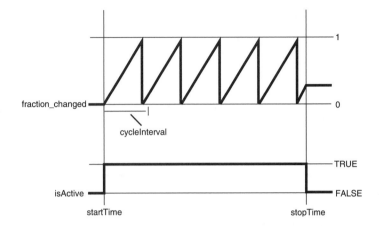

The TimeSensor also has a time eventOut, which continuously sends events when the timer is active, just like fraction_changed does. But it sends SFTime values, which are often useful when routed to a script for complex control tasks. The cycleTime eventOut also sends an SFTime event, but only at the beginning of a timing cycle. This event is generated at startTime and also after each cycleInterval. One example of its use can be seen in the boink.wrl file on the CD-ROM. The sounds of the objects bouncing are generated by the cycleTime event of the TimeSensor used to drive the animation.

Finally, the TimeSensor has an enabled exposedField, like all the other sensors. These fields and events can be used together in various ways to perform virtually any timer-related task needed in a VRML world.

Setting Events in the Future

In Chapter 9, when I showed you how to play an animation by connecting a TimeSensor to an interpolator, I showed you the timer starting either immediately or when a TouchSensor was activated. A TimeSensor begins its cycle at startTime, and often that value is to the current time because that is what the TouchSensor provides. But startTime can be set to any time in the past, present, or future. For instance, you can write a script that receives a touchTime event from a TouchSensor and then sets the startTime eventIn of a TimeSensor to one second before that time. If the cycleInterval of this timer is set to four seconds, the timer starts running immediately; however, it starts 25 percent of the way into the interval, and the first value generated by fraction_changed is 0.25.

If that same script sets startTime to two seconds past touchTime, the timer stays idle for two seconds, and then starts from the beginning of its interval. This delayed start feature is often useful when you want to have an automatic door stay open for a short time and then close

13

on its own, just like at the supermarket. Listing 13.1 is an example of a simple door animation in which the door, when touched, opens, and then closes four seconds later.

TYPE **Listing 13.1. VRML scene for door animation.**

```
DEF Touch TouchSensor { }
DEF Rotate Transform {
    center -2 0 0
    children Shape {
        appearance Appearance {
            material Material { }
        }
        geometry Box { size 4 9 0.1 }
    }
}
DEF OpenInterp OrientationInterpolator {
    key [ 0 1 ]
    keyValue [ 0 1 0 0, 0 1 0 -2 ]
}
DEF Open TimeSensor { cycleInterval 2 }

DEF CloseInterp OrientationInterpolator {
    key [ 0 1 ]
    keyValue [ 0 1 0 -2, 0 1 0 0 ]
}
DEF Close TimeSensor { cycleInterval 3 }

DEF S Script {
    eventIn SFTime touchTime
    eventOut SFTime startClose
    url "vrmlscript:
        function touchTime(value) {
            startClose = value + 4;
        }"
}

ROUTE Touch.touchTime TO Open.startTime
ROUTE Touch.touchTime TO S.touchTime
ROUTE Open.fraction_changed TO OpenInterp.set_fraction
ROUTE S.startClose TO Close.startTime
ROUTE Close.fraction_changed TO CloseInterp.set_fraction
ROUTE OpenInterp.value_changed TO Rotate .rotation
ROUTE CloseInterp.value_changed TO Rotate .rotation
```

13

For simplicity, I used two separate timers and interpolators and routed them both to the rotation field of the Transform, using VRML's fan-in feature. When the door is touched, the open animation begins, and the script runs and sets the close animation to begin at four seconds in the future. The door opens, delays, and then shuts again. Figure 13.3 shows the door as it is opening.

Figure 13.3.
Using the TimeSensor
node to control a door.

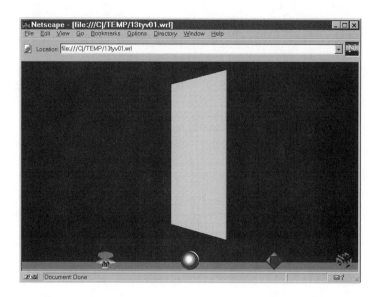

The same technique can be used with stopTime. Perhaps you have an animation running continuously, and you want to stop it five seconds after a button is pressed. You can achieve this result with the same technique, but with the script routing its output to the stopTime exposedField. Many interesting delayed start and stop behaviors can be obtained by combining the setting of both startTime and stopTime.

Using isActive to Indicate When a Timer Is Running

The isActive event is sent with a value of FALSE when the timer starts and with a value of TRUE when it stops. This event can be used for various tasks. For example, if you have a push-button that starts an animation, you might want to light the button while the animation is playing, and then extinguish the light when the animation is finished. Listing 13.2 is an example of how you can use isActive to carry out that task.

TYPE   **Listing 13.2. VRML scene using an isActive event.**

```
Transform {
    rotation 1 0 0 1.1
    children [
        DEF Touch TouchSensor { }
        Shape {
            geometry Cylinder { height 0.5 }
```

```
            appearance Appearance {
                material DEF Mat Material {
                    diffuseColor 0 0.1 0
                }
            }
        }
    ]
}

DEF T Transform {
    translation 0 5 0

    children [
        Shape {
            geometry Cone { }
            appearance Appearance {
                material Material {
                    diffuseColor 1 0 0
                }
            }
        }
    ]
}

DEF P PositionInterpolator {
    key       [ 0,     0.5,   1 ]
    keyValue [ 0 5 0, 4 5 0, 0 5 0 ]
}

DEF Time TimeSensor {
}

DEF LightControl Script {
    eventIn SFBool isActive
    eventOut SFColor color
    url "vrmlscript:
        function isActive(value) {
            if (value) color = new SFColor(0 1 0);
            else color = new SFColor(0 0.2 0);
        }"
}

ROUTE Touch.touchTime TO Time.startTime
ROUTE Time.fraction_changed TO P.set_fraction
ROUTE P.value_changed TO T.set_translation
ROUTE Time.isActive TO LightControl.isActive
ROUTE LightControl.color TO Mat.diffuseColor
```

Notice how I use the value of the isActive event to set the color to either bright green or dim green. Figure 13.4 shows the difference in shades of gray. Many other effects are possible. You might use isActive to control an audio clip, such as a clicking sound while a wheel-of-fortune is spinning.

Figure 13.4.

The isActive *event controls the lighting of the button.*

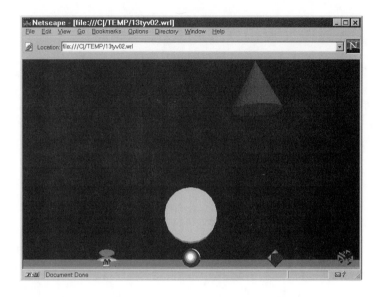

Using the `cycleTime` and `time` Outputs

The `fraction_changed` and `isActive` eventOuts are the most commonly used on the `TimeSensor`. But its two other eventOuts have many uses as well. The `cycleTime` eventOut is generated once, at the beginning of a cycle. If the timer has its `loop` field set to `TRUE`, this event is generated between each cycle as well. This field can be routed directly to other time-based nodes, such as `MovieTexture` and `AudioClip`. As mentioned earlier, you can use `cycleTime` to play an audio clip at each cycle of a repetitive animation.

The `time` output generates events continuously, just like `fraction_changed`. But it generates an `SFTime` event rather than an `SFFloat`. It is not used very often, because there is really no time-based node to which it can be routed directly, and the `fraction_changed` eventOut delivers a timestamp to a `Script` node eventIn, if time information is needed. But it is a reasonable alternative to `fraction_changed` when all you need is a source of continuous events for a script.

Summary

The `TimeSensor` forms the foundation of the timing capabilities of VRML. It can be used to control a simple continuous animation. Or it can be started when a sensor is activated, or at some time in the future, as with an alarm clock. The `stopTime` field can be used to interrupt a timing cycle, like the pause button on a VCR. It can be made to loop over and over for repetitive tasks, or to simply start at `startTime` and run for the number of seconds in

13

cycleInterval and then stop. Many types of outputs are available, from fraction_changed, which generates a ramp used most often in interpolated animations, to cycleTime, which can initiate other time-based nodes. Whether used to control a set of simple tasks or as one component of a complex, scripted system, the TimeSensor is one of the most useful of all the nodes available in VRML 2.

Q&A

Q Besides sunrises and sunsets, what other uses are there for a world clock?

A Some visionaries believe VRML worlds will take on content with a plot like a play or movie. These stories have a start and an end and a natural progression of events in between. Each object in the scene can perform its part based on the world clock. To the world visitor, this form of drama will add new possibilities. A user will be able to walk around the extended stage and watch events happen from different angles. In fact, for a mystery plot, it might make sense to play the world over and over while watching for different events that are happening at the same time. Historical reenactments would work well as VRML worlds with a world clock.

Q What else can I do with timers?

A Because you can stop and start timers, you can set up multiple timers for an object and turn them on and off. Add a script to the object and you have a way to randomly choose a timer and let an object perform that behavior for a while. Then, the object can take on another behavior as the script turns one timer off and another one on. With the right mix of interpolators and timers, you can make an object appear to take on a life of its own.

Q Are you suggesting a way to create artificial life in cyberspace?

A Yes, and I am not alone. There are lots of people interested in creating artificial life on the Web. VRML seems to be a great way to embody artificial life in a human-shaped object. The debate over the possibility of artificial life has made people think. Thinking about artificial life has led people to innovate some interesting VRML worlds with some far-out behaviors. A few more chapters to go and you'll have all the tools to add to the innovative world list.

13

Exercise

1. Create an egg timer with a button on top to start a three-minute cycle. Make the button light up when pressed, and have it extinguish when the cycle is complete. Have a clock hand go around a full revolution, returning to the upright position when the three-minute period has elapsed. Ring a bell or buzzer at the end of the cycle.

Answer

TYPE ### Listing 13.3. Answer to Exercise 1.

```
DEF B Transform {
    children [
        DEF TS TouchSensor { }
        Shape {
            appearance Appearance {
                material DEF B_MAT Material {
                    diffuseColor 0.2 0 0
                }
            }
            geometry Cylinder { }
        },
        DEF B_COLOR ColorInterpolator {
            key [0, .9999, 1]
            keyValue [1 0 0, 1 0 0, 0.2 0 0]
        },
        Sound {
            maxBack 1000
            maxFront 1000
            source DEF Audio AudioClip {
                url "elecbeep.wav"
            }
        }
    ]
    scale .5 .2 .5
    translation 0 1.65 0
},
DEF EGG Transform {
    children [
        Shape {
            appearance Appearance {
                material Material {
                    diffuseColor 1 1 1
                }
            }
            geometry Sphere { }
        }
    ]
    scale 1 1.6 1
},
DEF STAND Transform {
    children [
        Shape {
            appearance Appearance {
                material Material {
                    diffuseColor 1 1 .85
                }
            }
            geometry Cone { }
        }
    ]
```

```
        scale 1.6 1 1
        translation 0 -1 0
},
DEF CLOCKHAND Transform {
    children [
        Group {
            children [
                DEF CH Group {
                    children [
                        DEF Time_CH TimeSensor {
                            cycleInterval 180
                            loop FALSE
                        }
                    ]
                },
                DEF Move_CH OrientationInterpolator {
                    key [0, .25, .5, .75, 1]
                    keyValue [0 0 1 0,
                              0 0 1 -1.57,
                              0 0 1 -3.14,
                              0 0 1 -4.71,
                              0 0 1 -6.28]
                },
                DEF Pos_CH PositionInterpolator {
                    key [0, .25, .5, .75, 1]
                    keyValue [0 0 0,
                              -1 0 0,
                              0 0 0,
                              1 0 0,
                              0 0 0]
                }
            ]
        },
        Shape {
            appearance  Appearance {
                material  Material { diffuseColor  0 0 1 }
            }
            geometry Box {size .2 2 .2}
        }
        DEF Script_CH Script {
            eventIn SFBool isActive
            eventOut SFTime startTime
            url "vrmlscript:
                function isActive(value, ts) {
                    if (!value) startTime = ts;
                }"
        }
    ]
    center 0 -.9 0
    translation  0 1 1
}

ROUTE TS.touchTime TO Time_CH.set_startTime
ROUTE Time_CH.fraction_changed TO Move_CH.set_fraction
ROUTE Time_CH.fraction_changed TO B_COLOR.set_fraction
ROUTE Move_CH.value_changed TO CLOCKHAND.set_rotation
```

continues

Listing 13.3. continued

```
ROUTE B_COLOR.value_changed TO B_MAT.set_diffuseColor
ROUTE Time_CH.isActive TO Script_CH.isActive
ROUTE Script_CH.startTime TO Audio.startTime
```

☐ Because of code length, you can find the complete VRML file for the preceding exercise on the CD-ROM at \Source\Answers.

Day 14

Animated Viewpoints and Binding

In Chapter 7, "Viewpoints, Sound, and Anchors," I introduced you to the Viewpoint node. This node allows you to set the position and orientation of an interesting vantage point for the user. I showed you how to make these viewpoints available in the user interface of the browser so that visitors to your world could go to them. But VRML's animation capability extends to the control of viewpoints as well. You can animate the user's current viewpoint to take him or her on a guided tour of your world, with audio to point out the interesting sites. Viewpoints can be animated for elevators, buses, and moving sidewalks. They can also be used to pop a user to a new location instantly. The main facility used to control viewpoints is called *binding*, and I will explain this concept, as well as the nodes other than Viewpoint, that use it. Here is what I will cover today:

- ☐ The basics of viewpoint animation
- ☐ Binding the user to a viewpoint
- ☐ The binding stack
- ☐ Preserving the user's position during binding
- ☐ Other binding nodes

The Basics of Viewpoint Animation

When entering a world, a user is placed at the first Viewpoint node encountered in the file. From here, he can use the user interface to move freely about in the world. He is not tied to this entry viewpoint. But wouldn't it be powerful if you, the author of the world, could take control of the user's avatar and take him on a ride around the world? VRML provides you with a mechanism to do just that, and it is called *binding*. The reason binding exists in VRML is that giving you control over the user's movement requires that you send an event to some node. Events are the only mechanism available to assert control over a scene, so a node must be found to which events that can control the user's viewpoint can be sent. As it turns out, the Viewpoint node is the perfect candidate for this task.

Conceptually, the user looks at the scene through a virtual camera. This camera has a field of view, which sets the type of virtual lens to use (from wide angle to telephoto). It also has a position and an orientation to tell where it is and what part of the scene it is currently pointed at. The Viewpoint node provides initialization for all these, which is why a visitor's initial view of the scene is that of the first Viewpoint node encountered.

But that first encountered Viewpoint node provides more than the initial point of view. It embodies the user's camera. The camera and the Viewpoint are bound together. If you send an event to the position and orientation fields of the initial Viewpoint node, the user's view changes. You can create a guided tour by connecting interpolators to these fields. The user clicks a signpost or a button, a TimeSensor starts running, and the user is moved on a predefined path through the world. Listing 14.1 is a simple example of this capability. This example is a world with a box and a cone. When the user clicks either object, he or she is taken in close, around the object, and then finally back to his or her starting point.

TYPE **Listing 14.1. A world with a box and a cone.**

```
DEF VP Viewpoint { position 0 0 10 }

Group {
    children [
        DEF Touch TouchSensor { }
        Transform {
            translation 2 0 0
            children Shape {
                geometry Cone{ }
                appearance Appearance {
                    material Material {
                        diffuseColor 0 0.6 0
                    }
                }
            }
        }
```

14

```
        Shape {
            geometry Box { }
            appearance Appearance {
                material Material {
                    diffuseColor 0.2 0 0.6
                }
            }
        }
    ]
}

DEF O OrientationInterpolator {
    key      [ 0, 0.2, 0.4, 0.5, 0.6, 0.8, 1]
    keyValue [ 0 1 0 0, 0 1 0 0, 0 1 0 1.57,
               0 1 0 3.14, 0 1 0 4.71, 0 1 0 0,
               0 1 0 0 ]
}

DEF P PositionInterpolator {
    key      [ 0, 0.2, 0.4, 0.5, 0.6, 0.8, 1]
    keyValue [ 0 0 10, 0 0 5, 5 0 0, 0 0 -5,
               -5 0 0, 0 0 5, 0 0 10 ]
}

DEF Time TimeSensor {
    cycleInterval 20
}

ROUTE Touch.touchTime TO Time.startTime
ROUTE Time.fraction_changed TO P.set_fraction
ROUTE Time.fraction_changed TO O.set_fraction
ROUTE P.value_changed TO VP.set_position
ROUTE O.value_changed TO VP.set_orientation
```

You can try out this world yourself by running 14tyv01.wrl on the CD-ROM. Just click either object and you'll be taken on a 20-second tour of the box and cone. (See Figure 14.1.) Note that I added a PositionInterpolator and an OrientationInterpolator. They work in concert to move you around the objects and turn you so that you're always facing them. Now, in a simple scene like this, there is not much difference between animating the viewpoint, as I did here, and animating the objects themselves, as I showed you in Chapter 10, "Scripting." But in a real world, with lots of objects, terrain, and maybe other animations taking place, viewpoint animation is very useful.

14

Figure 14.1.

*Taking an automated
tour around two objects.*

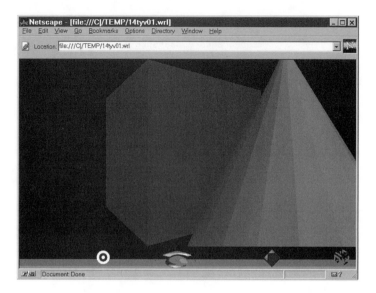

Binding the User to a Viewpoint

As I said in the preceding section, when the user enters the world, he or she is bound to the
first Viewpoint node encountered. Binding is an important concept in VRML, and it is used
for more than just the Viewpoint node, as you will see later in this chapter. Binding on entry
to the world is automatic, but you can also bind and unbind from other Viewpoint nodes in
the world. There are many reasons to do this, and most of them are rooted in the fact that
a Viewpoint node exists in a local coordinate space. This means that it is the child of a
Transform node, and thus, anything that affects that coordinate space also affects the user's
viewpoint. Listing 14.2 is a simple world with a blue sphere, representing the Earth, revolving
around a yellow sphere, representing the Sun.

TYPE   **Listing 14.2. Earth and Sun world.**

```
DEF VP Viewpoint { position 0 0 50 }

DEF T Transform {
    translation 20 0 0
    center -20 0 0

    children Shape {
        geometry Sphere{ }
        appearance Appearance {
            material Material {
                diffuseColor 0 0.4 0.8
            }
```

14

```
            }
        }
    }
    Shape {
        geometry Sphere{ radius 5 }
        appearance Appearance {
            material Material { }
            texture ImageTexture { url "sunspot.jpg" }
        }
    }

    DEF O OrientationInterpolator {
        key     [ 0, 0.25, 0.5, 0.75, 1 ]
        keyValue [ 0 1 0 0, 0 1 0 1.57, 0 1 0 3.14,
                   0 1 0 4.71, 0 1 0 0 ]
    }

    DEF Time TimeSensor {
        cycleInterval 20
        stopTime -1
        loop TRUE
    }

    ROUTE Time.fraction_changed TO O.set_fraction
    ROUTE O.value_changed TO T.set_rotation
```

This is a God's-eye view of the Sun and Earth. (See Figure 14.2.) You see the Earth slowly orbiting a (relatively) stationary Sun. But on Earth, it appears that the Sun rotates around the Earth, because the user's feet, and therefore his or her viewpoint, are tied to the Earth.

Figure 14.2.

A God's-eye view of the Sun and the Earth.

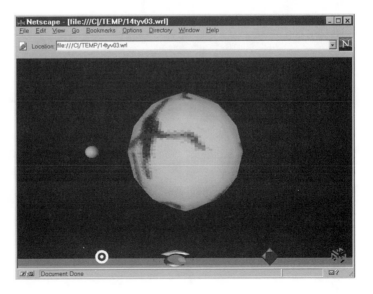

14

Now I will add a second Viewpoint to this world. This one is a child of the same Transform
that is being animated to move the blue sphere. When the user clicks the blue sphere, a bind
event is sent to that Viewpoint, and the view jumps to the Earth. If the user clicks the Sun,
he or she is taken back to the original viewpoint. Listing 14.3 gives the code for this viewpoint.

TYPE   **Listing 14.3. Adding a second** Viewpoint.

```
DEF VP Viewpoint { position 0 0 50 }

DEF T Transform {
    translation 20 0 0
    center -20 0 0

    children [
        DEF EarthTS TouchSensor { }
        Shape {
            geometry Sphere{ }
            appearance Appearance {
                material Material {
                    diffuseColor 0 0.4 0.8
                }
            }
        }
        DEF EarthVP Viewpoint {
            orientation 0 0.75 0.4 1.5708
            position 0 1.15 0
        }
    ]
}

Group {
    children [
        DEF SunTS TouchSensor { }
        Shape {
            geometry Sphere{ radius 5 }
            appearance Appearance {
                material Material { }
                texture ImageTexture { url "sunspot.jpg" }
            }
        }
    ]
}

DEF O OrientationInterpolator {
    key      [ 0, 0.25, 0.5, 0.75, 1 ]
    keyValue [ 0 1 0 0, 0 1 0 1.57, 0 1 0 3.14,
               0 1 0 4.71, 0 1 0 0 ]
}

DEF Time TimeSensor {
    cycleInterval 20
    stopTime -1
    loop TRUE
}
```

14

```
DEF S Script {
    eventIn SFTime bindToEarth
    eventIn SFTime unbindFromEarth
    eventOut SFBool bind
    url "vrmlscript:
        function bindToEarth() { bind = TRUE; }
        function unbindFromEarth() { bind = FALSE; }
    "
}

ROUTE Time.fraction_changed TO O.set_fraction
ROUTE O.value_changed TO T.set_rotation
ROUTE EarthTS.touchTime TO S.bindToEarth
ROUTE SunTS.touchTime TO S.unbindFromEarth
ROUTE S.bind TO EarthVP.set_bind
```

Figure 14.3 shows an image of the Sun from the vantage point of the Earth. If you run
14tyv03.wrl on the CD-ROM, you can switch between vantage points yourself. Notice that
the Sun seems to rotate in space. Even though the Sun is actually stationary and the Earth
is revolving around it, from your point of view, it is the Sun that is moving. It would appear
that you are truly the center of the universe from this view! You should also be able to tell why
I added texture to the Sun. From the Earth vantage point, it would be difficult to tell that
the Sun was moving without that texture!

Figure 14.3.

The Sun, from a
viewpoint on the Earth.

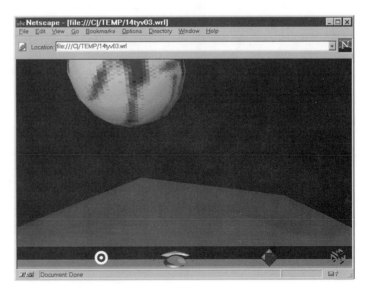

14

TIP

Notice that the Viewpoint is moving not because I am sending events to its position and orientation eventIns, as in the first example, but because its parent Transform is changing. This is the most common way to perform viewpoint animation when a physical object is being moved as well. This is so often the case that it is a good general practice to always animate the viewpoint in this way.

The Binding Stack

The example in the preceding section illustrates the basic concept behind binding a Viewpoint node. When you send a TRUE event to the bind eventIn, that viewpoint becomes the user's current view. Actually, the node that got the bind event becomes the active viewpoint, but any change in the user's current view is under your control, as I will explain shortly. But first, I want to mention the *binding stack*.

When you send a bind TRUE event, the Viewpoint that received the event becomes the active viewpoint. But the previous viewpoint does not go away. Any viewpoint that has ever been bound (and not unbound) resides in the viewpoint binding stack. The entry viewpoint is placed in this stack automatically. When you bind to a new viewpoint, it is placed above the previous viewpoint in the stack. When you unbind (by sending a bind FALSE event), it is removed from the stack, and the viewpoint that was below it becomes the active one. This allows you to nest viewpoints and their coordinate spaces. An unlimited number of viewpoints can be placed on this stack, but each viewpoint can occur in it only once. If a viewpoint somewhere in the middle of the stack is sent another bind TRUE event, it is simply moved to the top of the stack. (See Figure 14.4.)

Figure 14.4.

The Viewpoint *binding stack.*

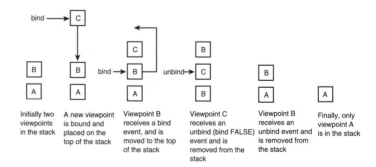

As an illustration of nesting viewpoints, take the example of the Sun and Earth shown previously. If they are rotating around the core of a spiral galaxy, you might initially be in space approaching the galaxy, outside its rotational influences. When you enter the galaxy, you might want to be carried around with its rotation, so you would bind to a viewpoint in that coordinate space. Then, when you approach the Earth, you might want to land on it, which would bind you to a viewpoint in its coordinate space.

Now there are three viewpoints in the stack: a viewpoint outside any animated coordinate space, the galaxy viewpoint, and the Earth viewpoint. The Earth viewpoint is at the top of the stack, so it is active. Your point of view makes it appear that the Earth is still and the Sun and the galactic core are rotating around you. If you get back into your spaceship and take off, you leave the Earth's coordinate space and unbind from its viewpoint. Now the galactic viewpoint is active and you are carried around with all the other objects revolving around the core. When you leave the galaxy, you unbind from its viewpoint and are left in a static top-level point of view.

Preserving the User's Position During Binding

If you tried the earlier galactic demonstration, you would find that whenever you bind to a new viewpoint, you would jump to its location. This would ruin the feel of this particular world. But the behavior of jumping during a bind can be disabled with the jump field. By default, jump is TRUE, so the user's view changes when it becomes active, as you saw in the preceding example. Setting jump to FALSE makes the viewpoint active, but the user's view does not change. This allows one of the most interesting uses for the Viewpoint node: transportation systems.

As you learned, VRML enables your avatar to walk up ramps and stairs. If you have a virtual department store with eight stories, you can have a central stairwell to allow visitors to explore all the floors. But just as in real life, stairs can quickly become tedious. An elevator is a modern convenience that is simple to duplicate in VRML, using a Viewpoint node and binding. If you put an elevator into your department store, complete with a call button and sliding doors, a visitor could wait for it, step in, and then push her desired floor. But when the elevator started to rise, you would not move, and the elevator would go up without you! This is because the terrain-following mechanism in VRML works in only one direction. When you move along stationary geometry, your vertical position is adjusted with every step, to maintain a constant height above the surface. But when an object you are standing on moves, you have not moved, so the terrain-following mechanism does not engage.

14

To solve the problem with the elevator, you can place a Viewpoint as a child of the same Transform that is moving the elevator. Then, when you step inside, a ProximitySensor can be used to execute a script that sends a bind TRUE event to this Viewpoint. But you don't want the user to suddenly jump when this bind happens, so you set jump to FALSE. The user is still attached to the viewpoint that is about to move up with the elevator, but your position and orientation are instantly and silently offset from that of the viewpoint so that you experience no distracting jump. When the elevator starts moving up, you go with it, instead of being left at the bottom of the shaft. You can move around inside the elevator, but collision detection keeps you from walking off until the doors open and you step off onto your new floor. After you step off, the same ProximitySensor that triggered the binding causes a bind FALSE event to be sent to the elevator Viewpoint. You are then attached to a static viewpoint again and can safely walk around. Figure 14.5 shows an elevator example you can explore by running elevator.wrl on the CD-ROM.

Figure 14.5.

A VRML elevator demonstration.

Other Binding Nodes

The Viewpoint is not the only node with a binding capability. Three other nodes have a bind eventIn as well: NavigationInfo, Background, and Fog. I will explain each in turn, but first I want to describe the binding capability in general. Each binding node type has its own binding stack, for a total of four. When you bind and unbind a Viewpoint, for instance, that action does not affect the binding status of the other three nodes. Each binding node also has the bind eventIn as well as an isBound eventOut. The isBound eventOut is issued when you

14

send it a bind TRUE or FALSE event to the node. It is also issued when the node is no longer active, because a new node was placed on top of the binding stack (isBound FALSE), or when it again becomes the active node, because a node above it was removed from the stack (isBound TRUE). This event can be used to turn on a light in an area when you bind to a viewpoint there. Or, it can be used to start and stop an eerie background sound when a Fog node is bound and unbound. The Viewpoint node also has a bindTime eventOut, provided as a convenience. It is sent when the isBound TRUE event is sent, but it is a SFTime value that can be routed directly to time-based nodes. It can be used to start a movie when you go to a viewpoint in which you're standing in front of a television, for instance.

I describe the Fog node in Chapter 17, "Special Effects." This node essentially allows you to bias the color to every visible object, which makes the world look foggy. When bound, it is influenced by the coordinate space containing it. This affects only the actual distance at which objects become completely obscured.

The Background node is another special-effect node, which I describe in Chapter 15, "Enriching Your Scene and Reusing Objects." It allows you to place a backdrop image or color behind all other objects to give the effect of a starry night or mountains in the distance. It is also influenced by its current coordinate space, which influences the rotation of the background. A simple way to have a star pattern that moves slowly across the sky is to make the active Background a child of a Transform node that is being rotated. Of course, you would have to make sure that your current viewpoint was not also a child of that same animation; otherwise, you would be spinning with the stars, and they would appear stationary!

When the NavigationInfo node is bound, all its fields become active. For instance, the avatarSize is specified so your avatar will take on the new size. The navigation type will change as well, so your user interface might change. Unlike with other bindable nodes, the size-related fields (such as avatarSize) do not depend on the coordinate space currently containing the node. Rather, they depend on the coordinate space containing the currently bound Viewpoint node. This is because all the fields of NavigationInfo relate to the viewer, which is controlled by the current viewpoint.

Summary

Viewpoint animation is another powerful tool to make your VRML worlds engaging. You can use it to take the user to interesting locations of your world, or you can create innovative transportation systems to help users get around. With binding, you can create a whole universe of relative coordinate spaces to make planets, stars, and entire galaxies for people to explore. You can bind other nodes as well, to create complete environments for different areas of your world.

14

Q&A

Q **If I take over the camera from the user by controlling the viewpoint, am I not taking away from the freedom of the user to use the VRML browser?**

A Sure, but there are many situations where the user wants to give up control. For example, a training world might help a user see how to navigate through a busy city or office complex. The viewpoint can be automated to show the way. By adding a button to the scene, you can let the user turn the viewpoint animation on and off. For a visitor new to a world, you might be surprised how often he or she relies on the viewpoint animation before wandering out on his or her own.

Q **Can viewpoint animation be used for anything other than taking a tour of the world?**

A Yes. The animation can reproduce the effect of an altered state of the visitor. The viewpoint can be shaken or staggered to represent the effect of being intoxicated or inebriated. The viewpoint can jump about to represent the behavior of a bird's view. I'm sure you can think of other special effects of matching the viewpoint behavior to an induced state of the user.

Q **Why are viewpoints bound on a stack?**

A Computers use a stack every time they run a subroutine in a computer program. Think about how you investigate an unknown place such as the woods or a cave. You walk in one direction until you get to a point where you don't want to walk anymore. You go back to a familiar place and then go in a new direction until that path is no longer interesting or becomes too scary. That's how the viewpoint binding stack works. It puts the most recent viewpoints on top and comes back to them first when the user wants to go back to a previous place.

Exercises

1. Create two transporters, one green and one blue. When you approach the green one so that it fills your field of vision, allow the user to click on the transporter and beam to inside the blue one. Create a shimmering effect for a few seconds while the transporting is in effect.

2. Place a button on the table of your house. When a visitor presses the button, he or she should be pulled back, far away from your house. The viewer should change to "EXAMINE" navigation mode so that he or she can examine the house as if it were a model.

Answers

TYPE **Listing 14.4. Answer to Exercise 1.**

```
Transform {
    translation -10 -18.3 4

    children [
        DEF PS ProximitySensor {
            size 1.2 1.75 1.2
        }
        DEF Transporter Transform {
            scale 0.3 0.3 0.3
            children [
                Transform {
                    translation 0 -3 0
                    children DEF FromPad Shape {
                        geometry Cylinder{
                            radius 2
                            height 0.2
                        }
                        appearance Appearance {
                            material Material {
                                diffuseColor 0 0.6 0
                            }
                        }
                    }
                }
                Transform {
                    translation 0 4 0
                    children USE FromPad
                }
                Collision {
                    collide FALSE
                    children Shape {
                        geometry IndexedFaceSet {
                            coord Coordinate {
                                point [ -1.4 -3 1.4, 1.4 -3 1.4,
                                        1.4 -3 -1.4, -1.4 -3 -1.4,
                                        -1.4 4 1.4, 1.4 4 1.4,
                                        1.4 4 -1.4, -1.4 4 -1.4 ]
                            }
                            coordIndex [ 0 4 5 1 -1, 1 5 6 2 -1,
                                2 6 7 3 -1, 3 7 4 0 -1 ]
                        }
                        appearance Appearance {
                            material DEF TP_MAT Material {
                                diffuseColor 0 0 0
                                specularColor 0 0 0
                                ambientIntensity 0
                                emissiveColor 0.6 0.6 0.6
                                transparency 1
                            }
```

continues

14

Listing 14.4. continued

```
                                }
                            }
                        }
                    ]
                }
            ]
        }

        Transform {
            translation 39.5 -5.5 -37

            children [
                DEF VP Viewpoint {
                    position        0 0.7 0
                    orientation     0 1 0  2.26747
                }
                USE Transporter
            ]
        }

        DEF TP_TRANSP ScalarInterpolator {
            key [ 0 0.4 0.6 1 ]
            keyValue [ 1 0 0 1 ]
        }

        DEF TP_COLOR ColorInterpolator {
            key [0, .05, .125, .2, .27,
                .35, .43, .4999, .5, .55,
                .625, .7, .77, .85, .93, 1]
            keyValue [.6 .6 .6,
                    1 1 1,
                    .2 .8 .2,
                    0 1 0,
                    0 0 0,
                    .2 .2 .7,
                    0 0 .2,
                    .2 .2 .2,
                    .2 .2 .2,
                    0 0 .2,
                    .2 .8 .2,
                    0 1 0,
                    0 0 0,
                    .2 .2 .7,
                    0 .2 0,
                    .6 .6 .6]
        },

        DEF Time TimeSensor {
            cycleInterval 10
        }

        DEF SwitchTime TimeSensor {
            cycleInterval 5
        }
```

14

```
DEF S Script {
    # Script to jump from the right pad to the left pad
    eventIn SFBool isActive
    eventOut SFBool bind
    url "vrmlscript:
        function isActive(value) {
            if (!value) bind = TRUE;
        }"
}

ROUTE PS.enterTime TO Time.startTime
ROUTE Time.fraction_changed TO TP_COLOR.set_fraction
ROUTE Time.fraction_changed TO TP_TRANSP.set_fraction
ROUTE TP_COLOR.value_changed TO TP_MAT.set_emissiveColor
ROUTE TP_TRANSP.value_changed TO TP_MAT.set_transparency
ROUTE PS.enterTime TO SwitchTime.startTime
ROUTE SwitchTime.isActive TO S.isActive
ROUTE S.bind TO VP.set_bind
```

Answer to Exercise 2 builds on the answer from Chapter 4, "Building Complex Objects," Exercise 1.

TYPE

Listing 14.5. Answer to Exercise 2.

```
DEF W NavigationInfo {
    type "WALK"
}
DEF E NavigationInfo {
    type "EXAMINE"
}
DEF VP Viewpoint { position -10 -3 -4.1
                   orientation 0 1 0 3.14 }
Group {
  children      [
    DEF BUTTON Transform {
       children [
         DEF TS TouchSensor { }
         Shape {
            appearance Appearance {
               material DEF B_MAT Material {
                  diffuseColor 0.2 0 0
               }
            }
            geometry Cylinder { }
         }
       ]
       scale .1 .01 .1
       translation -10 -3.76 -1.7
    }
    DEF TableBottom Transform {
```

14

continues

Listing 14.5. continued

```
        children
          Shape {
            appearance  Appearance {
                material        Material {
                  diffuseColor  0.3 0.3 0.0
                }
            }
            geometry Cylinder {}
          }
          translation -10 -4 -1.6
          scale .5 .2 .5
    }
    DEF TableTop Transform {
        children
          Shape {
            appearance  Appearance {
                material        Material {
                  diffuseColor  0.3 0.3 0.0
                }
            }
            geometry Cylinder {}
          }
          translation -10 -3.8 -1.6
          scale .8 .02 .8
    }
    DEF O OrientationInterpolator {
        key     [ 0, .01, 1 ]
        keyValue [ 0 1 0 3.14, 0 1 0 1.57, 0 1 0 1.57 ]
    }
    DEF P PositionInterpolator {
        key     [ 0, .01, 1 ]
        keyValue [ -10 -3 -4.1, 10 6 -10, 10 6 -10 ]
    }
    DEF Time TimeSensor {
        cycleInterval 1000
        startTime 0
        loop FALSE
    }
    ROUTE TS.touchTime TO Time.startTime
    ROUTE Time.isActive TO E.set_bind
    ROUTE Time.fraction_changed TO P.set_fraction
    ROUTE Time.fraction_changed TO O.set_fraction
    ROUTE P.value_changed TO VP.set_position
    ROUTE O.value_changed TO VP.set_orientation
```

☐ Because of code length, you can find the complete VRML files for the preceding exercises on the CD-ROM at \Source\Answers.

14

Day 15

Enriching Your Scene and Reusing Objects

You've learned and practiced the skills needed to create complex and interactive VRML scenes. This chapter should help you better organize large VRML projects. I will show you a way to take advantage of the built-in networking capabilities of your Web browser to use any VRML object made available on a Web server. I will demonstrate how to organize your VRML scenes into component files and then use a component in multiple VRML scenes through the use of the Inline node, another standard VRML 2 node. I'll emphasize often how one goal of VRML is to help developers create one efficient and shared cyberspace for everyone to enjoy. The chapter ends with a discussion of the Background node so that you can build a horizon for your worlds that will always be visible. Creating a background can make a dramatic difference in the look of your world.

In this chapter, you'll learn about the following topics:

- ☐ Combining objects from different sources
- ☐ Using simple VRML user-interface widgets
- ☐ Using a Background node for your world

Combining Objects from Different Sources

Take a look at your body in the mirror. Your body is a very complex object. Modeling a body in VRML is no simple task, yet if you were to spend the time to model it, you would like to be able to reuse your model the next time you needed to model a human being. As you will see, the Inline node is the feature of VRML that facilitates model reuse. But before you dig into the details of inlining, I want to help you better understand the full implications of object models, VRML, and the World Wide Web. This will become important background information for a complete discussion of inlining.

Continue thinking about modeling your body in VRML. If you were going to organize the modeling effort, you could subdivide your body parts into base objects. If I consider just the high-level objects that make up a human body, I can immediately see some redundancy in the modeling effort. I can model one leg and reuse that model for the other leg. One reason the Inline node was created is to help facilitate model reuse.

NOTE

> I consider the high-level objects of a human body to be the head, torso, right arm, left arm, right leg, and left leg. At lower levels of detail, the human body becomes even more symmetric. For example, a head has two ears, two eyes, two cheeks, and so on.

Next, think how wonderful it would be if a basic VRML model of the human form was already available on a Web server for you to use as a starting point. You could scale, transform, and texture the parts with information you gathered about your own body. For example, if your arms are longer than average, you could apply a scale factor of 1 1.1 1 to make the model arms 10 percent longer. You could create a texture map of your face and apply it to the available head model. Using the networking capability of a Web browser, the Inline node lets you access a VRML object anywhere on the Web and incorporate that object into the VRML file that contains the Inline node. In theory, every human object you ever encounter in cyberspace could be an adaptation of that same basic VRML model if everyone used an Inline node to access it within his own VRML world. Of course, many different human forms are found in cyberspace. To make that human model available to everyone who viewed a VRML scene with a human in it would require lots of network and computing resources. Yet it would be possible with VRML because of the Inline node.

15

NOTE

At this point, you might be thinking it would be easier to make a copy of the model than to use an `Inline` node to access the model each time. I seem to make lots of copies. But if the model is being improved or changed over time, inlining allows me to use the best available model each time.

TIP

Even if you copy a model from another source, you might want to keep it in a separate file so that you can reuse it in multiple scenes. As I will emphasize often, the `Inline` node lets you do this.

When visionaries speak of the power of inlining, they speak often about how it could organize cyberspace development. For example, if everybody was responsible for providing VRML models of the objects they knew better than anyone else, they could focus on improving those models over time. Everyone else would just use those models through an `Inline` node. We would build cyberspace faster and better that way because we would eliminate a lot of redundancy in modeling efforts.

This way of thinking suggests the need for a new naming convention, the Universal Resource Name (URN). As you will see, the `Inline` node uses a URL to find another VRML world on the Web. URLs were not created with persistency in mind. I have had a URL become invalid after I built a world using that object. That object mysteriously disappeared from my scene one day. As it turned out, the Webmaster at the other end decided there was a better way to organize the directory structure on that server. A URN uses a different approach to file access. Instead of focusing on the directory structure of the file system, a URN navigates a hierarchical name space, which a resolution service translates to the physical storage devices.

NEW TERM   A *name* is a text string given to uniquely identify an object. Every noun has a name whether generic or specific. George Washington is a name. Celery is a name. Wisconsin is a name.

NEW TERM A *resolution service* is a computer process that takes an input name and outputs a path and filename for that named object.

To make a URN structure work, a standard organization of all names must be devised and agreed on. Then, each browser that encounters a URN would know where to go to start looking for an object on the Web. A high-level name space could be moved around from place to place, but all browsers would be able to find it. Under that high-level name space, the hierarchy of subnames would always remain the same. The resolution service would quickly find the named object you requested. The necessary cataloging effort might start off with well-known objects and then evolve over time to include the model of yourself you created with your name attached. The idealistic conclusion would be that each name would map to one model, the best model available for that object.

I'll review the URN concept by way of an example. Say that I'm creating a VRML scene of a Spanish or Mexican plaza, and I want to get cute and include the Alamo in the scene. I could spend hours at the computer trying to create a realistic VRML model based on pictures in library books. Or, if I am lucky, I might find that a VRML model of the Alamo already exists on a server at the University of Texas. I go to the university's Web site using the identified URL, and I like the model I encounter. I then include the Alamo in my VRML world by inlining to it. If the University of Texas decides to change its directory structure, or if it gives the model to some other organization for upkeep, the Alamo will no longer appear in my VRML world. It has taken on a new URL. If I use a URN instead, it might look like this:

```
path://Famous Landmarks/US/Texas/Alamo.wrl
```

In this case, the Alamo should be in my VRML scene forever. My browser knows where to go to look for Famous Landmarks because it is one of a manageable number of high-level name spaces made public to browsers. When my browser sends me there, the resolution service looks up where to find the U.S. names, the Texas names, and the Alamo.

NOTE

In fact, if I learn the standard categorization scheme used, I might be able to find the Alamo by guessing the correct URN. I could then get there without performing a cumbersome search.

The point here is that inlining works well with a URN structure. VRML 2 is using URLs while the URN standard is in development.

I'll give you a quick recap of the capabilities of the Inline node, and then I'll provide the technical details:

- ☐ The Inline node provides a way to use a subcomponent of a scene contained in a separate file.
- ☐ This is an efficient way to organize subcomponents so that they can be used in multiple scenes.
- ☐ The Inline node provides a way to use a VRML object made available on any Web server.

Now, finally, look at the definition for the Inline node:

```
Inline {
  exposedField   MFString   url          []
  field          SFVec3f    bboxCenter   0 0 0
  field          SFVec3f    bboxSize     0 0 0
}
```

The Inline node is a grouping node similar to the Group node. The Inline node reads its children from anywhere in the World Wide Web. If a child cannot be located, the child is ignored, and the browser continues to the next child or node. You can specify multiple URLs, and your browser uses the first one it can find. This is one way to ensure against one URL becoming invalid. After a child is found, the complete file contents are added to the current scene as if they were listed in place of the Inline node.

To help your browser with rendering an inlined object, you can specify a bboxSize field and bboxCenter that the browser can use to determine whether the object is currently visible at the present viewpoint. This information can be used by a browser to speed up the rendering process whenever possible.

Using Simple VRML User-Interface Widgets

I mentioned using the Inline node to reuse an object model. I want to focus on a certain kind of reusable object model. An *interface widget* is an object that can be reused to facilitate interaction between your audience and your world. You want your audience to be able to interact with a scene in an intuitive manner. It should be obvious where interaction is possible. One way to make interaction opportunities obvious is to use objects a user will recognize. For example, light switches and elevator-button panels are readily recognized for their purpose. A second way to help a user is by using the same widget consistently throughout the world.

I will use an elevator control panel as a simple example of an interface widget you will be able to inline to from multiple worlds. Listing 15.1 is the VRML elevator control-panel object in the file lift.wrl.

TYPE **Listing 15.1. An elevator control panel interface widget.**

```
DEF overview Viewpoint {
    position      0 0 12
    orientation   0 0 1 0
    fieldOfView   0.785398
    description   "OVERVIEW"
}
```

continues

Listing 15.1. continued

```
DEF PAD Transform {
    children
        Shape {
          appearance Appearance {
            material Material { diffuseColor .5 .5 .5}
          }
          geometry Box { size  3 8 .5 }
        }
        translation 0 0 -.25
},
Group {
    children [
        DEF TS1 TouchSensor {}
        DEF BUTTON1 Transform {
            children
                Shape {
                  appearance Appearance {
                    material Material { diffuseColor 1 1 0}
                  }
                  geometry Box { size  1 1 .2 }
                }
                translation 0 2 0
        }
    ]
},
Group {
    children [
        DEF TS2 TouchSensor {}
        DEF BUTTON2 Transform {
            children
                Shape {
                  appearance Appearance {
                    material Material { diffuseColor 1 1 0}
                  }
                  geometry Box { size  1 1 .2 }
                }
                translation 0 0 0
        }
    ]
},
Group {
    children [
        DEF TS3 TouchSensor {}
        DEF BUTTON3 Transform {
            children
                Shape {
                  appearance Appearance {
                    material Material { diffuseColor 1 1 0}
                  }
                  geometry Box { size  1 1 .2 }
                }
                translation 0 -2 0
        }
    ]
}
```

15

15

The elevator panel is a simple VRML scene with four `Box` nodes. (See Figure 15.1.) The first `Transform` node defined as `PAD` contains a simple gray box `Shape`. I'll use it to represent a piece of metal that will contain the elevator buttons. The three `Group` nodes contain a `TouchSensor` node and a `Transform` node as children. Note how each `Transform` node contains an identical `Shape` node:

```
Shape {
   appearance Appearance {
       material Material { diffuseColor 1 1 0}
   }
   geometry Box { size  1 1 .2 }
}
```

Figure 15.1.

A simple elevator panel with three buttons.

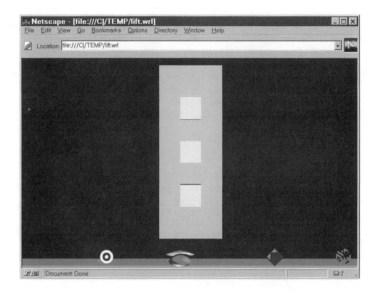

The `Shape` node identifies a simple box shape I will use for each elevator button. I use the `translation` field of the `Transform` node to put each button in an appropriate place on the elevator panel. The fact that the `Shape` node is identical in multiple places alerts me to consider using an `Inline` node instead. If I create the button shape as a separate VRML object in a separate file, I will be able to change the look and feel of my buttons in the future without having to change the elevator panel file. And if I create many different button objects, I will be able to change one line in the elevator panel file and use a different set of buttons. Finally, I will be able to use the buttons again in any other button-based widget I or someone else creates. See the power of the `Inline` node?

I will make the necessary changes for your review. First, I will create the button object in a separate VRML file in order to reuse it later. Listing 15.2 shows the VRML for file `button.wrl`.

TYPE **Listing 15.2. A button in its own** `.wrl` **file.**

```
DEF BUTTON Shape {
    appearance Appearance {
        material Material { diffuseColor 1 1 0}
    }
    geometry Box { size  1 1 .2 }
}
```

After I have the button as a separate file, I will modify my elevator panel widget file to use the Inline node to retrieve each button. Take a look at file panel.wrl in Listing 15.3.

TYPE **Listing 15.3. An elevator panel widget.**

```
DEF overview Viewpoint {
    position    0 0 12
    orientation    0 0 1  0
    jump        TRUE
    fieldOfView    0.785398
    description    "OVERVIEW"
}
DEF PAD Transform {
    children
        Shape {
            appearance Appearance {
                material Material { diffuseColor .5 .5 .5}
            }
            geometry Box { size  3 8 .5 }
        }
        translation 0 0 -.25
},
Group {
    children [
        DEF TS1 TouchSensor {}
        DEF BUTTON1 Transform {
            children
            Inline {
                url        ["button.wrl"]
                bboxCenter 0 0 0
                bboxSize    1 1 .2
            }
            translation 0 2 0
        }
]},
Group {
    children [
        DEF TS2 TouchSensor {}
        DEF BUTTON2 Transform {
            children
            Inline {
                url        ["button.wrl"]
                bboxCenter 0 0 0
                bboxSize    1 1 .2
            }
```

15

```
            translation 0 0 0
        }
]},
Group {
    children [
        DEF TS3 TouchSensor {}
        DEF BUTTON3 Transform {
            children
          Inline {
                url        ["button.wrl"]
            bboxCenter 0 0 0
            bboxSize   1 1 .2
          }
            translation 0 -2 0
        }
]}
```

Where I had previously used the Shape node, I now use the Inline node for my buttons. I have used a relative URL because I will keep my button.wrl file in the same file directory as the panel.wrl file. Remember that I could specify a complete URL to a different Web site if a library of interesting button models were made available to me on the Web.

As I design my elevator panel widget, I consider how someone else would use my object. I have enclosed TouchSensor nodes within my button Group node so that anybody who uses my elevator panel can actually use the buttons to interact with his or her scene.

NOTE

Creating widgets for optimum reuse requires planning for reasonable use considerations. I ask myself, *What would a reasonable VRML developer want to do with my widget?* If everyone takes the time to think that question through as he or she creates reusable objects, everyone benefits in the long run.

Next I will show you an example that uses the elevator panel widget I have created. If I take inlining to the limit, I can consider using my panel inside an elevator, which is inside an elevator shaft, which is inside a building. Perhaps you can imagine how to create the three additional files I would need to do that: lift.wrl, shaft.wrl, and building.wrl. For the sake of a simple illustration, I will put the elevator panel directly inside an elevator shaft. Listing 15.4 shows a VRML scene of an elevator shaft.

TYPE   **Listing 15.4. An elevator shaft without a panel.**

```
DEF SHAFT Transform {
    children
        Shape {
            appearance Appearance {
                material Material {  diffuseColor 1 0 0 }
            }
            geometry IndexedFaceSet {
                coord Coordinate {
                    point [
                        1 2 4.6,
                        1 0 4.6,
                        0.55 36 0.84,
                        -1 2 4.6,
                        -1 0 4.6,
                        -0.54 36 -0.71,
                        0.54 36 -0.71,
                        0.54 0 0.864,
                        -0.54 0 0.864,
                        0.54 -0.03 -0.71,
                        -0.54 -0.03 -0.71,
                        0.54 1.08 0.864,
                        -0.54 1.08 0.864,
                        -0.533 36 0.84
                    ]
                }
                coordIndex [
                    2,11,13,-1,
                    12,13,11,-1,
                    2,6,11,-1,
                    9,11,6,-1,
                    11,9,7,-1,
                    6,5,9,-1,
                    10,9,5,-1,
                    8,10,12,-1,
                    5,12,10,-1,
                    12,5,13,-1,
                    8,12,4,-1,
                    3,4,12,-1,
                    4,1,8,-1,
                    7,8,1,-1,
                    8,7,9,-1,
                    0,3,11,-1,
                    12,11,3,-1,
                    8,9,10,-1,
                    0,11,9,-1,
                    9,1,0,-1
                ]
            }
        }
    }
}
```

15

The elevator shaft VRML file (see Figure 15.2) contains a single Transform node that contains a Shape node with a red Material field and an Indexed Face Set-based geometry field within an appearance node field. I will put the shaft and panel together in a single VRML file using two Inline nodes. Listing 15.5 shows an example of the proper use of the Inline node.

Figure 15.2.
An elevator shaft without a panel.

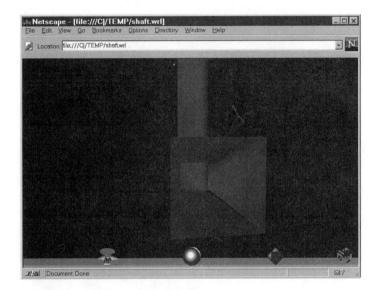

Listing 15.5. Inlining to the elevator shaft and panel.

```
DEF ELEVATOR_ENTRY Viewpoint {
    position    0 .5 12
    description     "ENTRY"
}
DEF ELEVATOR Transform {
    children [
    Transform {
        children
            DEF SHAFT Inline {
                url ["shaft.wrl"]
                bboxSize 2 40 6
            }
            translation     0 0 0
    },
    Transform {
        children
            DEF SHAFT Inline {
                url ["panel.wrl"]
                bboxSize 4 8 1
            }
            translation  .45 .6 -.696
            scale .04 .04 .04
    },
    ]
}
```

The newshaft.wrl file again emphasizes the power of the Inline node. You are able to put two completely different objects together by using an Inline node to import each file to the larger scene. (See Figure 15.3.) Because the files could have just as well come from any two places on the Web, I have used a different scale for the two objects. When this is the case, you need to scale, translate, and rotate your objects appropriately, to place each object according to your world coordinate system. I have chosen to translate and scale the panel object to conform to the coordinate system of the elevator shaft. If I then use this file in a larger building scene, I will probably have to transform this object to coordinate the system to the building world.

Figure 15.3.

An elevator shaft with the panel inserted.

I think you finally have enough to think about when considering the Inline node. I'll give you a break and end this chapter with a powerful node that does not have as many implications: the Background node.

Using a Background **Node for Your World**

A background image is an image that appears off in the distance, regardless of your current viewpoint. In a background image, the horizon changes as you rotate your viewpoint. Look out the nearest window. In the distance, you see a horizon. If you are running in a cornfield in the middle of the United States, the horizon does not get any closer as you move in any direction. Backgrounds add perspective for visitors to a VRML world. They help world visitors determine which way is up, if they rotate or spin a VRML model until they get lost.

15

15

Lost visitors can use background images to determine their orientation. If the ground plane is not horizontal as it should be, a user can make the appropriate adjustments until it is horizontal again. Often, you will use a Background node just to make your world appear more real or pleasing to the eye.

At first, the Background node looks complicated. As I present it to you, remember that the Background node allows for some flexible options. You don't have to use all the Background node fields at the same time, but instead, you can use a few fields together as a reasonable background technique. Take a look at the Background node definition:

```
Background {
    eventIn       SFBool     set_bind
    exposedField  MFFloat    groundAngle  []
    exposedfield  MFColor    groundColor  []
    exposedField  MFString   backUrl      []
    exposedField  MFString   bottomUrl    []
    exposedField  MFString   frontUrl     []
    exposedField  MFString   leftUrl      []
    exposedField  MFString   rightUrl     []
    exposedField  MFString   topUrl       []
    exposedField  MFFloat    skyAngle     []
    exposedField  MFColor    skyColor     [ 0 0 0 ]
    eventOut      SFBool     bind_changed
}
```

I'll describe each field from the top down. The set_bind field lets you send a TRUE or FALSE value through its eventIn. This binding feature is covered with respect to viewpoints in Chapter 14, "Animated Viewpoints and Binding." Through binding, you can dynamically change the current Background node in use if you list more than one Background node in your VRML file. A VRML viewer maintains a stack of backgrounds you can access as a visitor interacts with your world. The first Background node listed in your VRML file is the only background on the stack when a world is first opened. As another Background node is sent a set_bind event of TRUE, it is added to the top of the stack and becomes the active background. If you route a set_bind event of FALSE to the active background, that background is taken off the stack, and the background beneath it becomes active. In this manner, the background stack works similar to the viewpoint stack.

The groundAngle and groundColor fields work together. The simplest way to create an infinite ground plane is to use a single groundColor color. In the following example, the Background node creates an infinite, green ground plane in which y=0. You can add additional groundColor colors, but each additional groundColor set requires a corresponding groundAngle value. Because the skyAngle and skyColor fields work similarly, I will defer further explanation until later. Here's the example:

```
Background {
    groundColor  [0 1 0]
}
```

The next six fields allow you to place images in the infinite distance. These six fields make a cube that your viewpoint will always be within. The backUrl field uses a URL to an image that is at z=∞. The frontUrl field uses a URL to an image at z=∞. The rightUrl field uses a URL to an image at x=∞, and the leftUrl field uses a URL to an image at x=-∞. The topUrl and bottomUrl use URLs to images placed at y=∞ and y=-∞, respectively. You can use the same image for all six fields, or you can use different images to vary the horizon, depending on which way a visitor's viewpoint is oriented.

TIP

For a nice effect, define the right, left, back, and front images, but refrain from using the topUrl and bottomUrl to keep the sky and ground visible.

NOTE

Some graphics formats allow you to use a transparent color in your images. This way, you can create mountains and other distant objects, yet still allow the sky to be seen behind them.

The combination of skyColor and skyAngle fields lets you create a sky with varying color. As with the earlier groundColor example, you can use a single skyColor color to define a uniform sky color. Take a look at a more sophisticated example of using the sky fields:

```
Background {
    skyAngle      [.5, 1, 1.57]
    skyColor      [ 0 0 .6, 0 0 .7, 0 0 .85, 0 0 1 ]
}
```

The skyAngle value can range from 0 to π, in which 0 represents the point directly overhead, $\pi/2$ represents the ground horizon, and π represents the point directly below. The values between 0 and π represent angles off to infinity at relative concentric circles on an infinite sphere. In the preceding example, the sky color directly above is 0 0 .6. At about 30 degrees from overhead, the sky color becomes 0 0 .7. At 30 degrees up from the ground horizon, the sky color becomes 0 0 .85, and at the ground horizon, the sky becomes pure blue. In between those angles, the color is interpolated to create a smooth transition.

15

The groundColor and groundAngle fields work similarly except that a groundAngle of 0 is directly below and a groundAngle of π is directly overhead. The skyAngle and groundAngle fields contain lists whose members always increase in value reading from left to right. If your last list item is less than π, the region from your last list item to π is not defined.

NOTE

For both the sky and the ground field pairs, there will always be one more color set list item than for angle list items.

Finally, the binding_changed eventOut is active whenever a set_bind eventIn of TRUE is routed to the Background node. I will put this all together with a background example. Take a look at Listing 15.6 from the file bkexmpl.wrl on the CD-ROM.

TYPE **Listing 15.6. An elevator shaft with cloudy background.**

```
DEF ELEVATOR_ENTRY Viewpoint {
    position    0 .5 12
    description    "ENTRY"
}
Background {
    groundColor  [0 1 0]
    backUrl      ["clouds.jpg"]
    frontUrl     ["clouds.jpg"]
    leftUrl      ["clouds.jpg"]
    rightUrl     ["clouds.jpg"]
    topUrl       ["clouds.jpg"]
}
Transform {
    children
        DEF SHAFT Inline {
            url ["newshaft.wrl"]
        }
},
```

In the preceding example, I use five of the six URL-based fields in a Background node to create a cloudy background in all directions except below the user. I create a green ground plane and then use the elevator shaft I demonstrated earlier in the chapter with an appropriate viewpoint. (See Figure 15.4.)

Figure 15.4.

*An elevator shaft
enhanced with a cloudy
background.*

Summary

Inlining is a powerful capability of VRML that takes advantage of the structure of the World Wide Web. This chapter provided a discussion of Uniform Resource Names, yet technically explained the use of the Inline node using a url field. Through the Inline node, a VRML viewer can include in a scene any object available on a Web server anywhere on earth. Beyond that capability, the Inline node helps you organize your models for reuse in multiple VRML scenes. Background nodes also enrich your VRML scenes by providing the capability of creating a sky and ground plane. Using graphical images at infinite distances was also explained. A background image never changes as you move away from or toward it, yet it changes as you rotate your viewpoint. Because you experience backgrounds daily in the real world, backgrounds help your world appear more real.

Q&A

Q Is there a practical limit to how deep my nested inlines can go?

A From the standpoint of your file structure and your VRML browser's capabilities, there is no practical limit to the use of Inline nodes. But as long as you focus on inlining to a subcomponent from the more complex object, you will find that inlining is naturally nested only 10 or so levels deep for VRML models of real-world scenes.

15

15

Q In a VRML scene, if I inline to two different objects in two separate files with DEF statements that use the same name, how do I know which one the VRML browser will recognize as that name in my VRML scene if it encounters a subsequent USE statement?

A It won't recognize either one. When you inline to a file, all the DEF statements define names only within that specific file. You cannot use that name in another file. So, the good news is USE statements within each file will use the appropriate DEF statement for that file. The bad news is that you will have to reorganize how you inline to a file if you need to USE the object named in that file.

Q What about using ROUTE statements with names defined with a DEF statement?

A They are no exceptions. All the object names you want to use in a ROUTE statement must be defined in the same file as the ROUTE statement. So, inlining works best with static worlds that don't require ROUTE statements. But, inlining can always import complicated geometries such as those created using the IndexedFaceSet node and then use a DEF statement with the Inline node to name that geometry. Exercise 2 of this chapter will make you think about using both Inline nodes and ROUTE statements in the same file.

Q Isn't this a serious restriction to building the vision of a shared cyberspace that you speak about in this chapter?

A I have no doubt that future versions of VRML will improve VRML, so this is not considered a significant drawback. With the powerful scripts and server capabilities foreseen on the horizon, who knows how everyone will share nodes and events across the networks of tomorrow.

Exercises

1. Now that you understand inlining, go back to your answer to Exercise 1 of Chapter 12, "Movies, Switches, and Billboards," and break your VRML scene into reusable objects. Create a VRML scene that uses the Inline node to inline to your reusable object files. Compare your answer to the files I created when I used inlining with my answer to Exercise 1 of Chapter 12.

2. Using your house object from your answer to Exercise 1, create a second house by reusing your house object. Put your egg timer from Chapter 13, "Timing Events and Cycles," on a pedestal in one house and your table with a button from Chapter 14 in the other house. Make sure your egg timer and table button still work as they did in Chapters 13 and 14. Finally, add a background to your scene.

Answers

TYPE | **Listing 15.7. Answer to exercise 1.**

```
Group {
  children [
    DEF TERRAIN Inline {
        url ["terrain.wrl"]
    }
    DEF WELCOME_MAT Inline {
        url ["wellmat.wrl"]
    }
    Transform {
      children  DEF TREE_1 Inline {
          url ["tree1.wrl"]
      }
      translation  -1.41222 -15.3284 8.35686
    }
    Transform {
      children  DEF TREE_2 Inline {
          url ["tree2.wrl"]
      }
      translation  -4.03329 -15.3284 9.91395
    }
    Transform {
      children    USE TREE_1
      translation  -4.04862 -15.3284 8.36098
    }
    Transform {
      children    USE TREE_1
      translation  -4.07468 -15.3284 6.67403
    }
    Transform {
      children    USE TREE_2
      translation  5.38995 -15.3287 8.45525
      rotation    0 0 1  0
    }
    DEF HOUSE Inline {
        url ["house.wrl"]
    }
    DEF EXTRUSION_1 Inline {
        url ["extrusn1.wrl"]
    }
    DEF READING_LIGHT Inline {
        url ["readlite.wrl"]
    }
    DEF EXTRUSION_2 Inline {
        url ["extrusn2.wrl"]
    }
    DEF EXTRUSION_3 Inline {
        url ["extrusn3.wrl"]
    }
```

15

```
    DEF FURNITUREITEM_1 Inline {
        url ["furnitr1.wrl"]
    }
    DEF DOOR Inline {
        url ["door15.wrl"]
    }
    DEF HillTree Inline {
        url ["hilltree.wrl"]
    }
    Transform {
        translation 5 3 0
        children USE HillTree
    }
    Transform {
        translation -5 1 -3
        children USE HillTree
    }
  ]
}
```

TYPE **Listing 15.8. Answer to exercise 2.**

```
DEF W NavigationInfo {
    type "WALK"
}
DEF E NavigationInfo {
    type "EXAMINE"
}
DEF VP Viewpoint { position 4.2 0 0
                   orientation 0 1 0 1.57 }
Background {
    groundColor  [0 1 0]
    backUrl      ["clouds.jpg"]
    frontUrl     ["clouds.jpg"]
    leftUrl      ["clouds.jpg"]
    rightUrl     ["clouds.jpg"]
    topUrl       ["clouds.jpg"]
}
DEF Shelter Transform {
    children DEF HOUSE1 Inline {
        url ["house.wrl"]
    }
    translation 10.2 55 -11
    scale 3 3 3
}
Transform {
    children USE Shelter
    translation 25.8 0 0
}
DEF TBB Transform {
  children [
    DEF BUTTON Transform {
```

continues

Listing 15.8. continued

```
children [
  DEF TS2 TouchSensor { }
  Shape {
      appearance Appearance {
          material DEF B_MAT Material {
              diffuseColor 0.2 0 0
          }
      }
      geometry Cylinder { }
  }
  DEF O2 OrientationInterpolator {
      key      [ 0, .01, 1 ]
      keyValue [ 0 1 0 3.14, 0 1 0 1.57, 0 1 0 1.57 ]
  }
  DEF P2 PositionInterpolator {
      key      [ 0, .01, 1 ]
      keyValue [ -10 -3 -4.1, 10 6 -10, 10 6 -10 ]
  }
  DEF Time2 TimeSensor {
      cycleInterval 1000
      startTime 0
      loop FALSE
  }
]
scale .1 .01 .1
translation -10 -3.76 -1.7
}
DEF TableBottom Transform {
    children
      Shape {
        appearance  Appearance {
            material        Material {
              diffuseColor  0.3 0.3 0.0
            }
        }
        geometry Cylinder {}
      }
      translation -10 -4 -1.6
      scale .5 .2 .5
}
DEF TableTop Transform {
    children
      Shape {
    appearance  Appearance {
        material        Material {
          diffuseColor  0.3 0.3 0.0
        }
    }
    geometry Cylinder {}
  }
      translation -10 -3.8 -1.6
      scale .8 .02 .8
}
```

```
    ]
    translation 10.2 9.5 8
    scale 3 3 3
}
DEF Pedestal Transform {
        children
          Shape {
            appearance Appearance {
                material         Material {
                   diffuseColor  .1 .03 .03
                   }
            }
            geometry Cylinder {}
            }
            translation  15 -1 0
            scale .5 2 .5
}
Transform {
    children Inline { url 13tyve1.wrl }

    translation 15 2 0
    scale 0.5 0.5 0.5
}

# route statements for table button
ROUTE TS2.touchTime TO Time2.startTime
ROUTE Time2.isActive TO E.set_bind
ROUTE Time2.fraction_changed TO P2.set_fraction
ROUTE Time2.fraction_changed TO O2.set_fraction
ROUTE P2.value_changed TO VP.set_position
ROUTE O2.value_changed TO VP.set_orientation
```

☐ You can find the complete VRML files for the preceding exercises on the
CD-ROM at \Source\Answers.

Day **16**

Making Efficient Scenes

In the preceding chapter, I introduced you to the `Inline` and `Background` nodes. These VRML nodes are important because they provide powerful capabilities for organizing VRML objects and adding detail to your worlds. In this chapter, I will focus on making your VRML worlds more efficient. Efficient worlds load and render faster while maintaining the necessary detail for a believable scene. I will give you some guidelines to think about when modeling your VRML objects as I explain polygon budgets. You will learn that the `LOD` node changes the number of polygons used for an object at varying distances from the camera. I will explain why you might want to replace your objects with texture mapped billboards at far distances. Finally, I will discuss the `VisibilitySensor` node and its relevance on efficiency. If you can master these efficiency considerations, your audience will fully appreciate the VRML worlds you create.

In this chapter you'll learn about the following topics:

- ☐ Polygon complexity versus textures
- ☐ The `LOD` node
- ☐ Billboards for faraway objects
- ☐ Animation to give an object life
- ☐ The `VisibilitySensor`

Polygon Complexity Versus Textures

Every technology has a set of critical success factors on which producers of the technology compete. For example, the first computer manufacturers measured their progress by the number of instructions per second that their machines could process. Three-dimensional graphics-based technologies compete based on the number of polygons per second the graphics draw to a computer screen. Today, the competition is fierce as many companies try to deliver faster polygon rendering solutions through innovative hardware and software. Great advances are expected because of this competition. The number of polygons used in a VRML scene is the most relevant consideration for its performance. The faster the polygon rendering improves, the faster the VRML worlds will improve, as developers will be able to add more detail to their worlds and still provide a satisfying experience to a visitor.

As a VRML author, you have the responsibility of understanding the polygon rendering capabilities of the hardware and software combinations your audience will be using to view your world. Different VRML viewers render polygons at different speeds. Different computer hardware architectures render polygons at different speeds. Some visitors might buy a special graphics accelerator board for their computer specifically for speeding up the polygon rendering process. If you want everyone to visit your world, you might decide you can afford to use only 1,000 polygons in your scene before the rendering becomes too slow. If that is the case, I call that a polygon budget of 1,000 polygons.

 A *polygon budget* is the number of polygons an author or team of authors can afford to use in a VRML scene and still keep up with a reasonable rendering rate.

Generally, I will try my best to create a realistic world based on the number of polygons my worst-case visitor's VRML viewer can handle. If my world looks too simple or unrealistic at that polygon level, I will start to add polygons until I reach my least acceptable model. If I need 4,000 polygons to do that, I then document the minimum requirements for the world and let my visitors know up front what the minimum requirements are for a satisfying viewing experience. I will spend considerable time throughout this chapter teaching you the tricks I use to make the most of my polygon budget. These skills will always be relevant because by the time I can afford to use 20,000 polygons for my worst-case visitor, I will want to use 50,000. Everyone's worlds will be looking better as the technology improves, and I will want to compete for an audience.

The simplest trick I use is to replace polygon detail with textures. I can create my textures using sophisticated shading and coloring techniques so that they appear to have a lot of three-dimensional detail. Yet I can apply a texture to a simple rectangular polygon, a billboard. If I do a great job, I might be able to use one polygon in place of an object that otherwise would require 500 polygons. Sounds great, right? Well, nothing is that easy. There are things to consider when using this technique. First, a texture map begins to pixelate badly as I approach a textured object. I start to see dots of color that no longer appear realistic to me. Second, textures can take a lot of time to render each time a camera angle changes significantly.

WARNING

Consider that both the GIF and JPEG image files you use as textures can have significantly larger file sizes than the geometry they replace. Using them will require longer download times and longer load times, especially for those visiting your Web site with a 14.4 or 28.8 modem. They become most useful once the world has loaded in the browser and a user is moving about in the world.

16

The camera's angle to a texture changes most drastically when the camera is close to the object, especially when the image is starting to pixelate in the browser. In the preceding chapter, I introduced you to the Background node. Background images never pixelate because you never get closer to them. It is this feature of backgrounds that makes them such great nodes for adding detail to a scene. In fact, even if you use all six available background image fields, you are really using the equivalent of only six polygons for the whole background. Any other object that uses a texture and can be approached by a visitor can experience texture detail problems.

Using the LOD Node

If you are really in tune with these texture considerations, you might be brainstorming an idea here. You might be thinking, *If only I could use a texture map image for an object when I was far away from it and then replace it with a polygon model as my camera got closer.* If you are, you see the potential the LOD node provides. In fact, the LOD node allows you to specify as many different representations for the same object as you want. Using the node, you tell the VRML viewer which object model to use at which distance. So you can use high polygon modeled objects close to the user's current camera and then use lower polygon counts for objects farther away. Take a look at the LOD node definition:

```
LOD {
  exposedField   MFNode    levels    []
  field          SFVec3f   center    0 0 0
  field          MFFloat   range     []
}
```

LOD is short for levels of detail. The LOD node is potent. You use only three fields, yet you can define multiple objects within the levels field. Each child node in the levels field defines a level of detail for the same object that the VRML viewer can use when appropriate. The center field identifies the point in 3D space where the object is located, no matter which level of detail is being used. The range field lists multiple distance elements whereby the first element tells the viewer to use the first child node of the levels field until it is more than that distance away from the camera. The second child is used until the camera is farther than the second range field list element. The third child is used until the camera is farther than the third range field list element, and so on.

NOTE

The last child of the levels field does not require an associated range field list element. It is used no matter how far away the camera gets past the last range field list element.

I will demonstrate the LOD node through a simple example. Listing 16.1 is a VRML scene from the file 16tyv01.wrl:

Listing 16.1. A simple LOD example.

```
DEF overview Viewpoint {
    position    0 0 25
    fieldOfView    0.785398
    description    "STOPLIGHT"
}
LOD {
  levels [
          Transform {
            children
              Shape {
                appearance Appearance {
                    material Material { diffuseColor 1 0 0}
                }
                geometry Sphere {radius .4}
              }
          },
          Transform {
            children
              Shape {
                appearance Appearance {
                    material Material { diffuseColor 1 1 .8}
                }
                geometry Sphere {radius .4}
              }
          },
          Transform {
            children
              Shape {
                appearance Appearance {
                    material Material { diffuseColor 0 1 0}
                }
```

```
                geometry Sphere {radius .4}
            }
        },
    ]
    center   0 0 0
    range    [10,15]
}
```

This scene is a road warrior's nightmare. I have used the LOD node to change the color of a sphere as you approach it. The sphere is green, as long as you are at least 15 units away from it. It turns yellow as you get between 10 and 15 units away, and it turns red as you get closer than 10 units away. Remind you of something? Sure enough, it is a simple traffic-signal world, as shown in Figure 16.1.

Figure 16.1.

A simple traffic signal using the LOD *node.*

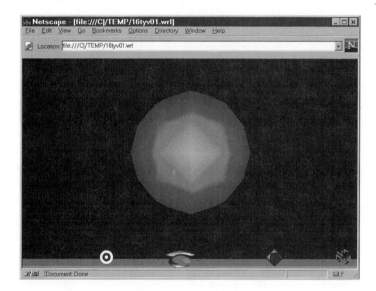

The scene is pretty simple. I start off with a Viewpoint node that starts the viewer 25 units away from the light. The light is green at that distance. The rest of the scene is one LOD node with three fields. First, the levels field contains three Transform nodes, each with a single Shape node child. The first Shape is a red sphere, the second is a yellow sphere, and the third is a green sphere. Second, the center field specifies the 3D location of the center of the sphere, which I have placed at 0 0 0. Remember that this will be the point of measurement for determining the current camera distance from the LOD objects. Finally, the range field identifies the distances at which the level of detail should change. Because I have created a range list of 10,15, the red sphere object will be visible up to 10 units, the yellow sphere object will be visible from 10 to 15 units, and the green object will be visible from 15 units off toward infinity.

The traffic-light example is a fun one that lets you see the LOD node in action. This type of use of the LOD node was available in the VRML 1 standard. With VRML 2, the LOD really has a better use. If you have been reading the chapters in order, you should have realized I could create the traffic light world with ProximitySensor nodes, ColorInterpolator nodes, and ROUTE statements. In fact, I would have if this were not just an example.

The LOD node's focus is on providing a VRML viewer alternative levels of detail to use for an object. As smarter browsers are created and VRML plug-ins are improved, VRML authors will provide multiple levels of detail for an object without specifying the range field. The VRML viewer will dynamically choose the appropriate level of detail based on the highest level of detail it can gracefully handle at that time. This will be an exciting development because each visitor to a world will get the best world possible for the technology he uses. In fact, some VRML viewers will use an existing range field as a suggestion or hint only and use their internal algorithms instead.

NOTE When you specify a range field in the LOD node, you are ensuring that each visitor to your world has the same experience in terms of polygon detail. This can be a drawback for power users, but it's a requirement for sharing technical drawings.

Consider the power of this concept from the preceding paragraph. Each time the camera moves, the VRML viewer can recalculate the distances to nearby objects and change the level of detail appropriately. The browser can determine the number of polygons it can comfortably render between changes in the camera and keep the world polygon count near that number. The visitor gets the most detail for objects nearby and much less detail for objects far away. Look around you. Your eyes work this way in the real world.

NOTE A side benefit of levels of detail is that a VRML viewer can be created that always loads the lowest level of detail first and then incrementally adds detail to the scene as time goes by. A visitor could begin exploring a world without waiting for the complexity to load.

It's time for another example. This time, I will give you an example that uses LOD in the way that will use the LOD node for its intended purpose and will take advantage of intelligent VRML viewers. In the preceding chapter, while introducing the Inline node, I created an elevator shaft that contained a panel of buttons. By the time I finished, I had a scene that

16

contained 44 polygons (20 for the shaft, 6 for each button, and 6 for the panel). If I then use this shaft inside a building inside a city, this level of detail would be appropriate only when a visitor's camera was near the building that contained the shaft. So I set up an LOD node for the shaft that contains three levels of detail. I create a second shaft object with similar dimensions, but much less detail. In fact, the scene in Listing 16.2 contains a box with six polygons.

TYPE **Listing 16.2. The elevator shaft at a low level of detail.**

```
DEF SHAFT Transform {
    children
      Shape {
         appearance Appearance {
            material Material { diffuseColor 1 0 0}
         }
         geometry Box { size  1 36 .72 }
      }
      translation 0 18 0
}
```

For the lowest level of detail, I will use a single rectangle and map an image texture on it. Take a look at the file shaft.gif in your Web browser. shaft.gif is an image file on the CD-ROM. I have taken a screen capture of the shaft at a great distance, created a GIF file with it that is 128×128 pixels in resolution, and added transparency to the pixels that are not part of the shaft object. Take a look at the complete VRML scene in Listing 16.3 and shown in Figure 16.2.

Figure 16.2.

The shaft at a low level of detail.

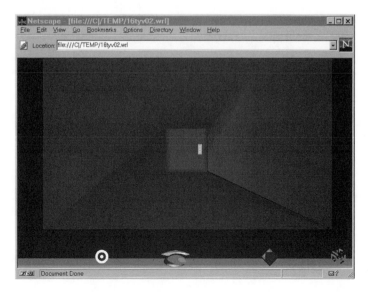

TYPE **Listing 16.3. An elevator shaft using three levels of detail.**

```
DEF overview Viewpoint {
    position    0 0 6
    fieldOfView    0.785398
    description    "OVERVIEW"
}
LOD {
  levels    [
      Transform {
        children
          DEF SHAFT Inline {
              url ["newshaft.wrl"]
              bboxSize 2 40 6
          }
      },
      Transform {
        children
          DEF SHAFT Inline {
              url ["shaftlow.wrl"]
              bboxSize 2 40 6
          }
      },
      Transform {
        children
          Shape {
              appearance Appearance {
                  texture ImageTexture { url ["shaft.gif"]}
              }
              geometry IndexedFaceSet {
                  coord Coordinate {
                      point [
                          -20 0 -80,
                          -20 40 -80,
                           20 40 -80,
                           20 0 -80
                      ]
                  }
                  coordIndex [
                      2,1,0,-1,
                      3,2,0,-1
                  ]
              }
          }
      },
    ]
    center    0 0 0
    range    [20,40]
}
```

The preceding example uses two high-level nodes, as does the traffic light example. The Viewpoint node puts the visitor six units away from and directly in front of the elevator shaft when the scene initially loads. The LOD node provides three levels of detail, centered at

16

0 0 0 and active in the range 0–20, 20–40, and 40–infinity. Each level of detail is defined in a Transform node. The first Inline node is active when a visitor is within 20 units of the shaft. At that distance, the elevator shaft appears in its full glory as I created it in Chapter 15, "Enriching Your Scene and Reusing Objects." Between 20 and 40 units away, the browser renders the stripped-down version of the shaft from this chapter. At any other distance, the textured rectangle is rendered.

Using Billboards for Faraway Objects

16

In the LOD example, I used an IndexedFaceSet to show an image in the distance. If you spent time exploring the world in a browser, you probably realized a potential problem with this technique. As you move from left to right, the imagemap moves. For some scenes, this movement might be too drastic. In fact, the farther off the object is supposed to appear relative to where the imagemap is actually positioned, the more camera movement will distort the user's sense of reality. In the elevator example, an image is placed near where it was supposed to appear so that the camera movement looks realistic.

Imagine, instead, if I wanted to place an image of foothills in the distance. This is a technique for improving the horizon in a world while providing a better sense of depth. I will set up a Background node with images of the Alps, Rockies, or some other tall mountain range. Then, I will create another image of smaller hills that I can place as a billboard in the distance in front of the mountains. The Billboard node enables me to rotate the image plane relative to the user's viewpoint. This keeps the user from perceiving the foothills as flat because the user always appears to be directly in front of the image. The farther I can place the billboard's contents in the distance, the better the technique works.

You have probably realized how many trade-off decisions a VRML author must make. This chapter is full of them. I will provide a table of them later in this chapter. If you are going to use the billboard technique for representing objects at a distance, you will have to consider where to place the image versus the size of the imagemap you will have to create. The farther away you want to place the image in your scene, the larger the bitmap file you will have to create. File sizes become important when you're considering the network transfer time of visitors coming to view your world over the Internet.

I have been speaking of billboards as you think of them in the real world. A billboard is usually a large, flat, rectangular wall that contains an advertisement. Advertisers only wish the billboard moved relative to your viewpoint so that you could see the ad head-on longer. The Billboard node has a more general use than advertising billboarding. The Billboard node is a grouping node. You can group as many children as you want as part of the billboard group. Yet the Billboard node moves all the objects in its children list relative to the camera. This camera-aware rotation is the Billboard node's strength. It just so happens that advertising, like billboarding, works well with the Billboard node. You can think of other ways to use the Billboard node creatively. Take a look at the Billboard node definition:

```
Billboard {
    eventIn        MFNode     add_children
    eventIn        MFNode     remove_children
    exposedField   SFVec3f    axisOfRotation   0 1 0
    exposedField   MFNode     children         []
    field          SFVec3f    bboxCenter       0 0 0
    field          SFVec3f    bboxSize         0 0 0
}
```

You can use two eventIn fields, add_children and remove_children, to add children to or remove children from the children field list. The axisOfRotation field specifies which way the group should rotate relative to changes in camera position. In all my worlds, I use X, Y, and Z for consistent purposes: X for left-right, Y for up-down, and Z for front-back. So I usually set the axisOfRotation to 0 1 0 to rotate the group around the up-down axis, my Y-axis. If I place my imagemaps at an angle, I modify the axisOfRotation to represent the same angle. This complicates matters, but it can make my foothills appear even more believable. The children field contains a list of children I want to include in the billboard. The field is an MFNode field type, identical to a Group node's children field. The bboxCenter and bboxSize fields help the browser determine how to load the group and whether the group is visible from the current viewpoint.

TIP

If you set the axisOfRotation to 0 0 0, the image will always face the camera from the same position no matter how the user explores the scene. This is a convenient exception built into the axisOfRotation field.

As an example, I will modify the third child of my LOD node in the preceding example to nest the imagemap inside a Billboard node. Take a look at the change:

```
Transform {
  children
      Billboard {
          axisOfRotation  0 1 0
          children [
              Shape {
                  appearance Appearance {
                      texture ImageTexture { url  ["shaft.gif"]}
                  }
                  geometry IndexedFaceSet {
                      coord Coordinate {
                          point [
                              -20 0 -80,
                              -20 40 -80,
```

16

```
                        20 40 -80,
                        20 0 -80
                    ]
                }
                coordIndex [
                    2,1,0,-1,
                    3,2,0,-1
                ]
            }
        }
    ]
    bboxCenter    0 20 -80
    bboxSize      40 40 .1
        }
}
```

I have nested the same Transform node inside a Billboard node. The Shape node is now a child of the Billboard. I set the axisOfRotation to 0 1 0, and added the appropriate bboxCenter and bboxSize values for the geometry of the billboard shape. You have seen how VRML nodes nest to produce the results you want. Add another nesting node to your growing list. You can nest the LOD node inside the Billboard node, or vice versa.

Using Animation to Give an Object Life

Sometimes you can get away with using fewer polygons for an object if the object is constantly moving. Animation uses significant computer processing, so you have a lot to think about in order to use animation as an efficiency trick. Most visitors will draw their attention to an animated object because it requires more attention. Remember the Flintstones? Every once in a while I would look at the background in a scene where Fred and Barney were doing their morning commute. The background was simple. One or two flat, basic mountains would fly behind them as they held a conversation in the foreground. My attention was always drawn to their eyes and mouths and body movement. The background did very little to add to or detract from my enjoyment of watching.

So even if you don't gain much efficiency from the reduction of polygons in the object you are animating by using animation, you might gain a lot by reducing the polygon count in all the other objects. Yes, another trade-off. I have summarized all the trade-offs mentioned in this chapter in Figure 16.3. You've learned everything you need to know to technically animate objects in this book.

Figure 16.3.
Some trade-off considerations for VRML authors.

Efficiency Consideration	trade-offs versus	
Polygon Detail	Realistic Appearance	Rendering Speed
Animation	Realistic Appearance	Rendering Speed
Billboarded Images	Distance from Scene Center	Image File Size
Realistic Scene Appearance	Animated Objects	Polygon Detail
# of Levels of Detail children	Scene Polygon Control	World Download Time

Using the `VisibilitySensor`

If you do decide to animate objects in your scene, you have no guarantee that your audience will watch your animations. Even if you did devise a clever method to keep an animated object on-screen at all times, you probably would not use it often. VRML scenes are meant to be explored. Movies and television do a great job of fixing an audience's point of view. The excitement of visiting a VRML scene is that you can move around as you want. In VRML, there is a node you can use to start or stop animations based on whether the animated object is visible. The `VisibilitySensor` node is very similar to other sensor nodes. Take a look at the `VisibilitySensor` definition:

```
VisibilitySensor {
  exposedField   SFVec3f   center    0 0 0
  exposedField   SFBool    enabled   TRUE
  exposedField   SFVec3f   size      0 0 0
  eventOut       SFTime    enterTime
  eventOut       SFTime    exitTime
  eventOut       SFBool    isActive
}
```

You identify the center of a box in 3D space that you want to keep track of by defining its location in the `center` field. Think of the box as the animation stage where your animated play takes place. As with all other sensors, you can enable the sensor through an `enabled` field. A `VisibilitySensor` is inactive when the `enabled` field is set to FALSE and is active when it is set to TRUE. Set the `size` field to reflect the dimensions of the box where your animation will take place. Then, each time the box comes in or out of a visitor's view, an `isActive` eventOut is triggered, and the appropriate `enterTime` or `exitTime` event is set. The `isActive` event is set to TRUE when the box becomes visible and is set to FALSE when it becomes invisible.

I hope you see how important this node becomes for complex animated scenes. Animation uses significant processing power on your computer—processing power that could be used to render better detail elsewhere. If you use the `VisibilitySensor` as intended, animations will use up processing power only when the animation is clearly visible to the user. Start your animations when your stage becomes visible, and stop them when it's out of view.

NOTE

Another use of the `VisibilitySensor` is to draw attention to an object when a bounding box nearby is visible. You can change its color, scale, or rotation to bring attention to it to try to steer a visitor's camera toward it.

16

NOTE

Determining whether a box is in view is no easy task. Sophisticated algorithms are used by the browser to determine visibility. The `VisibilitySensor` is guaranteed to realize when a part of the box is visible. It might err at times by determining that the box is visible when in fact it is not. Because you can't see the box at that time, no one will know the difference, but your computer will still use processing power when it really doesn't need to.

Summary

This chapter looked at ways to make your VRML scenes more efficient. As browsers become more intelligent and VRML evolves, the efficiency might be handled by the browser itself. Wouldn't it be great if the browser could take a high polygon model of an object and reduce the polygon count when necessary? Wouldn't it be great if it could take all the objects that were far away and dynamically translate them into imagemaps when appropriate? Unfortunately, these algorithms are difficult to get right. Besides, an average home computer is not ready to do all that processing yet anyway. So for now, you should use VRML nodes that tell the browser how to handle your scenes more efficiently.

I demonstrated the LOD node through the examples of a traffic light and an elevator shaft. The traffic light shows how to use the LOD node to change the characteristics of an object based on the camera's distance from it. With VRML 2, this task is better carried out with event routing methods. The elevator-shaft example shows how to reduce the number of polygons used for an object model based on how far away a visitor is from the object. When the object is far away, I use an imagemap rather than a 3D geometry to represent the object. The Billboard node works well with imagemaps because it dynamically rotates an image to face the camera. I discussed using animation to make up for a limited polygon budget. Lastly, I introduced the VisibilitySensor node and showed you how to use it to save processing on your visitor's computer.

By using the nodes in this chapter wisely, you will be able to compete with other authors using the same scant polygon budgets. By understanding the concepts in this chapter, you have developed an awareness of many technology issues of cyberspace.

Q&A

Q How do I determine how many levels of detail to use for an object?

A A good rule of thumb is to create a model for each power of 10—for example, an imagemap, a 10 polygon version, a 100 polygon version, and a 1000 polygon version. If your model has more than 1000 polygons, create a version for each 1000 (that is, 1000, 2000, 3000, and so on). Remember that a VRML 2.0-compliant browser should be able to take advantage of as many levels as you provide, and that every polygon you save by using an appropriate lower level of detail can be used in an object that is closer to the current viewpoint. So, bottom line—it depends on how many polygons you want to be able to save.

Q Can you show me more about the stage analogy?

A Sure. Take a look at this VRML scene outline:

```
DEF STAGE VisibilitySensor {
    Billboard {
        LOD {
            DEF HIGHRES Transform { animate here }
            DEF MIDRES Transform { less animation here }
            DEF LOWRES Transform { static here }
        }
    }
}
```

With a scene specified like this, I can consider it a stage. All the action happens within its boundaries, it has a high level of detail to someone watching from the front row and less detail to someone watching from the back row, and it faces anyone anywhere in the audience. I use the VisibilitySensor because there is no need to animate the play if the audience is looking elsewhere.

Q **Levels of detail are a lot of work. Isn't there a software package I can use to help me take a high level of detail model and scale it back to a lower level of detail?**

A That is a question I asked myself a lot over the last year. If you find one, please send me some e-mail as I have not found a reliable solution to the scale-down problem. The more I think about polygon reduction, the more I realize that it would be better for the VRML browser to do it on-the-fly. I suspect the algorithm would be quite sophisticated and inappropriate for current browser rendering-time constraints. Still, I suspect browsers will do some automatic polygon reduction for objects at a great distance and, perhaps, even create textures automatically at real great distances. These capabilities will probably come into fruition when our worlds are organized more as one continuous community and our computers incorporate specialized graphics hardware specifically designed for polygon rendering.

Exercise

1. Browse the world you created in Exercise 2 of Chapter 15, "Enriching Your Scene and Reusing Objects." Walk away from your houses while still keeping them in view. When they are far away, take a screen capture of the scene and create an imagemap from the screen capture. Create a VRML scene using a LOD node, where you inline to your full featured world at close distance, inline to a scene of two boxes from further away, and use a Billboard node with the imagemap from even further away. Create three viewpoints that face the houses from three different distances that show off the different levels of detail in your LOD node.

Answer

I loaded the file 15tyve2.wrl into my browser and walked backwards away from the house along the Z-axis. Once I got about 200 units away, I used the Print Scrn button on my keyboard to take a screenshot. (I was using Windows 95 at the time.) I pasted the screenshot from the clipboard to Microsoft Paint and cropped the image down to 128 by 128 pixels. I then used a graphics conversion program to save it as a .jpg file, houses.jpg.

I then created the two VRML scenes in Listings 16.4 and 16.5. The scene in Listing 16.4 is my LOD node that defines the three levels of detail the Exercise requests. The scene in Listing 16.5 is the simple two boxes I use for a mid-range model of the world.

TYPE   **Listing 16.4. Answer to Exercise 1: Overall VRML scene file.**

```
DEF VP1 Viewpoint { position 4 0 50
                    orientation 0 1 0 0
                    description "Up Close"
}
DEF VP2 Viewpoint { position 4 0 130
                    orientation 0 1 0 0
                    description "Mid Range"
}
DEF VP3 Viewpoint { position 4 0 180
                    orientation 0 1 0 0
                    description "Far Away"
}
LOD {
  levels    [
            Transform {
              children
                DEF SHAFT Inline {
                  url ["15tyve2.wrl"]
                  bboxSize 40 20 20
                }
            },
            Transform {
              children
                DEF SHAFT Inline {
                  url ["houseslo.wrl"]
                  bboxSize 40 20 20
                }
            },
            Transform {
              children
                Billboard {
                    axisOfRotation  0 1 0
                    children [
                      Shape {
                        appearance Appearance {
                          texture ImageTexture { url ["houses.jpg"] }
                        }
                        geometry IndexedFaceSet {
                          coord Coordinate {
                            point [
                                -20 0 0,
                          -20 30 0,
                           20 30 0,
                           20 0 0
                            ]
                          }
                          coordIndex [
                              2,1,0,-1,
                          3,2,0,-1
                            ]
                        }
                      }
                    ]
```

16

```
                    bboxCenter  0 20 0
                    bboxSize    40 30 .1
                }
        },
    ]
    center   0 0 0
    range    [80,150]
}
```

TYPE **Listing 16.5 Answer to Exercise 1: Mid-Range VRML file.**

```
Transform {
    children [
        Transform {
            children [
                DEF BOX Shape {
                    appearance Appearance {
                        material Material {diffuseColor 1 1 1}
                    }
                    geometry  Box {size 20 10 10}
                }
            ]
            translation 0 0 0
        },
        Transform {
            children USE BOX
            translation -22 0 0
        }
    ]
    translation 10 3 0
}
```

☐ You can find the complete VRML files for the preceding exercise on the CD-ROM at \Source\Answers.

Day **17**

Special Effects

Now that you have learned about most of the nodes VRML has to offer, it is time to learn some nifty tricks you can use to make your worlds more engaging. Some of these effects make scenes more efficient so that you can maintain an interactive frame rate while showing interesting content. Others give your world more realism and give visitors a more convincing illusion that this place really exists. Still others give your imagination tools to create unique and interesting additions to your virtual world. Here is what I will talk about today:

- ☐ Setting a visibility limit to reduce complexity
- ☐ Using fog
- ☐ Animation using texture coordinates
- ☐ Creating textures on-the-fly
- ☐ Changing backgrounds

Setting a Visibility Limit to Reduce Complexity

The NavigationInfo node has a visibilityLimit field. When a 3D scene is rendered, the objects rendered are contained in a *viewing frustum*. This is the rectangle surrounding all the objects that can be seen in the current view. The sides of this boundary are formed by the edges of the viewing window. The front and back are formed by the *near and far clipping planes*.

Objects closer than the near plane or farther than the far plane cannot be seen. You can think of the near clipping plane as being too close to your eye. In the real world, objects this close look blurry. In the virtual world, they are simply not rendered. In VRML, the near clipping plane is defined as one-half of the avatar radius, as set in the avatarSize field. Because you collide with objects that are at the avatar radius, setting the near clipping plane in this way means you can never get close enough for objects to disappear. The far clipping plane is set with the visibilityLimit field. By default, this field allows objects infinitely far away to be rendered. But far-away objects can take a significant amount of time to render, and they don't add much to the scene. So setting the visibilityLimit at some reasonable distance can improve rendering performance significantly.

The problem with setting the visibilityLimit is that it can cause distant objects, such as trees and mountains, to disappear, so you'll lose the nice backdrop for your world. The solution here is to use the Background node for this scenery, because it is always drawn, regardless of the value of visibilityLimit. Another solution is to somehow limit the distance a user can see. You could put two pieces of your world in separate valleys, with a mountain ridge between the two. You can set the visibilityLimit to prevent objects beyond the ridge from being seen. When standing on top of the ridge, you can use the LOD node to display low-complexity versions of both areas to keep performance high.

The binding capability of the NavigationInfo and Background nodes is very useful in this situation. When you are in each area, you can bind to nodes with an appropriate value for visibilityLimit and the proper background scene. When on top of the ridge, you can bind to a NavigationInfo node with a longer visibilityLimit, after the lowest LOD levels switch in and rendering performance is no longer an issue. In fact, you could even put an elevator at the base of the ridge to take you to the top. While ascending, you can bind in the nodes for the ridge. Because you're inside a closed elevator, you will not see any change in the scenery. When the elevator lets you off at the top, you'll see a new background and a longer visibilityLimit.

17

Using Fog

As I mentioned in Chapter 14, "Animated Viewpoints and Binding," VRML has a Fog node, which allows you to create the effect of a foggy day in your world. Here is its definition:

```
Fog {
  exposedField   SFColor    color             1 1 1
  exposedField   SFString   fogType           "LINEAR"
  exposedField   SFFloat    visibilityRange   0
  eventIn        SFBool     set_bind
  eventOut       SFBool     isBound
}
```

Adding fog is fast and efficient in VRML. The color value is added to the color calculation for each vertex of all objects in the scene. The amount of the color value factored in is dependent on the object's distance from the viewer. The farther away the object, the closer it gets to color. At the distance specified in visibilityRange, the object color is completely taken over by the color value. This color makes the object look flat and completely unaffected by lighting. If you make the background color equal to the colorvalue, the object completely blends into the background. The effect is such that as you walk away from the object, it fades more and more into the background until, at visibilityRange, it completely disappears. It is a good simulation of a foggy day.

Listing 17.1 is an example of three cones at different distances from the viewer, with a Fog node. I've left the background black with white fog so that you can still see the outline of the farthest object. Figure 17.1 shows what the scene looks like. The closest object is affected very little by the fog, the next object is somewhat affected, and the farthest object is completely affected.

Listing 17.1. Using the Fog node to show three cones at different distances.

TYPE

```
Fog { visibilityRange 14 }

DEF S Shape {
    geometry Cone { }
    appearance Appearance {
        material Material {
            ambientIntensity 0.1
            diffuseColor 0.9 0 0
            specularColor 0.9 0.4 0
            shininess 0.999
            emissiveColor 0 0 0
        }
    }
}
```

continues

Listing 17.1. continued

```
Transform {
    translation 3 0 -5
    children USE S
}

Transform {
    translation 7 0 -10
    children USE S
}
```

Figure 17.1.

Three cones, at different distances, affected by the Fog *node.*

Fog can be used effectively with the visibilityLimit field of the NavigationInfo node. Because nodes past the visibilityRange field of the Fog node cannot be distinguished from the background, you can set the visibilityLimit to the same value as visibilityRange, and objects beyond this limit will be neither seen nor drawn. The closer you set this limit, the foggier your world becomes, and fewer objects need to be rendered by the browser.

WARNING

As of this writing, the Fog node was still not implemented in the Windows 95/NT version of CosmoPlayer.

The fogType field allows you to set the way fog increases with distance. The default of "LINEAR" makes fog increase linearly. A linear increase means that an object twice as far away is twice as foggy. This type of increase is simple for the renderer to compute, but it does not give a very natural foggy appearance. Using a fogType of "EXPONENTIAL" gives a more natural fog behavior. In the real world on a foggy day, when you move away from an object, it starts out getting obscured very slowly, and then the rate of becoming more obscured increases. The "EXPONENTIAL" fogType simulates this effect. Objects still become totally obscured at the distance specified in visibilityRange, but objects in the middle distance look less obscured.

One other interesting trick you can perform with the Fog node is to use black fog. Simply set the color field to black (0 0 0) and leave the background at its default black color. Objects in the distance then fade to black, and the effect is that of walking around with a flashlight. Again, the closer you set the limit, the weaker your flashlight and the more efficient your rendering.

TIP

When you use fog, you must make the ground out of lots of little polygons, as I did with the SpotLight node example in Chapter 6, "Using Lights." That way, the fog fades properly on the ground plane, as well as on the objects. An easy way to get this effect is to use the ElevationGrid node with a large number of x and z grids. But as always, you make a trade-off: the complexity of the grid for rendering speed. A larger grid is slower to render, so the advantage of using the Fog node is lost. As in so many other areas of VRML, you have to make the right trade-off!

Animation Using Texture Coordinates

Now I will show you a fun trick. Imagine that you have a waterfall, complete with the sound of falling water. You can make this waterfall out of some geometry (perhaps an IndexedFaceSet) and then apply a water texture to it. But this texture is static, so it is not a very realistic waterfall. You could use a MovieTexture showing moving water, but that might take a while to download. I'll show you a simple water-animation method that is efficient and compact.

In Chapter 5, "Object Appearance," I showed you the TextureTransform node. With this node, you can set the transformation performed on the mapping between the texture and the object. Using an interpolator routed to the set_translation eventIn of this node, I can move the texture on the object. This eventIn is an SFVec2f. VRML does not have a built-in node to perform this interpolation, so I will show you how to do it with a Script node. Figure 17.2 shows the scene with the textured waterfall, and you can try this scene by running waterfall.wrl from the CD-ROM.

Figure 17.2.

A simulated waterfall created with the TextureTransform *node.*

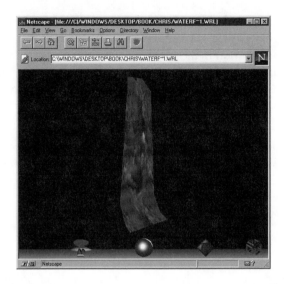

Listing 17.2 is the VRML code for Figure 17.2.

TYPE

Listing 17.2. A waterfall created with the TextureTransform **node.**

```
Group {
    children Shape {
        appearance Appearance {
        texture ImageTexture { url "clouds.jpg" }          textureTransform
        ➥DEF TT TextureTransform {
                scale 1.5 1.5
                center 0.5 0.5
            }
        }
        geometry Extrusion {
            crossSection    [ 0 2, 0 -1 ]
            scale [ 1 1, 1 1, 1 1, 0.6 0.6,
                    0.4 0.4, 0.4 0.4 ]
            spine [ 2 -5 0, 1 -5 0, 0 -4 0,
                    0 4 0, -1 5 0, -2 5 0 ]
        }
    }
}

DEF TS TimeSensor {
    cycleInterval 5
    stopTime -1
    loop TRUE
}

DEF S Script {
```

17

```
        eventIn SFFloat fraction
        eventOut SFVec2f translation
        field SFVec2f tt 0 0

        url "vrmlscript:
            function fraction(value) {
                tt[1] = value;
                translation = tt;
            }"
}

ROUTE TS.fraction_changed TO S.fraction
ROUTE S.translation TO TT.set_translation
```

The TextureCoordinate node can be used in a similar way. In fact, with this node you could stretch and squeeze the texture between any two vertices to simulate ripples on the water, lava flows, or even a whirlpool.

Creating Textures On-the-Fly

So far, you have learned about two ways to add texture to your worlds, the ImageTexture and the MovieTexture. Both of these nodes open a file (image or movie) and render the result on an object. But what if you could create an image in a VRMLScript program and then use that as an object texture? These are referred to as *procedural textures*, and with them you can create some very interesting and powerful effects. VRML allows you to do this with the PixelTexture node. Here is its definition:

```
PixelTexture {
    exposedField   SFImage   image     0 0 0
    field          SFBool    repeatS   TRUE
    field          SFBool    repeatT   TRUE
}
```

First note that this node has the repeatS and repeatT fields, just as the other texturing nodes do. But instead of having a url field, this node has an image field. This takes an SFImage value, which is a very special data type in VRML, created specifically to hold an image. In the VRML file format, this node must have at least three numbers. The first two are the X and Y dimensions of the image, in pixels. The next value is the number of *components* in the image. I talked about image components in Chapter 5, when I described the ImageTexture node. A one-component texture is a simple intensity map, and a three-component texture is a normal RGB image. Each of those texture types can have a transparency value or *alpha channel* associated with it. After the component value, you give integer values corresponding to the pixel values of the texture. You start with the lower-left pixel and give horizontal values, line after line, until you have defined all the lines in the image to the upper-right corner.

Pixel values are represented in *packed pixel* format. This means that one integer value holds all components of a single pixel. Values are typically represented in hexadecimal notation in the file (numbers prefixed with the characters 0x), because this allows the components to be easily separated out. For instance, the four-component value 0x908070FF has an alpha component of 0xFF, a red component of 0x90, a green component of 0x80, and a blue component of 0x70. To arrive at the normal color format, you would divide each of these values by 0xFF, which would yield an RGB value of 0.56 0.50 0.44 and an alpha value of 1.0.

NOTE   In the preceding example, an alpha value of 1.0 corresponds to a transparency value of 0.0, or "completely opaque." To convert from the alpha value, used in images, to a transparency value, used in the Material node, you simply subtract the value from 1.0.

NOTE   I will forgo a detailed discussion of hexadecimal numbers because image data is rarely represented in this way in the VRML file. Using a PixelTexture node with an image file is a much more efficient way of representing and transferring image data over the Web.

One interesting use you can make of the PixelTexture is in creating an SFImage value in a VRMLScript function and then sending it as an event to the PixelTexture node. VRMLScript has the capability to create an SFImage value for just this purpose. Here is an example of a VRMLScript function to do just that. This function creates a 16×16 image with black at the lower-left corner, white at the upper-right corner, and shades of red in-between:

```
function createImage() {
    myData = new MFInt32();    red = 0; // red increases vertically from 0 to
    ➡255
    for (y = 0; y < 16; ++y) {
        c = 0; // green and blue increase to the right
        for (x = 0; x < 16; x++) {
            gb = c*red; // this changes only the saturation
            myData[x][y] = (red<<24) + (gb<<16) + (gb<<8);
            c += 16
        }
        red += 16
    }

    myImage = SFImage(16, 16, 3, myData);
}
```

The image in myImage would then be sent to the image field of the PixelTexture node. In my example, I just created a 16×16 image for simplicity. But you can create much larger textures in this way. Using procedural textures like this has two advantages. First, if the texture is something you can generate on-the-fly, you can save the time it would take to download the image. Second, if the image is being generated by some interesting algorithm (mapping temperature in different areas of an engine over time, for instance), this algorithm can be executed over and over to create an animated texture.

Changing Backgrounds

The Background node provides backdrop colors or images for your worlds. Because its effects are so obvious, you can create many interesting effects with it. The first set of effects is created using the color capability of the node. You can set the sky color to be a range of shades to simulate a nice sunset. By animating this background color, you can create a day and night cycle. You can even play nice cricket noises at night. Listing 17.3 is an example in which I change the background through an entire cycle. I've placed a simple object in the middle of the scene to give it some interest. You can view this world by looking at 17tyv03.wrl on the CD-ROM.

TYPE **Listing 17.3. Background changed through an entire cycle.**

```
DEF B Background {
    skyAngle [ 1.4, 1.57 ]
    skyColor [ 0.3 0.3 0.6, 0.3 0.3 0.6, 0.7 0.3 0, 0.7 0.3 0 ]
    groundColor [ 0.2 0.1 0.1 ]
}

DEF S Shape {
    geometry Cone { }
    appearance Appearance {
        material Material {
            ambientIntensity 0.1
            diffuseColor 0.9 0 0
            specularColor 0.9 0.4 0
            shininess 0.999
            emissiveColor 0 0 0
        }
    }
}

DEF TS TimeSensor {
    stopTime -1
    loop TRUE
    cycleInterval 10
}

# interpolator for the lower half of the background color
DEF Interp1 ColorInterpolator {
```

continues

Listing 17.3. continued

```
        # 0 = midnight, 0.5 = noon, 1.0 = midnight
        # 0.25 = dawn, 0.75 = dusk
        key [ 0 0.25 0.5 0.75 1 ]
        keyValue [ 0 0 0, 0.7 0.3 0, 1 1 1, 0.7 0.3 0, 0 0 0 ]
}

# interpolator for the upper half of the background color
DEF Interp2 ColorInterpolator {
        # 0 = midnight, 0.5 = noon, 1.0 = midnight
        # 0.25 = dawn, 0.75 = dusk
        key [ 0 0.25 0.5 0.75 1 ]
        keyValue [ 0 0 0, 0.3 0.3 0.6, 0.5 0.5 0.8,
                   0.3 0.3 0.6, 0 0 0 ]
}

DEF S Script {
        eventIn SFFloat fraction
        eventOut MFColor color
        field SFNode interp1 USE Interp1
        field SFNode interp2 USE Interp2
        url "vrmlscript:
            function fraction() {
                color[0] = interp2.value_changed;
                color[1] = interp2.value_changed;
                color[2] = interp1.value_changed;
                color[3] = interp1.value_changed;
            }"
}

ROUTE TS.fraction_changed TO Interp1.set_fraction
ROUTE TS.fraction_changed TO Interp2.set_fraction
ROUTE TS.fraction_changed TO S.fraction
ROUTE S.color TO B.set_skyColor
```

Note the technique I used here. I have two interpolators changing the color of the sky and the color near the ground. I also route the fraction_changed output of the TimeSensor to the Script node. This triggers the script to build the MFColor value and send it to the Background node.

You can also switch Background nodes with different background images using its binding capability, as described in Chapter 14. In this way, you can have a simple background designed to be viewed out the window of a house from inside that house. Then, a ProximitySensor can switch to a better outdoor background when you leave the house. Because the background generates a rich backdrop for the world that renders very quickly, it is a very efficient way of adding interest and richness to your worlds.

17

Summary

VRML has many nodes that enable you to achieve interesting special effects. The `visibilityLimit` field of the NavigationInfo node provides an inexpensive way to eliminate far-away objects. Used in conjunction with hills to obscure distant objects, the Fog node can make far-off objects disappear in a haze, or the Background node can provide distant scenery. Animating texture coordinates with either the TextureTransform node or the TextureCoordinate node allows you to create other simple, yet interesting, effects, such as moving water or clouds. With the PixelTexture node, you can create textures on-the-fly, to save on download time, or to create algorithmic, animated textures. The Background node can have its color values animated to simulate the change between day and night, and different Background nodes can be bound to use backdrops appropriate for different parts of the world. All these effects allow you to add interest to your world without decreasing rendering performance.

17

Q&A

Q **Why can't I control fog visibility the way I can control a spatialized sound?**

A If you thought about this question during this chapter, you really are becoming a VRML expert. As I have explained the Fog node in this chapter, there really is no sense of location of the center of the fog. Fog is uniform wherever it is used in a VRML scene. The VRML Architecture Group considered adding a size field to the Fog node that would allow you to define fog in a manner similar to the minBack, maxBack, minFront, and maxFront fields of the Sound node. (See Chapter 7, "View-points, Sound, and Anchors," for a review of the Sound node. If you want to place fog in different locations at ground level such as clouds in the sky, you need to create a script that will take the current viewpoint position as an eventIn and determine the appropriate visibility as an eventOut. Take a look at Listing 17.4 after you have tried Exercise 1 in this chapter. Listing 17.4 presents a similar script that varies fog by time of day.

Q **So, if I understand the Fog node correctly, I could create a sandstorm by setting the color field to a light brown?**

A Right. You can create all kinds of effects with the Fog node. Try using the color `.3 .3 0` for a light brown fog to create a desert scene in a windstorm. Imagine using the color of cotton candy to create a world inside a piece of cotton candy. Consider using a bluegreen color for an underwater world.

Q **PixelTextures are rather tedious. Why wouldn't I just use an existing bitmap and route events to a TextureTransform node?**

A You can route events to a Transform node that contains a Shape with an ImageTexture node to produce many interesting techniques. Look at Listing 17.5

for an example after you have tried Exercise 2 of this chapter. Yet, once you define an `ImageTexture`, you no longer have access to each pixel on the image. You have to treat the bitmap as one uniform image for any transformations. The `PixelTexture` node gives you access to each individual pixel on the texture so you can write scripts that manipulate the texture at a lower level of detail. As computers get more powerful and better graphics acceleration is added to computer motherboards, you will see more action at the lowest level of detail in a VRML scene. The `PixelTexture` node is just one example of how the VRML 2 standard will take us well into the future.

Exercises

1. Add a `Fog` node to your house world, and animate it to make it foggy early in the day and clear later.

2. Add a stream next to your house. Animate the water texture on it to make it a rushing river.

Answers

TYPE   **Listing 17.4. Answer to Exercise 1.**

```
DEF F Fog {
  color              0.6 0.6 0.6
  fogType            "LINEAR"
  visibilityRange    100
}

DEF FogTS TimeSensor {
    stopTime -1
    loop TRUE
    cycleInterval 120
    # 2 minute days
}

DEF Interp ScalarInterpolator {
    key [ 0 0.5 1 ]
    keyValue [ 20 150 20 ]
}

ROUTE FogTS.fraction_changed TO Interp.set_fraction
ROUTE Interp.value_changed TO F.set_visibilityRange
```

17

Now I'll save the preceding code in a file called 17tyve1.wrl and add it to my world in Chapter 21, "Where to Go from Here," with an Inline node like this:

```
DEF MORNING_FOG Inline {
    url ["17tyve1.wrl"]
}
```

TYPE **Listing 17.5. Answer to Exercise 2.**

```
Viewpoint {
    position      -10.0473 -19.6837 25.022
    orientation   0.972642 -0.185814 -0.139428  0.126141
}

Inline { url "14tyve1.wrl" }

Transform {
    translation   2.15258 -24.771 -9.54302
    rotation      -0.00219377 0.999686 -0.0249765  3.1417
    scale  0.145221 1.20904 3.64254
    children [
        Shape {
    appearance Appearance {
      texture ImageTexture {
        url "water.gif"
      }

      textureTransform DEF TT TextureTransform {
        translation 0 0
        rotation    0
        scale       2 20
        center      0.5 0.5
      }
    }
    geometry IndexedFaceSet {
      coord Coordinate {
        point      [ -10 10 10,
                  10 10 10,
                  14.6126 1.10876 -11.5709,
                  -5.38744 1.10876 -11.5709,
                  8.49806 4.20742 2.30721,
                  -11.5019 4.20742 2.30721,
                  10 5.13217 5.01691,
                  -10 5.13217 5.01691,
                  5.24558 3.70158 -5.59115,
                  -14.7544 3.70158 -5.59115,
                  4.47459 4.43344 -0.865774,
                  -15.5254 4.43344 -0.865774 ]
      }

      coordIndex    [ 5, 7, 6, 4, -1, 7, 0, 1,
                  6, -1, 3, 9, 8, 2, -1, 9,
                  11, 10, 8, -1, 11, 5, 4, 10,
                  -1 ]
```

continues

Listing 17.5. continued

```
            ccw    TRUE
            solid TRUE
            creaseAngle 0.5
        }
            }
            ]
}
DEF Time_R TimeSensor {
    cycleInterval 10
    stopTime -1
    loop TRUE
}

DEF S Script {
    eventIn SFFloat fraction
    eventOut SFVec2f transform
    field SFVec2f temp 0 0

    url "vrmlscript:
        function fraction(value) {
            temp[1] = value;
            transform = temp;
        }"
}

ROUTE Time_R.fraction_changed TO S.fraction
ROUTE S.transform TO TT.set_translation
```

☐ You can find the complete VRML files for the preceding exercise on the CD-ROM at \Source\Answers.

17

Day 18

Collision

I have mentioned several times throughout this book the notion that VRML prevents users from walking through walls and keeps the avatar's feet on the ground when walking up or down hills or stairs. This is a major feature of VRML. It prevents the disorientation that would accompany penetrating seemingly solid objects. It also preserves the illusion that the world is tactile and substantial. Normally, these features are available without you, the author, doing anything. But you can turn them off and modify them to work differently for special purposes. You can also determine when collision occurs so that you can make a noise or open a secret door. Here is what I will cover today:

- [ ] How collision works
- [ ] Terrain following and gravity
- [ ] Collision sensing
- [ ] Collision proxy

How Collision Works

In the real world, if you try to walk through a wall, you are met with a most unpleasant realization that it can't be done. Walls in the real world are solid, which is why doors exist. You also can't walk through a table or statue, and even though it might look as though you should be able to, you can't walk through a glass window. But in a virtual world, objects are just the creation of the author. They really don't have substance. So, just as the computer must figure out how to draw all the objects in the scene from the current view, it also must determine which objects are solid and prevent the avatar (and, therefore, the current viewpoint) from going through them. In VRML, this is known as *collision detection.*

Implementing collision detection is not as easy as it might seem. When you tell the user interface of the browser to walk forward a step, it actually moves the viewpoint, instantly, from the current location to a point one step forward, and then rerenders. Performing this action over and over again is what gives a visitor to a virtual world the feeling of motion. Therefore, it's not enough to check whether an object is in the way at your new location; you must perform this check for the entire area that you could have been in as you moved from one spot to the next. (See Figure 18.1.)

Figure 18.1.

Collision detection in a virtual world.

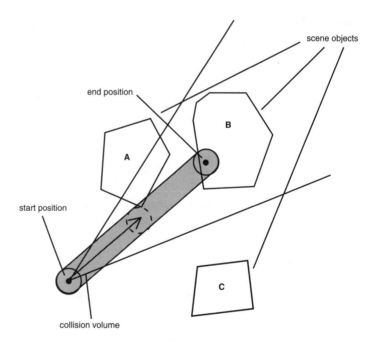

Remember, in VRML the avatar is a cylinder, so Figure 18.1 is a top view of a collision problem. As you can see, object B collides with the end position of the avatar, and object A collides with the path from the start to the end position. In this example, the avatar will collide at object A, because it is nearer to the start location, and the avatar will be positioned at the point of the dotted circle.

The previously described behavior is not dictated by VRML. Some browsers do a very quick collision test, comparing only the line of the center of movement. This test will miss the collision with object A, but it is legal in VRML. Other browsers do more accurate and complex tests to give the user a more natural feel when they're moving through the world. CosmoPlayer performs full volume collision and even slides off angled objects. In the example, the avatar would slide off object A and continue to move in the same direction, displaced enough to miss the object.

Terrain Following and Gravity

Going back to the real world, if you step off a balcony, you immediately begin falling to the ground, due to the inescapable effects of gravity. In a virtual world, gravity is no more automatic than collision. The browser must compute its effect and then adjust the avatar position accordingly. The feature of VRML that applies gravity is called *terrain following*. Its basic job is to keep the avatar's feet on the ground. If the avatar's feet leave the ground because of stepping off a ledge, terrain following uses gravity to pull it down until the feet land on something (virtually) solid. The test of whether the avatar has hit the ground is very similar to the test used for collision during forward motion, except that the collision volume is applied vertically rather than horizontally.

In addition to applying gravity and making the avatar fall to the ground, terrain following has one more test it must perform. An avatar in VRML always moves horizontally when walking. If you are walking toward an uphill slope, you are essentially walking into the side of that hill. I mentioned before that the avatarSize field of the NavigationInfo node has a step-height component. With this information, the terrain-following algorithm can detect the avatar boring into the side of the hill and decide if the slope is shallow enough (according to the step height) to allow the avatar to walk up the hill. If so, the avatar is raised up so that the avatar is no longer buried in the hill. As the avatar walks forward up the hill, he or she walks up the slope. When the avatar is walking downhill, the avatar's feet eventually leave the ground just by walking forward, and gravity naturally pulls it back down to the ground. In this way, avatars can walk up and down hills, ramps, and staircases.

In VRML, gravity is always applied in the negative y direction of the local coordinate space of the currently bound Viewpoint node. This means that you can walk on the ceiling of a room, as long as you bind to a viewpoint rotated 180°! Many interesting effects are possible with this feature. VRML really handles only flat worlds. Gravity always points down. But you can make it possible to walk on the surface of a sphere by simply changing the rotation angle of the Viewpoint's parent Transformation. You can do this in VRMLScript by using the vector difference of the SFRotation class, just as you did with the skyscraper placement example from Chapter 11, "Allowing Users and Objects to Interact." Listing 18.1 is an example that uses the position output from a ProximitySensor to constantly adjust the orientation of the viewpoint.

Listing 18.1. Constantly adjusting the viewpoint using ProximitySensor.

TYPE

```
DEF PS ProximitySensor { }

DEF VT Transform {
    children Viewpoint {
        position 0 102 5
    }
}

Shape {
    geometry Sphere { radius 100 }
    appearance Appearance {
        material Material {
            diffuseColor 0.5 0.5 1
            emissiveColor 0 0 0.5
        }
    }
}

# place a few objects on the sphere to make it interesting
Transform {
    translation 0 100 0
    children DEF S Shape {
        appearance Appearance {
            material Material { diffuseColor 0 0.8 0 }
        }
        geometry Cone { }
    }
}
Transform {
    translation 0 100 0
    center 0 -100 0
    rotation 1 0 0 1
    children USE S
}
Transform {
    translation 0 100 0
    center 0 -100 0
    rotation 1 0 0 -1
    children USE S
}

DEF S Script {
    eventIn SFVec3f position
    eventOut SFRotation rotation
    url "vrmlscript:
```

18

```
        function position(value) {
            rotation = new SFRotation(
                            new SFVec3f(0,1,0),
                            value);
        }"
}

ROUTE PS.position_changed TO S.position
ROUTE S.rotation TO VT.set_rotation
```

You can use this technique to create worlds on the outside of cylinders, the inside of a wheel (such as a space station), or even the inside of an extruded surface.

The rate at which gravity pulls you down is left up to the browser. Most browsers pull you down at about the same rate that gravity would on earth. Some browsers accelerate you as you fall—as you would in the real world—and others let you fall at a constant rate. The terrain-following and gravity features of VRML go a long way toward giving visitors to your world a feeling of reality.

Collision Sensing

The collision-detection and terrain-following features of VRML are enabled automatically. But you can use a Collision node to control various capabilities of these features. This node is one of the grouping nodes and, therefore, has a lot in common with the Group and Transform nodes. Here is its definition:

```
Collision {
  eventIn        MFNode    addChildren
  eventIn        MFNode    removeChildren
  exposedField   MFNode    children        []
  exposedField   SFBool    collide         TRUE
  field          SFVec3f   bboxCenter      0 0 0
  field          SFVec3f   bboxSize        -1 -1 -1
  field          SFNode    proxy           NULL
  eventOut       SFTime    collideTime
}
```

Like the other grouping nodes, Collision has children, bboxCenter, and bboxSize fields, and the addChildren and removeChildren eventIns. But the children of this node have their collision behavior controlled by the various fields of their parent Collision node. For instance, the collide flag can be used to disable collision detection entirely for the children. If this flag is set to FALSE, you can walk, or fall, right through these objects. This is an interesting effect for many purposes. You might make the smoke coming out of the fire from an object textured with a translucent smoke image. You can see it, but you also would want to walk right through it. The same might be true of water. Place a Collision node with collide set to FALSE and you can walk right through the waterfall example in the preceding chapter, perhaps into a hidden cave. In fact, you can use this feature for any atmospheric effect you create out of geometry that you don't want to have substance. Another example of when you would want to turn off collision is when you have secret portals hidden in blank walls.

Because collide is an exposedField, you can control it like any other behavior in VRML. You could, for instance, make a hidden doorway solid until some puzzle was solved, and then allow avatars to walk through it by sending a value of FALSE to the set_collide eventIn.

The collideTime eventOut is a very useful capability of the Collision node. Whenever your avatar collides with a child of a Collision node, its collideTime eventOut is generated. Because it sends a SFTime value, it can be routed directly to an AudioClip to play a bumping sound when you run into a wall. It can also be used to start an animation. Listing 18.2 is an example in which a tall cylinder falls over when you bump into it.

TYPE **Listing 18.2. A tall cylinder falls over when bumped into.**

```
DEF C Collision {
    children DEF T Transform {
        translation 0 4 0
        center 0 -5 0

        children Shape {
            appearance Appearance {
                material Material {
                    diffuseColor 1.0 0.5 0.5
                }
            }
            geometry Cylinder { height 10 }
        }
    }
}

DEF TS TimeSensor {
    cycleInterval 5
}

DEF OI OrientationInterpolator {
    key [ 0 0.3 0.5 0.7 0.8 0.9 0.95 1 ]
    keyValue [ 0 0 1 0,    0 0 1 0.3,
               0 0 1 0.8, 0 0 1 1.57,
               0 0 1 1.3, 0 0 1 1.57,
               0 0 1 1.5, 0 0 1 1.57 ]
}

ROUTE C.collideTime TO TS.startTime
ROUTE TS.fraction_changed TO OI.set_fraction
ROUTE OI.value_changed TO T.set_rotation
```

I was able to create this example without a `Script` node because the `collideTime` eventOut can be used to start an animation. Routing this output to a script would allow you to create even more interesting behavior with the `collideTime` eventOut.

Collision Proxy

The `Collision` node has three features in addition to the features it shares with the other grouping nodes: enabling and disabling collisions, generating an event when an object is collided with, and *collision proxies*. I talked about the first two features already. A collision proxy is geometry that is used in the collision test in place of the actual rendered geometry. Imagine that you have a table with a high level of detail. The edges of the top are rounded, and the legs have an intricate shape. This table might have a few hundred polygons, made this complex because it is an important object for your visitors to see. But colliding with hundreds of polygons is often very inefficient, and really unnecessary. A table leg might have many polygons because of the detail of a gentle curve. This might be important for rendering but certainly is not important for collision detection. A simple box surrounding the leg might be sufficient to solve this problem. The `proxy` field provides just this capability. It is an `SFNode`, which can have a single shape or a grouping node with an entire object hierarchy under it. Listing 18.3 is a simple example of a table with a proxy used for collision. Because the table is very complex, I have used an `Inline` node. Figure 18.2 shows what this scene looks like.

TYPE   **Listing 18.3. A table with a proxy used for collision.**

```
Collision {
    children Inline { url "table.wrl" }

    proxy Group {
        children [
            Transform {
                children DEF S Shape {
                    geometry Box {
                        size 4.15588 4.15589 4.15588
                    }
                }
                translation 2.49776 -1.37441 -2.90612
                scale        0.134072 0.802507 0.139992
            }               Transform {
                children USE S
                translation -3.30742 -1.37441 -6.27566
                scale        0.134072 0.802507 0.139992
            }               Transform {
                children USE S
                translation -3.29478 -1.37441 -2.90035
                scale        0.134072 0.802507 0.139992
            }               Transform {
```

continues

Listing 18.3. continued

```
              children USE S
              translation 2.79735 -1.37442 -6.33438
              scale        0.134072 0.802507 0.139992
     }              Transform {
              children USE S
              translation -0.396752 0.531491 -4.60492
              scale        1.77348 0.114698 1.18053
     }
  ]
 }
}
```

Figure 18.2.

A complex table with a simple collision proxy.

NOTE

In this scene, I have added the proxy geometry as visible, translucent boxes so that you can see where it is in relation to the real table. Proxies do not normally render.

Adding proxies to complex geometry allows you to reduce the overhead of the collision calculation. In extreme cases, you can include a proxy for the entire scene with very simple walls and simple incline planes in place of staircases. For simple geometry, though, the computational overhead is not great, so proxies might not be needed.

Summary

Collision is yet another of VRML's powerful features that make virtual worlds more realistic. When collision is used along with terrain following, worlds are easy and intuitive to navigate. The `Collision` node provides many additional functions, allowing you to tailor the collision capabilities of your world to suit your needs. You can switch off collision in certain parts of your world for special atmospheric effects or secret doors. You can sense when an object is collided with to start an animation or play a sound. And you can define simpler substitute objects for use for collision detection and terrain following. This proxy geometry can make the performance of collision tests, and, therefore, that of your entire virtual world, much faster.

Q&A

Q If you fall until you hit the floor, what happens if there is no floor below you? Why haven't I fallen forever in all the examples in this book that don't have a floor below?

A Some browsers, CosmoPlayer in particular, check to see whether a floor exists anywhere below you. If there is a floor, you fall to it. If not, the browser switches off the gravity feature until you are again over a floor.

Q Why is the handling of collisions VRML-browser specific?

A That seemingly basic question brings up some interesting philosophies of the VRML standard-setting process. VRML focuses on creating a standard way for authored scenes to be represented in a text-file format. The standard is important if everyone is to be able to visit all worlds using different browsers. Yet, the standard-setting committee believes in competition. Once a VRML file is loaded into the browser, each browser technology company can make its own interpretation of many actions in the world. This philosophy seems to bring out the best innovations in the browser producing companies. But, more importantly, it gives flexibility to each browser developer to make independent decisions about all the trade-offs that need to be considered. For example, if a developer decides to add intricate texturing routines to his browser, he may not have time left over in the frame-display loop to process intricate collision-detection routines. Yet, if collision detection is to be a selling point of the browser, the VRML standard leaves room for a browser developer to add all kinds of interesting reactions to the collision event. Hopefully, at some point in the near future, all the best routines will be in every VRML browser. At that point, the technology will have matured. Think about where spreadsheet programs are today versus ten years ago. Ten years ago, spreadsheet developers had to deal with many trade-offs. Now, all the best features are in all the spreadsheets. Time will dictate which features are most important in a VRML browser.

18

Q Are you suggesting yet another trade-off even in the standard setting process?

A Yes. A standard setting committee must walk the delicate line between not being specific enough and being too specific. If the standard is not specific enough, it will not be used because developers won't be able to create a rich enough product using the standard. If it is too specific, it will limit the future of that technology as new innovations don't fit well within the existing standard structure. The VRML standard setting process is a case study of success. All standard setting groups should look at how so many people worked together so well to create the VRML standard in a very short timeframe.

Exercises

1. Put a secret door in the back wall of your house.
2. Add a bumping sound to go off whenever you run into the floor or any of the walls of your house.

Answers

For Exercise 1, I use the `Transform` node for the house structure I created in Chapter 4, "Building Complex Objects." I replace the `Transform` for the house walls with two `Transform` nodes. The first is just the original geometry with an additional doorway placed in the back wall. The second is a door that fits exactly into the new doorway. The wall looks solid as it did before, but now the doorway is in a `Collision` node that lets the user walk right through it.

TYPE **Listing 18.4. Answer to Exercise 1.**

```
Transform {
    scale 2 2 2
    children
      Shape {
  appearance Appearance {
    material Material {
      diffuseColor        0.914894 0.444404 0.348914
    }
  }
  geometry IndexedFaceSet {
    coord Coordinate {
      point        [ -1 1 1,
                      -1 -1 1,
                       1 1 1,
                       1 -1 1,
                       1 1 -1,
                       1 -1 -1,
```

18

```
                       -1 1 -1,
                       -1 -1 -1,
                        1 2.68291 0,  #roof
                       -1 2.68291 0,  #roof
                       -0.334335 -0.995922 1,
                       -0.273211 1 1,
                        0.192442 1 1,
                        0.0190066 -0.994756 1,
                        0.019373 0.191373 1,
                       -0.333968 0.190208 1,
                       -0.334335 -0.995922 -1, #lowerleft
                        0.0190066 -0.994756 -1, #lowerright
                        0.019373 0.191373 -1,   #upperright
                       -0.333968 0.190208 -1,   #upperleft
                       -0.273211 1 -1,
                        0.192442 1 -1]
      }
      coordIndex    [ 20, 19, 16, 7, 6, -1, # add back door
                        18, 21, 4, 5, 17, -1, # add back door
                        19, 20, 21, 18, -1,   # add back door
                        6, 7, 1, 0, 9, -1,
                        2, 3, 5, 4, 8, -1,
                        0, 1, 10, 15, 11, -1,
                        13, 3, 2, 12, 14, -1,
                        14, 12, 11, 15, -1 ]

      ccw   FALSE
      solid FALSE
            convex FALSE
      creaseAngle   0.5
    }
      }
}
DEF SECRET_DOOR Collision {
  children [
   Transform {
    scale 2 2 2
    children
     Shape {
   appearance Appearance {
     material Material {
        diffuseColor  0.914894 0.444404 0.348914
     }
   }
   geometry IndexedFaceSet {
     coord Coordinate {
       point      [ -0.334335 -0.995922 -1, #lowerleft
                      0.0190066 -0.994756 -1, #lowerright
                      0.019373 0.191373 -1,   #upperright
                     -0.333968 0.190208 -1,   #upperleft
                       ]
     }
     coordIndex   [ 0, 3, 2, 1, -1 ] # solid back door
          colorIndex    [ ]
     ccw   FALSE
     solid FALSE
```

continues

Listing 18.4. continued

```
    creaseAngle    0.5
  }
    }
  }
]
collide FALSE
}
```

TYPE **Listing 18.5. Answer to Exercise 2.**

```
DEF C Collision {
  children [
      DEF HOUSE Inline {
          url ["house.wrl"]
      }
      Sound {
          maxBack 1000
          maxFront 1000
          source DEF Bump AudioClip {
              url "elecbeep.wav"
          }
      }
  ]
}
ROUTE C.collideTime TO Bump.startTime
```

☐ You can find the complete VRML files for the preceding exercise on the CD-ROM
at \Source\Answers.

18

Day 19

Prototyping

You've learned about the DEF and USE constructs for reusing pieces of a VRML scene. You've also learned about the Inline node, which allows you to place pieces of a world in a different file to better manage files and download time. Now I will show you the most powerful mechanism available in VRML for the sharing and managing of the scene. The prototyping mechanism allows you to collect pieces of a VRML scene so that they can be reused, but these parts can be made to look like any other VRML node. They can contain scripts to give them much more functionality than would be possible with the DEF mechanism. These prototypes can also be placed in separate files like the Inline node, but because they look like nodes, you can route to them and pass them to scripts. This gives you a complete extension mechanism for adding new nodes to VRML that will operate in any browser. Here is what I will cover in this chapter today:

- ☐ Prototyping concepts
- ☐ The PROTO node
- ☐ Using external prototypes
- ☐ Creating standard interfaces with prototyping
- ☐ Making a system of prototypes

Prototyping Concepts

VRML has 54 built-in nodes that let you do everything from defining simple shapes to creating complex animations and interactions. They certainly do not, however, perform every task you could ever want or need in a virtual world. But they can also be combined in many ways to perform the tasks for which any one node will not suffice. These combinations can be used to construct intricate geometric objects, complete with texture and articulated parts. Nodes can also be combined to provide building blocks of functionality not inherent in VRML. New interpolators are a good example of this. In Chapter 17, "Special Effects," I created an interpolator for multiple colors out of two existing interpolators and a Script node.

VRML nodes are like little reusable packages of functionality. This reusability is very powerful. If I create a Script node that performs some algorithm that is generally useful, I can copy that Script node into several worlds and use it there. But if I wanted to take my custom interpolator and use it in another world, I would have to collect all the nodes and routes and then tie them into my new world. If I collected all the right parts and connected them correctly, it would all work. But this is a tedious way to get the advantage of reusability. What is needed is a mechanism that enables you to put all the parts together under one name so that they can be reused as a package. The DEF facility can be used to a certain extent. As long as you can place all the nodes under a Group node, or other grouping node, you can name that top-level group and have a simple package of the desired functionality. However, you cannot place routes in this package, so it lacks the capability to represent many component types. The Inline node provides another type of packaging and has the capability to collect both nodes and routes. But both of these techniques lack the capability to give the package any sort of interface. The capability has to be fully self-contained, and this is very limiting.

Fortunately, VRML has provided a facility to create exactly what is needed, called *prototyping*, that gives authors the ability to collect nodes and routes and give them a standard interface. In fact, with prototyping, you can create extension nodes in VRML, which are added to the scene and used just like any of the built-in nodes.

The PROTO Node

The VRML prototyping mechanism consists of three parts: the *declaration*, the *implementation*, and the *instantiation*. The declaration is done using the PROTO keyword. It allows you to define the fields, exposedFields, eventIns, and eventOuts that will make up the interface to the new node. Here is the structure of a VRML prototype declaration:

```
PROTO name [ parameters ]
{
    implementation
}
```

The *name* will be used when the new extension node is instantiated, or used in a VRML world. It is like the name Transform or Viewpoint, except that it is defined by the user with the PROTO keyword. The *parameters* define the names, types, and default values for the fields and events that will make up the node's interface. They use the same format as the Script node, except that exposedFields can be defined in prototypes but not in the Script node. The *implementation* is the set of nodes and routes that implement the functionality of the extension node. Here is an example of how the Transform node would be written as a prototype:

```
PROTO Transform [
   eventIn       MFNode       addChildren
   eventIn       MFNode       removeChildren
   exposedField SFVec3f      center          0 0 0
   exposedField MFNode       children        []
   exposedField SFRotation   rotation        0 0 1  0
   exposedField SFVec3f      scale           1 1 1
   exposedField SFRotation   scaleOrientation 0 0 1  0
   exposedField SFVec3f      translation     0 0 0
   field         SFVec3f      bboxCenter      0 0 0
   field         SFVec3f      bboxSize        -1 -1 -1 ]
{
    # implementation goes here
}
```

Note how close that declaration is to the node definition format I have been using throughout this book. That should make writing your own prototype nodes an easy task.

The next part of the prototyping mechanism is the implementation. This is mostly just the set of nodes and routes that perform the desired function. But there needs to be a way to associate a field or event in the parameter list with an actual field or event of a node in the implementation. This is done using the IS keyword. The names in the parameter list don't really represent data values; they are just *aliases*, or placeholders, for fields or events in the implementation. The IS keyword is used to associate the parameter alias with the actual data value. Here is an example of a simple grouping node that takes only a children parameter:

```
PROTO MyGroup [ field MFNode myChildren [ ] ] {
    Group { children IS myChildren }
}
```

In this example, the myChildren parameter is associated with the actual children field of the Group node that implements MyGroup. Notice that myChildren is a field, whereas children is an exposedField. This example will associate only the field component of children, leaving the eventIn and eventOut components unassociated. When associating, you can associate a parameter with an entire exposedField or just one of its components. Table 19.1 describes the rules governing association.

Table 19.1. The prototype association rules.

	If the Parameter Is:			
	field	**eventIn**	**eventOut**	**exposedField**
The Actual Data Type May Be:				
field	yes	no	no	no
eventIn	no	yes	no	no
eventOut	no	no	yes	no
exposedField	yes	yes	yes	yes

Actually, the Transform node could not be implemented using the built-in nodes in VRML. Not even the Script node could duplicate its function. But one node that can be prototyped perfectly is the Inline node. Listing 19.1 shows what its prototype would look like.

TYPE   **Listing 19.1. The Inline node prototype.**

```
PROTO Inline [
    field    MFString url          []
    eventIn  MFString set_url
    eventOut MFString url_changed
    field    SFVec3f  bboxCenter 0 0 0
    field    SFVec3f  bboxSize    -1 -1 -1 ]
{
    DEF G Group {
        bboxCenter IS bboxCenter
        bboxSize IS bboxSize
    }

    DEF S Script {
        field    MFString url         IS url
        eventIn  MFString set_url      IS set_url
        eventOut MFString url_changed IS url_changed
        field    SFNode   myGroup      USE G

        url "vrmlscript:
            function doSetURL(myURL) {
                Browser.createVRMLFromURL(myURL,
                                          myGroup,
                                          "children");
            }

            function initialize() { doSetURL(url); }

            function set_url(value) {
                doSetURL(value);
                url = value;
                url_changed = value;
```

19

```
        }"
    }
}
```

The first thing to notice here is how the url is actually split into its three components: field, eventIn, and eventOut. This is because you cannot define exposedFields in a Script, so I have implemented the functionality of an exposedField with the separate components. The second thing to notice is that I have used an initialize function in the script. That's because you have to send out the original createVRMLFromURL request as soon as the node is loaded. Another interesting characteristic of this example is that it does not use routes at all! Most of the connections are done through association, and because the group node is passed to the script as a field, it need not be routed. This is rare, but happens occasionally, and it is a fine implementation of a prototype.

The third part of a prototype is its instantiation. This is where you actually include the prototyped node in your VRML file. You do this in exactly the same way that you add any other node. In fact, the power of prototyping is that prototyped nodes are identical in every way to standard nodes. You can route to and from them, and you can use DEF and USE to instantiate them. A prototyped node can be used anywhere the first node in its definition could be used. For example, Listing 19.2 is a simple example of a complete VRML scene that both defines and uses an AnimatedMaterial prototype. This prototype animates back and forth between red and green in the specified number of seconds.

Listing 19.2. VRML scene that defines and uses an
TYPE | AnimatedMaterial **prototype.**

19

```
PROTO AnimatedMaterial [ field SFTime seconds 1 ]
{
    DEF M Material { diffuseColor 1 0 0 }

    DEF TS TimeSensor {
        cycleInterval IS seconds
        stopTime -1
        loop TRUE
    }

    DEF CI ColorInterpolator {
        key [ 0 0.5 1 ]
        keyValue [ 1 0 0, 0 1 0, 1 0 0 ]
    }

    ROUTE TS.fraction_changed TO CI.set_fraction
    ROUTE CI.value_changed TO M.diffuseColor
}

Shape {
```

continues

Listing 19.2. continued

```
        appearance Appearance {
            material AnimatedMaterial { seconds 5 }
        }
        geometry Sphere { }
}
```

You can see this world by looking at 19tyv01.wrl on the CD-ROM. Notice that the AnimatedMaterial is used where a Material node would be used, because its first node is a Material. Prototyping allows you to package up lots of interesting functionality to make creation of the world easier or to create new nodes that can be used in various worlds.

Using External Prototypes

In the preceding example, I added the prototyped node at the top of the scene. If you wanted to reuse this node, you could certainly copy the entire prototype into each file where it was needed. However, VRML provides a simpler mechanism to make reusability more useful and flexible. It is called the EXTERNPROTO mechanism, and it allows you to include prototyped nodes from other files in your VRML world. If I place the prototyped node shown previously into a file called AnimatedMaterial.wrl, I could include it in any other world with this:

```
EXTERNPROTO AnimatedMaterial [ field SFTime seconds ]
"AnimatedMaterial.wrl"
```

The string given is simply a URL that is the file containing the PROTO node defining an AnimatedMaterial. Notice that the parameter does not have a default value. This is because the default is obtained from the PROTO node, so it is not allowed in the EXTERNPROTO. This is merely the declaration of a prototype that exists elsewhere. Its parameter list must match the prototype exactly, but the names of the EXTERNPROTO and the corresponding PROTO need not match. This way, you can include many different prototypes with the same original name. You simply make their names unique in the EXTERNPROTO declaration and use that name to create instances.

Creating Standard Interfaces with Prototyping

One powerful feature of the EXTERNPROTO mechanism is its capability to allow the creation of a standard interface to some set of VRML components. Imagine that you want to create a prototype for a set of doors. These doors can be wooden, glass, or even stone. They can have peepholes and can even squeak when they open, and they include working doorbells. The

19

interface to all these doors can be made the same. Here is an example of such a door prototype that specifies only the size in its interface:

```
EXTERNPROTO Door [ field SFVec2f size ]
"door.wrl"
```

I can then create a corresponding prototype, with this interface, that implements any type of door I want. I can then create three separate doors like this:

```
EXTERNPROTO StoneDoor [ field SFVec2f size ]
"stonedoor.wrl"

EXTERNPROTO WoodDoor [ field SFVec2f size ]
"wooddoor.wrl"

EXTERNPROTO GlassDoor [ field SFVec2f size ]
"http://someplace.com/doors/slidingGlassDoor.wrl"
```

Now I can include as many of each type of door as I want and can include them like any other shape in my world. Listing 19.3 is a sample implementation of a simple door.

Type **Listing 19.3. Implementation of a simple door prototype.**

```
PROTO Door [ field SFVec3f size ]
{
    DEF Touch TouchSensor { }
    DEF Rotate Transform {
        center -2 0 0
        children [
            Shape {
                appearance Appearance {
                    material Material { }
                    texture ImageTexture { url "oak.jpg" }
                }
                geometry Box { size IS size }
            }
        ]
    }

    DEF OpenInterp OrientationInterpolator {
        key [ 0 1 ]
        keyValue [ 0 1 0 0, 0 1 0 -2 ]
    }
    DEF Open TimeSensor { cycleInterval 2 }

    DEF CloseInterp OrientationInterpolator {
        key [ 0 1 ]
        keyValue [ 0 1 0 -2, 0 1 0 0 ]
    }
    DEF Close TimeSensor { cycleInterval 3 }

    DEF S Script {
```

continues

19

Listing 19.3. continued

```
        eventIn SFTime touchTime
        eventOut SFTime startClose
        url "vrmlscript:
            function touchTime(value) {
                startClose = value + 4;
            }"
    }

    ROUTE Touch.touchTime TO Open.startTime
    ROUTE Touch.touchTime TO S.touchTime
    ROUTE Open.fraction_changed TO OpenInterp.set_fraction
    ROUTE S.startClose TO Close.startTime
    ROUTE Close.fraction_changed TO CloseInterp.set_fraction
    ROUTE OpenInterp.value_changed TO Rotate .rotation
    ROUTE CloseInterp.value_changed TO Rotate .rotation
}
```

The most powerful use of this standard interface mechanism is in including prototyped nodes from several sites in your world. For instance, several companies might all make door prototypes that are actually portals to their own sites. When you open the door and walk through, you might be whisked away to that company's Web site, complete with an animated transition. Companies could add an animated logo over the doorway, or a catchy tune could be coming from another door to attract potential visitors. You could include any door without knowing about the contents because they all have a standard interface.

Making a System of Prototypes

Because you can define the interface to your prototyped nodes, you can give some of your prototypes the capability to understand and interact with others. If one of the parameters to a prototype you create is an SFNode field that takes a node that is another prototype you have defined, the first prototype can use the interface to the second. Using this technique, you can create an entire system of prototypes that work together to solve a problem. For instance, if you have a simple physics system with balls bouncing around inside a box, you can create a Ball prototype and a PhysicsBox prototype to contain the balls. The Ball prototype might understand how to move at a certain velocity through a fluid that adds friction and, therefore, slows the ball down over time. It might also understand how to change the direction of the ball when it strikes another object. The Ball prototype might look like the following:

```
EXTERNPROTO Ball [
    eventIn  SFFloat viscosity 0 # amount of friction
    eventOut SFVec3f currentPosition
    field    SFVec3f initialPosition 0 0 0
    field    SFVec3f initialForce 1 1 1
    field    SFFloat radius 1
    eventIn  SFTime  startTime
    eventIn  SFVec3f collision ]
"Ball.wrl"
```

After you create a ball with an initialPosition and initialForce, you send it a startTime, at which point it begins moving, being slowed over time by the value of viscosity. It continues moving until either it is stopped by friction or a collision event is received. The value of collision is the normal of the wall with which the ball collided, which influences the direction of the bounce. Actually, this normal would not have to be a wall; it could be perpendicular to the point of contact with another ball, allowing balls to bounce off each other.

You can also create the PhysicsBox prototype, which has an SFNode event as one of its parameters. This is an instance of a Ball node, which is added to the list and used in the physics simulation. Here is the prototype for the PhysicsBox:

```
EXTERNPROTO PhysicsBox [
    eventIn  SFNode  addBall
    field    MFNode  ballList [ ]
    field    SFVec3f size 1 1 1
    eventOut SFTime  startTime ]
"PhysicsBox.wrl"
```

To use this system, you would add the following scene to the file containing the preceding prototype declarations:

```
DEF TS TouchSensor { }
DEF PB PhysicsBox {
    size 20 20 20
    ballList [
        Ball {
            initialPosition 1 2 3
            initialForce 0.5 0.1 0.1
        }
        Ball {
            initialPosition 3 3 4
            initialForce 0.1 0.5 0.4
        }
        Ball {
            initialPosition 5 2 1
            initialForce 0.3 0.6 0.2
        }
    ]
}

ROUTE TS.touchTime TO PB.startTime
```

Now when you click the box, the simulation starts. The startTime eventIn of the PhysicsBox is sent as an event to all the balls in the ballList. The PhysicsBox has a TimeSensor that runs a script at each time step. The script reads the position of each ball and sees whether the ball intersects with a wall or another ball. If it does, the script computes the perpendicular vector of that wall or the point of contact between the two balls. The ball then changes its velocity vector to simulate bouncing off the wall or the other ball. New balls can be added with the addBall eventIn. A new ball is immediately sent the time the add event was received so that it can immediately start moving. This would be an extremely simplistic simulation, but it can

19

be made more complex without changing the interface. For instance, you could make the balls squish when they strike a surface to simulate soft rubber balls, or you could change the color of a wall as it is struck. You could even imagine creating a 3D Ping-Pong game using this system!

Summary

The prototyping mechanism of VRML gives you a powerful tool for adding new, reusable functionality to your worlds. A prototype consists of the declaration, with the PROTO keyword and parameters making up the interface; the implementation, with all the nodes and routes making up the prototype definition; and the instantiation, in which the new node is actually put to use. The EXTERNPROTO mechanism allows you to include prototypes by adding their declaration and placing their implementation in a separate file. This can make creation of VRML scenes much simpler because pieces can be developed separately and then assembled. Standard interfaces allow you to create many different prototypes that share an interface, to allow you to separate the form from the function of the node. Entire prototype systems can be constructed to interact with each other in interesting ways.

Q&A

Q So, prototyping is the answer to many of my questions from previous chapters, right?

A Yes. The PROTO statement becomes the ultimate extender of the VRML language because anyone can, in effect, add to the list of available VRML nodes by creating a prototype. For example, when you asked me why there weren't more primitive geometry nodes in VRML, I said it was because the IndexedFaceSet was the catch-all. Well, it is also because you can define your own VRML primitive geometry nodes by prototyping objects you create from the existing nodes. For example, the answer to Exercise 1 in this chapter prototypes the house with a secret door I showed you in Exercise 1 of Chapter 18, "Collision." I could now create a simple House node by creating a prototype and calling it a primitive geometry that everyone could use when creating basic houses. It would work very similarly to the Box node.

Q But how does the browser developer anticipate my prototypes to have them render as fast as possible in the browser?

A OK. You see there is a catch. It might be possible for the browser developer to take a shortcut to rendering your prototyped node if he or she were aware of its existence. The hope is that most other nodes that are created from existing VRML 2.0 standard nodes will render in a reasonable amount of time because a lot of thought was put into creating the standard set of nodes.

Q **But, won't there be new nodes that arise with different needs because VRML will be used for new purposes?**

A Yes. There will be a VRML 3, VRML 4, and so on, which will continue to create new standard nodes where there is a demonstrated need for that specific node type. This is exactly how the HTML standard has progressed over time.

Q **If prototyping is so powerful, is there an example of anyone using it to extend VRML in a truly innovative way?**

A I am sure there are many examples, but the one that comes to mind is the Living Worlds standard-setting group, which is extending VRML 2 to be able to keep track of shared objects across multiple VRML worlds. For example, the group's vision includes extending VRML 2 through the PROTO statement to allow you to take an object from one world and leave it in another one. The group has lots of interesting ways they are extending VRML 2 in a standard manner. If you are interested, look at their Web site at `http://www.livingworlds.com/`. If the link is no longer active, search for Living Worlds in your favorite search engine, or look for a book on the subject at your favorite computer book store.

Exercises

1. Create prototypes for some of the objects you have created in other chapters so they can be used by other authors.

2. Make the teleporter created in Chapter 14, "Animated Viewpoints and Binding," into a prototype, and make it take you to a URL specified in the interface. Put three of these teleporters around your property, and have them take you to your three favorite Web sites.

Answers

For Exercise 1, I'll show you how I create a prototype for the secret door exercise in Chapter 18. I have chosen to make the house scale and house color open for the user to define.

TYPE **Listing 19.4. Answer to Exercise 1.**

```
PROTO HouseWithSecretDoor [
    field    SFVec3f   scale 1 1 1
    field    SFColor   diffuseColor 0.5 0.5 0 ]
{
    Transform {
      children [
        Transform {
          children
```

continues

Listing 19.4. continued

```
        Shape {
    appearance Appearance {
      material Material {
        diffuseColor IS diffuseColor
      }
    }
    geometry IndexedFaceSet {
      coord Coordinate {
        point [ -1 1 1,
                -1 -1 1,
                 1 1 1,
                 1 -1 1,
                 1 1 -1,
                 1 -1 -1,
                -1 1 -1,
                -1 -1 -1,
                 1 2.68291 0,  #roof
                -1 2.68291 0,  #roof
                -0.334335 -0.995922 1,
                -0.273211 1 1,
                 0.192442 1 1,
                 0.0190066 -0.994756 1,
                 0.019373 0.191373 1,
                -0.333968 0.190208 1,
                -0.334335 -0.995922 -1,  #lowerleft
                 0.0190066 -0.994756 -1, #lowerright
                 0.019373 0.191373 -1,   #upperright
                -0.333968 0.190208 -1,   #upperleft
                -0.273211 1 -1,
                  0.192442 1 -1]
      }
          coordIndex [ 20, 19, 16, 7, 6, -1, # add back door
                       18, 21, 4, 5, 17, -1, # add back door
                       19, 20, 21, 18, -1,   # add back door
                       6, 7, 1, 0, 9, -1,
                       2, 3, 5, 4, 8, -1,
                       0, 1, 10, 15, 11, -1,
                       13, 3, 2, 12, 14, -1,
                       14, 12, 11, 15, -1 ]
      ccw FALSE
      solid FALSE
      creaseAngle 0.5
        convex FALSE
        }
      }
    }
    DEF SECRET_DOOR Collision {
      children [
        Transform {
          children
            Shape {
          appearance Appearance {
            material Material {
              diffuseColor IS diffuseColor
```

```
              }
            }
          geometry IndexedFaceSet {
            coord Coordinate {
              point [ -0.334335 -0.995922 -1,  #lowerleft
                       0.0190066 -0.994756 -1, #lowerright
                       0.019373 0.191373 -1,   #upperright
                      -0.333968 0.190208 -1,   #upperleft
                         ]
            }
            coordIndex [ 0, 3, 2, 1, -1 ] # solid back door
            ccw    FALSE
            solid  FALSE
            creaseAngle 0.5
          }
            }
          }
        ]
        collide FALSE
      }
    ]
    scale IS scale
  }
}
```

TYPE **Listing 19.5. Answer to Exercise 2: Create the Prototype.**

```
PROTO Teleporter [
    field     MFString url [ ]
    field     SFColor  diffuseColor 0.6 0.6 0 ]
{

Transform {
    children [
        DEF PS ProximitySensor {
            size 1.2 1.75 1.2
        }
        DEF Transporter Transform {
            scale 0.3 0.3 0.3
            children [
                Transform {
                    translation 0 -3 0
                    children DEF FromPad Shape {
                        geometry Cylinder{
                            radius 2
                            height 0.2
                        }
                        appearance Appearance {
                            material Material {
                                diffuseColor IS diffuseColor
                            }
                        }
                    }
                }
```

continues

Listing 19.5. continued

```
                        }
                    Transform {
                        translation 0 4 0
                        children USE FromPad
                    }
                    Collision {
                        collide FALSE
                        children Shape {
                            geometry IndexedFaceSet {
                                coord Coordinate {
                                    point [ -1.4 -3 1.4, 1.4 -3 1.4,
                                            1.4 -3 -1.4, -1.4 -3 -1.4,
                                            -1.4 4 1.4, 1.4 4 1.4,
                                            1.4 4 -1.4, -1.4 4 -1.4 ]
                                }
                                coordIndex [ 0 4 5 1 -1, 1 5 6 2 -1,
                                             2 6 7 3 -1, 3 7 4 0 -1 ]
                            }
                            appearance Appearance {
                                material DEF TP_MAT Material {
                                    diffuseColor 0 0 0
                                    specularColor 0 0 0
                                    ambientIntensity 0
                                    emissiveColor 0.6 0.6 0.6
                                    transparency 1
                                }
                            }
                        }
                    }
                ]
            }
        ]
    }

    DEF TP_TRANSP ScalarInterpolator {
        key [ 0 0.4 0.6 1 ]
        keyValue [ 1 0 0 1 ]
    }

    DEF TP_COLOR ColorInterpolator {
        key [0, .05, .125, .2, .27,
            .35, .43, .4999, .5, .55,
            .625, .7, .77, .85, .93, 1]
        keyValue [.6 .6 .6,
                1 1 1,
                .2 .8 .2,
                0 1 0,
                0 0 0,
                .2 .2 .7,
                0 0 .2,
                .2 .2 .2,
                .2 .2 .2,
                0 0 .2,
                .2 .8 .2,
```

```
               0 1 0,
               0 0 0,
               .2 .2 .7,
               0 .2 0,
               .6 .6 .6]
},

DEF Time TimeSensor {
    cycleInterval 10
}

DEF SwitchTime TimeSensor {
    cycleInterval 5
}

DEF S Script {
    eventIn SFBool isActive
    field MFString url IS url
    url "vrmlscript:
        function isActive(value) {
            if (!value) Browser.loadURL(url);
        }"
}

ROUTE PS.enterTime TO Time.startTime
ROUTE Time.fraction_changed TO TP_COLOR.set_fraction
ROUTE Time.fraction_changed TO TP_TRANSP.set_fraction
ROUTE TP_COLOR.value_changed TO TP_MAT.set_emissiveColor
ROUTE TP_TRANSP.value_changed TO TP_MAT.set_transparency
ROUTE PS.enterTime TO SwitchTime.startTime
ROUTE SwitchTime.isActive TO S.isActive

}
```

19

TYPE **Listing 19.6. Answer to Exercise 2: Use the Prototype.**

```
EXTERNPROTO Teleporter [ field MFString url []
                         field SFColor  diffusecolor  ]
"Teleport.wrl"

Transform {
   children [
      translation 2 0 5
      Teleporter {
      url ["houses.wrl"]
         diffusecolor 1 0 1
      }
}
Transform {
   children [
      translation 10 0 0
      Teleporter {
      url ["13tyve1.wrl"]
```

continues

Listing 19.6. Answer to Exercise 2: Use the Prototype.

```
              diffusecolor 1 1 0
        }
}
Transform {
  children [
      translation -10 0 0
      Teleporter {
      url ["03tyve1.wrl"]
          diffusecolor 0 1 1
      }
}
```

☐ You can find the complete VRML files for the preceding exercise on the CD-ROM at \Source\Answers.

19

Day 20

Creating a Composite Multimedia Document

Now that you have learned the details of creating VRML 2 worlds, you can focus on enhancing Web pages by integrating VRML worlds with HTML text. The HTML 3.2 standard adds frames to the growing list of markup tags. With frames, you can display multiple Web documents in separate frames through your HTML 3.2–compliant Web browser. One frame can display a VRML world while one or more other frames provide text and navigation aids to help your audience read about and interact with your VRML world. The result is a very intuitive, responsive, and aesthetic presentation to your audience.

In this chapter you'll learn about the following topics:

☐ How frames work

☐ Creating frames using standard HTML tags

☐ Choosing the best options for your VRML frame

☐ Using the Anchor node in VRML to communicate with the HTML

☐ Using the <A> tag in HTML to communicate with a VRML frame

How Frames Work

A frame is a rectangular area of a Web page that can be navigated independently from the rest of the page. If you use a window-based operating system, you might have heard the word *pane* before. Think of a pane as a frame, and vice versa. File-management software uses frames. One frame shows you a directory of file folders you can access from your hard drive. Another frame shows you the file contents of each folder, based on which folder you have currently selected in the file folder frame. A third frame is sometimes added to preview each file through a file viewer available in that frame. Within a Web browser, each frame can display a different document and can change which document is currently displayed.

I'll help you investigate frames by way of an example that I'll build from scratch. Imagine that the year is 2020. An astronomer named Galner has discovered a unique trio of planets in a distant galaxy called Helvetica. I have been asked to create a Web site to present information about the planets. I decide to use VRML to display a model of the planets that I will design using the VRML 2 techniques outlined in Chapters 1–19. You've seen that VRML is a powerful language for presenting three-dimensional content. Yet the site would be lacking without some narration to accompany the VRML model. I could use an audio track or perhaps a movie to narrate a trip through the planets. A text presentation would allow the audience to absorb the material at their own pace and review specific information at any time.

Using frames, I can provide all four (three-dimensional model, audio, video, and text) media. Each frame I create can contain a separate document that can be navigated independently. I decide to use three frames to present information about the three planets, which are referred to as GX1, GX2, and GX3. One frame will contain a VRML model of the planets, another will contain an index to the text material, and a third will contain narrative with specific documentation on each planet. Figure 20.1 shows the Galner System Web site using frames.

Figure 20.1.

A VRML scene of three spheres in a frame, with a narrative frame and an index frame to add text to the presentation.

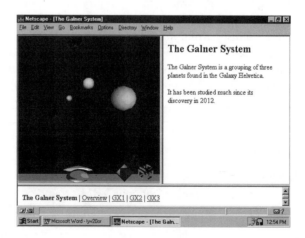

The upper-left frame contains the VRML world. The upper-right frame contains narrative text that changes as a visitor interacts with the site. The bottom frame contains an index of hyperlinks to the HTML-based narrative documents.

Frames add some flexibility to the presentation style. Consider the index of hyperlinks to each planet in the lower frame. Without using frames, a Web visitor would lose direct access to the index whenever he or she scrolled down within a document or clicked a hyperlink. With frames, I can place an index in a nonscrollable frame, which will always be immediately available for navigating the Web site. Each time someone clicks a link in the index, I can open the appropriate document in the narrative text frame. Every time I open the narrative, I can move to a viewpoint in the VRML frame that best relates to the narrative. Therefore, I can coordinate the frames to work together to best present the material.

NOTE   Frames were first introduced to the Web by Netscape in its Navigator 2.0 browser before frames were a part of standard HTML.

HTML 3.2 defines the tags and attributes I'll use to create multiple frames and set up communication among frames. Similarly, VRML 2 defines node fields and routing events that I'll use to communicate with other frames. My audience will be able to click an object in the VRML frame, and I will open the related text in the narrative frame. At the same time, I can move to a different viewpoint in the VRML to focus best on the object being described in the narrative frame.

NOTE   VRML use is enhanced in a framed environment. The VRML world is smaller when rendered in a frame than when it's one complete document. A smaller world renders faster and animates with less flicker when it's being explored.

20

TIP   I can use the frame to fix the dimensions of the VRML world. For technical illustrations, framing ensures that the scale is always intact without horizontal or vertical distortion.

Because you must use HTML to create a framed Web site, I have assumed that you understand the basics of HTML tags. If you don't have any experience with HTML, you can still build simple frame sites using the examples that follow. HTML is an ASCII-based standard, the same as VRML. You can use an ASCII editor to create, modify, and save HTML files. HTML files should have the extension `.htm` or `.html` so that your Web browser will recognize them as HTML documents. For more information, read Laura Lemay's book called *Teach Yourself HTML 3.2 in a Week*, published by Sams.net.

Creating Frames Using Standard HTML Tags

A Web browser will use frames to display multiple documents simultaneously whenever it opens a frame definition document. The frame definition document creates the frames, defines the size and behavior of each frame, and assigns a file and a name to each frame. Listing 20.1 shows the HTML tags for the Galner System's frame definition document located in file `galner.htm` on the CD-ROM.

TYPE

Listing 20.1. HTML tags for the Galner System frame definition document.

```
<HTML>
<HEAD>
<TITLE>The Galner System</TITLE>
<FRAMESET ROWS="*,50">
   <FRAMESET COLS="*,300">
      <FRAME SRC="galner.wrl" NAME="VRML" NORESIZE>
      <FRAME SRC="overview.htm" NAME="DESC">
   </FRAMESET>
   <FRAME SRC="gxindex.htm" NAME="INDEX" SCROLLING=NO>
</FRAMESET>
</HEAD>
</HTML>
```

NEW TERM   The *frame definition document* is the HTML page that contains the layout of the frames and the names of the documents that will fill the frames.

The `<FRAMESET>` and `</FRAMESET>` tags replace the familiar `<BODY>` and `</BODY>` tags when you use a frame presentation style. The frameset tag tells the browser you want to display multiple documents in frames rather than as a singular document body. The frameset tag sets the number of frames, the size of each frame, and the layout of the frames. Using a ROWS attribute, the example sets up two horizontal frames, the bottom one being 50 pixels in height. By using the asterisk as a wildcard, I am telling the browser to fill the rest of the browser window with the top frame.

20

NOTE The number of frames created by a <FRAMESET> tag is defined by the number of elements in the ROWS or COLS size list. For example, ROWS=100,*,*,50 creates four frames because the list contains four elements.

TIP Use at least one * list item when using the ROWS or COLS attribute to allow flexibility for different monitor resolutions or window sizes. The browser will assign all leftover space equally to each item specified as an asterisk.

Because I want to split the top frame, I embed <FRAMESET> and </FRAMESET> tags immediately after the first one. Using a COLS attribute, the example splits the upper horizontal frame into two vertical frames. The right frame will be 300 pixels in width. The left frame will fill the rest of the horizontal space in the browser window for the first row of frames. In all, I have defined three frames using the <FRAMESET> and </FRAMESET> tags. For each frame in the framesets, I use a <FRAME> tag to identify the file to be displayed in the frame and to assign a name to the frame. The SRC attribute requires a URL to the file I want to display in that frame. The NAME attribute allows me to assign a name to that frame. I'll use the name later to tell the browser that I want a hyperlink to open in that particular frame.

In the preceding example, I assign the galner.wrl file to the upper-left frame and name the frame VRML. I assign the file overview.htm to the upper-right frame and name the frame DESC. I assign the file gxindex.htm to the bottom frame and name the frame INDEX. After all the frames are filled, I close off <FRAMESET> with the requisite </FRAMESET>.

NOTE The order of the <FRAMESET> and <FRAME> tags is significant. The <FRAME> tag always defines the next frame that has yet to be defined. The definition order is top-down, left to right, in the same order as you are reading this text. After a frame has been defined, any embedded <FRAMESET> tag subdivides the next frame in order that has not been defined with a <FRAME> tag. So, if I reversed the line order of the second <FRAMESET> tag and the first <FRAME> tag, the bottom frame, rather than the top one, would be subdivided. The DESC frame would be the left frame of the bottom row rather than the right frame of the top row.

20

Additional attributes of interest are associated with the <FRAME> tag. I used the SCROLLING=NO attribute for the INDEX frame because I want the index to always be visible. Without a SCROLLING attribute being specified, a frame is dynamically scrollable when the contents of the frame require it. I used the NORESIZE attribute on the VRML frame to keep that frame a fixed size and maintain model scale. I'll defer any further details on HTML options for a frame definition document to a book on HTML scripting.

NOTE If you expect visitors who use older Web browsers, investigate the <NOFRAME> and </NOFRAME> tags to provide an alternative nonframed presentation to that audience.

Choosing the Best Options for Your VRML Frame

By default, each frame you create is scrollable as needed and is resizable by each visitor. If you are presenting a three-dimensional model as I am doing, you might spend a lot of time and effort writing your VRML to maintain the scale of your model to the real world. Using a frame, I can fix the frame's dimensions so that a visitor can't resize it and distort the scale. You can accomplish this task by including the NORESIZE attribute within your <FRAME> tag for the VRML frame and specifically identifying the frame dimensions in the ROWS and COLS attributes of the framesets.

NOTE Always consider that visitors to your Web site will be using many kinds of monitors with different resolutions.

Using the Anchor Node to Communicate with the HTML

Up to this point, I have defined the frames and have given them names. Now I can set up communication channels between the frames. I can modify the VRML world file to interact with the other frames and can modify the HTML files to communicate with the VRML and each other. I'll review the file structure for this project in Figure 20.2.

20

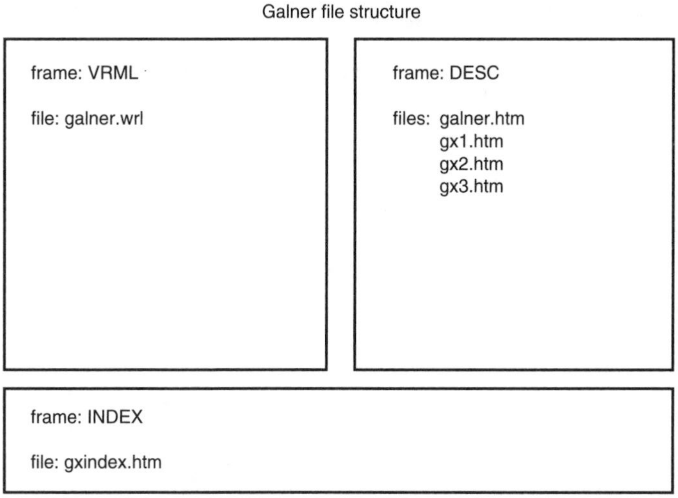

Figure 20.2.

The file structure for the Galner System Web site.

Galner file structure

```
frame: VRML

file: galner.wrl
```

```
frame: DESC

files:  galner.htm
        gx1.htm
        gx2.htm
        gx3.htm
```

```
frame: INDEX

file: gxindex.htm
```

Because this is a book about VRML, I'll start by modifying the VRML. With what you have learned in this book, you could create a really awe-inspiring model of the three planets of the Galner System. You would use texture maps, animation, and lighting to provide a very impressive model. Those added features would divert your attention from this chapter's teachings. So, instead, I'll start with a simple VRML model, as shown in Listing 20.2.

TYPE   **Listing 20.2. A VRML scene with three spheres.**

```
DEF OVERVIEW Viewpoint {
    position    0 0 6
    orientation    0 0 1 0
    fieldOfView    0.785398
    description    "OVERVIEW"
}
Transform {
    children
            Shape {
                appearance Appearance {
                    material Material { diffuseColor 1 1 0}
                }
                geometry Sphere {radius .4}
            }
        translation 0 1 0
},
Transform {
    children
            Shape {
                appearance Appearance {
                    material Material { diffuseColor 0 1 1}
                }
```

continues

Listing 20.2. continued

```
                    geometry Sphere {radius .7}
                }
        translation 2 0 1
    },
    Transform {
        children
                Shape {
                    appearance Appearance {
                        material Material { diffuseColor 0 1 .3}
                    }
                    geometry Sphere {radius .3}
                }
            translation -2 0 -3
    }
```

I'll modify the file from the top down. First, I'll add three additional viewpoints to the VRML scene to focus on each planet. I'll move to these viewpoints whenever a reader clicks a planet in the VRML or clicks a planet link in the index frame. I'll use the jump field for each viewpoint to route a set_bind eventIn to the viewpoint from a TouchSensor I will add shortly. The jump field is an exposed field that can have a value of TRUE or FALSE. When the jump field is set to TRUE, the viewpoint's set_bind eventIn is active. When the set_bind event occurs, the browser moves to that viewpoint, effectively moving it to the top of the viewpoint stack.

The viewpoints are created with the appropriate field values to show off each planet in the center of the VRML frame:

```
DEF GXA Viewpoint {
    position      0 1 3
    orientation   0 0 1 0
    jump          TRUE
    fieldOfView   0.785398
    description   "GX1"
}
DEF GXB Viewpoint {
    position      2 0 4
    orientation   0 0 1 0
    jump          TRUE
    fieldOfView   0.785398
    description   "GX2"
}
DEF GXC Viewpoint {
    position      -2 0 0
    orientation   0 0 1 0
    jump          TRUE
    fieldOfView   0.785398
    description   "GX3"
}
```

I'll define the viewpoints as GXA, GXB, and GXC to save the GX1, GX2, and GX3 names for the Anchor node definitions. The Anchor node allows me to open an HTML document when I click an object in the VRML scene. Yet, at the same time, I want to use a TouchSensor node to route events to the planet viewpoints. To associate both an Anchor and a TouchSensor with each of the planets, I'll place them both within a Group node. The appropriate Group node for GX1 is similar to the Group nodes for GX2 and GX3, so I'll just focus on the GX1 Group node:

```
Group {
    children [
        DEF TS1 TouchSensor {}
        DEF GX1 Anchor {
            url ["GX1.htm"]
            parameters ["target=DESC"]
            children [
                Transform {
                    children
                        Shape {
                            appearance Appearance {
                                material Material { diffuseColor 1 1 0}
                            }
                            geometry Sphere {radius .4}
                        }
                    translation 0 1 0
                }
            ]
        }
    ]
},
```

The first child of the Group node is the TouchSensor, which I'll define as TS1. The second child, the Anchor node, I'll define as GX1. The Anchor node uses three fields. The url field specifies the file I want to open when the user clicks the yellow planet in the VRML model. For the site, the file GX1.htm contains the narrative on the planet GX1. The parameters field directs the browser to open the file in the frame named DESC, the narrative frame, which is created by the frame definition document. The third field associates the planet to the Anchor and TouchSensor nodes through the use of a Transform, which defines the planet's shape, appearance, and translation.

Finally, I can create the three ROUTE statements that will route the TouchSensors' isActive eventOut to the Viewpoints' set_bind eventIn to jump to an appropriate viewpoint for the planet selected by the user:

```
ROUTE TS1.isActive TO GXA.set_bind
ROUTE TS2.isActive TO GXB.set_bind
ROUTE TS3.isActive TO GXC.set_bind
```

Listing 20.3 shows the VRML world in its entirety.

TYPE | **Listing 20.3. The VRML scene after changes.**

```
DEF OVERVIEW Viewpoint {
    position      0 0 6
```

continues

Listing 20.3. continued

```
            orientation    0 0 1  0
            jump           TRUE
            fieldOfView    0.785398
            description    "OVERVIEW"
    }
    DEF GXA Viewpoint {
            position       0 1 3
            orientation    0 0 1  0
            jump           TRUE
            fieldOfView    0.785398
            description    "GX1"
    }
    DEF GXB Viewpoint {
            position       2 0 4
            orientation    0 0 1 0
            jump           TRUE
            fieldOfView    0.785398
            description    "GX2"
    }
    DEF GXC Viewpoint {
            position       -2 0 0
            orientation    0 0 1 0
            jump           TRUE
            fieldOfView    0.785398
            description    "GX3"
    }
    Group {
        children [
            DEF TS1 TouchSensor {}
            DEF GX1 Anchor {
                url ["GX1.htm"]
                parameters ["target=DESC"]
                children [
                    Transform {
                        children
                            Shape {
                                appearance Appearance {
                                    material Material { diffuseColor 1 1 0}
                                }
                                geometry Sphere {radius .4}
                            }
                        translation 0 1 0
                    }
                ]
            }
        ]
    },
    Group {
        children [
            DEF TS2 TouchSensor {}
            DEF GX2 Anchor {
                url ["GX2.htm"]
                parameters ["target=DESC"]
                children [
```

20

```
                 Transform {
                    children
                       Shape {
                          appearance Appearance {
                             material Material { diffuseColor 0 1 1}
                          }
                          geometry Sphere {radius .7}
                       }
                    translation 2 0 1
                 }
              ]
           }
        ]
     },
     Group {
        children [
           DEF TS3 TouchSensor {}
           DEF GX3 Anchor {
              url ["GX3.htm"]
              parameters ["target=DESC"]
              children [
                 Transform {
                    children
                       Shape {
                          appearance Appearance {
                             material Material { diffuseColor 0 1 .3}
                          }
                          geometry Sphere {radius .3}
                       }
                    translation -2 0 -3
                 }
              ]
           }
        ]
     }

     ROUTE TS1.isActive TO GXA.set_bind
     ROUTE TS2.isActive TO GXB.set_bind
     ROUTE TS3.isActive TO GXC.set_bind
```

Using the <A> Tag in HTML to Communicate with a VRML Frame

You've learned how to enhance VRML to take advantage of frames. Now you'll focus on the HTML. In all, I have six HTML documents in the Web site. You've seen the frame definition document that creates the frames. I'll need one document for the index. And I'll create four narrative documents. One narrative document will provide an overview of the Galner System. The other three definition documents will provide separate descriptions of the three planets. Listing 20.4 shows the HTML tags for the index document, file gxindex.htm on the CD-ROM.

TYPE   **Listing 20.4. HTML for the INDEX frame.**

```
<HTML>
<HEAD>
</HEAD>
<BODY>
<B>The Galner System</B> ¦
<A HREF="overview.htm" TARGET="DESC">Overview</A>
¦ <A HREF="GX1.htm" TARGET="DESC">GX1</A>
¦ <A HREF="GX2.htm" TARGET="DESC">GX2</A>
¦ <A HREF="GX3.htm" TARGET="DESC">GX3</A>
</BODY>
</HTML>
```

Because the index contains no <P> or <BR> tags, the links will all appear on one horizontal line of text. Each <A> tag contains an HREF attribute with a URL as its value. Each URL refers to one of the four narrative documents. The TARGET attribute tells the browser to open the hyperlink in the DESC frame rather than in the index frame itself. I'll provide text for each link: Overview, GX1, GX2, and GX3. Then, I'll close each <A> with </A>. The vertical pipe symbol (¦) makes a simple border between links on the same line.

Next, I'll take a look at the HTML tags for the narrative document GX1.htm in Listing 20.5.

TYPE   **Listing 20.5. HTML for the DESC frame.**

```
<HTML>
<HEAD>
<TITLE>Overview</TITLE>
<SCRIPT>
function viewpoint() {
top.VRML.location.href="galner.wrl#GXA"
}
</SCRIPT>
</HEAD>
<BODY onLoad="viewpoint()">
<H2>GX1</H2>
GX1 is the brightest of the three planets.  Yellow in hue, an inordinate
amount of sulphur is found within its crust.
<P>
Circumference: 20,000 miles<BR>
Day Length: 14.3 hours<BR>
</BODY>
</HTML>
```

This document contains a simple HTML body but requires some additional tags to take advantage of the frames. I'll add an onLoad attribute to the <BODY> tag. The onLoad attribute takes as its value a function that is defined within <SCRIPT> and </SCRIPT> tags. I want to change the VRML viewpoint whenever a user opens a different narrative by using the index.

20

In the viewpoint function within the script tag, I can move to the appropriate viewpoint within the VRML file. I'll add the #GXA bookmark to the end of the galner.wrl URL to tell the VRML viewer to move to the GX1 planet's viewpoint. If the VRML viewer did not accept the standard bookmark syntax, I would have to create four separate VRML files. Each file would be similar yet would list the appropriate viewpoint for that planet first. The bookmark method has an obvious advantage: The user won't have to wait for a new VRML file to load every time a new narrative is chosen.

Another option would be to create one or more functions that communicate with the available eventIns in the VRML scene. This scripting capability allows me to create a wide variety of interactions with a VRML world from other frames in a Web site. Each VRML viewer can provide a different API for use to communicate with the VRML world that is loaded in a frame, yet standard APIs will not lag far behind.

TIP

When using VRML with frames, don't provide any links that open outside of the frames created by your frame definition document. Most VRML browsers reload a VRML scene from scratch when a user moves on to a document outside of the frames and subsequently comes back to the frames environment.

Summary

Frames are proving to be a successful presentation style for text and graphical information. Information-browsing tools, such as operating-system file managers, groupware views, and popular Web browsers, are all incorporating frames into the latest versions. VRML scenes take advantage of frames to provide a multimedia presentation to a Web visitor by adding text-based narrative. Information content in each frame is navigated independently, yet frames can communicate with each other to provide a well-choreographed and intuitive presentation. Throughout this chapter, I built a Web site using frames. The necessary changes were made to the HTML tags and VRML nodes. With just a few changes, I was able to take advantage of the frames created by a frame definition document. The frameset and frame tags that are needed to create frames were explored. I ended with a vision of future enhancements I might attempt through an available VRML viewer's API. I'll further build this vision in Chapter 21, "Where to Go from Here."

20

Q&A

Q Can I have multiple VRML frames present at the same time?

A Yes. Each frame is an independent decision. You can create a Web site where two or more frames display VRML scenes simultaneously. You can then communicate between the VRML scenes by using the eventIns and eventOuts of each.

Q Can I mix file types in the same frame?

A Yes. A frame that starts by displaying a VRML scene need not continue to display VRML. It could just as well open an HTML document based on a visitor's interaction with other frames or the browser menu bar. Just be aware that browser plugins must reload a frame whenever its file type is opened in a frame. Try to limit this distraction as much as possible.

Q Many sites are converting to a frame presentation style lately. Is this a fad, or are frames really that attractive?

A Frames are really that attractive. I'll agree that they have caused some problems on older computers, because they require more processing power. But Netscape is doing the work behind the scenes in their LiveConnect architecture to allow programmers to connect frames in powerful ways. The Internet is still too slow for a lot of the "fast twitch" video games to be played in multiplayer mode, but Netscape is building on the scripting paradigm that would allow a game presentation style using frames. In fact, if you are interested in using an avatar to visit multiuser worlds, multiuser browsing tools are becoming available with frames. With this set up, one frame shows you the world you are investigating, one frame presents you with tools to use in the world, and another frame becomes a chat frame for communicating with the other world visitors.

Exercise

1. Create an HTML-based frame definition document in which one frame is a VRML world containing three objects: a cube, a sphere, and a cone. Provide three viewpoints in the world to correspond with the three objects. Create two text-based frames. One should provide navigation among the three objects, and the other should describe each object in a paragraph with an appropriate heading. Be creative in your frame placement.

Answer

Step 1: Create the frame definition document, `shapes.htm`

TYPE | **Listing 20.6. Answer to Exercise 1.**

```
<HTML>
<HEAD>
<TITLE>VRML Primitives</TITLE>
<FRAMESET ROWS="*,50">
<NOFRAMES>
</NOFRAMES>
<FRAMESET COLS="*,300">
<FRAME SRC="shapes.wrl" NAME="VRML">
<FRAME SRC="cube.htm" NAME="DESC">
</FRAMESET>
<FRAME SRC="shapendx.htm" NAME="INDEX">
</FRAMESET>
</HEAD>
</HTML>

Next, the VRML world, shapes.wrl:
DEF cubeview Viewpoint {
    position              0 1 3
    orientation     0 0 1  0
    jump                 TRUE
    fieldOfView     0.785398
    description     "Cubeview"
}
DEF coneview Viewpoint {
    position              2 0 4
    orientation     0 0 1 0
    jump                 TRUE
    fieldOfView     0.785398
    description     "Coneview"
}
DEF sphereview Viewpoint {
    position             -2 0 0
    orientation     0 0 1 0
    jump                 TRUE
    fieldOfView     0.785398
    description     "Sphereview"
}
Group {
   children [
       DEF TS1 TouchSensor {}
       DEF GX1 Anchor {
           url ["cube.htm"]
           parameters ["target=DESC"]
```

continues

20

Listing 20.6. continued

```
                    children [
                        Transform {
                            children
                                Shape {
                                    appearance Appearance {
                                        material Material { diffuseColor 1 1 0}
                                    }
                                    geometry Box {size .8 .8 .8}
                                }
                            translation 0 1 0
                        }
                    ]
                }
            ]
        },
        Group {
            children [
                DEF TS2 TouchSensor {}
                DEF GX2 Anchor {
                    url ["cone.htm"]
                    parameters ["target=DESC"]
                    children [
                        Transform {
                            children
                                Shape {
                                    appearance Appearance {
                                        material Material { diffuseColor 0 1 1}
                                    }
                                    geometry Cone { height .8
                                    bottomRadius .5}
                                }
                            translation 2 0 1
                        }
                    ]
                }
            ]
        },
        Group {
            children [
                DEF TS3 TouchSensor {}
                DEF Sphere Anchor {
                    url ["sphere.htm"]
                    parameters ["target=DESC"]
                    children [
                        Transform {
                            children
                                Shape {
                                    appearance Appearance {
                                        material Material { diffuseColor 0 1 .3}
                                    }
                                    geometry Sphere {radius .3}
                                }
                            translation -2 0 -3
                        }
```

20

```
        ]
      }
    ]
}
ROUTE TS1.isActive TO cubeview.set_bind
ROUTE TS2.isActive TO coneview.set_bind
ROUTE TS3.isActive TO sphereview.set_bind
Then, our index, shapendx.htm:
<HTML>
<HEAD>
</HEAD>
<BODY>
<B>VRML Primitives </B> ¦
 <A HREF="cube.htm" TARGET="DESC">Cube</A>
 ¦ <A HREF="cone.htm" TARGET="DESC">Cone</A>
 ¦ <A HREF="sphere.htm" TARGET="DESC">Sphere</A>
</HTML>
And, finally, our narrative:
Cone.htm:
<HTML>
<HEAD>
<TITLE>Overview</TITLE>
<SCRIPT>
function viewpoint() {
top.VRML.location.href="shapes.wrl#coneview"
}
</SCRIPT>
</HEAD>
<BODY onLoad="viewpoint()">
<H2>Cone</H2>
The cone is a VRML primitive with a circular bottom and pointed top.
<P>
Node Name: Cone<BR>
fields: height and bottomRadius<BR>
</BODY>
</HTML>
Cube.htm:
<HTML>
<HEAD>
<TITLE>Overview</TITLE>
<SCRIPT>
function viewpoint() {
top.VRML.location.href="shapes.wrl#cubeview"
}
</SCRIPT>
</HEAD>
<BODY onLoad="viewpoint()">
<H2>Cube</H2>
The Cube is a VRML primitive with six sides.  It can be easily stretched in the
X, Y, or Z direction by using the size field.
<P>
Node Name: Box<BR>
fields: size<BR>
</BODY>
</HTML>
```

20

continues

Listing 20.6. continued

```
Sphere.htm:
<HTML>
<HEAD>
<TITLE>Overview</TITLE>
<SCRIPT>
function viewpoint() {
top.VRML.location.href="shapes.wrl#sphereview"
}
</SCRIPT>
</HEAD>
<BODY onLoad="viewpoint()">
<H2>Sphere</H2>
The Sphere is a VRML primitive that is shaped like a ball
<P>
Node Name: Sphere<BR>
fields: radius<BR>
</BODY>
</HTML>
```

☐ You can find the complete VRML files for the preceding exercise on the CD-ROM
at \Source\Answers.

Day 21

Where to Go From Here

You should now be a master of VRML content creation. I have shown you virtually every node available, and how those nodes can be used together in an infinite variety of ways to let you express your greatest dreams. You are now ready to create vast, creative expanses of your own with VRML 2. But what does the future hold? Where will VRML and 3D on the Web be in a year, five years, or even ten years? It's time to explore some possibilities of that future and predict where all this fledgling technology will take us. Here is what I will talk about today:

- ☐ Short-term goals
- ☐ The future of VRML
- ☐ Cyberspace

Short-Term Goals

VRML is a very new technology. It is so new that none of the browsers available today implement all of its features. This is not the fault of any programmers working on VRML browsers; it's just that VRML is so new that no one has had sufficient time to create a finished product. We are in what programmers like to call the *beta period*, when browsers are available only with the caveat that they are not yet complete and might not be fully stable. Therefore, the first and most important short-term goal of VRML is to deliver on its promise of allowing users to explore animated, interactive virtual worlds on the World Wide Web.

Beyond that first step, browsers must give authors more power to create rich and compelling worlds. Several technologies will help achieve this goal, solidifying VRML as a major force for the Web of the future. I will discuss what I believe are the three most important technologies to ensure this success.

External Authoring Interface

In Chapter 20, "Creating a Composite Multimedia Document," I showed you how to integrate VRML with an HTML document to create a true multimedia experience. But this was done with the simple mechanisms of Anchor nodes and named Viewpoint nodes, which limited the amount of interaction that was possible. For instance, using these mechanisms, it is impossible to start an animation in the VRML world by pressing a button on the HTML page. You also cannot activate a TouchSensor in VRML and use the event to highlight a line of text on the HTML page. But a new mechanism that is just becoming available, called the *External Authoring Interface* (EAI), will allow these interactions and more.

The EAI allows you to write a Java applet and place it on the HTML page, which can send events to the VRML world. These look like any event routed inside the scene, and they give the same type of control. For instance, a Java-controlled button can be made to send the equivalent of the TouchSensor's touchTime event to a TimeSensor to start an animation. Likewise, the Java applet can be set up to be notified when a node in the VRML scene sends an eventOut. In this way, a TouchSensor in the scene can cause the applet to highlight some text in a window under its control.

Using Java in Script Nodes

In all the Script node examples I showed you, I used VRMLScript, a lightweight language that is a subset of JavaScript. VRMLScript is extremely easy to write but is limited in expressive power, due to its very nature as a lightweight language. Java is the most popular choice for a powerful, full-featured language inside Script nodes, due to its similarity to C++ and the fact that scripts written in Java run on all platforms. Browsers that support both the EAI and Java in Script nodes give authors the greatest flexibility in creating any type of content imaginable. No browser supports both yet, but the popularity of both makes this future support inevitable.

21

Graphics Hardware to Boost Performance

The single biggest problem in VRML is the lack of inexpensive hardware on which to explore worlds with acceptable performance. You might have seen some of the 3D games, such as DOOM and Quake, that are becoming available. These have good performance on simple PCs, but they are very specialized and can take advantage of many tricks to make game play more fluid. Because VRML is more general, achieving this performance is much more difficult. Looking at VRML on higher-end graphics computers with specialized hardware gives you a glimpse into the future of 3D performance. The fluid motion and rendering quality outpace even specialized 3D games running on the PC.

Work is being done on many hardware fronts to alleviate this problem. Computer vendors are realizing the potential for 3D and are responding with affordable graphics hardware to give VRML much higher performance. At the same time, the basic speed of a PC is quickly rising. Together, these advances promise to put high-performance rendering into the hands of every PC owner.

Consumer products manufacturers are not sitting idly by. Several companies are beginning to offer game machines with 3D graphics hardware. Others have plans to put similar hardware right into your TV set. These promise to bring down the cost of exploring VRML worlds so that anyone can afford it.

The Future of VRML

This is an exciting time for VRML. I'm sure that by the time you read this book, new browsers will be available, and the current browsers will be more feature-rich and stable. But with the excitement also comes frustration. Making compelling content is difficult when products are changing so fast. But those who are now creating content will have some beautiful results a year from now, according to my VRML crystal ball.

One Year Out

As I said before, I believe that the most important change we will see in the next year will be the wide availability of good-quality stable and compatible VRML browsers. With that will naturally come the first batch of really exciting and rich virtual environments. There will be game worlds, virtual shopping malls, and online museums. Some of these will be created purely for pleasure; others will be proving that 3D on the Web can be a compelling tool for business. When VRML catches the eye of the business community, its growth, which is very rapid right now, will become extraordinary. The commercialization of this technology troubles some, mostly from an artistic point of view. But while business will use 3D to sell, it will also stimulate the availability of tools for content creation and better hardware for browsing. This brings me to my next prediction: better tools.

21

Some good tools for VRML authoring are available today. But many more are needed. I believe that over the next year you will see 3D Web tools to fit every niche, suitable for everyone from the professional graphics artist to the casual user. Forces are at work outside the VRML community that are giving users a wider choice of platforms for both browsing and creating Web content. Because of this, I believe that the new VRML tools will be available on many kinds of platforms, using many new technologies such as Java and HTML, to supply novel and flexible solutions to the problem of creating content for the new rich medium of VRML.

Finally, I am quite sure many interesting and sometimes bizarre applications for VRML will be seen. You can already see historic sites, where you can view the reconstruction of an ancient city, and sites showing what a decaying neighborhood will look like after a proposed renovation. Of course, not all sites will have such high ideals. Games will no doubt dominate VRML in the short term. A few holiday sites are popping up, with fun experiences for Halloween, Christmas, or New Year's. Then there's the site where you can create your own coffin, with a full 3D visualization. I'm sure the technology will show much progress over the next year. But what about the next milestone? What will happen in the next five years?

Five Years Down the Virtual Road

The way begins to get a bit murky this far down the path into the future. But assuming that the Web grows at the expected rate, VRML should be quite embedded in our everyday lives. I mean that quite literally. Many manufacturers are talking about placing computer hardware into television sets. Just plug the TV into the cable connection and you have access to the world. It's hard to imagine the Internet surviving such a crush of new subscribers. When 75 percent of the homes in the world are online, the traffic of people talking, browsing, and exploring at all hours of the day or night will be unimaginable. But these big problems will be solved as they always have been. Necessity is the mother of invention, so someone will come up with solutions just in time to avert a major world crisis!

This connectivity will be wonderful for VRML. With good 3D graphics hardware available free inside your TV set, everyone will be able to have rich virtual experiences that we can only dream of today. Five years is not quite enough time to make this experience available to everyone, but the effort will have made great progress by then. Multiuser virtual environments will be common, complete with lifelike, animated avatars and the ability to walk up to someone, hand him a briefcase full of information, and chat with him about the weather. Anyone with a few cyberbucks will be able to buy a little homestead on this virtual landscape and set up shop, or just create a fortress of solitude, free from the noise and influences of the virtual city.

Business on the Web will be in full swing by then. You'll be able to have all your cash online, so you'll be able to swing into the cybermall, try some new pants on your avatar, and buy the

21

pants with your cyberbucks. Back in the real world, your pants will still take a couple of days to get to you, but you won't care because you'll be too busy trying to be a corporate tycoon in a new, multiplayer business game.

But VRML and the Web won't be all high-tech fun and games. You'll be able to cruise around a model of that new lodge in the National Park you've been wanting to visit. That way, you can check out the view from various rooms before making a reservation and travel plans to get away from the TV and spend some quality time relaxing in the real world. Just like many technologies before it, such as the telephone and the airplane, VRML, and the Web in general, will eventually blend into society and become an ordinary tool. But it will be an amazingly powerful tool that will entertain you when you want entertainment and help you when you need help.

The Distant Future

Looking out beyond five years is largely pointless. With developments happening as fast as they are, something that we can't now imagine will surely come on the scene and will completely change the landscape (both real and virtual). The only thing you can say with certainty is that VRML is changing rapidly and, by all indications, will continue to do so well into the future.

Cyberspace

Many people in the VRML community view the highest aspirations of VRML to be the creation of *a fully immersive cyberspace environment.* This would be an alternate universe inside the Web where you can interact with the world and with others, just as you would in the real world. This environment would have unlimited possibilities for information gathering, learning, working, and playing, in ways that would be impossible elsewhere. Several steps are necessary to reach this goal, but those steps are already beginning to take shape.

As I mentioned earlier, the big advance from VRML 1 to 2 was in adding life to the virtual world. You've now seen how to make objects move and how to allow buttons to be pressed, but the world is still a lonely place. In your visits to traditional Web sites, you might have seen *hit counters*—those little displays of the number of people who have visited the site. There might well be several people browsing the site at the same time you are, but you have no obvious indication of this fact. Several companies, however, are trying to remedy this situation, at least for your visits to virtual worlds. In doing so, they are taking VRML to the next level.

21

Step 1: Multiuser Environments

In browsing HTML pages, you really have no sense of spatial orientation. By that I mean you are not really located anywhere *on* that page. The page just exists, and you are reading it. But when walking in a VRML world, you have a definite position and orientation. This information about you can be transmitted to other people visiting that space, and they can actually see your avatar as it moves around. Their information can be transmitted to you, so you can see them as well. You all will effectively be occupying the same space, with your avatars representing each of you.

I've talked about avatars several times throughout this book. Your avatar is your personification in the virtual world through which you are wandering. In VRML, your avatar is a cylinder, with your viewpoint sitting on top. If you're looking at the scene through the eyes of your avatar (which all current VRML browsers do), you'll never see this cylinder, so its simplistic shape doesn't matter much. All it really does is give the browser something with which to perform collision testing so that you don't go walking through walls. But if others can see you, the look of your avatar (and more important to you, the look of another person's avatar) matters a great deal. VRML worlds that allow multiple visitors to visit at the same time and see each other are called *multiuser environments*. They are a big step toward a vastly improved cyberspace. Several companies are scrambling to make multiuser technology available. Today, this work is in its infancy. The look of an avatar is limited, and users can interact only by *chatting*—typing or speaking to nearby avatars. If you press a button that starts an animation, other visitors to the world will not see it start.

Step 2: Shared Behaviors

The second step toward the dream of cyberspace is referred to as *shared behaviors*, and it has to do with letting others see your interactions with the world. This step will also make *articulated avatars* available. Others will see your legs move when you walk and your lips move when you talk, and you'll be able to command your avatar to smile, shake hands, and wave good-bye. When this happens, the virtual world will look more realistic because avatars will look less like robots and more like participants in a shared experience. There have even been some early demos of discotheques, where avatars can dance together!

The biggest problem with sharing behaviors in this way has to do with consistency. If you pressed a button to open a door and I pressed another button to close it, is the door open or closed? The obvious answer would seem to be "whoever pressed the button last." But this means every participant in the world must have the same notion of time. Ideally, I would see you press the button at the same instant you really pressed it, so when I pressed my button it would be easy to tell who acted first. But your action is sent to me over a network—and all networks have *high latency*, which means they take a long time to send information around. If I had to wait for a message indicating that you pressed your button before I was allowed to press mine, we could guarantee the order in which the interactions occurred, but the system would be unacceptably slow. Many techniques have been proposed to solve the consistency problem, but more work is needed in this area before a general solution is found.

Step 3: Persistence

After the problems of shared behaviors are solved, a fundamental mechanism will still be missing from this virtual environment. When you enter a virtual world today, everything is in its initial state. If you click a bird to make it fly away, the next time you visit the world the bird will be back. That is because no mechanism exists to make the world remember the changes you have made to it. This problem is compounded because someone else visiting the world might have made the bird fly away, so you would have to remember his changes as well. This mechanism, known as *persistence*, is the third step along the road to cyberspace. Persistence would allow you to walk into a world carrying a statue you just created, place it in the center of the plaza, and then leave. Anyone else who wandered into the plaza, at any time in the future, would be able to admire your creation. Someone could then tip over the statue, and all those viewing it would see it crash to the ground. The statue would stay tipped over from then on, until someone came along to set it upright again.

Persistence has many of the same problems to solve as shared behaviors. If two people try to pick up an object in the world, you must decide who gets it. But another problem to solve is where to keep the information that an object has been added to or subtracted from the world. Another problem is how to control access to the world. If I happen to own the plaza world, I would probably have permission to add a statue to it. But I probably would not want someone else to come in and tip over the statue or walk away with it.

Step 4: Seamless Environments

There is a fourth and final step in the creation of cyberspace. All the worlds I've shown you have been small and self-contained. If you wanted to visit another world, you would walk through a portal that would load the new world, or you would click an Anchor node, which would cause the new world to replace the one in which you were standing, with an unceremonious flash during the transition. But to get to a truly virtual universe, *seamless environments* are needed. This feature would allow you to go from one VRML world to another by walking down a road or climbing on a bus. To you, it would seem as though you were moving through one continuous virtual universe, even though your travels might take you to VRML content on dozens of machines around the real world.

All the steps to build this universe are in the works right now. When this undertaking is all complete, it will change the Web from a reference library to an experiential environment. Cyberspace is only one of the many applications looming in VRML's future, but it is certainly the most fanciful and enticing.

21

Summary

At the time of this book's writing, the Nintendo 64 is just making its way onto the store shelves in North America. This little "game machine" gives us a glimpse at the future of 3D Web content. Not everyone will have an avatar that looks like Super Mario, and hopefully not all our VRML worlds will have wild cartoon landscapes. But having any 3D technology become a basic part of our society will require a small box that everyone can afford, with hardware that is specially designed for the task of browsing 3D worlds. The Nintendo 64 is a very important first step in that direction.

There are many uses for VRML, from large multimedia Web sites to the visualization of your dream house you want to show to your friends. I hope this book helps you realize your 3D visions so that you can share them with others. Stay tuned to the progress of VRML. It really is in its infancy, and we are all lucky enough to watch it grow from the very start.

Have fun!!!

Q&A

Q How can I keep up with all the changes taking place with VRML and other virtual reality technologies?

A No one can keep up completely nowadays. I recommend surfing the Internet to see what all the top companies are up to. Open up your favorite search engine in your Web browser and search on **VRML** and **Virtual Reality**. Also, read the online magazines devoted to VRML. If you can, download the latest beta copies of each browser and take a tour with them. Keep a list of the features of each browser. Spend some time thinking about the algorithms required to make a browser work. Keep a link to the VRML Consortium home page and other VRML-related organizations. And, by all means, go to the conferences where all the best ideas are presented and discussed. You'll never run out of things to think about, because VRML is involved in so many different disciplines, including education, scientific visualization, communication, psychology, physiology, anthropology, and entertainment, to name a few.

Exercise

1. Using the momentum you've gained throughout this book, put the finishing touches on your house and plan your next project. Go ahead and put your home world in a frame and add some narrative text for your audience in a second frame. Let your creativity go wild!

Answer

Whatever you've done, I'm sure it looks great. Now, keep it up.

21

APPENDIX A

VRML Node Reference

Introduction

VRML consists of 54 built-in nodes. Each node consists of fields and event values. Some fields contain a list of other nodes; therefore, VRML allows you to create a hierarchical structure of nested nodes. VRML has three types of nodes. Grouping nodes can contain a list of other nodes (children). Children nodes can be contained in the children lists. Attribute nodes must be contained in a specific field of a specific node. They add attributes to shapes, sounds, and so on.

This reference lists all VRML nodes in alphabetical order. It first lists the node description. The format of this description is similar to the way the node would be written in a VRML file. The node name is listed first, followed by an open brace, followed by all the fields the node contains, ending with a close brace. But rather than using the file format to describe each field, the more descriptive format used to define fields in a Script node is used here. The format for each field is:

```
class type name [initial value]
```

The *class* is the class specifier (field, exposedField, eventIn, or eventOut). The *type* is the type specifier (one of the field names from Appendix B, "VRML Field and Event Types"). The *name* is the name of the field, used in the file format. The *initial value* is used only for the field and exposedField classes, and specifies the initial value of that field. The initial value specified in this reference is the default value for that field.

Each entry also contains a short description of the node and of each field. Finally, the place in the file format where each node may appear is listed, along with related nodes.

Anchor

```
Anchor {
  eventIn       MFNode   addChildren
  eventIn       MFNode   removeChildren
  exposedField  MFNode   children        []
  exposedField  SFString description      " "
  exposedField  MFString parameter       []
  exposedField  MFString url             []
  field         SFVec3f  bboxCenter      0 0 0
  field         SFVec3f  bboxSize        -1 -1 -1
}
```

Fields and events

addChildren	Adds the passed nodes to children.
removeChildren	Removes the passed nodes from children.
children	The list of children of the Anchor node.
description	A string describing the contents of url.
parameter	A string passed to the browser, indicating special handling.
url	The URL to be loaded when Anchor is activated.
bboxCenter	Center of the axis-aligned box encompassing all the children of this node.
bboxSize	Total size of the axis-aligned box encompassing all the children of this node.

Description:

The Anchor grouping node causes a URL to be fetched over the network when the viewer activates (for example, clicks) some geometry contained within the Anchor's children. If the URL pointed to is a legal VRML world, that world replaces the world of which the Anchor is a part. If non-VRML data type is fetched, it is up to the browser to determine how to handle that data; typically, it will be passed to an appropriate general viewer.

The Anchor node can appear in the top level of the file or as a child of a grouping node.

See also: Group, Transform in this Appendix.

Appearance

```
Appearance {
  exposedField SFNode material          NULL
  exposedField SFNode texture           NULL
  exposedField SFNode textureTransform  NULL
}
```

Fields and events

material	A Material node
texture	An ImageTexture, MovieTexture, or PixelTexture node
textureTransform	A TextureTransform node

Description:

The Appearance node specifies the visual properties of geometry by defining the material, texture, and textureTransform nodes. The value for each of the fields in this node can be NULL. However, if the field is non-NULL, it must contain one node of the appropriate type.

The Appearance node can appear in the appearance field of a Shape node.

See also: Shape, Material, ImageTexture, MovieTexture, PixelTexture, TextureTransform in this Appendix.

AudioClip

```
AudioClip {
  exposedField  SFString description        " "
  exposedField  SFBool   loop              FALSE
  exposedField  SFFloat  pitch             1.0
  exposedField  SFTime   startTime         0
  exposedField  SFTime   stopTime          0
  exposedField  MFString url               []
  eventOut      SFTime   duration_changed
  eventOut      SFBool   isActive
}
```

Fields and events

description	A string to use in a browser-dependent way to describe the sound.
loop	If TRUE, the sound plays over and over as long as startTime is greater than stopTime or stopTime is less than startTime and stopTime is in the future. If FALSE, the sound plays once and stops.
pitch	A value multiplied by the normal playing rate to speed up or slow down the sound.
startTime	The absolute time to start the sound.
stopTime	The absolute time to stop the sound.
url	The location of the sound data to play.
duration_changed	When the sound has loaded, this event is sent with the duration, in seconds, of the sound.
isActive	When the sound starts, a TRUE event is sent. When the sound stops, a FALSE event is sent.

Description:

An AudioClip node specifies audio data that can be referenced by other nodes that require an audio source.

The AudioClip node can appear in the source field of a Sound node.

See also: Sound, MovieTexture in this Appendix.

Background

```
Background {
   eventIn       SFBool    set_bind
   exposedField  MFFloat   groundAngle  []
   exposedField  MFColor   groundColor  []
   exposedField  MFString  backUrl      []
   exposedField  MFString  bottomUrl    []
   exposedField  MFString  frontUrl     []
   exposedField  MFString  leftUrl      []
   exposedField  MFString  rightUrl     []
   exposedField  MFString  topUrl       []
   exposedField  MFFloat   skyAngle     []
   exposedField  MFColor   skyColor     [ 0 0 0 ]
   eventOut      SFBool    isBound
}
```

Fields and events

set_bind	When this event is received, this node becomes the current Background node.
groundAngle	This is a list of angles delimiting one ground color from another in the groundColor list. An angle of 0° is straight ahead, and positive angles continue down. There must be one less than the number of colors in groundColor.
groundColor	The list of colors for the ground. The first color is at 0° (straight ahead), and colors continue down from the horizon. Each color past the first is at the angle specified in groundAngle.
backUrl	The location of the image file to use for the back of the background-image cube.
bottomUrl	The location of the image file to use for the bottom of the background-image cube.
frontUrl	The location of the image file to use for the front of the background-image cube.
leftUrl	The location of the image file to use for the left side of the background-image cube.
rightUrl	The location of the image file to use for the right side of the background-image cube.
topUrl	The location of the image file to use for the top of the background-image cube.
skyAngle	This is a list of angles delimiting one sky color from another in the skyColor list. An angle of 0° is straight up, and positive angles continue down. There must be one less than the number of colors in skyColor.

skyColor	The list of colors for the sky. The first color is at 0° (straight up), and colors continue down from there. Each color past the first is at the angle specified in skyAngle.
isBound	This event is sent with a value of TRUE when this node becomes the current Background node, and with a value of FALSE when this node is no longer the current Background node.

Description:

The Background node is used to specify a color backdrop that simulates ground and sky, as well as a background texture, or panorama, that is placed behind all geometry in the scene and in front of the ground and sky. Background nodes are specified in the local coordinate system and are affected by the accumulated rotation of their parents.

The Background node can appear in the top level of the file or as a child of a grouping node.

See also: Viewpoint, Fog, NavigationInfo in this Appendix.

Billboard

```
Billboard {
  eventIn      MFNode   addChildren
  eventIn      MFNode   removeChildren
  exposedField SFVec3f  axisOfRotation   0 1 0
  exposedField MFNode   children         []
  field        SFVec3f  bboxCenter       0 0 0
  field        SFVec3f  bboxSize         -1 -1 -1
}
```

Fields and events

addChildren	Adds the passed nodes to children.
removeChildren	Removes the passed nodes from children.
axisOfRotation	Combined with a point at the origin, this defines a line about which the children are rotated to remain pointing at the viewer. A value of 0 0 0 is a special case that rotates the children about the origin to maintain screen alignment regardless of orientation.
children	The list of children of this node.
bboxCenter	Center of the axis-aligned box encompassing all the children of this node.
bboxSize	Total size of the axis-aligned box encompassing all the children of this node.

Description:

The Billboard node is a grouping node that modifies its coordinate system so that the Billboard node's local Z-axis turns to point at the viewer.

The Billboard node appears in the top level of the file or as a child of a grouping node.

See also: Group, Transform in this Appendix.

Box

```
Box {
  field    SFVec3f size  2 2 2
}
```

Fields and events

size   The size of the box along each of the three major axes.

Description:

The Box node specifies a rectangular box in the local coordinate system centered at 0,0,0 in the local coordinate system and aligned with the coordinate axes.

The Box node can appear in the geometry field of a Shape node.

See also: Shape, Cone, Cylinder, Sphere in this Appendix.

Collision

```
Collision {
    eventIn       MFNode    addChildren
    eventIn       MFNode    removeChildren
    exposedField  MFNode    children       []
    exposedField  SFBool    collide        TRUE
    field         SFVec3f   bboxCenter     0 0 0
    field         SFVec3f   bboxSize       -1 -1 -1
    field         SFNode    proxy          NULL
    eventOut      SFTime    collideTime
}
```

Fields and events

addChildren	Adds the passed nodes to children.
removeChildren	Removes the passed nodes from children.
children	The list of children of this node.
collide	If TRUE, all children of this node are collided. If FALSE, collision testing is skipped for these children.
bboxCenter	Center of the axis-aligned box encompassing all the children of this node.
bboxSize	Total size of the axis-aligned box encompassing all the children of this node.
proxy	A node with which collision testing is performed instead of the children geometry. This can be a grouping node containing an entire scene hierarchy. It is used to allow collision with simpler geometry.
collideTime	When the avatar collides with any children of this node, this event is generated.

Description:

By default, all objects in the scene are collidable. The browser detects geometric collisions between the user's avatar and the scene's geometry, and prevents the avatar from "entering" the geometry. The Collision node is a grouping node that may turn off collision detection for its descendants, specify alternative objects to use for collision detection, and send events signaling that a collision has occurred between the user's avatar and the children of the Collision node.

The Collision node can appear in the top level of the file or as a child of a grouping node.

See also: Group, Transform, NavigationInfo in this Appendix.

Color

```
Color {
  exposedField MFColor color  []
}
```

Fields and events

color   The list of colors to be used on each vertex of a vertex-based
                             shape.

Description:

The Color node defines a set of RGB colors to be used in the fields of another node.

The Color node can appear in the color field of an IndexedFaceSet, ElevationGrid, IndexedLineSet, or PointSet.

See also: IndexedFaceSet, ElevationGrid, IndexedLineSet, PointSet in this Appendix.

ColorInterpolator

```
ColorInterpolator {
    eventIn        SFFloat set_fraction
    exposedField MFFloat key            []
    exposedField MFColor keyValue       []
    eventOut       SFColor value_changed
}
```

Fields and events

set_fraction	When this event is received, an interpolated value_changed event is sent. Value is interpolated from the key and keyValue fields.
key	The list of keys, corresponding to set_fraction values received.
keyValue	The list of key values, which are used to interpolate the value_changed output when a set_fraction eventIn is received. Each key value corresponds to a key.
value_changed	This value is generated with the current interpolated output whenever a set_fraction eventIn is received.

Description:

The ColorInterpolator node interpolates among a set of color key values to produce a value_changed event. The number of colors in the keyValue field must be equal to the number of values in the key field. A linear interpolation, using the value of set_fraction as input, is performed in HSV space.

The ColorInterpolator node can appear in the top level of the file or as a child of a grouping node.

See also: Material, ScalarInterpolator, OrientationInterpolator in this Appendix.

Cone

```
Cone {
  field    SFFloat    bottomRadius 1
  field    SFFloat    height       2
  field    SFBool     side         TRUE
  field    SFBool     bottom       TRUE
}
```

Fields and events

bottomRadius	Radius of the bottom of the cone.
height	Height from the base of the cone to the peak.
side	If TRUE, the sides of the cone are visible; if FALSE, they are invisible.
bottom	If TRUE, the bottom of the cone is visible; if FALSE, it is invisible.

Description:

The Cone node specifies a cone that is centered in the local coordinate system and whose central axis is aligned with the local Y-axis.

The Cone node can appear in the geometry field of a Shape node.

See also: Shape, Box, Cylinder, Sphere in this Appendix.

Coordinate

```
Coordinate {
  exposedField MFVec3f point  []
}
```

Fields and events

point   The list of points defining the vertices of vertex-based
                             shapes.

Description:

The Coordinate node defines a set of 3D coordinates to be used in the coord field of vertex-based geometry nodes.

The Coordinate node can appear in the coord field of an IndexedFaceSet, IndexedLineSet, or PointSet.

See also: IndexedFaceSet, IndexedLineSet, PointSet in this Appendix.

CoordinateInterpolator

```
CoordinateInterpolator {
  eventIn       SFFloat set_fraction
  exposedField  MFFloat key          []
  exposedField  MFVec3f keyValue      []
  eventOut      MFVec3f value_changed
}
```

Fields and events

set_fraction	When this event is received, an interpolated value_changed event is sent. Value is interpolated from the key and keyValue fields.
key	The list of keys, corresponding to set_fraction values received.
keyValue	The list of key values, which are used to interpolate the value_changed output when a set_fraction eventIn is received. There must be an even multiple of key values corresponding to each key. The number of values sent for each value_changed eventOut is equal to the number of key values divided by the number of keys.
value_changed	This value is generated with the current interpolated output whenever a set_fraction eventIn is received.

Description:

The CoordinateInterpolator node linearly interpolates among a set of MFVec3f values. This would be appropriate for interpolating coordinate positions for a geometric morph.

The CoordinateInterpolator node can appear in the top level of the file or as a child of a grouping node.

See also: NormalInterpolator, Coordinate in this Appendix.

Cylinder

```
Cylinder {
  field     SFBool     bottom   TRUE
  field     SFFloat    height   2
  field     SFFloat    radius   1
  field     SFBool     side     TRUE
  field     SFBool     top      TRUE
}
```

Fields and events

bottom	If TRUE, the bottom of the cylinder is visible. If FALSE, it is invisible.
height	Height from the centerline of the cylinder.
radius	Radius of the cylinder.
side	If TRUE, the sides of the cylinder are visible. If FALSE, they are invisible.
top	If TRUE, the top of the cylinder is visible. If FALSE, it is invisible.

Description:

The Cylinder node specifies a capped cylinder centered at the origin in the local coordinate system and with a central axis oriented along the local Y-axis.

The Cylinder node can appear in the geometry field of a Shape node.

See also: Shape, Box, Cone, Sphere in this Appendix.

CylinderSensor

```
CylinderSensor {
  exposedField SFBool     autoOffset TRUE
  exposedField SFFloat    diskAngle  0.262
  exposedField SFBool     enabled    TRUE
  exposedField SFFloat    maxAngle   -1
  exposedField SFFloat    minAngle   0
  exposedField SFFloat    offset     0
  eventOut     SFBool     isActive
  eventOut     SFRotation rotation_changed
  eventOut     SFVec3f    trackPoint_changed
}
```

Fields and events

autoOffset	If TRUE, the offset field is updated with the current rotation angle when the user finishes manipulating. If FALSE, the offset is not changed.
diskAngle	The angle at which the sensor switches between disk and cylinder behavior.
enabled	If TRUE, the sensor is enabled and can be activated by the user. If FALSE, the sensor cannot be activated.
maxAngle	The maximum angle value the sensor will output.
minAngle	The minimum angle value the sensor will output.
offset	The offset to be added to every angle output by the sensor.
isActive	When the sensor is activated, a TRUE event is sent. When the sensor is deactivated, a FALSE event is sent.
rotation_changed	Sent when the user activates the sensor and whenever the pointing device is moved while the sensor is activated. The value is the rotation value of the imaginary cylinder being manipulated.
trackPoint_changed	Sent when the user activates the sensor and whenever the pointing device is moved while the sensor is activated. The value is the current point on the surface of the imaginary cylinder.

Description:

The CylinderSensor maps pointing-device (for example, mouse) motion into a rotation on an invisible cylinder that is aligned with the Y-axis of its local space.

The CylinderSensor node can appear in the top level of the file or as a child of a grouping node.

See also: PlaneSensor, SphereSensor, TouchSensor in this Appendix.

DirectionalLight

```
DirectionalLight {
  exposedField SFFloat ambientIntensity  0
  exposedField SFColor color             1 1 1
  exposedField SFVec3f direction         0 0 -1
  exposedField SFFloat intensity         1
  exposedField SFBool  on                TRUE
}
```

Fields and events

ambientIntensity	The intensity applied to all objects affected by this light.
color	The color applied to all objects affected by this light.
direction	The direction this light is pointing.
intensity	The intensity of the color being generated by this light.
on	If TRUE, this light will affect all objects within its coordinate space. If FALSE, it will not affect any objects.

Description:

The DirectionalLight node defines a directional light source that illuminates along rays parallel to a given three-dimensional vector.

The DirectionalLight node can appear in the top level of the file or as a child of a grouping node.

See also: PointLight, SpotLight in this Appendix.

ElevationGrid

```
ElevationGrid {
    eventIn       MFFloat   set_height
    exposedField  SFNode    color           NULL
    exposedField  SFNode    normal          NULL
    exposedField  SFNode    texCoord        NULL
    field         MFFloat   height          []
    field         SFBool    ccw             TRUE
    field         SFBool    colorPerVertex  TRUE
    field         SFFloat   creaseAngle     0
    field         SFBool    normalPerVertex TRUE
    field         SFBool    solid           TRUE
    field         SFInt32   xDimension      0
    field         SFFloat   xSpacing        0.0
    field         SFInt32   zDimension      0
    field         SFFloat   zSpacing        0.0
}
```

Fields and events

set_height	Sets the values in the height field.
color	A Color node.
normal	A Normal node.
texCoord	A TextureCoordinate node.
height	The y values for the grid of points.
ccw	If TRUE, the object is visible from the top (looking down from the Y-axis). If FALSE, the object is visible from the bottom.
colorPerVertex	If TRUE, values in the color field are applied to each vertex. If FALSE, they are applied to each face of the grid.
creaseAngle	When the normal field is NULL, this determines the angle between faces above which you will see creases.
normalPerVertex	If TRUE, values in the normal field are applied to each vertex. If FALSE, they are applied to each face of the grid.
solid	If TRUE, only the front side of the object is visible (as determined by the ccw field). If FALSE, both sides are visible.
xDimension	The number of grid points in the X dimension.
xSpacing	The number of units between each grid point in the X direction.
zDimension	The number of grid points in the Z dimension.
zSpacing	The number of units between each grid point in the Z direction.

A

Description:

The ElevationGrid node specifies a uniform rectangular grid of varying height in the XZ plane of the local coordinate system. The geometry is described by a scalar array of height values that specify the height of a rectangular surface above each point of the grid.

The ElevationGrid node can appear in the geometry field of a Shape node.

See also: Shape, Extrusion, IndexedFaceSet in this Appendix.

Extrusion

```
Extrusion {
    eventIn MFVec2f    set_crossSection
    eventIn MFRotation set_orientation
    eventIn MFVec2f    set_scale
    eventIn MFVec3f    set_spine
    field   SFBool     beginCap      TRUE
    field   SFBool     ccw           TRUE
    field   SFBool     convex        TRUE
    field   SFFloat    creaseAngle   0
    field   MFVec2f    crossSection  [ 1 1, 1 -1, -1 -1, -1 1, 1 1 ]
    field   SFBool     endCap        TRUE
    field   MFRotation orientation   0 0 1 0
    field   MFVec2f    scale         1 1
    field   SFBool     solid         TRUE
    field   MFVec3f    spine         [ 0 0 0, 0 1 0 ]
}
```

Fields and events

set_crossSection	Sets the values in the crossSection field.
set_orientation	Sets the values in the orientation field.
set_scale	Sets the values in the scale field.
set_spine	Sets the values in the spine field.
beginCap	If TRUE, the cap at the start of the figure (at the first spine point) is rendered; if FALSE, it is not.
ccw	If TRUE, the object is visible from the outside. If FALSE, the object is visible from the inside.
creaseAngle	When the normal field is NULL, this determines the angle between faces above which you will see creases.
crossSection	The shape of the cross section, in the XZ plane.
endCap	If TRUE, the cap at the end of the figure (at the last spine point) is rendered; if FALSE, it is not.
orientation	The rotation to be applied to the cross section at each spine point. This is relative to the default orientation at each spine point (determined by the spine vertex before and after this point).
scale	The scale to be applied to the cross section at each spine point.
solid	If TRUE, only one side of the object is visible (determined by the ccw field). If FALSE, both sides are visible.
spine	The shape of the spine along which the cross section is extruded.

Description:

The Extrusion node specifies geometric shapes based on a two-dimensional cross section extruded along a three-dimensional spine. The cross section can be scaled and rotated at each spine point to produce a wide variety of shapes.

The Extrusion node can appear in the geometry field of a Shape node.

See also: Shape, ElevationGrid, IndexedFaceSet in this Appendix.

Fog

```
Fog {
  exposedField SFColor  color            1 1 1
  exposedField SFString fogType          "LINEAR"
  exposedField SFFloat  visibilityRange  0
  eventIn      SFBool   set_bind
  eventOut     SFBool   isBound
}
```

Fields and events

color	The fog color.
fogType	The fog type, either "LINEAR" or "EXPONENTIAL".
visibilityRange	The distance beyond which objects are completely obscured by fog.
set_bind	When this event is received, the node becomes the current Fog node.
isBound	This event is sent with a value of TRUE when this node becomes the current Fog node, and with a value of FALSE when this node is no longer the current Fog node.

Description:

The Fog node provides a way to simulate atmospheric effects by blending objects with the color specified by the color field based on the objects' distances from the viewer. The distances are calculated in the coordinate space of the Fog node.

The Fog node can appear in the top level of the file or as a child of a grouping node.

See also: Background, NavigationInfo, Viewpoint in this Appendix.

FontStyle

```
FontStyle {
  field MFString family       "SERIF"
  field SFBool   horizontal   TRUE
  field MFString justify      "BEGIN"
  field SFString language     " "
  field SFBool   leftToRight  TRUE
  field SFFloat  size         1.0
  field SFFloat  spacing      1.0
  field SFString style        "PLAIN"
  field SFBool   topToBottom  TRUE
}
```

Fields and events

family	The font family (SERIF, SANS, or TYPEWRITER).
horizontal	If TRUE, each string of text is rendered horizontally. If FALSE, each string is rendered vertically.
justify	The justification to use. This field can have two string values. The first is the justification along the major axis (as determined by horizontal) and the second is the justification along the minor axis. Values can be BEGIN, FIRST, MIDDLE, or END.
language	A string identifying the language of the strings. This is used to select the proper characters in the rare instance that multiple characters can be rendered.
leftToRight	If TRUE, the strings are rendered left to right. If FALSE, the strings are rendered right to left. This could be the major axis or minor axis, depending on the value of horizontal.
size	The size of a character. This is usually the character height, although it is font-dependent. This value also determines the amount of space between subsequent lines of text.
spacing	The size field is multiplied by this value to determine the actual distance between subsequent text lines.
style	The font style (PLAIN, BOLD, ITALIC or BOLDITALIC).
topToBottom	If TRUE, the strings are rendered top to bottom. If FALSE, the strings are rendered bottom to top. This could be the major axis or minor axis, depending on the value of horizontal.

Description:

The FontStyle node defines the size, font family, and style of text's font, as well as the direction of the text strings and any specific language rendering techniques that must be used for non-English text.

The FontStyle node can appear in the fontStyle field of a Text node.

See also: Text in this Appendix.

Group

```
Group {
  eventIn       MFNode  addChildren
  eventIn       MFNode  removeChildren
  exposedField MFNode  children        []
  field         SFVec3f bboxCenter      0 0 0
  field         SFVec3f bboxSize        -1 -1 -1
}
```

Fields and events

addChildren	Adds the passed nodes to children.
removeChildren	Removes the passed nodes from children.
children	The list of children of this node.
bboxCenter	Center of the axis aligned box encompassing all the children of this node.
bboxSize	Total size of the axis aligned box encompassing all the children of this node.

Description:

A Group node is equivalent to a Transform node without the transformation fields.

The Group node can appear in the top level of the file or as a child of a grouping node.

See also: Transform in this Appendix.

ImageTexture

```
ImageTexture {
   exposedField MFString url     []
   field        SFBool   repeatS TRUE
   field        SFBool   repeatT TRUE
}
```

Fields and events

url	The location of the image data.
repeatS	If TRUE, the texture is repeated over the surface of the object in the texture's S direction (which corresponds to the X direction). If FALSE, it is displayed only once, and the edges of the texture are repeated horizontally over the rest of the object.
repeatT	If TRUE, the texture is repeated over the surface of the object in the texture's T direction (which corresponds to the Y direction). If FALSE, it is displayed only once, and the edges of the texture are repeated vertically over the rest of the object.

Description:

The ImageTexture node defines a texture map by specifying an image file and general parameters for mapping to geometry.

The ImageTexture node can appear in the texture field of the Appearance node.

See also: Appearance, PixelTexture, MovieTexture, TextureTransform, TextureCoordinate in this Appendix.

IndexedFaceSet

```
IndexedFaceSet {
  eventIn       MFInt32 set_colorIndex
  eventIn       MFInt32 set_coordIndex
  eventIn       MFInt32 set_normalIndex
  eventIn       MFInt32 set_texCoordIndex
  exposedField  SFNode  color              NULL
  exposedField  SFNode  coord              NULL
  exposedField  SFNode  normal             NULL
  exposedField  SFNode  texCoord           NULL
  field         SFBool  ccw                TRUE
  field         MFInt32 colorIndex         []
  field         SFBool  colorPerVertex     TRUE
  field         SFBool  convex             TRUE
  field         MFInt32 coordIndex         []
  field         SFFloat creaseAngle        0
  field         MFInt32 normalIndex        []
  field         SFBool  normalPerVertex    TRUE
  field         SFBool  solid              TRUE
  field         MFInt32 texCoordIndex      []
}
```

Fields and events

set_colorIndex	Sets the values in the colorIndex field.
set_coordIndex	Sets the values in the coordIndex field.
set_normalIndex	Sets the values in the normalIndex field.
set_texCoordIndex	Sets the values in the texCoordIndex field.
color	A Color node.
coord	A Coordinate node.
normal	A Normal node.
texCoord	A TextureCoordinate node.
ccw	If TRUE, the object is visible from the top (looking down from the Y-axis). If FALSE, the object is visible from the bottom.
colorIndex	The list of indexes into the color list. Colors are applied to each vertex or each face as determined by the colorPerVertex field. Sets of indexes for each face (list of indexes terminated by a -1) must match those in the coordIndex field.
colorPerVertex	If TRUE, values in the color field are applied to each vertex. If FALSE, they are applied to each face of the grid.
convex	If TRUE, all faces must be convex or the results will be undefined. If FALSE, faces may be concave or convex.

continues

Fields and events

coordIndex	The list of indexes into the coordinate list that make up the vertices of each face. Multiple faces can be included by terminating each index list with a -1.
creaseAngle	When the normal field is NULL, this determines the angle between faces above which you will see creases.
normalIndex	The list of indexes into the normal list. Normals are applied to each vertex or each face as determined by the normalPerVertex field. Sets of indexes for each face (list of indexes terminated by a -1) must match those in the coordIndex field.
normalPerVertex	If TRUE, values in the normal field are applied to each vertex. If FALSE, they are applied to each face of the grid.
solid	If TRUE, only the front side of the object is visible (as determined by the ccw field). If FALSE, both sides are visible.
texCoordIndex	The list of indexes into the texture coordinate list. Texture coordinates are applied to each vertex. Sets of indexes for each face (list of indexes terminated by a -1) must match those in the coordIndex field.

Description:

The IndexedFaceSet node represents a 3D shape formed by constructing faces (polygons) from vertices listed in the coord field, indexed by the coordIndex field. Coordinates are specified in the local coordinate system and are affected by parent transformations.

The IndexedFaceSet node can appear in the geometry field of a Shape node.

See also: Shape, ElevationGrid, Extrusion in this Appendix.

IndexedLineSet

```
IndexedLineSet {
  eventIn        MFInt32 set_colorIndex
  eventIn        MFInt32 set_coordIndex
  exposedField   SFNode  color           NULL
  exposedField   SFNode  coord           NULL
  field          MFInt32 colorIndex      []
  field          SFBool  colorPerVertex  TRUE
  field          MFInt32 coordIndex      []
}
```

Fields and events

set_colorIndex	Sets the values in the colorIndex field.
set_coordIndex	Sets the values in the coordIndex field.
color	A Color node.
coord	A Coordinate node.
colorIndex	The list of indexes into the color list. Colors are applied to each vertex or each face as determined by the colorPerVertex field. Sets of indexes for each face (list of indexes terminated by a -1) must match those in the coordIndex field.
colorPerVertex	If TRUE, values in the color field are applied to each vertex. If FALSE, they are applied to each face of the grid.
coordIndex	The list of indexes into the coordinate list that make up the vertices of each face. Multiple faces can be included by terminating each index list with a -1.

Description:

The IndexedLineSet node represents a 3D geometry formed by constructing polylines from 3D points specified in the coord field, indexed by the coordIndex field. Coordinates are specified in the local coordinate system and are affected by parent transformations.

The IndexedLineSet node can appear in the geometry field of a Shape node.

See also: Shape, IndexedFaceSet, PointSet in this Appendix.

Inline

```
Inline {
  exposedField MFString url         []
  field        SFVec3f  bboxCenter  0 0 0
  field        SFVec3f  bboxSize    -1 -1 -1
}
```

Fields and events

url	The location of the VRML file to be loaded and inserted into the scene in place of this node.
bboxCenter	Center of the axis-aligned box encompassing all the children of this node.
bboxSize	Total size of the axis-aligned box encompassing all the children of this node.

Description:

The Inline node is a grouping node that reads its children data from the location specified in the url field.

The Inline node can appear in the top level of the file or as a child of a grouping node.

See also: Anchor in this Appendix.

LOD

```
LOD {
  exposedField MFNode  level   []
  field         SFVec3f center  0 0 0
  field         MFFloat range   []
}
```

Fields and events

level	The list of nodes to display at each level. One node in the list is displayed at each range entry. The first level is the nearest range, the last is the farthest.
center	The point in the local coordinate space to use to determine the distance from the viewer. This distance is used to determine the level to display.
range	The list of ranges at which the level should switch. There should be one less range value than there are levels. Ranges are specified in increasing order.

Description:

The LOD node specifies various levels of detail or complexity for a given object, and provides hints for browsers to automatically choose the appropriate version of the object based on the distance from the user.

The LOD node can appear in the top level of the file or as a child of a grouping node.

See also: Switch in this Appendix.

Material

```
Material {
  exposedField SFFloat ambientIntensity   0.2
  exposedField SFColor diffuseColor        0.8 0.8 0.8
  exposedField SFColor emissiveColor       0 0 0
  exposedField SFFloat shininess           0.2
  exposedField SFColor specularColor       0 0 0
  exposedField SFFloat transparency        0
}
```

Fields and events

ambientIntensity	The base intensity of the object. This value is multiplied by the diffuseColor to set the minimum color over the entire surface of the object.
diffuseColor	The object color affected by light striking the object, but not by the angle of incidence of that light.
emissiveColor	The object color that has the appearance of being emitted by the object.
shininess	The coefficient that affects how narrow the angle of incidence of the light striking the object must be to create a shiny spot on the object. Lower shininess values distribute the specular color over a larger area of the object, while higher values restrict the specular color over a small area.
specularColor	The object color affected by the shininess factor.
transparency	The amount of transparency in this object. Lower values are less transparent. A value of 1 is completely transparent.

Description:

The Material node specifies surface material properties for associated geometry nodes that are used by the VRML lighting equations during rendering.

The Material node can appear in the material field of an Appearance node.

See also: Appearance, Color, Normal in this Appendix.

MovieTexture

```
MovieTexture {
  exposedField SFBool    loop              FALSE
  exposedField SFFloat   speed             1
  exposedField SFTime    startTime         0
  exposedField SFTime    stopTime          0
  exposedField MFString  url               []
  field        SFBool    repeatS           TRUE
  field        SFBool    repeatT           TRUE
  eventOut     SFFloat   duration_changed
  eventOut     SFBool    isActive
}
```

Fields and events

loop	If TRUE, the movie plays over and over as long as startTime is greater than stopTime or stopTime is less than startTime and stopTime is in the future. If FALSE, the movie plays once and stops.
speed	A value multiplied by the normal playing rate to speed up or slow down the movie.
startTime	The absolute time to start the movie.
stopTime	The absolute time to stop the movie.
url	The location of the movie data to play.
repeatS	If TRUE, the texture is repeated over the surface of the object in the texture's S direction (which corresponds to the X direction). If FALSE, it is displayed only once, and the edges of the texture are repeated horizontally over the rest of the object.
repeatT	If TRUE, the texture is repeated over the surface of the object in the texture's T direction (which corresponds to the Y direction). If FALSE, it is displayed only once, and the edges of the texture are repeated vertically over the rest of the object.
duration_changed	When the sound has loaded, this event is sent with the duration, in seconds, of the sound.
isActive	When the sound starts, a TRUE event is sent. When the sound stops, a FALSE event is sent.

Description:

The MovieTexture node defines a time-dependent texture map (contained in a movie file) and parameters for controlling the movie and the texture mapping. A MovieTexture can also be used as the source of sound data for a Sound node.

The MovieTexture node can appear in the texture field of an Appearance node or the source field of a Sound node.

See also: Appearance, Sound, PixelTexture, ImageTexture, TextureTransform, TextureCoordinate in this Appendix.

NavigationInfo

```
NavigationInfo {
  eventIn       SFBool    set_bind
  exposedField  MFFloat   avatarSize        [ 0.25, 1.6, 0.75 ]
  exposedField  SFBool    headlight         TRUE
  exposedField  SFFloat   speed             1.0
  exposedField  MFString  type              "WALK"
  exposedField  SFFloat   visibilityLimit   0.0
  eventOut      SFBool    isBound
}
```

Fields and events

set_bind	When this event is received, this node becomes the current NavigationInfo node.
avatarSize	The size of the avatar, used in collision detection. This field can have up to three values. The first is the radius of the avatar cylinder, the second is the height of the cylinder, and the third is the maximum height of an object over which the avatar may step.
headlight	If TRUE, the browser headlight is turned on. If FALSE, the headlight should be turned off.
speed	The average travel speed of the user through the world, in meters per second.
type	The type of navigation to use in this world. Standard values are WALK, EXAMINE, NONE.
visibilityLimit	The distance beyond which the browser may choose not to render objects. A value of 0 indicates that the browser must render objects infinitely far away.
isBound	This event is sent with a value of TRUE when this node becomes the current NavigationInfo node, and with a value of FALSE when this node is no longer the current NavigationInfo node.

Description:

The NavigationInfo node contains information describing the physical characteristics of the viewer and viewing model. For purposes of scaling the avatarSize and speed, the current NavigationInfo node is considered to be a child of the current viewpoint—regardless of where it is located in the file.

The NavigationInfo node can appear in the top level of the file or as a child of a grouping node.

See also: Background, Fog, Viewpoint, Collision in this Appendix.

Normal

```
Normal {
  exposedField MFVec3f vector  []
}
```

Fields and events

vector   A list of normal vectors for use in vector-based objects.

Description:

The Normal node defines a set of 3D surface normal vectors to be used in the vector field of some geometry nodes.

The Normal node can appear in the normal field of an ElevationGrid or IndexedFaceSet node.

See also: IndexedFaceSet, ElevationGrid in this Appendix.

NormalInterpolator

```
NormalInterpolator {
  eventIn       SFFloat set_fraction
  exposedField MFFloat key            []
  exposedField MFVec3f keyValue       []
  eventOut      MFVec3f value_changed
}
```

Fields and events

set_fraction	When this event is received, an interpolated value_changed event is sent. Value is interpolated from the key and keyValue fields.
key	The list of keys, corresponding to set_fraction values received.
keyValue	The list of key values, which are used to interpolate the value_changed output when a set_fraction eventIn is received. There must be an even multiple of key values corresponding to each key. The number of values sent for each value_changed eventOut is equal to the number of key values divided by the number of keys.
value_changed	This value is generated with the current interpolated output whenever a set_fraction eventIn is received.

Description:

The NormalInterpolator node interpolates among a set of MFVec3f values, suitable for transforming normal vectors. All output vectors will have been normalized by the interpolator.

The NormalInterpolator node can appear in the top level of the file or as a child of a grouping node.

See also: CoordinateInterpolator, Normal in this Appendix.

OrientationInterpolator

```
OrientationInterpolator {
   eventIn       SFFloat    set_fraction
   exposedField  MFFloat    key          []
   exposedField  MFRotation keyValue        []
   eventOut      SFRotation value_changed
}
```

Fields and events

set_fraction	When this event is received, an interpolated value_changed event is sent. Value is interpolated from the key and keyValue fields.
key	The list of keys, corresponding to set_fraction values received.
keyValue	The list of key values, which are used to interpolate the value_changed output when a set_fraction eventIn is received. Each key value corresponds to a key.
value_changed	This value is generated with the current interpolated output whenever a set_fraction eventIn is received.

Description:

The OrientationInterpolator node interpolates among a set of SFRotation values. An orientation represents the final position of an object after a rotation has been applied.

The OrientationInterpolator node can appear in the top level of the file or as a child of a grouping node.

See also: ScalarInterpolator, PositionInterpolator, ColorInterpolator, Transform in this Appendix.

PixelTexture

```
PixelTexture {
  exposedField SFImage   image     0 0 0
  field        SFBool    repeatS   TRUE
  field        SFBool    repeatT   TRUE
}
```

Fields and events

image	The inline image data.
repeatS	If TRUE, the texture is repeated over the surface of the object in the texture's S direction (which corresponds to the X direction). If FALSE, it is displayed only once, and the edges of the texture are repeated horizontally over the rest of the object.
repeatT	If TRUE, the texture is repeated over the surface of the object in the texture's T direction (which corresponds to the Y direction). If FALSE, it is displayed only once, and the edges of the texture are repeated vertically over the rest of the object.

Description:

The PixelTexture node defines a 2D image-based texture map, contained in the image field, as an explicit array of pixel values and parameters controlling the mapping of the texture onto the geometry.

The PixelTexture node can appear in the texture field of an Appearance node.

See also: Appearance, MovieTexture, ImageTexture, TextureTransform, TextureCoordinate in this Appendix.

PlaneSensor

```
PlaneSensor {
  exposedField SFBool  autoOffset            TRUE
  exposedField SFBool  enabled               TRUE
  exposedField SFVec2f maxPosition           -1 -1
  exposedField SFVec2f minPosition           0 0
  exposedField SFVec3f offset                0 0 0
  eventOut     SFBool  isActive
  eventOut     SFVec3f trackPoint_changed
  eventOut     SFVec3f translation_changed
}
```

Fields and events

autoOffset	If TRUE, the offset field is updated with the current translation value when the user finishes manipulating. If FALSE, the offset is not changed.
enabled	If TRUE, the sensor is enabled and can be activated by the user. If FALSE, the sensor cannot be activated.
maxPosition	The maximum position value the sensor will output.
minPosition	The minimum position value the sensor will output.
offset	The offset to be added to every position output by the sensor.
isActive	When the sensor is activated, a TRUE event is sent. When the sensor is deactivated, a FALSE event is sent.
trackPoint_changed	Sent when the user activates the sensor and whenever the pointing device is moved while the sensor is activated. The value is the current point on the surface of the imaginary plane.
translation_changed	Sent when the user activates the sensor and whenever the pointing device is moved while the sensor is activated. The value is the translation value on the imaginary plane being manipulated.

Description:

The PlaneSensor node can appear in the top level of the file or as a child of a grouping node.

See also: CylinderSensor, SphereSensor, TouchSensor in this Appendix.

PointLight

```
PointLight {
  exposedField SFFloat ambientIntensity  0
  exposedField SFVec3f attenuation        1 0 0
  exposedField SFColor color              1 1 1
  exposedField SFFloat intensity          1
  exposedField SFVec3f location           0 0 0
  exposedField SFBool  on                 TRUE
  exposedField SFFloat radius             100         .
}
```

Fields and events

ambientIntensity	The intensity applied to all objects affected by this light.
attenuation	The attenuation affecting this light over distance. The three numbers indicate constant, linear, and exponential attenuation.
color	The color applied to all objects affected by this light.
intensity	The intensity of the color being generated by this light.
location	The location of this light in the local coordinate space.
on	If TRUE, this light will affect all objects within its coordinate space. If FALSE, it will not affect any objects.
radius	The radius of influence of this light. Objects beyond this distance are not affected.

Description:

The PointLight node specifies a point-light source at 3D location in the local coordinate system. A point source emits light equally in all directions; that is, it is omnidirectional.

The PointLight node can appear in the top level of the file or as a child of a grouping node.

See also: DirectionalLight, SpotLight in this Appendix.

PointSet

```
PointSet {
  exposedField  SFNode  color    NULL
  exposedField  SFNode  coord    NULL
}
```

Fields and events

color	A Color node.
coord	A Coordinate node.

Description:

The PointSet node specifies a set of 3D points in the local coordinate system with associated colors at each point. Only the emissiveColor field of the associated Material node or the color field of the PointSet node affects the point colors.

The PointSet node can appear in the geometry field of a Shape node.

See also: Shape, IndexedFaceSet, IndexedLineSet in this Appendix.

PositionInterpolator

```
PositionInterpolator {
    eventIn      SFFloat set_fraction
    exposedField MFFloat key          []
    exposedField MFVec3f keyValue     []
    eventOut     SFVec3f value_changed
}
```

Fields and events

set_fraction	When this event is received, an interpolated value_changed event is sent. Value is interpolated from the key and keyValue fields.
key	The list of keys, corresponding to set_fraction values received.
keyValue	The list of key values, which are used to interpolate the value_changed output when a set_fraction eventIn is received. Each key value corresponds to a key.
value_changed	This value is generated with the current interpolated output whenever a set_fraction eventIn is received.

Description:

The PositionInterpolator node linearly interpolates among a set of SFVec3f values. This is appropriate for interpolating a translation.

The PositionInterpolator node can appear in the top level of the file or as a child of a grouping node.

See also: ScalarInterpolator, OrientationInterpolator, ColorInterpolator, Transform in this Appendix.

ProximitySensor

```
ProximitySensor {
    exposedField SFVec3f     center      0 0 0
    exposedField SFVec3f     size        0 0 0
    exposedField SFBool      enabled     TRUE
    eventOut     SFBool      isActive
    eventOut     SFVec3f     position_changed
    eventOut     SFRotation  orientation_changed
    eventOut     SFTime      enterTime
    eventOut     SFTime      exitTime
}
```

Fields and events

center	The center of the region being sensed.
size	The size of the region being sensed.
enabled	If TRUE, the sensor is enabled and can be activated by the user. If FALSE, the sensor cannot be activated.
isActive	When the sensor is activated, a TRUE event is sent. When the sensor is deactivated, a FALSE event is sent.
position_changed	Sent when the user enters the sensed region and whenever the user moves while inside the region. The value is the position of the user in the coordinate space of the sensor.
orientation_changed	Sent when the user enters the sensed region and whenever the user moves while inside the region. The value is the orientation of the user in the coordinate space of the sensor.
enterTime	Sent when the user enters the sensed region. The value is the current time.
exitTime	Sent when the user exits the sensed region. The value is the current time.

Description:

The ProximitySensor node generates events when the user enters, exits, and moves within the defined region in space.

The ProximitySensor node can appear in the top level of the file or as a child of a grouping node.

See also: TouchSensor, Collision, VisibilitySensor in this Appendix.

ScalarInterpolator

```
ScalarInterpolator {
  eventIn       SFFloat set_fraction
  exposedField MFFloat key          []
  exposedField MFFloat keyValue     []
  eventOut      SFFloat value_changed
}
```

Fields and events

set_fraction	When this event is received, an interpolated value_changed event is sent. Value is interpolated from the key and keyValue fields.
key	The list of keys, corresponding to set_fraction values received.
keyValue	The list of key values, which are used to interpolate the value_changed output when a set_fraction eventIn is received. Each key value corresponds to a key.
value_changed	This value is generated with the current interpolated output whenever a set_fraction eventIn is received.

Description:

The ScalarInterpolator node linearly interpolates among a set of SFFloat values. This interpolator is appropriate for any parameter defined using a single floating point value, such as width, radius, and intensity.

The ScalarInterpolator node can appear in the top level of the file or as a child of a grouping node.

See also: PositionInterpolator, OrientationInterpolator, ColorInterpolator in this Appendix.

Script

```
Script {
  exposedField MFString url              []
  field         SFBool   directOutput   FALSE
  field         SFBool   mustEvaluate   FALSE
  # And any number of:
  eventIn        eventTypeName eventName
  field          fieldTypeName fieldName initialValue
  eventOut       eventTypeName eventName
}
```

Fields and events

url	The location of the script to be loaded. This may be a local script if the vrmlscript: or javascript: protocols are used.
directOutput	If TRUE, this script may send events directly to any SFNodes to which it has access. If FALSE, it may not send events directly.
mustEvaluate	If TRUE, this script must always be evaluated whenever it has pending eventIns. If FALSE, event processing may be deferred if this script does not affect any visible portion of the world.

Description:

The Script node is used to program behavior in a scene. Script nodes typically receive events that signify a change or user action, execute code to perform some computation in response to this event, and send events to other parts of the scene.

The Script node can appear in the top level of the file or as a child of a grouping node.

See also: TimeSensor, TouchSensor in this Appendix.

Shape

```
Shape {
  exposedField SFNode appearance NULL
  exposedField SFNode geometry   NULL
}
```

Fields and events

appearance	An Appearance node.
geometry	Any one of the geometric nodes (for example, IndexedFaceSet, Extrusion).

Description:

The Shape node is used to create rendered objects in the world. The node specified in the geometry field is rendered with the specified appearance.

The Shape node can appear in the top level of the file or as a child of a grouping node.

See also: Appearance, IndexedFaceSet, Extrusion, Group, Transform in this Appendix.

Sound

```
Sound {
  exposedField SFVec3f  direction     0 0 1
  exposedField SFFloat  intensity     1
  exposedField SFVec3f  location      0 0 0
  exposedField SFFloat  maxBack       10
  exposedField SFFloat  maxFront      10
  exposedField SFFloat  minBack       1
  exposedField SFFloat  minFront      1
  exposedField SFFloat  priority      0
  exposedField SFNode   source        NULL
  field        SFBool   spatialize    TRUE
}
```

Fields and events

direction	The direction the sound is pointing.
intensity	The intensity of the sound. A value of 1 indicates maximum intensity.
location	The location of the sound source in the local coordinate space.
maxBack	The distance to the back of the sound (in the direction opposite the direction field), beyond which sound can no longer be heard.
maxFront	The distance to the front of the sound (in the direction of the direction field), beyond which sound can no longer be heard.
minBack	The distance to the back of the sound (in the direction opposite the direction field), beyond which the sound begins to fade, reaching zero intensity at maxBack.
minFront	The distance to the front of the sound (in the direction of the direction field), beyond which the sound begins to fade, reaching zero intensity at maxFront.
priority	The priority of the sound, with 1 being the highest priority. If the sound hardware can play all the sounds required, this field is used to prioritize them for selection.
source	An AudioClip or MovieTexture node.
spatialize	If TRUE, the sound should be spatialized by moving it from one speaker to the other based on the position of the sound relative to the viewer. If FALSE, the sound is not spatialized.

Description:

The Sound node describes the positioning and spatial presentation of a sound in a VRML scene. The sound may be located at a point and emit sound in a spherical or ellipsoid pattern, in the local coordinate system. The Sound node can also describe an ambient sound that tapers off at a specified distance from it.

The Sound node can appear in the top level of the file or as a child of a grouping node.

See also: AudioClip, MovieTexture in this Appendix.

Sphere

```
Sphere {
  field SFFloat radius   1
}
```

Fields and events

radius   The radius of the sphere.

Description:

The Sphere node specifies a sphere centered at the origin in the local coordinate system.

The Sphere node can appear in the geometry field of a Shape node.

See also: Shape, Box, Cone, Cylinder in this Appendix.

SphereSensor

```
SphereSensor {
  exposedField SFBool     autoOffset        TRUE
  exposedField SFBool     enabled           TRUE
  exposedField SFRotation offset            0 1 0 0
  eventOut     SFBool     isActive
  eventOut     SFRotation rotation_changed
  eventOut     SFVec3f    trackPoint_changed
}
```

Fields and events

autoOffset	If TRUE, the offset field is updated with the current rotation when the user finishes manipulating. If FALSE, the offset is not changed.
enabled	If TRUE, the sensor is enabled and can be activated by the user. If FALSE, the sensor cannot be activated.
offset	The offset to be added to every rotation value output by the sensor.
isActive	When the sensor is activated, a TRUE event is sent. When the sensor is deactivated, a FALSE event is sent.
rotation_changed	Sent when the user activates the sensor and whenever the pointing device is moved while the sensor is activated. The value is the rotation value of the imaginary sphere being manipulated.
trackPoint_changed	Sent when the user activates the sensor and whenever the pointing device is moved while the sensor is activated. The value is the current point on the surface of the imaginary sphere.

Description:

The SphereSensor node maps pointing-device (for example, mouse) motion into spherical rotation about the center of its local space. The SphereSensor uses the descendant geometry of its parent node to determine if a hit occurs. The feel of the rotation is as if you were rolling a ball.

The SphereSensor node can appear in the top level of the file or as a child of a grouping node.

See also: CylinderSensor, PlaneSensor, TouchSensor in this Appendix.

SpotLight

```
SpotLight {
  exposedField SFFloat ambientIntensity   0
  exposedField SFVec3f attenuation        1 0 0
  exposedField SFFloat beamWidth          1.570796
  exposedField SFColor color              1 1 1
  exposedField SFFloat cutOffAngle        0.785398
  exposedField SFVec3f direction          0 0 -1
  exposedField SFFloat intensity          1
  exposedField SFVec3f location           0 0 0
  exposedField SFBool  on                 TRUE
  exposedField SFFloat radius             100
}
```

Fields and events

ambientIntensity	The intensity applied to all objects affected by this light.
attenuation	The attenuation affecting this light over distance. The three numbers indicate constant, linear, and exponential attenuation.
beamWidth	The angular width from the centerline of the light's direction to the edge of the full-intensity cone of light.
color	The color applied to all objects affected by this light.
cutoffAngle	The angular width from the centerline of the light's direction to the edge of the cone beyond which no light shines. In the area between the full-intensity cone (defined by beamWidth) and the cutoff cone, light drops off linearly.
direction	The direction this light is pointing.
intensity	The intensity of the color being generated by this light.
location	The location of this light in the local coordinate space.
on	If TRUE, this light will affect all objects within its coordinate space. If FALSE, it will not affect any objects.
radius	The radius of influence of this light. Objects beyond this distance are not affected.

Description:

The SpotLight node defines a light source that emits light from a specific point along a specific direction vector and constrained within a solid angle.

The SpotLight node can appear in the top level of the file or as a child of a grouping node.

See also: DirectionalLight, PointLight in this Appendix.

Switch

```
Switch {
  exposedField    MFNode  choice       []
  exposedField    SFInt32 whichChoice  -1
}
```

Fields and events

choice	The list of nodes from which to choose. No more than one node from the list is rendered.
whichChoice	The index of the chosen node. If this value is -1, no node is chosen.

Description:

The Switch node is a grouping node that allows zero or one of the nodes specified in the choice field to be rendered.

The Switch node can appear in the top level of the file or as a child of a grouping node.

See also: Transform, Group, LOD in this Appendix.

Text

```
Text {
  exposedField  MFString string    []
  exposedField  SFNode   fontStyle NULL
  exposedField  MFFloat  length    []
  exposedField  SFFloat  maxExtent 0.0
}
```

Fields and events

string	The list of strings to render.
fontStyle	A FontStyle node.
length	The length of each string. An attempt will be made to force each string to the length in the corresponding length list entry. If not enough entries are provided for the number of strings, the last length entry is used for the remaining strings. A length of 0 indicates that this string should not have its length restricted.
maxExtent	The maximum length of all strings. If any string is longer than this value, its length is forced to this value. But if a string is shorter, its length is not affected.

Description:

The Text node specifies a two-sided, flat, text, string object positioned in the X-Y plane of the local coordinate system based on values defined in the corresponding FontStyle node.

The Text node can appear in the geometry field of a Shape node.

See also: Shape, FontStyle in this Appendix.

TextureCoordinate

```
TextureCoordinate {
  exposedField MFVec2f point  []
}
```

Fields and events

point   The list of two-dimensional texture coordinates, for use in
                         vertex-based shapes.

Description:

The TextureCoordinate node specifies a set of 2D texture coordinates used by vertex-based geometry nodes to map from textures to the vertices.

The TextureCoordinate node can appear in the texCoord field of an IndexedFaceSet or ElevationGrid node.

See also: IndexedFaceSet, ElevationGrid, TextureTransform in this Appendix.

TextureTransform

```
TextureTransform {
    exposedField SFVec2f  center       0 0
    exposedField SFFloat  rotation     0
    exposedField SFVec2f  scale        1 1
    exposedField SFVec2f  translation  0 0
}
```

Fields and events

center	The center of rotation.
rotation	The angle to rotate the two-dimensional texture coordinates, in radians.
scale	The amount to scale the texture coordinates in the S and T dimensions.
translation	The amount to translate the texture coordinates in the S and T directions.

Description:

The TextureTransform node defines a 2D transformation that is applied to texture coordinates, and affects the way textures are applied to the surface of geometry.

The TextureTransform node can appear in the textureTransform field of an Appearance node.

See also: Appearance, TextureCoordinate in this Appendix.

TimeSensor

```
TimeSensor {
  exposedField SFTime    cycleInterval 1
  exposedField SFBool    enabled       TRUE
  exposedField SFBool    loop          FALSE
  exposedField SFTime    startTime     0
  exposedField SFTime    stopTime      0
  eventOut     SFTime    cycleTime
  eventOut     SFFloat   fraction_changed
  eventOut     SFBool    isActive
  eventOut     SFTime    time
}
```

Fields and events

cycleInterval	The amount of time it takes for the timer to complete one cycle. The fraction_changed eventOut takes this much time to go from 0 to 1 when the time is running.
enabled	If TRUE, the timer is enabled and will run when the appropriate values are sent to startTime and stopTime. If FALSE, the timer will not run.
loop	If TRUE, the movie plays over and over as long as startTime is greater than stopTime or stopTime is less than startTime and stopTime is in the future. If FALSE, the movie plays once and stops.
startTime	The absolute time to start the movie.
stopTime	The absolute time to stop the movie.
cycleTime	This event is sent at the start of each time interval (as determined by cycleInterval). This event is sent once when loop is FALSE and repeatedly when loop is TRUE.
fraction_changed	This event is sent continuously with a SFFloat value while the timer is running. The value starts at startTime with a value of 0, and increases to 1, taking the number of seconds in cycleInterval to complete the cycle. If loop is TRUE, this cycle repeats over and over until stopTime is reached.
isActive	When the timer starts, a TRUE event is sent. When the timer stops, a FALSE event is sent.
time	This event sends the current time continuously whenever the timer is running.

Description:

The TimeSensor node generates events as time passes. It can be used to drive continuous simulations and animations, periodic activities (for example, one per minute), and/or single occurrence events, such as an alarm clock.

The `TimeSensor` node can appear in the top level of the file or as a child of a grouping node.

See also: `TouchSensor`, `PositionInterpolator`, `Script` in this Appendix.

TouchSensor

```
TouchSensor {
  exposedField SFBool  enabled TRUE
  eventOut     SFVec3f hitNormal_changed
  eventOut     SFVec3f hitPoint_changed
  eventOut     SFVec2f hitTexCoord_changed
  eventOut     SFBool  isActive
  eventOut     SFBool  isOver
  eventOut     SFTime  touchTime
}
```

Fields and events

enabled	If TRUE, the sensor is enabled and can be activated by the user. If FALSE, the sensor cannot be activated.
hitNormal_changed	Sent whenever the user is over the geometry being sensed (as indicated by isOver). The value is the surface normal at the point under the pointing device.
hitPoint_changed	Sent whenever the user is over the geometry being sensed (as indicated by isOver). The value is the point on the object under the pointing device.
hitTexCoord_changed	Sent whenever the user is over the geometry being sensed (as indicated by isOver). The value is the texture coordinate on the object at the point under the pointing device.
isActive	When the sensor is activated, a TRUE event is sent. When the sensor is deactivated, a FALSE event is sent.
isOver	When the pointing device is over the geometry being sensed, a TRUE event is sent. When the pointing device is no longer over the geometry, a FALSE event is sent.
touchTime	This event is sent when isActive goes FALSE while isOver is TRUE. The value sent is the current time.

Description:

The TouchSensor node tracks the location and state of the pointing device and detects when the user points at or clicks on geometry contained in the children of its parent group.

The TouchSensor can appear in the top level of the file or as a child of a grouping node.

See also: CylinderSensor, PlaneSensor, SphereSensor, TimeSensor in this Appendix.

Transform

```
Transform {
    eventIn        MFNode      addChildren
    eventIn        MFNode      removeChildren
    exposedField  SFVec3f     center            0 0 0
    exposedField  MFNode      children          []
    exposedField  SFRotation  rotation          0 0 1  0
    exposedField  SFVec3f     scale             1 1 1
    exposedField  SFRotation  scaleOrientation  0 0 1  0
    exposedField  SFVec3f     translation       0 0 0
    field         SFVec3f     bboxCenter        0 0 0
    field         SFVec3f     bboxSize          -1 -1 -1
}
```

Fields and events

addChildren	Adds the passed nodes to children.
removeChildren	Removes the passed nodes from children.
center	The center of rotation.
children	The list of children of this node.
rotation	The axis and angle to rotate the children of this node.
scale	The amount to scale the children of this node are the X, Y, and Z dimensions.
scaleOrientation	The axis and angle by which the object should be prerotated before applying the scale value. After scaling, the object is rotated back to its original orientation by applying the inverse of the scaleOrientation.
translation	The amount to translate the children of this node in the X, Y, and Z directions.
bboxCenter	Center of the axis-aligned box encompassing all the children of this node.
bboxSize	Total size of the axis-aligned box encompassing all the children of this node.

Description:

The Transform node is a grouping node that defines a coordinate system for its children that is relative to the coordinate systems of its parents.

The Transform node can appear in the top level of the file or as a child of a grouping node.

See also: Group, Shape in this Appendix.

Viewpoint

```
Viewpoint {
   eventIn       SFBool      set_bind
   exposedField SFFloat      fieldOfView     0.785398
   exposedField SFBool       jump            TRUE
   exposedField SFRotation   orientation     0 0 1  0
   exposedField SFVec3f      position        0 0 10
   field        SFString     description     " "
   eventOut      SFTime      bindTime
   eventOut      SFBool      isBound
}
```

Fields and events

set_bind	When this event is received, this node becomes the current Viewpoint node.
fieldOfView	The angle to use for the field of view. Larger values give the effect of a wide angle lens. Smaller values give the effect of a telephoto lens.
jump	If TRUE, the user's view jumps to the position and orientation when this node is bound. If FALSE, the user's view does not change during a bind.
orientation	The orientation to be set when the user binds to this viewpoint when jump is TRUE, or when the user sets this viewpoint with a browser specific user interface. The orientation is relative to the coordinate space of this Viewpoint.
position	The position to be set when the user binds to this viewpoint when jump is TRUE, or when the user sets this viewpoint with a browser specific user interface. The position is relative to the coordinate space of this Viewpoint.
description	A string to use in a browser dependent way to describe this viewpoint. If this string is left at its default value, this viewpoint will never appear in any browser viewpoint menu.
bindTime	This event is sent when this node becomes the current Viewpoint node. The value is the current time.
isBound	This event is sent with a value of TRUE when this node becomes the current Viewpoint node, and with a value of FALSE when this node is no longer the current Viewpoint node.

Description:

The Viewpoint node defines a specific location in a local coordinate system from which the user might view the scene. When a Viewpoint is at the top of the viewpoint stack, the user's view is conceptually re-parented as a child of the Viewpoint. All subsequent changes to the viewpoint's coordinate system change the user's view.

The Viewpoint node can appear in the top level of the file or as a child of a grouping node.

See also: Background, NavigationInfo, Fog in this Appendix.

VisibilitySensor

```
VisibilitySensor {
  exposedField SFVec3f center   0 0 0
  exposedField SFBool  enabled  TRUE
  exposedField SFVec3f size     0 0 0
  eventOut      SFTime  enterTime
  eventOut      SFTime  exitTime
  eventOut      SFBool  isActive
}
```

Fields and events

center	The center of the region being sensed.
enabled	If TRUE, the sensor is enabled and will send events when activated. If FALSE, the sensor will not send events.
size	The size of the region being sensed.
enterTime	Sent when the sensed region becomes visible. The value is the current time.
exitTime	Sent when the sensed region is no longer visible. The value is the current time.
isActive	When the sensor becomes active, a TRUE event is sent. When the sensor is no longer active, a FALSE event is sent.

Description:

The VisibilitySensor node detects visibility changes of the defined rectangular box as the user navigates the world. VisibilitySensor is typically used to detect when the user can see a specific object or region in the scene, and to activate or deactivate some behavior or animation in order to attract the user's attention or to improve performance.

The VisibilitySensor node can appear in the top level of the file or as a child of a grouping node.

See also: ProximitySensor, TouchSensor, Collision in this Appendix.

WorldInfo

```
WorldInfo {
  field MFString info  []
  field SFString title ""
}
```

Fields and events

info	These strings are for user-defined information, such as authorship and copyright.
title	This is the title of the world, and is used in a browser-dependent way to identify the world to the user.

Description:

The WorldInfo node contains information about the world. It has no effect on the visual appearance or behavior of the world—it is strictly for documentation purposes.

The WorldInfo node can appear in the top level of the file or as a child of a grouping node.

See also: NavigationInfo in this Appendix.

APPENDIX

B

VRML Field and Event Types

Introduction

There are two general classes of fields and events in VRML: fields/events that contain a single value (where a value may be a single number, a vector, or even an image), and fields/events that contain multiple values. Single-valued fields/events have names that begin with SF. Multiple-valued fields/events have names that begin with MF.

Multiple-valued fields/events are written as a series of values enclosed in square brackets, and separated by whitespace (for example, commas). If the field or event has zero values, only the square brackets ([ ]) are written. The last value may optionally be followed by whitespace (for example, a comma). If the field has exactly one value, the brackets may be omitted and just the value written. For example, all of the following are valid for a multiple-valued MFInt32 field named foo containing the single integer value 1:

```
foo 1
foo [1,]
foo [ 1 ]
```

SFBool

A field or event containing a single Boolean value. An SFBool is written as TRUE or FALSE. For example,

```
fooBool FALSE
```

is an SFBool field, fooBool, defining a FALSE value.

The initial value of an SFBool eventOut is FALSE.

SFColor/MFColor

SFColor specifies one RGB (red-green-blue) color value, and MFColor specifies zero or more RGB values. Each color is specified as three floating point numbers (red, then green, then blue), in the range 0.0 to 1.0. For example,

    fooColor [1.0 0. 0.0, 0 1 0, 0 0 1]

is an MFColor field, fooColor, containing the three primary colors: red, green, and blue.

The initial value of an SFColor eventOut is 0 0 0. The initial value of an MFColor eventOut is [ ].

SFFloat/MFFloat

SFFloat specifies one floating point number, and MFFloat specifies zero or more floating point numbers. For example,

```
fooFloat [ 3.1415926, 12.5e-3, .0001 ]
```

is an MFFloat field, fooFloat, containing three floating point values.

The initial value of an SFFloat eventOut is 0.0. The initial value of an MFFloat eventOut is [ ].

B

SFImage

The SFImage field or event defines a single, uncompressed, two-dimensional, pixel image. SFImage fields and events are specified as three integers representing the width, height, and number of components in the image, followed by width×height hexadecimal values representing the pixels in the image, separated by whitespace:

```
fooImage <width> <height> <num components> <pixels values>
```

A one-component image specifies one-byte hexadecimal values representing the intensity of the image. For example, 0xFF is full intensity, and 0x00 is no intensity. A two-component image puts the intensity in the first (high) byte and the alpha (opacity) in the second (low) byte. Pixels in a three-component image have the red component in the first (high) byte, followed by the green and blue components (0xFF0000 is red). Four-component images put the alpha byte after red/green/blue (0x0000FF80 is semi-transparent blue). A value of 0x00 is completely transparent, and 0xFF is completely opaque.

Each pixel is a single unsigned number. For example, a 3-component pixel with value 0x0000FF may also be written as 0xFF (hexadecimal) or 255 (decimal). Pixels are specified from left to right, bottom to top. The first hexadecimal value is the lower left pixel and the last value is the upper-right pixel.

For example,

```
fooImage 1 2 1 0xFF 0x00
```

is a one pixel wide by two pixel high one-component (that is, grayscale) image, with the bottom pixel white and the top pixel black. And

```
fooImage 2 4 3 0xFF0000 0xFF00 0 0 0 0 0xFFFFFF 0xFFFF00
              # red     green  black.. white     yellow
```

is a two pixel wide by four-pixel-high RGB image, with the bottom left pixel red, the bottom right pixel green, the two middle rows of pixels black, the top left pixel white, and the top right pixel yellow.

The initial value of an SFImage eventOut is 0 0 0.

SFInt32/MFInt32

The SFInt32 field and event specifies one integer value, and the MFInt32 field and event specifies zero or more integer values. SFInt32 and MFInt32 values are represented by an integer in decimal or hexadecimal (beginning with 0x) format. For example,

```
fooInt32 [ 17, -0xE20, -518820 ]
```

is an MFInt32 field containing three values.

The initial value of an SFInt32 eventOut is 0. The initial value of an MFInt32 eventOut is [ ].

B

SFNode/MFNode

The SFNode field and event specifies a VRML node, and the MFNode field and event specifies zero or more nodes. The following example illustrates valid syntax for an MFNode field, fooNode, defining four nodes:

```
fooNode [ Transform { translation 1 0 0 }
          DEF CUBE Box { } ]
```

An SFNode field may contain the keyword NULL to indicate that it is empty.

The initial value of an SFNode eventOut is NULL. The initial value of an MFNode eventOut is [ ].

SFRotation/MFRotation

The SFRotation field and event specifies one arbitrary rotation value, and the MFRotation field and event specifies zero or more arbitrary rotation values. They are represented as four floating point values separated by whitespace. The first three values specify a normalized rotation axis vector about which the rotation takes place. The fourth value specifies the amount of right-handed rotation about that axis, in radians. For example, an SFRotation containing a 180 degree rotation about the Y-axis is

```
fooRot 0.0 1.0 0.0  3.14159265
```

The initial value of an SFRotation eventOut is 0 0 1 0. The initial value of an MFRotation eventOut is [ ].

SFString/MFString

The SFString and MFString fields and events contain strings formatted with the UTF-8 universal character set. SFString specifies a single string, and MFString specifies zero or more strings. Strings are represented as a sequence of UTF-8 characters enclosed in double quotes (for example, "string").

Any characters (including newlines and #) may appear within the quotes. To include a double quote (") character within the string, precede it with a backslash (\). To include a backslash character within the string, type two backslashes. For example,

```
fooString [ "One, Two, Three", "He said, \"Immel did it!\"" ]
```

is an MFString field, fooString, with two valid strings.

The initial value of an SFString eventOut is "". The initial value of an MFRotation eventOut is [ ].

SFTime

The SFTIme field and event specifies a single time value. Time values are represented as floating point numbers, specified as the number of seconds from a specific time origin. Typically, SFTime fields and events represent the number of seconds since Jan. 1, 1970, 00:00:00 GMT.

The initial value of an SFTime eventOut is -1.

B

SFVec2f/MFVec2f

An SFVec2f field or event specifies a two-dimensional vector. An MFVec2f field or event specifies zero or more two-dimensional vectors. An SFVec2f or MFVec2f value is represented as a pair of floating point numbers separated by whitespace. For example,

```
fooVec2f [ 42 666, 7, 94 ]
```

is an MFVec2f field, fooVec2f, with two valid vectors.

The initial value of an SFVec2f eventOut is 0 0. The initial value of an MFVec2f eventOut is [ ].

SFVec3f/MFVec3f

An SFVec3f field or event specifies a three-dimensional vector. An MFVec3f field or event specifies zero or more three-dimensional vectors. An SFVec3f or MFVec3f value is represented as three floating point numbers separated by whitespace. For example,

```
fooVec3f [ 1 42 666, 7, 94, 0 ]
```

is an MFVec3f field, fooVec3f, with two valid vectors.

The initial value of an SFVec3f eventOut is 0 0 0. The initial value of an MFVec3f eventOut is [ ].

APPENDIX

C

Glossary

Absolute URL

Also called a complete URL, an absolute URL lists a protocol, name, and path to a file. The file can then be found from anywhere on the Web. The alternative, a relative URL, defines the path to a file relative to the current directory displaying the file in which the URL is referenced. An example of an absolute URL would be `http://www.company.com/division/dept/world.wrl`.

ActiveVRML

Microsoft's proposal for VRML 2. An alternative for adding action and interaction to a VRML 1.0 scene. Microsoft now calls this ActiveX Animation.

Alias

An alternative string reference to an object. It is used in VRML 2 for parameter passing in prototypes.

Alpha channel

Also called a transparent pixel color, it allows one color in an image to be see-through.

Ambient color

The color used in a material node to represent color picked up from the surrounding environment, such as the color of a nearby object that is reflecting light.

Ambient light

The color of the omnipresent light source in the world, such as in a room at sunset.

Ambient sound

The predominant background sound heard everywhere at once, such as interstate traffic off in the distance.

Anchor

Used both in VRML and HTML to assign a hyperlink to an object in the world or on the page. VRML uses an `Anchor` node. HTML uses the `<A>` and `</A>` tags.

Application Programming Interface (API)

The set of functions made available to a programmer to use a program or group of programs. An API allows the programmer to call functions without having any control over the source code for those functions. In VRML, a major technological development for allowing an author to make the browser or VMRL viewer do something on his or her behalf.

Assignment statement

A line of script that assigns a value to a variable using the = operator.

Attenuation

The drop-off rate of brightness of light or volume of sound as distance from the source increases.

Audio clip

A file containing a digital recording of sound, such as voice or music.

Avatar

A visual representation of the body of a visitor to a virtual world.

Axis of rotation

The straight line defined between point 0,0,0 and another X,Y,Z location around which rotation occurs.

Background

The image at, or color of, the infinite horizon. In VRML, the object or objects that can never be approached by a visitor.

Behavior

The movement of an object controlled by a VRML file or related script file, such as a traffic signal changing colors.

Beta period

The period of time a software product is available for trial usage while the bugs are worked out and the performance and usability are monitored.

Billboard

A group of objects in a VRML scene that follow the user's current viewpoint. A Billboard is most often a texture map used for advertising or objects off in the distance.

Binding

The event that gives priority to a specific node that can be one of many of the same type, such as a viewpoint or background image.

Binding stack

The part of a VRML viewer that maintains the order nodes are bound. It's called a stack because each binding puts that node as highest priority, yet all other nodes retain their relative priorities. Each unbinding removes the highest priority item.

Boolean operator

An operator that allows logical expressions to be evaluated as true or false.

Browser

The software that coordinates access to the Web and appropriately loads files requested by the user.

Cartesian Coordinate System

A popular method of representing a point in three-dimensional space as used in VRML. Every point is defined relative to an X-,Y-, and Z-axis.

Class specifier

A keyword that defines how an object is stored in computer memory and affected by other objects.

Clipping plane

A plane that defines the border of visible and invisible objects in a VRML scene. All objects not within the visible border are considered clipped and are not rendered.

Collision detection

The capability of a VRML viewer to determine whether one object is sharing its space with another object, including the user's avatar.

Collision proxy

An alternative, usually simpler, geometry associated with an object for use in collision detection.

Composition

The act of putting things together, such as putting an object together from smaller pieces or putting a script together from multiple functions.

Compound statement

A script statement that includes logical operators or multiple mathematical operators usually separated by pairs of parentheses.

Concatenation

The act of putting two or more text strings together, one following the other to make one string. VRMLScript concatenates two strings using the + operator.

Conditional expression

An expression that can be evaluated as true or false at time of execution, usually associated with the if statement.

Connectivity

A relative term describing the number of events that associate nodes together through a cause-and-effect relationship.

Convex

The characteristic of an object such that it has a caved-in appearance, such as a contact lens. In VRML, an object is convex if any two points on the object can be connected without hitting a third point.

Coordinate

A point in three-dimensional space defined in VRML by x, y, z distances relative to the point $0,0,0$ and parallel to the X-, Y-, and Z-axes.

Coplanar

The characteristic of an object such that all points on a face exist in a single geometric plane.

Crease angle

The angle formed between two objects that touch each other. It's also used to define the angle between both ends of a viewer's field of vision.

Cross section

The face obtained by intersecting a plane with an object and filling in the area within the points of intersection.

Cyberspace

A place existing solely within computer representation. It's often referred to as the single large place defined by all computer representations that exist.

Cycle

The time a clock or timer is active from start to finish, or until reaching the start value again.

Cylinder behavior

The behavior an object exhibits by appearing to exist on the lengthwise surface of a cylinder.

CylinderSensor

A sensor shaped as a cylinder that senses whether the current viewpoint is within its area.

Default

The behavior an object exhibits in absence of any additional information.

Dereferencing operator

The operator that takes one object out of a container of multiple related objects and returns it to a script.

Diffuse color

The color an object has in absense of direct, reflected, or emitted light.

Disk behavior

The behavior an object demonstrates by appearing to exist on the top or bottom surface of a cylinder.

Drag sensor

The capability of a VRML scene to sense the movement of the primary pointing device when moving on top of an object.

Dynaboard

A series of textures applied at different angles to make an object appear three-dimensional.

Elevation grid

A ground plane as defined by squares in the X and Z directions and the Y height of each point at the corner of each square.

Ellipsoidal volume

A volume of space existing within the area of an ellipsoid. In VRML, it's used to define the area of audible sound coming from a single source.

Emmissive color

The color an object emits as if radiating light.

Event

Anything significant that happens in a VRML world to be recognized and reacted to by the VRML viewer.

eventIn

The event that comes into a VRML node to change a field in that node.

eventOut

The event that comes out of a VRML node when a field in the node or the binding of the node has changed.

Exposed field

A field that has an associated eventIn and eventOut associated with it by its definition.

Expression

Any series of characters in a script that can be evaluated to a single value such as a + b/c.

External Authoring Interface (EAI)

See Application Programming Interface. The EAI is the Application Programming Interface for an author to use to connect HTML documents with VRML worlds through the use of a scripting language.

Extrusion

A three-dimensional object created by taking a face and moving it while filling in the area swept out by the movement.

Face

A coplanar area defined by connecting multiple points in a logical order.

Fan-in

A situation that happens when multiple eventOuts, routed to the same eventIn, are activated at the same time.

Fan-out

A situation that happens when an eventOut, routed to multiple eventIns, is activated.

Field

A component of a node that further defines the attributes of that node.

Field of view

The area visible from the current camera location.

Fixed font

A font that allots the same horizontal space for each character, irrespective of the width of the character itself.

Flicker

The irritating ability to identify individual frames of a movie instead of a smooth, flowing experience.

Flipbook animation

An animation made out of multiple images shown in quick succession.

Fog

A setting in VRML that adds a certain color value to every pixel rendered in the current frame.

Font

A set of all characters that have the same look and feel, such as in a typeset for a newspaper column.

Frame

A two-dimensional rendering of a three-dimensional model in order to show it on a screen—or, in HTML, a subwindow under independent user control that is part of a frameset.

Frame definition document

An HTML document that creates frames and defines names and characteristics for each frame.

Frameset

A vertical or horizontal set of frames.

Function

A scripting component that takes parameters as input, performs some processing, and returns output.

Grouping node

A node that contains multiple nodes as children.

Header line

The first line in a text file that identifies the text file type, such as the use of the <HTML> tag in HTML.

Headlight

The default light a VRML browser uses in absence of any other light in the scene. A light attached to the top of an avatar's head like a coal-miner's light.

High latency

A situation in which a user has to wait a while before the results of some action take place. For VRML on the Internet, multiuser worlds are likely to exhibit this behavior.

Hit point

The point a pointing device identifies on an object, such as a texture map.

HTML

The Hypertext Markup Language; the scripting language with which Web pages are written.

http:

The identifier for the hypertext transport protocol used in absolute URLs to request information from a server on the Web.

Hyperlink

An object that, once selected by a pointing device, takes the user to another location or file on the Web.

Illumination

The effect a light source has on an object it shines on.

Imagemap

A texture where different regions or zones of the image are mapped for a different purpose, such as different hyperlinks.

Immersive

The extent to which a user experiences the simulation rendered by a computer.

Inlining

The act of bringing in additional information from a separate file when a line in a file is encountered, such as another object when encountering the `Inline` node in VRML.

Instantiation

The act of making an object or variable active in computer memory.

Interface type

The current toolset for a specific method available to navigate in and interact with a VRML scene.

Interface widget

A VRML object created to be used and reused within a scene with the purpose of adding capabilities to the browser.

Interpolation

The capability of a mathematical calculation to estimate a value between two known values based on the distance of it from the two known values.

Inventor

A text file format created by Silicon Graphics that became the basis for VRML 1.

JavaScript

A scripting language that follows the syntax of the Java programming language created by Sun Microsystems.

JPEG

Also know as JPG, a popular image file format created by the Joint Photographic Expert Group.

Justification

The placement of a block of text relative to the right and left margins.

Justified (text)

A form of justification that adds spacing between words in order to place text flush against the right and left margins simultaneously.

Key values

The set of values that are to be used in interpolating continuous values on one or more line segments.

Keys

The set of values that place the key values on a timeline. In VRML, the timeline goes from 0 to 1 so that each key has a value between 0 and 1.

Kiosk

A publicly available multimedia computer and stand used to display information about a person, place, or event.

Level of detail

A characteristic of the number of polygons used when modeling an object. In VRML, the LOD node chooses from among multiple representations of the same object based on the distance from the object to the camera.

Linear interpolation

The simplest form of interpolation whereby the two known points are considered on a line that goes through the point being interpolated.

Local coordinate system

The coordinate system used for modeling an object in a VRML scene. Usually, the local coordinate system is scaled to the world coordinate system for an object included in the scene.

Morphing

An advanced form of interpolation that works on multiple coordinates simultaneously to make an object change smoothly to become another object.

Motion capture

A form of creating a digital behavior by recording key point locations during an exhibition of that behavior in the real world.

Movie texture

A 2D movie image that can be applied to an object in a VRML scene.

Moving Worlds

The name of the winning proposal for the basis of the VRML 2 standard.

MPEG

Also know as MPG, a popular movie image file format created by the Motion Pictures Expert Group.

Multiuser environment

A virtual world that can be visited by multiple users at the same time with a sense of presence usually embodied by an avatar.

Name space

A group of names from a similar category, such as geographic names.

Node

An object that is connected to other objects in a scene graph. In VRML, nodes are the building blocks used to author a scene.

Normal

The perpendicular line away from the plane of an object face.

Normalized

A normal line segment that is defined with a length of one comprised of three components, X, Y, and Z, representing distances from the point 0,0,0 along each axis.

Null

A value represented by filling bits of zero into a location in computer memory, conveniently used for assigning no value to a variable.

Operator precedence

Rules governing the order of evaluation of component expressions in a compound statement within a script.

Optimization

A method of revising a script or scene file in order to make it perform better when running in computer memory.

Orientation

The direction an object faces or moves in three-dimensional space, such as the current camera's focal point.

Parameters

Variables or values used by a function or node created for a specific purpose.

Performance

A characteristic of how well a process takes advantage of available computer processing capabilities to do its task.

Persistance

The capability of an object or variable to stay in the same state over time.

Perspective

The capability of an object to identify its distance from the camera and relative to all other objects around it.

Pitch

The speed at which a sound clip is played.

Pixel

The smallest component of a texture that can be colored independently. It is short for picture element.

Pixelation

An unfortunate occurance when a texture map begins to look more like a bunch of colored dots than an integrated image.

PlaneSensor

A sensor that maps all events in terms of a single plane.

Plug-in

An add-in software module that adds capabilites to a Web browser specific to a certain file type.

Polygon budget

The number of polygons to be used for a VRML scene as decided upon before creation begins.

Primitive (object)

A single node, three-dimensional object defined without referring to its coordinates.

Procedural texture

An image wherein all pixels are defined in the VRML file and that can receive events to modify the texture on-the-fly, creating an image behavior.

Property node

A node that adds a certain attribute to all its parent nodes.

Prototypes

A syntactic definition of an object and its available routing that can be instantiated by anyone who wants to use it in a VRML scene.

Proximity

The closeness of two objects, such as the camera and another object in a scene.

Radians

A unit of measure used with angles. There are approximately 6.28 radians in a circle.

Ramp output

Any mathematical output that increases continuously over time.

Relative URL

A URL that locates one file on the Web based on the location of the current file being used, as opposed to an absolute URL.

Rendering

The act of taking a snapshot of objects in a scene based on a viewpoint in time and drawing that snapshot to a computer screen.

Resolution service

A computer process that finds a resource on the Web based on its name.

Right hand rule

A method of determining the direction of rotation of an object by curling the fingers of the right hand around its axis of rotation.

Route

A connection of an eventOut of one node in a scene graph to an eventIn of another node in order to process an event that occurs in a scene.

Sans-serif font

Any font that excludes horizontal handles during character formation in order to create a simpler looking character. The handles, called serifs, help a reader follow text horizontally while reading.

Scalar

Any variable type that accepts just one value at a time.

Scale

The unit of measure used when discussing the absolute size of an object relative to the whole scene.

Scene graph

The graph created by connecting all the nodes in a VRML text file in a way that demonstrates the hierarchical relationship of all nodes.

Scope

The range of influence of a variable or node in a script or scene graph.

Script

A process a computer can execute by reading statements that are written following the syntax rules of a computer language.

Seamlessness

The experience by a virtual world visitor that everything encountered in the world is part of a single whole.

Sensor

A node in a VRML scene that is able to tell when a condition is true based on time, actions, or distances changing in the world.

Serif font

A character set that includes small, horizontal handles at the top and bottom of characters when forming them. The handles, called serifs, help a reader follow text horizontally while reading.

Shared behavior

A behavior that multiple users can see once put in motion by a single user's actions.

Spatialized

A feature of sound that makes it appear to come from a single source location in a scene.

Specular color

The color an object shows when light is cast upon it.

SphereSensor

A sensor shaped as a sphere that senses whether the current viewpoint is within its area.

Spine

The line or curve that runs through the middle of an object, such as an extrusion.

Sprites

Two-dimensional representations of objects using images instead of three-dimensional geometries.

State

The current value of all variables or attributes associated with an object at a point in time.

Static object

An object in a VRML scene that demonstrates no behaviors or movement at any time.

Switch node

A node that changes which child node is used in a scene based on the current value of its index.

Tag

A string of characters used in an HTML file to apply an attribute to text in the file or create an object for inclusion in the page.

Terrain following

The capability of an avatar to walk around in a scene similar to real world, pedestrian navigation.

Texture

A 2D digital image applied to an object in order to add visual detail to the object.

Texture mapping

A characteristic of how an image is applied to an object.

Transform

A specification for how an object should change from its current space, such as its size, location, and orientation.

Trigger

A preexisting condition that, when encountered, makes an event occur.

Type specifier

A text string that identifies how a variable is represented and used in computer memory.

Uniform Resource Locator (URL)

A text string used to find a file on the Internet and to set up a protocol by which to send the contents of the file back to its requestor.

Uniform Resource Name (URN)

A text string that finds a file on the Internet by object name instead of by filename.

UTF8

A standard for representing characters in computer memory used predominantly on the Web because of its international character set.

VRML Architecture Group (VAG)

A group of individuals responsible for the creation and proliferation of the VRML standard. Its purpose was overtaken by the VRML Consortium in early 1997.

Variable

A text string used in a script to create and refer to a location in computer memory.

Vector

A variable type that organizes multiple values of the same type in a convenient package.

Vertex

A coordinate used in the creation of a 2D or 3D object.

Viewing frustum

The shape used by a VRML browser to identify what is visible by the camera at any point in time.

Viewpoint

A specific point in three-dimensional space where a camera can be placed and oriented on demand.

Virtual reality

A computer simulation that can be experienced as a physical place and that interacts with the user's senses to create an alternative reality.

Virtual Reality Modeling Language (VRML)

A language used to create three-dimensional content on a Web site. It is also a file format for saving a three-dimensional model.

Visibility

The characteristic of an object in a scene that describes whether the object can be seen or not.

VRML 1

The first official standard for the Virtual Reality Modeling Language

VRML 1.1

The first attempt to standardize additional features beyond VRML 1. It never became a standard, but helped identify the need to take a different direction for the VRML 2 standard.

VRMLScript

A simple scripting language that can be used within the VRML file itself.

Wireframe

The image of a three-dimensional object created by displaying the edges of the polygons that make up the object, but not the area within the edges themselves.

World coordinate system

The coordinate system to be used for the final VRML scene. All objects to be used in the scene are transformed to comply with this measurement system.

World Wide Web

The servers and connections between servers that contain and deliver the information shared over the Internet.

www-vrml

The original mailing list server used to collaboratively create the VRML 1 standard and discuss its validity and verification.

APPENDIX

D

What's on the CD-ROM?

On the *Teach Yourself VRML 2 in 21 Days* CD-ROM, you will find all the sample files that have been presented in this book, along with a wealth of other applications and utilities.

NOTE | Please refer to the readme.wri file on the CD-ROM (Windows) or the Guide to the CD-ROM (Macintosh) for the latest listing of software.

Windows Software

VRML and 3D Graphics

- ☐ Ez3D VRML authoring demo
- ☐ Pioneer
- ☐ NuGraf Rendering System
- ☐ Polytrans
- ☐ Fractal Design Painter demo
- ☐ VRML 2 specification

HTML Tools

- ☐ Microsoft Internet assistants for Access, Excel, PowerPoint, Schedule+, and Word
- ☐ Hot Dog 32-bit HTML editor
- ☐ HoTMeTaL HTML editor
- ☐ HTMLed HTML editor
- ☐ InContext Spider demo
- ☐ InContext Web analyzer demo

Graphics Utilities

- ☐ MapThis imagemap utility
- ☐ Paint Shop Pro 3.12
- ☐ SnagIt screen capture utility
- ☐ ThumbsPlus image viewer and browser

Explorer

☐ Microsoft Internet Explorer v3.01 for Windows 95 and NT 4

Utilities

☐ Microsoft viewers for Excel, PowerPoint, and Word
☐ Adobe Acrobat viewer
☐ Microsoft PowerPoint animation player and publisher
☐ WinZip for Windows NT/95
☐ WinZip Self-Extractor

Macintosh Software

VRML and 3D Graphics

☐ VRML 2 specification
☐ Strata StudioPro Blitz demo
☐ Strata Vision demo
☐ Strata Media Paint demo

HTML Tools

☐ BBEdit 3.5.1
☐ BBEdit 4 demo
☐ HTML Web Weaver v2.5.2
☐ WebMap v1.01f imagemap creator
☐ HTML.edit v1.7
☐ HTML Editor for the Macintosh v1.0
☐ Images and backgrounds

Graphics, Video, and Sound Utilities

☐ Graphic converter v2.1.4
☐ GIFConverter v2.3.7
☐ Fast player v1.1

☐ Sparkle 2.4.5

☐ SoundApp v1.5.1

Utilities

☐ ZipIt for Macintosh

☐ ScrapIt Pro

☐ Adobe Acrobat

About Shareware

Shareware is not free. Please read all documentation associated with a third-party product (usually contained with files named `readme.txt` or `license.txt`) and follow all guidelines.

INDEX

Symbols

A

C

Laura Lemay's Web Workshop: 3D Graphics and VRML 2

Laura Lemay, Kelly Murdock, and Justin Couch   *Covers the Internet*

This is the easiest way for readers to learn how to add three-dimensional virtual worlds to Web pages. It describes the new VRML 2 specification, explores the wide arrray of existing VRML sites on the Web, and walks the readers through the process of creating their own 3D Web environments.

CD-ROM contains the book in HTML format, a hand-picked selection of the best VRML and 3D graphics tools, plus a collection of ready-to-use virtual worlds.

Contains complete coverage of VRML 2!

Teaches how to create 3D worlds on the Web.

Price: $39.99 USA $56.95 CDN   User Level: Casual—Accomplished
ISBN: 1-57521-143-2 400 pp.   7 3/8 x 9 1/8 09/01/96 Internet–Graphics/Multimedia

Laura Lemay's Web Workshop: Graphics and Web Page Design

Laura Lemay, Jon Duff, and James Mohler   *Covers the Internet*

With the number of Web pages increasing daily, only the well-designed will stand out and grab the attention of those browsing the Web. This book illustrates, in classic Laura Lemay style, how to design attractive Web pages that will be visited over and over again.

CD-ROM contains HTML editors, graphics software, and royalty-free graphics and sound files.

Teaches beginning and advanced-level design principles.

Price: $55.00 USA $77.95 CDN   User Level: Accomplished   500 pp.
ISBN: 1-57521-125-4   7 3/8 x 9 1/8   08/01/96   Internet–Online/Communications

Laura Lemay's Web Workshop: JavaScript

Laura Lemay and Michael Moncur   *Communications/Online–Internet*

Readers will explore various aspects of Web publishing—whether JavaScripting and interactivity or graphics design or Netscape Navigator Gold—in greater depth than the Teach Yourself books.

CD-ROM includes the complete book in HTML format, publishing tools, templates, graphics, backgrounds, and more.

Provides a clear, hands-on guide to creating sophisticated Web pages.

Covers JavaScript

Price: $39.99 USA $56.95 CDN   User Level: Casual—Accomplished
ISBN: 1-57521-141-6   400 pp.   7 3/8 x 9 1/8   09/01/96

Laura Lemay's Web Workshop: Microsoft FrontPage

Laura Lemay & Denise Tyler   *Internet–Web Publishing*

This is a clear hands-on guide to maintaining Web pages with Microsoft's FrontPage. Written in the clear, conversational style of Laura Lemay, it is packed with many interesting, colorful examples that demonstrate specific tasks of interest to the reader.

CD-ROM included!

Teaches how to maintain Web pages with FrontPage.

Includes on the CD-ROM all the templates, backgrounds, and materials needed!

Covers FrontPage

Price: $39.99 USA $56.95 CDN   User Level: Casual - Accomplished
ISBN: 1-57521-149-1 672 pp.   7 3/8 x 9 1/8   09/01/96

Laura Lemay's Web Workshop: Creating Commercial Web Pages

Laura Lemay, Brian K. Murphy, & Edmund T. Smith　　　　　　　*Internet–Business*

Filled with sample Web pages, this book shows how to create commercial-grade Web pages using HTML, CGI, and Java. In the classic clear style of Laura Lemay, author of the best-selling *Teach Yourself Java*, it details not only how to create the page, but how to apply proven principles of design that will make the Web page a marketing tool. CD-ROM includes all the templates in the book, plus HTML editors, graphics software, CGI forms, and more.

Illustrates the various corporate uses of Web technology—catalogues, cutomer service, and product ordering.

Covers the Web

Price:$39.99 USA　　$56.95 CDN　　User Level: Accomplished
ISBN: 1-57521-126-2　　　528 pp.　　7 3/8 x 9 1/8　　　09/01/96

Laura Lemay's Web Workshop: ActiveX and VBScript

Laura Lemay, Paul Lomax, & Rogers Cadenhead　　　　*Internet–Programming*

ActiveX is an umbrella term for a series of Microsoft products and technologies that add activity to Web pages. Visual Basic Script is an essential element of the ActiveX family. This book is a compilation of individual workshops that show the reader how to use VBScript and other ActiveX technologies within their Web site. CD-ROM contains the entire book in HTML format; a hand-picked selection of the best ActiveX development tools, scripts, templates, backgrounds, borders, and graphics.

Covers ActiveX and VBScript

Price:$39.99 USA　　$56.95 CDN　　User Level: Casual — Accomplished
ISBN: 1-57521-207-2　　450 pp.　　7 3/8 x 9 1/8　　12/01/96

Laura Lemay's Web Workshop: Netscape Navigator Gold 3

Laura Lemay & Ned Snell　　　　　　　　　　　　*Internet–General*

Netscape Gold and JavaScript are two powerful tools to create and design effective Web pages. The included CD-ROM contains editors and code from the book, making the reader's learning experience a quick and effective one.

Teaches how to program within Navigator Gold's rich Netscape development environment.

Covers Web Publishing

Price: $39.99 USA　　$53.99 CDN　　User Level: Casual—Accomplished
ISBN: 1-57521-128-9　　400 pp.　　7 3/8 x 9 1/8　　06/01/96

Teach Yourself Web Publishing with HTML 3.2 in 14 Days, Professional Reference Edition

Laura Lemay　　　　　　　　　　　　　　*Internet–Web Publishing*

This is the updated edition of Lemay's previous bestseller, *Teach Yourself Web Publishing with HTML in 14 Days, Premier Edition.* In it, readers will find all the advanced topics and updates—including, adding audio, video, and animation—to Web page creation.

CD-ROM included.

Explores the use of CGI scripts, tables, HTML 3.2, the Netscape and Internet Explorer extensions, Java applets and JavaScript, and VRML.

Covers HTML 3.2

Price: $59.99 USA　　$81.95 CDN　　User Level: New—Casual—Accomplished
ISBN: 1-57521-096-7　　1,104 pp.　　7 3/8 x 9 1/8　　06/01/96

Add to Your Sams.net Library Today
with the Best Books for Internet Technologies

ISBN	Quantity	Description of Item	Unit Cost	Total Cost
1-57521-143-2		Laura Lemay's Web Workshop: 3D Graphics and VRML 2 (Book/CD-ROM)	$39.99	
1-57521-125-4		Laura Lemay's Web Workshop: Graphics and Web Page Design (Book/CD-ROM)	$55.00	
1-57521-141-6		Laura Lemay's Web Workshop: JavaScript (Book/CD-ROM)	$39.99	
1-57521-149-1		Laura Lemay's Web Workshop: Microsoft FrontPage (Book/CD-ROM)	$39.99	
1-57521-126-2		Laura Lemay's Web Workshop: Creating Commercial Web Pages (Book/CD-ROM)	$39.99	
1-57521-207-2		Laura Lemay's Web Workshop: ActiveX and VBScript (Book/CD-ROM)	$39.99	
1-57521-128-9		Laura Lemay's Web Workshop: Netscape Navigator Gold 3 (Book/CD-ROM)	$39.99	
1-57521-096-7		Teach Yourself Web Publishing with HTML 3.2 in 14 Days, Professional Reference Edition (Book/CD-ROM) (Hardcover)	$59.99	
		Shipping and Handling: See information below.		
		TOTAL		

Shipping and Handling: $4.00 for the first book, and $1.75 for each additional book. If you need to have it NOW, we can ship product to you in 24 hours for an additional charge of approximately $18.00, and you will receive your item overnight or in two days. Overseas shipping and handling adds $2.00. Prices subject to change. Call between 9:00 a.m. and 5:00 p.m. EST for availability and pricing information on latest editions.

201 W. 103rd Street, Indianapolis, Indiana 46290

1-800-428-5331 — Orders   1-800-835-3202 — FAX   1-800-858-7674 — Customer Service

Book ISBN 1-57521-193-9

Installing the CD-ROM

The companion CD-ROM contains all the source code and project files developed by the authors, plus an assortment of evaluation versions of third-party products. To install, please follow these steps.

Windows 95 / NT 4 Installation Instructions

1. Insert the CD-ROM into your CD-ROM drive.
2. From the Windows 95 or NT 4 desktop, double-click the My Computer icon.
3. Double-click the icon representing your CD-ROM drive.
4. Double-click the icon titled setup.exe to run the CD-ROM installation program.

Windows NT 3.51 Installation Instructions

1. Insert the CD-ROM into your CD-ROM drive.
2. From File Manager or Program Manager, choose Run from the File menu.
3. Type *drive*\setup and press Enter, where *drive* corresponds to the drive letter of your CD-ROM. For example, if your CD-ROM is drive D:, type D:\SETUP and press Enter.
4. Follow the on-screen instructions.

Macintosh Installation Instructions

1. Insert the CD-ROM into your CD-ROM drive.
2. When an icon for the CD appears on your desktop, open the disc by double-clicking its icon.
3. Double-click the icon named Guide to the CD-ROM, and follow the directions that appear.